Hermann Kappelhoff
Front Lines of Community

Cinepoetics

Edited by
Hermann Kappelhoff and Michael Wedel

Volume 1

Hermann Kappelhoff
Front Lines of Community

Hollywood Between War and Democracy

Translated by
Daniel Hendrickson

DE GRUYTER

ISBN 978-3-11-070911-7
e-ISBN (PDF) 978-3-11-046808-3
e-ISBN (EPUB) 978-3-11-046733-8
ISSN 2569-4294

Library of Congress Control Number: 2018934555

Bibliographic information published by the Deutsche Nationalbibliothek
The Deutsche Nationalbibliothek lists this publication in the Deutsche Nationalbibliografie;
detailed bibliographic data are available on the Internet at http://dnb.dnb.de.

© 2020 Walter de Gruyter GmbH, Berlin/Boston
This volume is text- and page-identical with the hardback published in 2018.
Cover image: „Shell shocked soldier awaiting transportation away from the frontline". Don McCullin / Contact Press Images / Agentur Focus
Typesetting: Integra Software Services Pvt. Ltd.
Printing and binding: CPI books GmbH, Leck

www.degruyter.com

Preface

The Limits of Community: This is the title of a famous book written by the philosopher Helmuth Plessner during the twenties of the last century. The book deals with the opposition between democratic societies, based on the difference of opinion, and those forms of government that claim a communal "we," divested of all dissent. His plea for the calming procedures of the institutionalized processes of democratic forms of government and against the mobilization of nationalist or communist feelings of community was historically confirmed to such a harrowing degree that for a long time the idea of political community seemed to have been completely discredited.

Only toward the end of the last century did the term community surface again, starting from debates in French philosophy, a phenomenon that has held to this day. Although I will not explicitly be thematizing this debate (Jean-Luc Nancy, Jacques Rancière, etc.) here, it does form a frame of reference for the fundamental arguments and perspectives that are developed over the course of this book.

I will, however, explicitly refer to a writer who might initially seem out of context in any discussion within continental European philosophy centered around an understanding of politics and community. In fact, it was a book by an American philosopher that urgently showed me how much the understanding of democracy in American liberalism is marked by an idea of the political that is at core an idea of political community. The electoral success of Donald Trump in 2016 has brought this book an attention that is as belated as it is overwhelming. It is a lecture by Richard Rorty, published in 1998 under the title: *Achieving our Country*. Rorty calls for a return to the liberal idea of American history as a history of a permanent struggle to "improve our country." In his view, its driving force should neither be sought in general principles of human justice nor in the evolutionism of the free competition of economic, political, or social forces. Rather, the talk of "our country" always already requires deciding for solidarity with a "we" of the political community. The question then, of who can participate in this "we" – socially, politically, culturally, economically – who belongs and who does not, is the driving force behind the permanent struggle over the boundaries of community.

Like Helmuth Plessner – but now portending the opposite – Rorty speaks of an affective bond to the community, a fundamental feeling for the sense of commonality, which, much like the familial bond, is the actual incitement for 'Achieving our Country.' And he chooses – which is also what makes it a central reference point for this book – films about platoons, the smallest military unit, as an example to understand how American society seeks to come to an understanding about the sense of commonality.

For me, Rorty's understanding of the sense of commonality was a final building block with which in turn my reading of the Hollywood war film could be worked out. Indeed, my extensive studies on the Hollywood war film – through all its historical and aesthetic changes in media – always came to the same conclusion: The fundamental social conflict around which the films were crystallized as a genre of Hollywood cinema consists in the irresolvable contradictions inherent to the sense of commonality itself. The "we" implicit in "our country" presents itself on the one hand quite literally as an embattled front line, the course of which is as arbitrary as it is unstable; on the other hand, it collapses inward into mutually exclusive claims by competing communities, whose frontline positions are no less warlike than those of transnational conflicts. Among the internal frontline positions, perhaps the most radical is the one between military communitization and the democratic community. At any rate, in my view, war films open up a historical perspective in which the permanent battle over the boundaries of community can be reconstructed as an inner conflict within liberal democracy.

To reach such a goal I am relying on another great representative of American liberalism, namely Stanley Cavell. In particular, I am thinking of his writings about the comedies of remarriage. As is well known, Cavell reads these films as reflections that probe into the conditions under which democratic relations of mutual recognition are possible. And perhaps, with the platoon films – as Rorty calls them – Hollywood has developed a cinematic metaphor that achieves, with regard to the front lines of political communities, what the metaphor of the twice married couple contributes to the paradigm of civil democratic agreement.

The present book therefore deals with the idea of American democracy – but not as an objectively historical object in the history of ideas or of politics, but as an approach to a sense of commonality, as it might confront spectators today in the Hollywood war films of an earlier time period. To me at least, the reconstruction of such a sense of commonality in film analysis seems to opens up historical consciousness in the first place, which the films of Frank Capra, John Ford, William Wyler, or Sam Fuller and many others bring into our present day.

The films are a cultural legacy, artifacts of a critical state of emergency. They attest to a struggle over the political self-conception of a nation, one that reflects on its beginnings during the state of emergency of war in order to found itself anew, over and over again. This can be understood quite literally. Indeed, self-reflection – I am borrowing here from a highly idiosyncratic interpreter of American liberalism, namely Hannah Arendt – on self-defined beginnings is the basic form of political action. It refers to acting into an undefined future, by which a political tradition is grounded, without itself being able to rest on any foundation. For this action setting a beginning, modernity developed the idea of revolution. If we follow Hannah Arendt's analysis in *On Revolution*, the American Revolution can in turn be distinguished from all those that followed it by how this action was carried out. The revolutionary upheaval was not primarily determined by conquering state power in war or civil war. It was carried out much more as a declaration of the claim to freedom by its citizens in order to regulate the possibility of state force. The revolution was carried out as a promise with which the power concentrated in state institutions was bound to a single goal: the pursuit of individuals to secure their happiness.

The circumstance that the state would not be allowed any interests in its own right, which could be defended in world politics, might all too easily seem to be isolationism in advance of the two world wars. Obviously, the American population had to give up something that citizens of other states would not even have been conceded. Namely a sense of commonality that allows the state as such no life of its own, which could least offset the everyday lives of its citizens. At any rate, that is the view of things conveyed through Hollywood war films; they make very palpable how state force ends up in the sharpest contradiction to liberal democracy, when military mobilization encompasses a society in its totality.

The state of emergency that is war reverses the principle of 'pursuit of happiness' into its opposite. The focus of all social efforts is no longer the everyday lives of individuals, but the interests of the state, of social institutions. The state now, in the form of military bodies, lays claim to the bodies and lives of individuals.

By examining just this state of exception, this book deals with war only to the degree that war allows the state to demand of its citizens everything meant to be protected, and which provided the reason for the state in the first place, for the formation of a state power in procedures, laws, and institutions. The focus of the book, therefore, is on the fundamental antagonism between forms of military communitization and liberal political society, which Rorty speaks of in *Achieving Our Country*. This antagonism is also the topic of Hollywood war films – it is their actual subject. The focus is on films that become legible as witnesses to this antagonism. They describe the celebration of a society at war as the crisis, the demise, or the renewal of just that political community that marks its beginnings in the American Revolution.

It is these films that first provide us with the possibility of calling the "we" of a political community into question, a community that we tend to take quite deliberately as "our western democracy." The films open up the internal perspective of experiencing a "we," which we ourselves can only belong to as spectators – thus remaining utterly excluded from the experiential world of the "we" of the films. Cavell has understood this kind of participation of non-participants as a specific form of how cinematic images produce meaning.

The films are thus not only unfamiliar to us due to their historical distance; in their unfamiliarity they create, for their part, the necessary distance to the self-conception of a political community on which they are founded and to which they refer – a self-conception that we have always already overlooked when we unconditionally take it to be our own. The sense of commonality as a specific feeling for the social only emerges in the difference to other presents and other cultures. Therein lies the specific potential of the historical consciousness of cinematic images.

This means that films create for me the possibility of a methodological alienation with which political ideas, notions, and conceptions of another present and culture can be dislodged from what was always already known. At any rate, it is in this sense that I am attempting to position them as an instrument of a thinking which sees itself obligated equally to (cultural) history and to theory. This is why I also pursue an eminent methodological interest in this book by attempting to position film analysis and genre theory as cultural-philosophical disciplines.

For all the interest in the theory of the political, in that of liberalism in general and the tradition of American pragmatism in particular, this is why my endeavors are initially and above all concerned with films as concrete witnesses of what we can understand, along with Richard Rorty, as the historical experiment of a liberal, democratic society. The history of such an experiment cannot be narrated as an unbroken arc that links a difficult yesterday with a better tomorrow. Indeed, as little as it can be narrated as the history of a self-consolidated "we." It is much more the history of a permanent renewal of unredeemed promises, which continually recalibrates the limits of community by incorporating new things and excluding others.

One of the constitutive fictions of any formation of community is the notion that the enemy is threatening from outside. Whole genre genealogies of Hollywood can be brought into the field to work against this fiction. They reveal ever new front lines that lead deep into the interior of the community itself. Seen in this way, it would be possible to establish completely different perspectives to pursue the same cognitive interests. The eradication of the Native Americans, slavery, or the Civil War could then just as easily function as leading topics on which the frontline procedures of community in film history(ies) could be reconstructed, such as the comedy of remarriage or the family melodrama. The genres of Hollywood cinema – and also their successors in the history of media – always describe battles around the changing boundaries of the sense of commonality. Indeed, it has always and in any future been open, that is, embattled and disputed, who or what can lay claim to being an individual that may pursue his happiness.

In our time, the ambivalence that is part and parcel of any sense of commonality cannot be stressed often enough. Indeed, not only is Rorty's call to liberal democracy based on the belief in an American sense of commonality. A new racially tinged American nationalism, which was strikingly evident in the recent presidential election, also appeals to the "we" of "our country." If I have chosen the war film genre as an exemplary object, then it is due to the radicalism with which this profound ambivalence itself becomes the topic here.

Berlin, August 2017

Contents

Acknowledgments —— xiii

A Shell-Shocked Face: Prologue —— 1

1 **Repair Work on the Sense of Commonality** —— 9
1.1 A Snapshot of History: Three War Films at the Turn of the Century —— 9
  SAVING PRIVATE RYAN: the sentimental scene of commemorating war —— 11
  WINDTALKERS: the first American – conceived in the plural —— 15
  THE THIN RED LINE: the singular face —— 21
1.2 Richard Rorty and the Pursuit of Happiness —— 29
  Picking up the thread again —— 29
  A feeling for the communal: sense of commonality —— 30
  Poetic making, political acting —— 33
  Describing and redescribing: the plurality of modes of media experience —— 35
1.3 Poetic Calculation and Political Critique: A Film-analytical Comparison —— 37
  APOCALYPSE NOW: a new architecture of cinematic spaces —— 38
  PLATOON: the melody of psychic consonance —— 43
  Genre films as cultural practice —— 45
1.4 Propaganda, Avant-garde, and Genre Films —— 48
  A comparative case study —— 48
  TAG DER FREIHEIT: the media technology of fusion —— 51
  PRELUDE TO WAR: "What put us in the uniform?" —— 56
  Genre films and democracy —— 64
  The constitutive conflict —— 65
  Film analysis as a poetology of film —— 70

2 **The Poetology of Genre Films** —— 73
2.1 Stanley Cavell's Genre Theory —— 73
  Types and individualities —— 73
  Genres as media of a shared perception of the world —— 75
  The historicity of genre cinema —— 77
2.2 On the Critique of the Poetics of Genre —— 80
  Classical and post-classical —— 80

	Taxonomies of rule-governed poetics —— 82
	A mode of industrial production —— 85
	A mode of representation —— 86
	A mode of aesthetic experience —— 89
2.3	Modes and Modalities (Gledhill) —— 91
	Beyond the taxonomies of rule-governed poetics —— 93
	Genre and affect dramaturgy —— 96
	The historical dynamic of poetic making —— 98
	The Hollywood war film as a paradigmatic object —— 101
2.4	What is a Poetics of Affect? —— 101
	Approaches from cognitive psychology: appraisal —— 104
	Mood cues —— 106
	Emotion, feeling, affect —— 108
	A reflexive feeling (Dewey) —— 110
	Spectator feeling —— 113
2.5	Expressive Movement: A Methodological Concept —— 115
	Expressive movement as temporal form —— 118
	The war film and the historical dynamic of genre cinema —— 123
	Pathos scenes: The affect-dramaturgical framework of the Hollywood war film —— 127
	Genre history and history —— 135
3	**The Emergence of the War Film Genre: A Construction of its Poetological Origins** —— 139
3.1	Genre and Film Document —— 139
	Found footage —— 139
	The experiential space of war films —— 146
3.2	Document and Propaganda —— 153
	DECEMBER 7TH —— 154
	The affect-dramaturgical concept —— 155
	Staged reminiscence rather than historical document —— 158
	The face of the invisible enemy —— 161
	Contradictory perceptual politics —— 163
3.3	The Media Practice of Military Collectivization —— 164
	The affect rhetoric of THE BATTLE OF MIDWAY —— 164
	Sentimental pathos versus military pathos —— 168
	Feigning and falsifying: historical knowledge —— 171
	Sentiment versus document —— 174
	What does the film document document? —— 176

3.4	Affective Mobilization —— 178	
	Affect dramaturgies in the range of action and melodrama —— 179	
	GUNG HO!: The mobilization film —— 180	
	The transformation of needy individuals into soldiers —— 183	
	Peripety: switching from action to melodrama —— 185	
	Fighting spirit and the willingness to suffer: a dramaturgical comparison —— 189	
	BATAAN: the pathos of the victim in military collectivization —— 192	
	Audiovisual composition and the affective dynamic —— 193	
	The apotheosis: fusion of separated visual spaces —— 199	
	The emergence of the genre from the perception politics of war films —— 203	
3.5	On the Historicity of Film Images —— 206	
	A succession of automatic world projections (Cavell once again) —— 208	
	The split in perception in the act of viewing films —— 210	
	A specific temporality of film images —— 215	
	WITH THE MARINES AT TARAWA: a memory image on film —— 216	
	The even-tempered registering gaze —— 217	
	Elegy of remembering —— 219	
	Physical presence rather than action —— 221	
	The horror: forms of paranoid perception —— 224	
	Narrative enclosure —— 225	
	Film memory —— 228	

4 Genre and History —— 233

4.1 John Ford's THEY WERE EXPENDABLE: The Matrix of a New Genre —— 233
 Back to genre films —— 233
 An affect-dramaturgical analysis —— 235
 Act I: dissolution and initiation —— 240
 Act II: phantasmagorias of love and death —— 246
 Act III: the cycle of separation and reformation —— 252
 Act IV: the memory image —— 256
4.2 Cultural Memory and Confabulations of Memory —— 260
 Reconstruction of a much-discussed term —— 262
 The relation of memory and political identity (Assmann) —— 263
 Collective memory and individual recollection —— 268
 Confabulations of memory —— 269
 Celebration and ritual —— 270

4.3 Interlocking Affects: SANDS OF IWO JIMA —— 272
   The disillusionment of the feeling for military community —— 273
   The ramifying of affects —— 277
   Making history —— 280
   Genre theory as a poetology of producing history —— 284
4.4 Commemorating the Dead and Community —— 288
   A WALK IN THE SUN: a requiem —— 288
   The formal vocabulary of political sensibility (Koselleck) —— 292
   The talk of war and the myth of community —— 294
   THE STEEL HELMET: the perspective of the dead —— 296
   The miracle of survival —— 300
   THE BIG RED ONE: an image of annihilation —— 302
   The community of survivors —— 304
4.5 The Irresolvable Conflict —— 307
   The irate taxi driver —— 308
   Celebrating war: JARHEAD —— 313
   Military communitization: FULL METAL JACKET —— 318
   The immortal body: the corps —— 322
   The heroic epic: PATTON —— 326
   The present of military communities —— 330

Genre and Sense of Commonality: An Epilogue —— 333
   The Pixelated Revolution —— 333
   THE WAR TAPES —— 335
   REDACTED —— 338
   Moral judgments and transformations in genre poetics —— 340
   A new figure of victim —— 342
   The sensus communis and aesthetic judgment —— 344
   Sensus communis as sense of commonality (Arendt) —— 347
   Genre cinema as a space of experiencing competing senses of the communal —— 349

Bibliography —— 353

Name index —— 367

Film index —— 369

Subject index —— 371

Acknowledgments

For this book, I want to thank all the students and PhD candidates who have accompanied me through seminars and lectures, workshops, PhD colloquia, and research projects: for inspiring me, teaching me in many ways, and supporting me in my work on this rather vast field. I am thinking of the participants of the first seminars and lectures at the Freie Universität Berlin, and of those student assistants, graduate students, and research associates whose committed work facilitated the development of methods that allowed for the exploration of such a broad area of research in the first place. I would like to express my gratitude to Jan-Hendrik Bakels, Hye-Jeung Chung, Sinan Ertugrul, Sarah Greifenstein, Matthias Grotkopp, Michael Lück, Christian Pischel, Thomas Scherer, Franziska Seewald, Anna Steininger, and to all those who, as a research group, have developed with me the methodical groundwork to institute comparative quality analyses of a broad film-historical corpus on a digital basis (eMAEX). I would also like to thank David Gaertner, Cilli Pogodda, and Eileen Rositzka, who – on this basis – have sought to theoretically redefine the field of the Hollywood war film with me. I am greatly indebted to them for numerous suggestions and factual clarification, and also to Danny Gronmaier, Hanno Berger, and Jasper Stratil, whose well-informed comments and critical readings accompanied my finishing of the text.

Finally, I want to thank all those (both on the part of the publisher and in loyal and collegial support) who have helped the text over the last obstacles of reading and re-reading in order to turn it into a richly illustrated book: Stella Diedrich at De Gruyter, as well as Hannes Wesselkämper, Eileen Rositzka, Matthias Grotkopp, and Hauke Lehmann.

Last but not least, I would like to thank Daniel Hendrickson for his patient work translating the book, and Daniel Illger for his understanding editorial work.

A Shell-Shocked Face: Prologue

A shell-shocked face

A famous photo: It shows a soldier, his eyes wide open but vacant. He doesn't seem to be in his right mind, stunned, but not mad, paralyzed, but not dead (see Fig. 1). "Shell-shocked Marine" is the caption, as if the flash from the grenade were just an intensification of photographic lighting technology. Indeed, one could take the caption to refer not only to the face represented there, but also to the form of media used to represent it. At any rate, it seemed to me that the photo got its intensity from the fact that its subject is aligned with the media principle of photography in a quite peculiar way: the time of the face, frozen in the grenade explosion, can be grasped as movement frozen in the moment of a flash of light. Movement here does not mean just any movement in space, but exactly that intensive interplay of micro-facial movements that allow us to perceive the front of a head as a face in the first place.

When this image first caught my eye in a book on the work of Don McCullin, I was in fact interested in the face itself as a form of representation in a wide variety of arts and media. I was searching for examples by which the patterns of facial expression could be described as a specific expressivity of movement that was fundamental to cinematic visuality. That this expressivity was in no way bound to the film image could be seen in the long history of representing faces: from the Faiyum mummy portraits through Christian icons on up to modern painting. And even the conventions of photographic portraiture were aimed at creating the illusion of the movement of facial expression, the living expression of sensation. The intensity with which the photo confronts the spectator as a shell-shocked face is thus very much an effect of its poetic operation.

But this intensity had another very different reference point for me. For an affective quality seemed to be revealed in the shell-shocked face of the photograph, a quality in which I once again recognized a pattern of sensation that I had encountered shortly beforehand in a film. The film was Terrence Malick's THE THIN RED LINE (1998). The look in the soldier's eyes in the photo touched the same aesthetic nerve; and it was not just a matter of related subject matter. In the one as in the other example, what I encountered was a kind of "face" that could not be entirely grasped as a subject or a motif, indeed, it could not even be grasped at the level of representation at all.

What became clear in the photo was that faces do not represent any fixable entity; that what is manifest in them is much more a specific type of movement figuration that we directly grasp as a temporal form of affect. The photo shows

https://doi.org/10.1515/9783110468083-001

Figure 1: Shell-shocked US soldier awaiting transportation away from the frontline, Têt offensive, Hué, Vietnam, February 1968, Don McCullin.

a face from which the facial quality has been obliterated at a single blow along with this temporal form, the dynamic play of the movement of densely packed micro-impulses.

For its part, the film THE THIN RED LINE presented several examples of exactly this temporal form as it mixed its audiovisual images into ever new movement configurations. At any rate, it seemed clear to me that the film transformed the shell-shocked face into another temporality, that of the film image – the screen itself became a face on which the moment of blinding horror extends infinitely, moment for moment, in a finely graded play of sensation within the time of the spectator's perception.

In McCullin's photo the face is fixed as a transitional moment between living sensation, horror, and the impassivity of insentient rigidity. As if the fear of the person hit by the grenade fire were a kind of paradoxical sensation of one's own death – a real living sensation, but still somehow beyond one's own perception: That's it, my death. In the film, this transition is formed as a fluid metamorphosis in which bodies become separated and singled out in ever new convolutions, soon to merge back once again into the battling troop as individual entities, the landscape, and the enemy lodged within the landscape.[1] It is a continual mutation in which the face of the individual changes into that of the troop, which is in turn lost in the face of the landscape, in order to bring forth new series of individual faces.

The duration of this episode of sensation is monadically encapsulated in the photograph of the shell-shocked face. For the photograph does not capture some singular, isolated moment within this duration; rather, it compacts the preceding and following moments of the affect into layers of facial expression laid on top of one another, and all movement has given way: the blazing fear in the moment of the explosion, the horror of the detonation, with which this fear congeals into the crystalline structure of the shell-shocked face. The movement of congelation itself is the face, which becomes the metamorphosis of figurations of kinesthetic expression as they merge into one another in the film.

The representation of faces in a wide variety of media – and this was what I learned from this encounter between a photo and a film – makes it possible to study a form of dynamic movement figuration to which we can attribute a number of visual expressive patterns that we experience as affective and

---

[1] One might think of Plessner's laughing and crying here, which both represent transitions to a corporeal experience in which the subject experiences itself as a blurry boundary to mere organic life. Cf. Helmuth Plessner, "Zur Hermeneutik nichtsprachlichen Ausdrucks," in *Gesammelte Schriften VII: Ausdruck und menschliche Natur*, Frankfurt am Main 1982, 459–478.

affecting. This is the sense in which Gilles Deleuze speaks of the face as a paradigm of the affection-image.[2] For Deleuze, affects designate the power of bodies mutually to affect one another. They designate the temporal form of the event in which bodies are connected up into new corporal figurations. Affects come into their own as aesthetic sensations in a wide variety of temporal patterns and morphological dynamics of symbolic representations; whether these be the representations of faces in painting, in film, or in photography, or simply figurations of movement that in turn can appear in all variations of visual, sculptural, and performative manners of representation. Affection-images do not refer to feelings or emotions, but function as generic forms that generate and transform feelings, allowing them to circulate between various bodies. Affection-images do not give expression to any subjective sensation of feeling, but link separated, contingent acts of subjectivization in their expressivity: for instance, when the affect befalls a cinema spectator in the form of a photo, which awakens in the spectator a feeling that had been implanted in him or her shortly beforehand as a film, and which connects her or him up to the anonymous masses of those who encounter the face in the photo and the one in the film in a similar manner.

The interest in these aesthetic processes, in which the feeling of the individual joins up with a communitarian feeling, is the first reason that I am concerned with war films here. For I do take the subject matter for significant, inasmuch as the media representation of war is founded in a particular way on aesthetic practices and processes that serve the purpose of forming and deploying feelings of community. My interest thus applies to the circulating affection-images of these representations of war, which are meant to relate the sensations of individual spectators to a communally shared, collective feeling.

When, spurred on by this interest, I turned to the Hollywood war film genre, it quickly became clear that a specific type of affection-image is in fact represented in the shell-shocked face, a type that is obviously of great significance for the genre. At any rate, this type can be traced in ever new variations throughout the genre's films: It is the stunned astonishment of Montgomery Clift in FROM HERE TO ETERNITY (Fred Zinnemann, 1953) and the face of the man running berserk in FULL METAL JACKET (Stanley Kubrick, 1987). It is the insistent astonishment of Martin Sheen and the coldness of Colonel Kurtz's controlled cruelty in APOCALYPSE NOW (Francis Ford Coppola, 1979). It is the paralyzed face of Tom Hanks in SAVING PRIVATE RYAN (Steven Spielberg, 1998) and the flashing self-consciousness of Nick in THE DEER HUNTER (Michael Cimino, 1978). And

---

2 Gilles Deleuze, *Cinema 1: The Movement-Image*, London 1986, 87ff.

time and again it is the image of the soldier's suffering, emphatically pointed out and supplied with the mythic signs of sacrifice, as in THE STEEL HELMET (Samuel Fuller, 1951), in PLATOON (Oliver Stone, 1986) and in HAMBURGER HILL (John Irvin, 1987).

The pathos formula of the war film genre

The focus of these films is not war heroes or heroic deeds; the focus is much more the melodramatic depiction of the suffering individual soldier. The shell-shocked face forms the signature of the Hollywood war genre; it can be read throughout the films as a deeply ambivalent emblem. On the one hand, it is the imago of the sacrifice, in which the horror, the agony of the soldier has been shaped into the subject matter of an evocative and meaningful icon of suffering. On the other hand, it presents a film image that seeks to bear witness to this suffering as nothing other than pure, physical suffering; it is a witness to an annihilated human life, to which no meaning can be attributed any more. On the one hand then, this face becomes a symbol that refers to the mythology of community, which finds its own worth confirmed in the sacrifice of the individual. On the other hand, it points to the sheer immeasurable quantity of photographic and film images that document the victims of violence in the wars and mass murders of the past century.

On the one hand a mythical emblem of community, on the other a document of crime, on the one hand a symbol, on the other a witness – the ambivalent image of the soldier's suffering articulates a contradiction that lies quite literally in the foundations of America's political culture. Indeed, the annihilation of individual life violates the central value that founds the goal of political community itself. Today, nearly 70 years after the Second World War, this concerns western culture as a whole – albeit in a less explicitly political sense.

Alternating between a mythical image of sacrifice and an image that attests to the moral violation of the political community's values through this community, the shell-shocked face articulates a deep moral ambiguity in all its variations. It equates moral indignation with devout remembrance, accusation with the pathos of commemorating the fallen who had sacrificed themselves to maintain the political community. This ambiguous pathos in the American war film genre is perfectly exemplified in McCullin's photograph. We can thus see the shell-shocked face as the pathos formula that has generated and structured the genre as such, as a genre.

We should state that pathos formulas are in no way meant as iconographic subjects or motifs, which can then form serial entities that can be traced straight through the various manifestations of visual culture.³ Rather, in this case as well, it is a matter of circulating affects; of passions – namely pathos – which get transferred with these forms to a community – whether that be conceived as an audience or as a religious or political community. For Aby Warburg, who coined the term 'pathos formula,' certain primal affects function as generic factors that have been expressed in the history of visual culture in countless series of dynamic movement figurations. Even if we do not share this cultural-anthropological reasoning, the term allows us to link aesthetic serialities, for example genres, to the affective economies of forms of cultural community.

From the perspective to be developed here, pathos formula quite generally means a generic principle with which serially recurring expressivities are to be referred back to specific realms of affect in a cultural community. Pathos formulas are connected with the tension-laden affect constellations and constitutional conflicts of the community in each case. Speaking with Deleuze, they can be conceived as a specific type of image, that is, affection-images,⁴ which can be developed in serial replication into forms of a communitarian feeling. My understanding of the pathos formula is thus not directed at archetypal forms of affect (primal fears, pain ...), but seeks to understand affects per se as generic forms of collective sensation, which are manifest in series of expressivities.

In the recurrent re-staging of the pathos formula in media we can grasp a reworking of the affective collision, newly applied every time, that confronts us in the ambiguity of the shell-shocked face. If the image of sacrifice in the war film links back to archaic rituals of forming community, the pathos of commemorative mourning and collective memory, the image, being a testament to the crime, simultaneously refers to the violation of the goals that the political community has set for itself; it is directed at the pathos of moral indignation, the rage that is turned against any attempt to endow meaning. The iconography, the dramaturgy of conflict, the narrative of the the genre develop along this collision of affect. This is the sense in which the variations of the pathos formula in the shell-shocked face structure the history and poetics of the Hollywood war film genre.

While I do not wish to be hasty in comparing the media practice of watching films with cultic actions and rituals, I would like to work out one ritual aspect of this practice in the following, an aspect that can help us understand the generic

---

3 This is the sense in which Bronfen and others use the term. Cf. Elisabeth Bronfen, *Specters of War: Hollywood's Engagement with Military Conflict*, New Brunswick 2012.
4 Cf. Gilles Deleuze and Félix Guattari, *A Thousand Plateaus: Capitalism & Schizophrenia*, Minneapolis 1987; see also their *What is Philosophy?*, New York 1994.

function of the pathos formula and its serial ramification in the war film genre. The Hollywood war film, I would hypothesize, is oriented to a form of collectivity that can be understood as an affective basis of the political, as a sense of commonality. Understanding and terminologically defining this sense of commonality in its relation to the sphere of politics is the basic goal of my examination of the Hollywood war film genre.

This requires the prior task of defining the generic function of the pathos formula in order to develop an affect-theoretical understanding of the poetics of genre – instead of the typical understanding of genre as a taxonomy of texts, deducing the genre from their history. The Hollywood war film genre is an exemplary place to work out this affect-theoretical understanding; indeed, within a clearly delimited time period (1940 to 1945) and a quite homogeneous media technological *dispositif* (the cinema of the 1950s) and a fully developed genre system (Hollywood), we can observe how a new genre developed from the propaganda and informational films made by government offices and entertainment films mad in Hollywood. Looking at the process of how this genre emerged, it should be possible to study the dynamic of transformations in which the Hollywood genre system reacted to the appearances of crisis in a democracy at war. To the degree that the Hollywood war film can be defined at all by a peculiar kind of pathos, this is closely associated with the affect-economic crises in the structures of political community.

The pathos formula of the shell-shocked face corresponds to a crisis in the forms of political community, which are obviously manifest in western culture after the excesses of state violence in the genocides and wars of the twentieth century. The stark contradiction between the meaningful death of the sacrifice *for* and the meaningless death of the individual *due to* the political community is an irresolvable, affect-laden conflict for any society that does not call on any higher authority than that of the ordinary life of numerous individuals in its political action. Consequently, the Hollywood war film does not develop as a heroic genre, but as a melodramatic one. This speaks to the formation of an aesthetic pleasure – the delight in sentimentality – that is not initially granted any political dignity at all. But the question of the relation between the feeling of the communal, the sense of commonality, and that of politics, is closely linked to the question of how the various modalities of aesthetic pleasure contribute to this sense of commonality.

The example of the war film genre makes it obvious that the media practices and symbolic forms by which a society secures its political coherence are marked by just those modalities of experience that are usually attributed to the genres of art and entertainment culture. At any rate, the strategies of mise-en-scène and the poetic concepts of Hollywood's war film genre are always related to the network of "affective connectors"⁵ in a culture that pursues an emphatic idea of political community – irrespective of whether the individual films seek to confirm, mobilize, criticize, reject, or renew these affective collectivizations in their pathos. Because this never happens as pure reflection, but is always conveyed through an enjoyment of becoming-affected, I speak of the poetics of affect in the Hollywood war film. In the following, I would thus like to attempt to work out the ritual aspect as an exemplary poetics of the media practice of cinema, in which a given society refers to itself as a political community.⁶

I would first like to turn to the recent history of Hollywood genres to clarify these reflections, sketching out the essential features of the poetics of a few war films. They are films that were screened for a worldwide audience at the end of the last century but that developed a highly specific social perspective based on the American nation as a political community. I would like to consider these films in the light of some ideas that Richard Rorty was developing at the same time. In his lecture from 1998, the American philosopher developed concepts about the political community of the nation that – in analogy to the films discussed – mark that brief historical moment in which the political ideal of the United States of America seemed once again to be gaining that culturally binding force that it had lost since the Vietnam War – only to land very quickly in a difficult crisis⁷ once again.

---

5 Cf. Albrecht Koschorke, *Körperströme und Schriftverkehr: Mediologie des 18. Jahrhunderts*, Munich 1999, 15.
6 Cf. Joseph Vogl, "Einleitung," in his edited volume *Gemeinschaften: Positionen zu einer Philosophie des Politischen*, Frankfurt am Main 1994, 7–27.
7 Richard Rorty, *Achieving Our Country: Leftist Thought in Twentieth-century America*, Cambridge 1998.

1 Repair Work on the Sense of Commonality

1.1 A Snapshot of History: Three War Films at the Turn of the Century

Since the mid-seventies, the Hollywood war film has almost been synonymous with films about the Vietnam War. Only at the turn of the new millennium did large-scale Hollywood productions emerge that once again looked back to the Second World War: SAVING PRIVATE RYAN (Steven Spielberg, 1998) tells of the first days of the invasion in Normandy; Terrence Malick's THE THIN RED LINE, also from 1998, and John Woo's WINDTALKERS from 2002 refer back to different stages of the war in the Pacific. If the Vietnam films had been about what was probably the greatest moral crisis of the United States in the last century, the Second World War, as a historical topos of the nation, stands for the exact opposite. In this war, the USA not only became the undisputed military-economic leader of the western world, it also took on – despite Hiroshima and Nagasaki – moral-political leadership.

This suggested the idea that this turn to the Second World War was politically motivated. At the end of the twentieth century it became necessary once again – as was popularly believed – to bolster the moral prestige that the United States had achieved in the greatest moral and human catastrophe of a century familiar with catastrophes. At any rate, these films, which were made before the attacks on the World Trade Center and the quickly ensuing wars in Afghanistan and Iraq, instigated a new discussion about the media representation of war and its cultural and political function. In a certain sense, we can say that this discussion continues to this day. It is animated by ever new media forms of warfare, in which the various wars take shape.

On the one hand, the interest in images of war is an immediate effect of the way contemporary wars appear in the media. On the other, and precisely in light of the turn of the millennium, it became clear that even the greatest crimes and catastrophes of humanity – the Holocaust, the World Wars, the atom bomb – fade as memories when the eyewitnesses begin to die. War films, and the discussion of war films, are thus closely linked, particularly in Europe, to a discussion about collective memory and cultural remembrance.

Correspondingly, the discussion about the war film – in part a result of the films I have just named – primarily circled around the question of the media and practices of collective memory. Hollywood's politics of memory was especially discussed in relation to SAVING PRIVATE RYAN. Already with SCHINDLER'S LIST (1993) Spielberg had presented a film that inserted the historical testament of the Holocaust as a melodramatic staging of genre cinema into the popular historical image of Hollywood. SAVING PRIVATE RYAN also presents itself as a telling rearrangement of historical facts and visual documents. But the question was not primarily about historical knowledge or cultural forms of memory; in fact, Spielberg's history films were discussed as examples of a post-classical blockbuster cinema, which – under the sign of the end of history – put aesthetic experience in place of historical consciousness.[1] But it does not seem very sensible to me to oppose history in this way with spectacularly staged acts of remembrance. An image of history also remains linked to the poetic processes of its production and presentation, even if it is subject to the operations of scholarship.

In fact, SAVING PRIVATE RYAN, WINDTALKERS, and THE THIN RED LINE each engage with media factors and poetic processes in highly specific ways, which is the basis of the historical image of the Second World War; an image of history that is quite overwhelmingly determined by photographic and film documents. So, not only in their subject matter, but also in their arrangement of dramatic conflict, the films revert to the stereotypes and visual standards that had been used to shape the classical Hollywood war film over three decades. At any rate, what these films have in common – and do not share, for instance, with productions such as PEARL HARBOR (Michael Bay 2001) or WE WERE SOLDIERS (Randall Wallace, 2002) – is that rather than referring to historical positionings they refer to pictures and documents, which themselves belong to a past time. SAVING PRIVATE RYAN, for instance, ostensibly borrows from the screen epic THE LONGEST DAY (Ken Annakin/Andrew Marton/Bernhard Wicki/Darryl F. Zanuck) from 1962; but above all the film refers to countless film documents that were created during the landing of the allied forces at Normandy.

In no way do I understand this recourse to the previous visual documents as any self-sufficient postmodern poetics of pastiche; the films are much more concerned with the audiovisual images as the circulating testaments of a historical catastrophe that is fading in the memory of the living generation. I would like to discuss how this is presented in detail by means of three film-analytical sketches.

---

1 Drehli Robnik brought the results of this discussion into his work on the combat film. He convincingly demonstrated how Spielberg re-stages the European campaign in the simulated remembrance acts of blockbuster movies as an act of rescuing Jews. (It hurts! – Where? – Don't know! – Good, here you have a spectacle, that shows you the source of your pain.) Cf. Drehli Robnik, *Kino, Krieg, Gedächtnis: Affekt-Ästhetik, Nachträglichkeit und Geschichtspolitik im deutschen und amerikanischen Gegenwartskino*, unpublished dissertation: Amsterdam 2007, http://dare.uva.nl/document/50897 (August 17, 2013). On the relation between historical evidence and aesthetic experience, cf. also: Rick Altman, *Film/Genre*, London 1999, 188ff.

I begin with Spielberg's SAVING PRIVATE RYAN before turning to John Woo's WIND-TALKERS and finally to Terrence Malick's THE THIN RED LINE.

SAVING PRIVATE RYAN: the sentimental scene of commemorating war

One family, three generations ... parents, children, grandchildren. A field of graves, endless, unrestricted by any horizon. The montage forms an impression that is already implied by the architecture of the military cemetery. Gravestone after gravestone is lined up in diagonal rows; each of them can be singled out and enumerated in itself, but seeing them all together like this, they all add up to an image of the literal innumerability of the dead. The white monuments are as homogenous as the uniforms of soldiers, the only difference being that between the Christian cross and the Jewish Star of David.

A close-up shows the face of the veteran (see Figure 2). This introduces a flashback, which begins with the event testified to by the innumerable stony witnesses in the graveyard: the great loss of life at Omaha Beach. The sound design, the sound of the landing boat, already pulls the spectators into the visual space, even before the ramps are opened and the infantrymen at the front of the boat are relinquished to enemy fire.

With no establishing action, the theme of the next 20 minutes starts with a bang. The first rows of soldiers die as a living shield, making it possible for those following to advance, step by step, row by row, onto the beach peppered with mines and fencing. The troops push onto the land, while the individual soldiers, tattered and shot to pieces, head toward the prize made possible by this movement.

Within its first twenty minutes, SAVING PRIVATE RYAN draws on all the registers of audiovisual rhetoric that the cinema has developed for battle scenes to put this monstrosity on the screen. A montage of dissociated spatial and sound perspectives opens up a space of chaotic perception; the camera moves between diffusely attributable shots, just above or below the water, like a swimmer – or a drowning person; sometimes obstructed by the water spraying up; sometimes the smeared spurts of blood make the lens itself visible. What we see gets detached from any attributable perspective, becomes distant, viewed as through a glass pane. Even the level of sound is composed out of an impression of multiple perspectives, moving between the muteness of the soldiers falling into the water and the deafening noise of the explosions.

Finally, the audio perspective opens up to the emptiness of a muffled echo chamber; the effect is like the self-perception of the inner sounds of our body, like what we hear when we hold our ears closed. In fact, this echo chamber, shut

Figure 2: The face (SAVING PRIVATE RYAN).

off to the outside, is the first perspective clearly attributed to an individual body. The turmoil of the battle becomes a horror film; mute cries, thudding inaudible shots, soundless grenade explosions, bodies torn to pieces. We see the protagonist's face: a shell-shocked face.

As a whole, the staging of the scene is aimed at producing the largest possible discrepancy between the perspective of a living individual, enclosed and disorientated in the events of the battle, and the cinematographic description of that battle. The paralyzed face joins these two perspectives to each other.

Enclosed within the thunder of shots, then in the quietness of this foreign body, a peculiar form of subjective perspective unfolds for the spectator; he senses himself to be physically quite near, and at the same time he is kept at an absolute distance – as the counterpart to the traumatized face. The camera simulates the fragmented view of overextended perception, while nonetheless maintaining the position of the sovereign spectator.[2] What the troops manage to achieve only through great suffering and sacrifice is possible for him without any effort whatsoever. Seeing and hearing the whole time, the spectator criss-crosses through the spatial simulation of the chaotic perceptual consciousness of a body dazzled and numbed by horror and pain; he finds a first narrative foothold when he sees the face of the star, Tom Hanks, associated with the muffled echo chamber, which surrounds him in the movie seat (much like the interior view of the shell-shocked face). A dialogue is initiated; first still without sound, then comes the first exchange of words. Little by little a figuration of plot is formed from the scenario of horror: "How can we crack that bunker up there?" When the soldiers overtake the beach, scale the bluffs, and take the bunker, the spectator finds himself in the action space of a clear reality, once again securely in the space of classical narrative cinema.

The transition into the mode of narration is marked by a precise cusp. Only at the moment when it becomes possible to catch a glimpse of the enemy by means of a mirror does the narrative perspective become stable.[3] The journey into the interior of the country, the landscape of Normandy, the reconnaissance patrol with the special mission, the decisive battle, all of this takes place in the mirror of the classical Hollywood war film and of the audiovisual documents of the Second World War, which circulate in the media.

We understand the flashback as a movement of memory, described not only in the fiction of the character, but also on the real level of the film spectator.

---

[2] Thomas Elsaesser and Michael Wedel view the post-classical war film as a new body genre. Cf. Thomas Elsaesser and Michael Wedel, "The Hollow Heart of Hollywood: Apocalypse Now and the New Sound Space" in *Conrad on Film*, ed. Gene M. Moore, Cambridge 1997, 151–175. Cf. also: Hermann Kappelhoff, "Shell shocked face: Einige Überlegungen zur rituellen Funktion des US-amerikanischen Kriegsfilms," in *Verklärte Körper*, ed. Nicola Suthor, Erika Fischer-Lichte, Munich 2006, 69–89.

For an analysis of Spielberg's film in terms of character psychology or plot logic, cf. Albert Auster, "'Saving Private Ryan' and American Triumphalism," in *The War Film*, ed. Robert Eberwein, New Brunswick/London 2005, 205–213; Jeanine Basinger, "Combat Redux," in *The World War II Combat Film: Anatomy of a Genre*, ed. Jeanine Basinger, New York 2003, 253–262.

[3] Cf. Drehli Robnik, "Körper-Erfahrung und Film-Phänomenologie," in *Moderne Film Theorie*, ed. Jürgen Felix, Mainz 2002, 246–280.

What for the character is a passage through a trauma, behind which the space of memory opens up, functions for the spectator as a mirror reversal of the sequence of action in the classical war film. There, the agony of the soldiers, the shell-shocked face, is the *last* image; here it is placed at the beginning. In the spatial simulation of the chaos of a catastrophe that overstrains every individual consciousness, the presentation of this face forms the *first* crystallization on which an episodic action can gradually become anchored, the germ of a narrative, of a genre tale.

The same reversal also takes place on the level of the dramatic conflict. While the opening sequence offers up all possible means of cinematic representation in order to allow the unbearable act of violence to be grasped by the senses, an act which consists of literally employing the life and limb of the individual as the medium of the onward motion of the troops, the film's plot reverses this order. It is not the individual who dies for the intangible community, but the mission of saving the individual life that brings death to nearly the entire unit. With this story, Spielberg seems to resolve the fundamental conflict of the classical war film, that between providing an image of sacrifice and testifying to an act of violence, in a paradoxical way of reading the founding act of the nation. The right of the individual to life, liberty, and the pursuit of happiness, this highest value of the political community, is secured and maintained through the sacrificial death of innumerable individuals. In fact, however, the face of the weeping veteran among his family transfers the historical pathos of the shell-shocked face into a sentimental image of remembrance. The soldier, who comes back to the graveyard, thinks of his commander's last words: "Earn this."

After nearly everyone has fallen so that he, James Ryan, can keep the right to life and liberty, this last order seems as terrible to us as the image of the battle at the beginning of the film. But the guilt that this survivor has to deal with consists only in bringing to an end the platoon's mission, for which the others died. He owes the dead nothing more than to use his life and liberty to pursue happiness. This is why, at the end of the film, it is not the pathos formula of the shell-shocked face that we see, but the weeping face of the remembering survivor.

The surviving soldier at the grave of his fallen comrades, his face, the tears turned away from the family; the wife, the children, the grandchildren stand slightly off in the background, their gaze fixed on the weeping man. This scene is also a reprise of another scene; we might think of it as the primal scene of bourgeois sensibility. Indeed, here Spielberg is reconstructing a scene of pathos-laden remembrance, and its serial repetition almost designates the *movens* of sentimental entertainment culture: the family gathered at the father's deathbed, merging into a community, their feelings focused in the same direction as they empathetically gaze at the dying man. In his play *Le Père de famille* (1758), Diderot deployed this scene as the prototype of the sentimental theater with the purpose of newly re-staging it over and over again in order to awaken in the audience the idea of a community connected to one another by the bond of their shared sensations.[4] For the sensitive bourgeoisie, this bond was sentimental compassion. Seen in this way, it is in fact the primal scene of an art and entertainment culture that constructs media in order to configure affects. At any rate, the closing scene of SAVING PRIVATE RYAN could not have been better arranged to illustrate the character of the absorbed beholder, which Michael Fried has developed as the type-case for this subjectivity.[5]

SAVING PRIVATE RYAN lets the war film end in this scene of sentimental remembrance. In fact, Private Ryan's family, positioned in a half-circle in the background of the image, confronts the film spectator as a community, literally drawing him or her into their circle; indeed, they are connected through the shared gaze at one and the same scene of someone weeping at a graveside – as if the circle of community were closing around the mourning face together with the gaze of the anonymous audience in front of the screen. The montage breaks up the figuration with a line crossing in order to link this community of sentimental remembrance in a circular sequence of shots directly with the symbol of the nation: the flag of the United States of America.

WINDTALKERS: the first American – conceived in the plural

WINDTALKERS begins with a prologue that plays out a narrative stereotype of the classical war film. Joe Enders (Nicolas Cage), the commander of a platoon, compels his men to hang on through a crushing attack; Enders is the only one to survive the attack, hit by a grenade explosion and only seemingly dead. The conception of the character varies the basic dramatic conflict in a thoroughly conventional way. Feelings of guilt keep the survivor from getting on with his life; he is no longer capable of pursuing happiness. This characterizes the figure of the sacrifice, and this type has increasingly come to define the genre since the Vietnam War: the soldier traumatized by his culpable act.[6]

In the end, the starting constellation, the culpable act in militarily correct behavior, is reversed. The film finds its apotheosis in the stereotype of the

---

4 Cf. Hermann Kappelhoff, *Matrix der Gefühle: Das Kino, das Melodrama und das Theater der Empfindsamkeit*, Berlin 2004, 63–83, as well as 98–102, 107–109 and 148–151.
5 Cf. Michael Fried, *Absorption and Theatricality: Painting and Beholder in the Age of Diderot*, Berkeley 1980.
6 Cf. the chapter on the Iraq War film in this book.

sacrificing hero, who puts the lives of his comrades over his own: the soldier, carrying his dying comrades on his back away from enemy fire, thus coming to his own death. This time it is the commander, the white American, who saves the life of his friend, a Navajo.

I quote from a summary:

> In the Pacific War the marines Joe Enders (Nicolas Cage) and "Ox" Henderson (Christian Slater) are given the secret order to act as a kind of bodyguard for the radio operators Ben Yahzee (Adam Beach) and Charlie Whitehorse (Roger Willie). The two Navajos are in possession of a special code that must under no circumstances fall into enemy hands. The grim battle over the island of Saipan bonds the men together. And it is only a matter of time before the two protectors of the code speakers are confronted with the terrible question: Would they give their all to protect the code?[7]

The special code is the language of the Native Americans, the Navajos. As much as it might give us pause to contemplate that it is precisely the language of the natives, whose almost complete annihilation forms the foundation of the nation, which now provides a decisive strategic advantage in the battle against the Japanese, the director, John Woo, is not content to leave it at that. Even the circumstance that the Navajos physically resemble the Japanese enemies more than they do their white comrades cannot be taken as merely anecdotal. Both refer much more to a rather marginal narrative of the genre that WINDTALKERS is working with. Indeed, in the classical US war film, ethnic heterogeneity is regularly highlighted as one of the fundamental characteristics of the American army. It goes without saying that this topos was due to the pragmatic demands of propaganda during the Second World War, which made it necessary to represent the widest possible number of ethnicities (with the exception of African American soldiers) in the personnel of the film. With this topos WINDTALKERS is certainly singling out a characteristic element of the American nation, which defines itself in its political self-understanding by permanently and dynamically refiguring a community that can be consummated beyond all ethnic and religious boundaries.

In fact, this can be taken as a statement of the film's subject matter. One by one, the different ethnic backgrounds of individual soldiers come forth; so that the initial contrast between Navajos and white Americans breaks apart into multiple figurations of many individuals of various backgrounds. Among them all, the Navajos are in fact the only true Americans, indeed, Native Americans. Here, the idea of a political community meant to traverse the oppositions of ethnicities and religions acquires a specific turn. From the film's perspective, the

---

7 Content information of the German DVD edition, distributed by MGM.

other ethnicities initially always appear to be menacing, foreign, and adversarial; but they are only transitional appearances in determining the dynamically expanding boundaries of the community. Admittedly, this historical dynamic is ultimately determined by military force, the racist roots of which are in clear evidence. So just as the initial antagonism in the platoon between Navajos and the other Americans transitions into a community of individuals who are foreign to one another but are connecting by a growing bond of friendship, the war against the Japanese appears as a further stage of the dynamic reconfiguration of the political community. The war in WINDTALKERS becomes a metaphor for racist violence, the repression of which defines the political goal of this community.[8]

The interpretation of war as the basis for a dynamic collectivization of ethnicities that are foreign and hostile to one another has found a telling rhetorical intensification in the film. After every battle – almost like winding down after work – we see the decimated troops at the graves of their just fallen comrades. The soldiers chat after burying the dead, they relax, they receive their commendations, they go into a rage, haunted by the voices of the dead, they take off from here to their next battle. We see the horde of men transform: living bodies become fields of crosses and steel helmets – while the friendships between the survivors become closer and closer. Like the refrain of a ballad, the recurring battles structure the arrival of a community that seems to get its power from the increasing number of the dead.

WINDTALKERS stages the process of this collectivization in the friendship between the two main characters: Joe Enders and Ben Yahzee. Their relationship begins with great disconcertment and remains defined by a battle in which one of them struggles for distance, the other for recognition, in order finally to end in literal fusion. Their faces are staged as radical antagonists: the one empty, stony, a mask of the choked power of sensation – a shell-shocked face; the other open, always laughing. It seems to have an overabundance of precisely the powers of sensation that have been obliterated from the face of Enders. Joe Enders therefore is

---

[8] Michael Wedel also thematizes WINDTALKERS as a film focused on the question of community. In order to do so, he primarily draws on Nancy's theories. This constitutes a fundamental difference from what I understand as a political community in this text. Cf. Michael Wedel, "Körper, Tod und Technik – Der postklassische Hollywood-Kriegsfilm als reflexives »Body Genre«," in *Körperästhetiken: Filmische Inszenierungen von Körperlichkeit*, ed. Dagmar Hoffmann, Bielefeld 2010, 77–100.

From the perspective that I am attempting to develop here, the war film in fact appears to be a genre that confronts two incompatible models of community: that of the political community and that of the military community. On the term 'military community', cf. Kappelhoff, "Shell shocked face."

also given the mission to protect the Navajo, because, as is shown in the prologue, he acquired this stoniness as a quite particular qualification in battle. It would not be past him to kill the one entrusted to him if he threatened to fall into enemy hands.

This melodrama of love between friends finds its counterpart in the representation of the war action. In blinding speed, a highly mobile camera links series of unattributable views together with blurry, internally moving medium shots and wild pans to form an elaborate landscape of war. It culminates in long shots that look like computer animated paintings. These are images of classic Hollywood cinema, from John Ford's westerns to Sam Fuller's war epics, estranged through the rhetoric of action cinema into a kind of high-tech realism. In the film's final rescue operation, both sides, the melodrama and the action film, come together. Enders saves the Navajo from enemy fire instead of taking him away from the clutches of the enemy with a deadly shot.

One might see the rescue of the Indian as an ironic commentary on the military code of honor of "no man left behind." This complies with the impression that the scenes of winding down after battles between the increasing graves at the camp above all emphasize the deep ambivalence of this promise of indissoluble bonds. The death of the individual is the medium of soldierly solidarity. But the irony goes deeper; it refers to the political community. In the apotheosis described, WINDTALKERS links back to the topography of a narrative tradition in which the history of colonizing the American continent was poetically formed into a myth of the birth of the nation, an image of the historicity of "our country."

"A key scene in almost every Vietnam movie" – so it is said – is the helicopter that flies away leaving a GI behind. "The traumatology of the new war film is built up on the experience of leaving behind and being left behind."[9] This scene is certainly much older than the Vietnam War film. The solider abandoned among the enemy – threatened with torture and desecration – continues a motif that reaches back to the very beginnings of American culture: the narrative of the suffering and martyrdom of prisoners captured by savages, the scenario of the puritanical 'captivity narratives.'

The poetic phantasm of the captivity narratives conform – here I am drawing on Winfried Fluck's functional history of the American novel[10] – to the basic

---

9 Georg Seeßlen, "Von Stahlgewittern zur Dschungelkampfmaschine. Veränderungen des Krieges und des Kriegsfilms," in *Kino und Krieg: Von der Faszination eines tödlichen Genres*, eds. Ernst Karpf and Doron Kiesel, Arnoldshainer Filmgespräche 6, Frankfurt am Main 1989, 15–32, here 26 and 27.
10 Winfried Fluck, *Das kulturelle Imaginäre: Eine Funktionsgeschichte des amerikanischen Romans 1790–1900*, Frankfurt am Main 1997.

schema of the imagination of the historical that is cultivated in popular narrative forms. According to this schema, the topography of the historical image is structured by two other motifs. The first is war against the foreign, uncivilized race; this topos is historically marked by the Indian Wars. Here the enemy is positioned outside the communal world as the menacing other. The second is the struggle against the technocratic rule of bureaucracy and state power, which threatens the freedom of the individual and his pursuit of happiness. Historically, this struggle is positioned by the War of Independence, the American revolution against the forms of rule in old Europe. But the topos is very quickly related to an enemy that lives inside the community itself, and that threatens to choke the life out of this community through the excesses of bureaucracy and state despotism.

Martyrdom, the individual physical suffering of the one lost alone in the wilderness; the enemy as the menacing outside of the other race or culture; the conflict between individual claims to freedom and growing technocratic rule: this is the outline – according to Winfried Fluck – of the basic topography proposed by the popular narrative forms of American culture in order to connect the idea of the nation with an idea of history.[11] This topography still provides the dramaturgical pattern of the Hollywood war film genre.

The scenes in which Ben Yahzee is rescued and Joe Enders dies follow this poetic phantasm. They form a variation on the constellation of characters that came into world literature with James Fenimore Cooper's *The Last of the Mohicans* (1826): the friendship between the last of the Mohicans and the frontiersman. This friendship spans the gulf that divides the inhabitable settlers' areas from the woods where the foreigners dwell. It is the clearing in the no-man's-land between the races who had been turned enemy in war and the area under the control of the old technocratic powers. Cooper's narrative of a friendship beyond the war of enemy races describes the beginning of a new form of community. But this beginning is also already linked to the ambivalence of the victim and the criminal, mourning and culpability. In the friendship between the frontiersman and the last Mohican, this ambivalence found its form of pathos.

WINDTALKERS stages this double figure literally as one body fused in battle. Except that in this film, it is not the native who has to die, but the non-native American. Instead of obeying orders and killing Ben, Enders puts himself under attack to drag his wounded friend out of the line of fire, carrying him away on his back. We see a grotesque figure – Enders is also hit by shots – assembled out of body parts and bleeding wounds, which can only lumber forward with great difficulty. It hobbles, creeps, crawls out of the thick of battle in the war film and into

---

11 Cf. ibid.

the apotheosis of the melodrama. The dying soldier remembers his Italian roots, and with this remembrance all the powers of sensation seem to return to his face.

Much like Spielberg seeks to resolve the ambivalent pathos of the war film in a sentimental scene, John Woo transfers the pathos scene of friendship into a melodramatic figuration. But unlike in Spielberg, this is no internalized sense of remembrance, but an analytical set up. The reversal of the positions, the play with the poetic topography of the primal narrative of the nation, gives the pathos an ironic distance and allows for the ambiguity to come forth even more strongly (see Figure 3). In its representation of the Second World War, WINDTALKERS develops the image of history itself as a poetic form, in which a society imagines itself as a community. It thus refers much more to the contemporary issues of a multiethnic, postcolonial society than to the significance of the Second World War for just this historical image of this society.

Figure 3: Melodramatic figuration (WINDTALKERS).

The film contrasts the self-image of a political community that sees itself as neither an ethnic nor a religious unit with the narrative of the war between races. It thus allows communitization itself to appear as a deeply ambivalent process of violence, a constantly shifting frontal progression, a moving frontier between what is one's own and what constitutes and marks the foreigner.

When, at the ending – before the grandiose backdrop of Monument Valley, which became the iconographic signature landscape of the myth of genesis of

America in the western genre – Private Ben Yahzee completes the mourning ritual of the native Americans. This happens in a very similar way to SAVING PRIVATE RYAN, under the gaze of his wife and his son. It is a different American family. Dressed in the traditional clothing of the Navajos, high above the location of so many films about the wars on the Indians, the family creates a highly unreal appearance. A reflection of the cinema in which the image of America's history seems to be corrected in a similar way as it is through the story of rescuing the soldier James Ryan. The frontiersman gets his last respects from his friend, the Native American.

While Spielberg in fact attempts to integrate the American European campaign into the historical image of the United States with the sentimental scene of mourning (a war that saved the lives of individuals[12]), John Woo reverses the poetics of the narrative of the birth of the nation itself against historical facticity. According to this poetic, the societal dominance of the white race is only a temporary appearance in the becoming of the community – a becoming that sketches out its historical shape in the topography of narratives of war against the foreign races, of the martyrdom of the sacrifice, and of the victory of freedom over the rule of technocracy.

THE THIN RED LINE: the singular face

Terrence Malick's THE THIN RED LINE also takes up the poetics of this talk of war. He transfers it into a lyrical form. Right from the beginning, he varies the theme: Why is there still war at the foundation of the most peaceful relationship? Why this division into two fighting powers everywhere? There dark-haired children, here light-skinned soldiers; there mothers of color, holding their children on their hips as they carry them home from the beach, here the steel grey gunboat that the soldiers maneuver right into the middle of the South Seas paradise. The film's prologue shows idyllic nature. Like a cathedral of light, it surrounds the kind of everyday life that the soldiers had left behind when they became members of the military corps. We see soldiers playing with children, dancing, bodies floating in the water; they are reflected in the foreign gazes of women carrying their children home from the riverbanks to the village. It seems to be the epitome of peace, even if the dread with which one of the women speaks of being afraid of the strangers already portends something else. The gunboat turns up in front of the village; it takes the fugitive soldiers, who had left their unit without permission, back to war.

---

12 Cf. Robnik, *Kino, Krieg, Gedächtnis*.

If WINDTALKERS is based on the narrative of the Indian wars and James Fenimore Cooper's historical novels, then THE THIN RED LINE is connected to the philosophical essays of Ralph Waldo Emerson and Henry David Thoreau. In fact, we get the impression that these bacchanal observations of nature translate American transcendentalism into a cinematographic hymn.

The camera moves through the landscape of the South Seas island like the philosophizing walker in Thoreau's *Walden* does through the woods of Massachusetts. Indeed, it produces an encounter with nature as an image that does not correspond to conventional representations of nature at all. It produces it, as Dana Polan writes, as the image of a purely subjective experience: "The long waves of grass ... become here a pure space of experience as we see nothing but endless fields with no advance, no logic, no fixities of point of view."[13] The film unquestionably follows a poetics that behaves quite differently from that of classical narrative cinema.[14] The images of the landscape and the battles are like the characters, their faces, their gestures and actions are themselves elements of a lyrical reflection, of a monologue folded into itself, which cannot be attributed to any individual subject. It belongs neither to the characters nor to any narrator, not to the author nor to the spectator either – and yet it links each of these elements, framing them all in a floating, expanding state that is contended in transitory first-person moments.

In doing so, the film proves to be a strict transposition of the narrative strategy of the novel *The Thin Red Line* (1962). In the style of laconic realism, James Jones depicts a landscape, a situation, an atmosphere in broad strokes; the outward qualities of the characters are broadly outlined in a similar way. This also brings them that much closer to the authorial narrator in the form of his speech. Indeed, in diction and perspective, this speech is much like that of the characters, even in

---

[13] Dana Polan, "Auteurism and War-teurism: Terence Malick's War Movie," in *The War Film*, ed. Robert Eberwein, New Brunswick 2005, 53–62.

[14] Dana Polan has described this form as follows: "The narration in THE THIN RED LINE both originates in various characters and goes beyond them, creating a floating perspective that in keeping both with the film's epic pretense and its poetic ambition to represent unities of the human and of the natural beyond all artificial divisions. Not only does the narration say things we do not necessarily imagine the particular characters to be capable of saying, but it also seems to waft beyond any particular character's perception, becoming a virtually pan-individual disquisition on war and existence." (Polan, "Auteurism and War-teurism," 59) This is as wrong as it is right in its observation. The characters are not narrated human beings, but a splintered and scattered eye, a folded subjectivity, which can be related to the narration of action and acting characters as difference, not as disintegration.

CF. ALSO Michel Chion, *The Thin Red Line*, London 2004.

1.1 A Snapshot of History: Three War Films at the Turn of the Century — 23

passages of interior monologue. It jumps directly to another character, motivated merely by a change in viewpoint, a fleeting dialogue, or by the simple circumstance that the other character has moved into the field of vision of the other who is momentarily not speaking. The novel thus approximates the authorial narrative of free indirect discourse, as Bakhtin defined it and as Pasolini then expounded it in relation to film.[15] This entails the narrator mimicking the diction, word choice, and perceptual methods of the characters, without entirely abolishing the difference between narrating speech and narrated character. This poetic procedure allows Jones to link up a wide variety of vantage points, modes of perception and sensation with each other so that the image of the military community arises in the form of speech itself. In the end there are fifteen, eighteen, or even twenty equal protagonists between whom the novel's speech circulates. The troop itself, the C-Company, can thus take shape as an entanglement of voices, perceptions, and sensations, as a sensing, expressive body. And new voices continually turn up, even down to the very last pages.

Malick's film follows this poetic procedure when, in off-voices and in the camera, it aligns itself with the faces and gestures, the voices and speech of the soldiers on the screen, without ever becoming quite identical to them. Rather, the film articulates a kind of astonishment,[16] which does not belong to any individual face, but is transferred from one face to the next; it does not mark any standpoint, nor any personal entity of sensations, experiences, and evaluations.

This astonishment is realized in the face of the soldier, who recognizes in bewilderment that he has been hit and is dying, and is then transferred to the compassionate gaze of the one trying to console him. It lingers for a moment in the timid horror of the inexperienced boy, who may indeed not want to avert his gaze from the terror of the defiled corpse, it loses its contours in the ecstasy of the gunman who has just killed someone for the first time. It becomes detached from the human body, transitioning through a movement that gets lost in the clouds blown by the wind, the waving grass, the slipping of shadows. It is the movement of the light filtering through the leaves, of the transforming light, joined with the sometimes strutting, sometimes flowing carpet of sound made by the music.

---

15 Pier Paolo Pasolini, "The 'Cinema of Poetry,'" in *Heretical Empiricism*, ed. Louise K. Barnett, Bloomington/Indianapolis 1988, 167–186. Italian original: "Il 'cinema di poesia,'" in idem, *Empirismo eretico*, Milan 1981, 167–187.
16 Astonishment is the expression of an affect that is intimately connected with the experience of thinking, of reflection. (Deleuze writes about astonishment [*admiration*] in *The Movement-Image*, 88).

The landscape in this film resembles the model of old "nature," which we know from museums and old poems, only in the foreground. It corresponds much more to what Balázs discovered in the close-up, the movement of affect with no relation to space.

> Landscape is a physiognomy, a face that all at once, at a particular spot, gazes out at us, as if emerging from the chaotic lines of a picture puzzle. A face of a particular place with a very definite, if also indefinable, expression of feeling, with an evident, if also incomprehensible, meaning. A face that seems to have a deep emotional relationship to human beings. A face that is directed towards human beings.[17]

In fact, nature in THE THIN RED LINE appears as an impersonal, non-human face. Malick's film articulates the impressions of a variously formed sensing, feeling, and thinking, in which ever new viewpoints and speaking perspectives arise – a cinematic hero's song, reporting on the wars of the twentieth century like they were horrors from a far away past.

THE THIN RED LINE projects the lyrical emphasis of Emerson's "nature," the celebration of a direct view of a divine universal soul in nature, onto the poetic surface of the talk of war. What thus arises is a cinematic vision of history: a flow of gazes, gestures, faces that is brought into the living, bodily present of a perceiving, sensing, and thinking spectator. It is the photos of war reporters, from the World Wars to Vietnam – including the photo of the paralyzed GI – and the faces in shadows, taken from films that were made shortly after the war: elegiac ballads such as Lewis Milestone's A WALK IN THE SUN (1945), which present portraits of fallen heroes in small chamber plays and, if necessary, superimpose the images of battle as found footage from innumerable documentaries. THE THIN RED LINE develops a vision of history in which the photo and film documents of the wars of the twentieth century coalesce into a multi-voiced speech that rises up from all the war novels and news coverage, the letters and the war diaries. They add up into fleeting, first-person oriented figurations – sometimes in off-camera speech, sometimes dialogically splintering off, sometimes as the interior monologue of individual characters – only to lose themselves again right away in the movement of metamorphosis of the camera's gaze. As if the endless series of photo and film faces from the so well documented wars of the past century themselves formed a flow of memories, which crystallize for moments in scenes and characters, only always to turn back into the flow of indeterminate speech without fixed origin.

The soldiers land in the morning sun, they draw into the interior of the island, encountering the strangers, the indigenous person, who does not see

---

17 Béla Balázs, *Early Film Theory: Visible Man and The Spirit of Film*, Oxford 2010, 53.

1.1 A Snapshot of History: Three War Films at the Turn of the Century — 25

them, wordlessly passing by. On a muggy afternoon, they come across rotting corpses, in the evening light they see the wounded and dead from the last fight. The next morning the battle begins. Like strophes from a traditional epic, each of the new sequences falls into place. The uniform, flowing time seems similar to space, 'with no advance, no logic, no fixities of point of view': a movement without space, organized by the faces of soldiers, much like the Homeric epic is organized by meter and recurring turns of phrase. As if the events narrated were as long ago as the war of the Greeks against the Trojans. But what is destroyed is not the proud securing of the enemy city; it is the idyllic peacefulness of the village on this South Seas island. At the beginning the inhabitants of this village remain uninvolved in the face of the battle that the warring troops carry into their country from a world far away; at the end their community has also fallen to the war. At the beginning, they are part of nature in the midst of war, presented by the film as an utterly imperturbable beauty: the swimming children, the estranged smiles of the woman – we do not know if these are directed at the camera team – the singing villagers under the roof of a light-flooded cathedral of trees, the man that passes by the troops as if they did not exist. At the end the village – an Indian camp after the cavalry has pulled out – is desolated, the villagers antagonized, the household objects are in pieces. When the company finally retreats to the landing boat, past the graveyards of the fallen, we can once again speak of this foreign face: the voice, which does not clearly belong to any narrator, any character, nor any author, asks us not to ignore him when we encounter him.

This might be taken to mean the disturbing gaze of the women in the islander's village, or the gaze of the man who refused to look at the soldiers as they were marching to the interior of the island. But perhaps it could also be a face that we saw right at the beginning: soldiers standing in crowded rows in front of washbasins and mirrors. There is a stifling constriction under the deck of the battleship that is taking the troops to war. A very young man, almost still a child: he speaks of his fear, it is not entirely clear to whom. Perhaps to his immediate superior, First Sergeant Edward Welsh (Sean Penn); he briefly stops shaving to look at the boy. At the very end we see this nameless soldier for the second time. Once again, he is on the ship; this time it is meant to be transporting the soldiers back home. Crushed in between innumerable unfamiliar faces, about whom we know as little as we do about him, we now see him standing on the upper deck in daylight. Once again he delivers a monologue, and once again we do not know to whom. This uncertainty seems to define the play of features itself. We see a face that does not know if there is anyone who is looking at it; or whether it is astonished or unsettled to be seen so suddenly, becoming aware of his own face on the screen, laid bare before a mass of viewers ...

For this audience, the face becomes the appearance of exactly that nature that the film stages as a cinematographic anthem in the prologue and the epilogue;

a nature that the military causes to vanish when it forms soldiers out of young men, the organs of a troop. Instead of a shell-shocked face we see the soldiers swarming in the light of the morning sun. We also see the face – as numerous as it is unique, as nameless as it is particular, as anonymous as it is individual (see Figure 4). Faces that speak of hope, precarious and vulnerable because it belongs

Figure 4: Paradisiac nature (THE THIN RED LINE).

Figure 4: (Continued)

to the living bodies of the young soldier that speaks for it. He speaks of a future beyond idyllic nature, but also beyond the military community:

> Somethin' I can come back to. Some kind of foundation. I mean, I don't know what, you know, what your plans are, but ... I'm determined now. I've been through the thick and thin of it. You know, I may be young, but I've lived plenty of life. I'm ready to start living it good. You know, my daddy always told me it's gonna get a lot worse before it gets better. You know, cos life ain't supposed to be that hard when you're young. Well, I figure after this the worst is gonna be gone. It's time for things to get better. That's what I want. That's what's gonna happen. I'm getting older now. By no means old, but older.[18]

The young man's words are like the caption under a photo. They articulate the beauty of the dawn light breaking out over the faces – hundreds of faces: diverse, similar, unfamiliar, close, identical, endlessly non-identical. The words seem to articulate that feeling that we, the spectators, think we can grasp in the innumerable faces of the soldiers, jostling about in the sunlight on the ship's upper deck. We think we can understand their feelings – but we would certainly not be in any position to recognize even one of the innumerable faces if we were to encounter it on the street.

Three films – SAVING PRIVATE RYAN, WINDTALKERS, THE THIN RED LINE – they examine the idea of America, the idea of a democratic nation in view of its historical destiny and its current social conflicts. In doing so, they reconstruct the poetic logic and the thematics of a genre that emerged directly from the political question of America's entry into the Second World War, and they

---

18 Timecode: 02:32:47–02:33:38.

reveal the basic topography of a historical narrative that in its concrete formation is as specific for this society as it is general in its function. Indeed, it is one of the platitudes of cultural theory that every society has to construct its own history in order to achieve political identity. What is less evident is that such constructions follow poetics that more or less explicitly stage a "talk of war," which always – according to Foucault, which I will come back to later – represents a narrative of the war between the races: "It is the first discourse in postmedieval Western society that can be strictly described as being historico-political."[19]

The films re-stage the standard film images of war as an image of history in which the current society looks for its political dimension as a community. Each in their own way, the films provide a way to grasp the war film genre as a form of aesthetic experience, in which the experience of history is linked up with feelings of belonging, of affective bonds to a community – a collectively borne destiny. They re-stage history as a cinematographic visual space in which innumerable anonymous biographies and family stories find their shared frame of reference. Now this definition of the genre is no less ambivalent than its pathos-oriented basic model. Indeed, the feeling of belonging to a community justifies the ethnocentrism that the talk of war as a discourse of a "war of races" – following Foucault – had always had as its goal.

It makes no difference whether the films re-stage documentary or fictional predecessors; they are always modeling an image of history that refers to the great political catastrophes of the past century, over the course of which the meaning that history can give to a society at all was fundamentally altered. Given this set up, the poetic practices with which a society seeks to open up its historical reality as a political community seem no less suspect than the idea of affective collectivities that provide the reason for such a community.

The films presented here thus touch on questions that one would rather not pose, at least from a European viewpoint, without at least securing the terrain beforehand by establishing moral values. But the fact that they appeal to just such an affective collectivity in the pathos of the way they are staged does not seem to me to be an issue that can be morally evaluated.

SAVING PRIVATE RYAN, WINDTALKERS and THE THIN RED LINE do indeed clearly aim to restore American (or western) patriotism, but this does not make them reactionary per se. Rather, they seem – if I may make this unsupported claim – to respond to the historical constellation at the end of the century, in

---

19 Michel Foucault, *"Society Must Be Defended": Lectures at the Collège de France*, 1975–76, New York 2003, 51–52.

which political possibilities seemed to be within reach for a brief moment, but which were quickly negated by the concrete politics of war. In the following I would like to bolster this speculative thesis by extending the analysis of films through a reading of a philosophical book, the object of which is exactly the political state of this contemporary constellation.

1.2 Richard Rorty and the Pursuit of Happiness

At the same time that SAVING PRIVATE RYAN and THE THIN RED LINE were released, Richard Rorty published an engaged and critical reading of the thinking of the American Left. His book *Achieving Our Country* proclaims the fundamental failure of the Left – two years before George W. Bush became president of the United States and during a period of seemingly unlimited growth and affluence. After Vietnam, the Left had maintained at a critical distance to its own country, restricting itself to the spectator role rather than further developing its socio-political agenda, which was as necessary as it was unachieved. Rorty does concede that the break with the political establishment, even with the liberal Democrats, over the course of the debate about the Vietnam War was as justified as it was inevitable. But he condemns the moral rigor with which the Left gave up the historically evolved, common basis in political goals and values, which is what constitutes the American nation as a political community in the first place. Instead of further pursuing these goals, also against technocratic enforcement of power and populist *ressentiment*, the Left retreated into a cultural critique that was as fundamentalist as it was academic. They had indeed achieved great success in their efforts to curtail racist and sexist discrimination; but they had moved away from the idea of progress, with which the American nation had sought to realize itself historically as a political community. In doing so they had also discarded the historical promise that this political community represents for those who had been denied this belonging.[20]

Picking up the thread again

Rorty unfolds his diagnosis within the tradition of American philosophy: William James, Walt Whitman, and above all John Dewey are the keepers of a politically

---

[20] Cf. Richard Rorty, *Achieving Our Country: Leftist Thought in Twentieth-Century America*, Cambridge 1998, 39f.

grounded "patriotism," in which the principle of the pursuit of happiness gets a particular socio-political stamp. In this reading, the founding act of the nation is understood as a historical mandate to realize a liberal political community, and its boundaries of solidarity are to be permanently reconfigured and extended. From this perspective, the nation becomes the idea of a political community that persists as an interminable historical work-in-progress in the contingent vicissitudes of history. For this community precisely does not command any fixed self-image that could stipulate its origin or its historical goal. From this perspective, the pursuit of happiness is reinterpreted in a history of permanently redefining the boundaries that separates the We of the community from those who do not belong. The boundaries of the community are themselves dynamic; they are moving frontiers. Herein lies the genuine field of action of a way of thinking and acting politically that – throughout colonialism and the Indian wars, slavery and the Civil War, throughout everyday horrors and major political crimes – sought to piece together the broken thread over and over again. The decision consists – and this is the topic of the speech by the anonymous soldiers in THE THIN RED LINE – in taking up this thread anew and continuing to spin a future from it, a future that is indeed completely unpredictable, but nonetheless malleable. *Achieving Our Country*, like Malick's film, is a call to do just this; this means, for instance, continuing to think that it might be possible to form political communities with institutions that have no other goal than to protect the freedoms of each of those nameless individuals so that they can pursue their happiness. This of course presumes a sense of commonality for which ordinary social, sexist, or racist discrimination is reason enough to call the borders of the community into question, time and time again. This is exactly why Rorty stresses that "emotional involvement with one's country ... is necessary if political deliberation is to be imaginative and productive."[21] All effective political action, however compartmentalized it might be in political campaigns and legal issues, is based on a feeling of community that is capable of bridging cultural differences and moral transgressions.

A feeling for the communal: sense of commonality

This understanding of the "sense of commonality,"[22] of the feeling for the communal, speaks to a fundamental problem that concerns all democracies today. How can modern societies have any relation at all to themselves as political

---

21 ibid., 3.
22 ibid., 101.

communities? Indeed, they have to claim political responsibility for the polity on the one hand, without being able to call on any universally valid idea of community on the other.

On the one hand, no political body can get by without solidarity, without a "sense of commonality"; on the other hand, common sense and the sense of commonality cannot be grounded in anything other than in the value that the community itself represents. If a polity renounces the appeal to a sense of commonality, it subjects itself to the purely technocratic calculations of administration and power; if, however, it relies on a metaphysically, genealogically, morally, or historico-philosophically grounded idea of community, it will find itself on the frontlines of fundamental claims to power and exclusionary maneuvers.[23]

Time and again, Rorty stresses that the right to freedom, life, and the pursuit of happiness are the politically desired goals of the state, which cannot be legitimated outside of politics. He thus disassociates himself from the idea that a political community could be grounded in inalienable rights and moral principles, even if one establishes these rights – as does communitarianism – taking communality itself to be a universal human characteristic. It makes no difference whether legitimation is sought in the history of the people, in the emancipation of a collective subject, or in universal rights or some absolute outside of all history. For Rorty there can be no a priori justification of action that would precede politics.[24]

Politics can only be carried out in the appeal to solidarity with the convictions and values of a historically contingent community. And it is just this appeal that Rorty calls the "sense of commonality," the feeling of being connected with the community: "that we substitute a 'merely' ethical foundation for our sense of community – or, better, that we think of our sense of community as having no foundation except shared hope and the trust created by such sharing."[25] Community is therefore the affective agreement to a historically developed political body, which is defined by shared values and hopes, appraisals, and attitudes to the world. This is also why this theoretical position – there is the "priority of democracy to philosophy" – cannot be separated from the political conviction that the scope of moral action and individual freedom is the result of the history of liberal

---

[23] Cf. Richard Rorty, *Objectivity, Relativism, and Truth*, Cambridge 1995; Rorty, *Achieving Our Country*, and Richard Rorty, "A Defense of Minimalist Liberalism," in *Debating Democracy's Discontent: Essays on American Politics, Law, and Public Philosophy*, ed. Anita L. Allen, Milton C. Regan, New York 1998, 117–125.
[24] Cf. Richard Rorty, "The Priority of Democracy to Philosophy" in *Objectivity, Relativism, and Truth*, 175–196.
[25] Richard Rorty, "Solidarity or Objectivity?" in *Objectivity, Relativism, and Truth*, 21–34, here 33.

democracy. "Moral progress" is "a history of making rather than finding, of poetic achievement by 'radically situated' individuals and communities."[26]

Rorty inserts his own thinking into this history, pragmatically defining politics as a progressive making, the only aim of which is to expand the boundaries of solidarity, the we-feeling,[27] which facilitates and protects the free self-determination of the individual. Moral progress is the history of political beginnings, to which one can join up ever more actions, socio-political interventions and reflections.[28] It is the constantly necessary improvement of real, given circumstances, as compartmentalized as it may be:

> To accept the contingency of starting-points is to accept our inheritance from, and our conversation with, our fellow-humans as our only source of guidance [...] We shall lose what Nietzsche called ‚metaphysical comfort', but we may gain a renewed sense of community. Our identification with our community – our society, our political tradition, our intellectual heritage – is heightened when we see this community as ours rather than nature's, shaped rather than found, one among many which men have made. In the end, the pragmatists tell us, what matters is our loyalty to other human beings clinging together against the dark, not our hope of getting things right.[29]

The only foundation that this history of making can rest on is the "sense of commonality." This means both the political ideas associated with *common sense* and the feeling of connectedness, the *sense of commonality*.[30] Neither the one nor the other can be justified in any way but through political thinking and acting. The political community itself can call on nothing other than the self-established goal of its consolidation; it can only confirm and reconfirm this in the appeal to a generally shared feeling of solidarity and belonging. Decisions about its dignity can only be made in view to the future: How far can we manage to continue extending the boundaries of solidarity? How far can the community be reconfigured over and over again?

Such a "history of making" is above all a matter of perception and naturalization of the foreign. It "is a matter of detailed description of what unfamiliar people are like and of redescription of what we ourselves are like"[31]. This is the

---

[26] Rorty, "The Priority of Democracy to Philosophy," 189.
[27] Cf. Richard Rorty, *Contingency, Irony, and Solidarity*, Cambridge 1989, 190 f.
[28] Hannah Arendt coins this formulation in view of the American Revolution. See her *On Revolution*, New York 1963.
[29] Richard Rorty, "Pragmatism, Relativism, Irrationalism," in *Consequences of Pragmatism*, ed. Richard Rorty, Minneapolis 1982, 160–175, here 166.
[30] The English expression *common sense* only reproduces one part of the sense of the German term "Gemeinsinn," as it is defined by Kant for instance. This is why Rorty uses two terms: "common sense" and "sense of commonality."
[31] Rorty, *Contingency, Irony, and Solidarity*, xvi.

function in which Rorty positions poetic, artistic practice. He defines it through a strict correlation of poetics and politics.

Poetic making, political acting

Politics and poetics – in western culture since Aristotle these terms have designated two strictly separate practices and discourses, defined by different logics, systems of reference, and operating rules. And yet, the correlation between politics and poetics has been and continues to be discussed over and over again in view of how we understand the political.[32] Rorty also positions himself in this tradition of western democratic theory when he defines poetic practice through its political function. He assumes that we constantly invent new vocabularies and descriptive tools in order to increase the sensibility with which we perceive others as "fellow sufferers" and reconfigure our common world. 'Novels, cinema, television,' much like political or philosophical arguments, are 'vehicles of moral change,' which make it possible to effect a direct change in the sense of commonality by creating new forms of description.[33]

The relation between poetics and politics thus not only concerns artistic production, but every form of political thinking and acting. But the reconfiguration of the schemata that we perceive as a common world also has another side for Rorty. He speaks of the eccentric self-conceptions and idiosyncratic acts of subjectivization that constitute the core of poetic activity. The poetic inventions of forms, metaphors, and images with which the common world can be described as new and different at the same time bring to bear that free self by which all progress is measured. To put it another way, poetics and politics designate two mutually referencing aspects of the political, two ways of "making," of the poiesis of moral progress.

The decisive issue for Rorty is that these poetic proposals of idiosyncratic languages do indeed define the goal of liberal politics – namely securing precisely the freedom to self-development – but not their justification. Like religious belief, poetic language games are strictly assigned to the realm of the private and thus elude the need for legitimation necessary to the implementation of political power.

---

[32] This problem marks the current discussion of democracy. In this context, we should point to the debate about the term of the political in contrast to the term politics. Cf. Giorgio Agamben, et al., *Demokratie? Eine Debatte*, Frankfurt am Main 2012. Cf. also Anja Streiter, "Die Frage der Gemeinschaft und die 'Theorie des Politischen'" in *Die Frage der Gemeinschaft. Das westeuropäische Kino nach 1945*, eds. Hermann Kappelhoff and Anja Streiter, Berlin 2012, 21–37; Uwe Hebekus and Jan Völker, *Neue Philosophien des Politischen zur Einführung*, Hamburg/Berlin 2012.
[33] Cf. Rorty, *Contingency, Irony, and Solidarity*, 16.

Rorty develops a highly idiosyncratic way of reading the romantic utopia of art. He speaks of the "liberal utopia" of a "poeticized culture,"[34] in which the question of what is true, what is good, and what is real has entirely become the question of pluralistically competing re-inscriptions of the shared reality of a community. Such a community could always understand itself as a reality that is made, that is poetically produced, in such descriptions and redescriptions. Politically, it is defined solely through the goal of creating and securing the freedom of every single one of its fellow citizens. Which ultimately means nothing more than the possibility of exerting oneself in just this way: through the reworking of an eccentric vocabulary, a new metaphor of describing the world. Freedom here is thus realized to the degree to which nothing other than one's own poetic faculty and the privacy of other citizens limits the possibilities of such descriptions.

The metaphor that Rorty uses to conceive these relations is that of the republic of free and talented writers. In the plurality of their writing styles, ever new realities of the community arise, which are then extended and altered in new writings and new connections to old descriptions. On the one hand, they engender themselves in this making as eccentric egos, which seek to distinguish themselves from the 'we' of the community; in order, on the other hand, to expand and intensify the solidarity of cohesion through an increased sensibility, created through writing and reading, for the life of the others, the foreign persons, the foreign communities. This metaphor describes all communal life as a matter of politics; whereas from Rorty's point of view, questions of the community are to be resolved through new descriptions. The "possibility of a liberal utopia [...] a post-metaphysical culture [...] would settle [...] for narratives which connect the present with the past [...] and with utopian futures."[35] Political action is defined solely by the goal of facilitating and expanding the freedom of this making – without this action itself being justified any further. It is literally groundless, without any foundation beyond a concrete, historically situated and unfolding polity.

It is easy to overlook that this pragmatic reading of the sense of commonality is precisely not due to any optimistic view of the moral progress of liberal polities. Rorty's elaborations on Orwell's *1984* (1949) make it clear that even political thought itself is one of the torture victims that Orwell writes about. Rorty takes on the role of this victim in formulating the following sentences: "I no longer have a self to make sense of. There is no world in which I can picture myself as living, because there is no vocabulary in which I can tell a coherent story about

---

34 Cf. the third chapter of ibid.
35 ibid., xv–xvi.

myself."³⁶ It is as if a political thought were speaking here that had itself survived the worst atrocities of the last century, albeit not without consequential damages. He speaks more of these consequences a few pages later: "I do not think that we liberals *can* now imagine a future of "human dignity, freedom and peace." That is, we cannot tell ourselves a story about how to get from the actual present to such a future."³⁷

Describing and redescribing: the plurality of modes of media experience

The films that I have presented – SAVING PRIVATE RYAN, WINDTALKERS, and THE THIN RED LINE – seem to conform in their cinematic poetics to the political diagnosis developed in Rorty's reading. For these films, the crisis of the sense of commonality designates the social field of their aesthetic intervention. They seek to reactivate a feeling of political belonging, not without putting their own spin on the idea of political community. The films thus stand in a tradition of political thought that Rorty clearly outlines once again. Indeed, they allow the idea of a liberal, democratic polity – for all its moral failure and all its culpability – to appear in the line of historical becoming as a political utopia.

At the end of a century of the most destructive and reprehensible wars, in which moral testing was as triumphant as moral failure was devastating, the films attempt to restore an affective solidarity that binds the individual to the political community. SAVING PRIVATE RYAN, WINDTALKERS, and THE THIN RED LINE are about repairing the sense of commonality. They are interventions in the affective balance of a political community. These interventions do not rely on having a good argument; they are not carried out on the level of discursive reasoning, but as the pathos of cinematographic staging. The films intervene on the level of the modalities of aesthetic experience. They imply poetic concepts of cinematic ways of experiencing things, which refer to forms of feeling themselves as the affective basis of the community.

This distinction would not apply to Rorty. For him there is no reason to distinguish the representational modes of literature, of pictures, of music, or of the audiovisual image. Indeed, ultimately, he always imagines poetic making as writing, and descriptions are always taken to be written texts. Even less does he see the necessity of distinguishing between various modes of experience, such as between the mode of knowledge and the mode of aesthetic pleasure.

---

36 Ibid., 179.
37 Ibid., 181–82.

In his view, the arts designate an ensemble of poetic techniques that, each according to their modality, behave indifferently to a "history of making." Solidarity is based on the ability to perceive others as similar to myself. So, all that is necessary is the growing awareness of the particularity of others so that I experience them as related to me and feel myself in solidarity with them for this reason alone.

Rorty can imagine the permanent revision of the boundaries of community without actually having to alter the feeling of community; indeed, it represents a cultural-historical endowment that is to be expanded merely in its object field. The appeal to a sense of commonality would thus manage quite well without having any relation at all to aesthetic processes.

But it is hard to imagine how the sensibility might be increased or the perception of the communal world changed without the sensation of perception itself becoming an object of modulation. Even the most prosaic of literary descriptions that makes visible what no one had seen before can hardly be reduced to an expanded intellectual horizon, to a surplus of knowledge and information. New visibilities – Rorty shows this quite impressively in his interpretations of literary texts – are due to a changed feeling for the common world; they assume new affects and percepts, which are the focus of poetic endeavors, in order to generalize them. One would therefore have to look into the media practices and modalities in which the feeling for the commonly shared world itself becomes the primary object of poetic making.

That such a distinction between various modes of experience is of great significance in view of the films being discussed here will become resoundingly clear as soon as we make any efforts to qualify the films morally. We cannot come to any meaningful evaluation without referring to the aesthetic experience that these films are for us. It is not this experience, but the film-poetic construction that structures such an experience that can be analytically evaluated. One can criticize it if one reconstructs it as a specific poetic concept and places it in a relationship to similar poetic proposals. Such a critique will hardly refer to what is already common to all comparable films. In our case, this is the cinematic representation of recently past or currently raging wars on the one hand and the re-staging of pre-existing basic patterns of pathos on the other; both, namely, define – I will come to this later – the poetics of the genre. What is decisive for such a comparison is the difference between the various formations of the aesthetic matrix of the cinematic mode of experience, with which the film staging gives a particular stamp to the pathos of the war film genre. The aesthetic formation of pathos determines the ethos of the films.

In the following, I would like to sketch out such a comparison by means of certain examples.

1.3 Poetic Calculation and Political Critique: A Film-analytical Comparison

It is surely not by chance that Rorty speaks of "platoon films" when he looks for examples for the meaning of the "sense of commonality."[38] He may even actually have thought of PLATOON, the film by Oliver Stone from 1986. Certainly he had the Vietnam War film in mind, a group of films that deal with exactly that political constellation that Rorty thematizes in his reading. Of all these films, it was PLATOON that turned most decidedly and explicitly to restoring the feeling of community. This can be seen on the one hand in the subject matter – the platoon is represented as a community that spans ethnic and cultural oppositions in its cohesion, and also moral culpability and transgression – on the other hand it can be seen in the calculations of how the film is staged. Indeed, the film is obviously calculated to be a media event, at which cinematic experience is meant to be publicly displayed as an act of collective grieving.

If we compare PLATOON with Francis Ford Coppola's APOCALYPSE NOW for instance, we clearly see how much the film resorts to narrative strategies that reach back to the heyday of the genre in the late forties and fifties and how these strategies are called on as conventionalized rhetorical figures of affectation. Oliver Stone himself aspired to this comparison when he claimed that his film would finally portray a realistic image of the experience of war from the viewpoint of the soldiers.[39] But the political attitude of the film does not rest on the question of whether PLATOON, APOCALYPSE NOW, or any other film is an adequate representation of the social crisis that ended in the events of war, the race riots, and the political assassinations of the sixties. Rather, the films should be analyzed and assessed as the poetic attempt to create adequate forms of perception and communication, with which society can find some relation to the consequences of these events in the basic affect texture of the political community.

I would first like to delve more thoroughly into the staging concept of APOCALYPSE NOW, in order then to make clear, in a cursory comparison with PLATOON, that every moral-political evaluation affects the formation of the cinematic mode of experience.

---

38 Cf. Rorty, *Achieving Our Country*, 100f.
39 "That's why I wanted to make *Platoon*; I felt that the truth of this war had not been shown [...] But I didn't approach *Platoon* as a genre film, but rather as real life [...] I was dealing with raw experience." Charles L.P. Silet (ed.), *Oliver Stone: Interviews*, Jackson 2001, 39–49, here 39f.

APOCALYPSE NOW: a new architecture of cinematic spaces

Granted, the reception of APOCALYPSE NOW at the time of its release tended to see the poetic concept of the film as the unbounded aestheticism of the New Hollywood. The gigantic proportions of the production, the reports and rumors of the catastrophes, accidents, and setbacks during shooting made this itself seem like a war being fought to open up a new terrain of cinematic possibilities. Using all the available means of the film industry, an optical-acoustic visuality was installed that sought to close in aesthetically on the perceptual dimensions of war as a cinematic form – which critics sometimes rejected and sometimes praised.[40] The "spatial machine of the cinema"[41] would position the spectator in a mythical dimension of experience, which would reveal to him the horror of war as aesthetic pleasure. Now the equation of the destructive power of war technology and the aesthetic pleasure of perceptual possibilities in the cinema do indeed seem to me to address a fundamental modality of the war film genre; but it does not affect the decisive shift that the staging strategies of APOCALYPSE NOW entailed for the pathos of the genre.

We get a much clearer view of this if we bring to mind a level of staging that at first seems highly conventional: namely, the construction of the characters. Protagonist and antagonist are related to one another in a way that allows the entire film to appear as a gradual convergence of the two, in order – in the mimetic alignment of the first and the ritual killing of the other – to be fused in the end: Colonel Kurtz (Marlon Brando), who defects from the army and sets up a reign of terror in the depths of the Cambodian jungle, and Captain Willard (Martin Sheen), who has been secretly charged with tracking Kurtz down and killing him. In relation to the film as a whole, both characters appear to be two opposing entities of one and the same consciousness.

The tie that indissolubly binds the two is made up of the strands of three different poetic concepts: Joseph Conrad's story *Heart of Darkness* (1899) shows the travelers following the course of a river into the interior of the African continent, there to meet the colonial master as an archaic figure of terror. Michael

---

[40] Cf. Karsten Visarius, "Wegtauchen oder Eintauchen? Schreckbild, Lockbild, Feindbild: Der inszenierte Krieg" in *Kino und Krieg*, eds. Ernst Karpf and Doron Kiesel, 9–13; Rainer Gansera: "Krieg und Geilheit, die bleiben immer in Mode" (Shakespeare), in Karpf and Kiesel, eds., *Kino und Krieg*, 33–46; Ernst Karpf, "Kriegsmythos und Gesellschaftskritik. Zu Coppolas 'Apocalypse Now'" in Karpf and Kiesel, eds., *Kino und Krieg*, 106–112.

[41] Hans-Thies Lehmann, "Die Raumfabrik – Mythos im Kino und Kinomythos," in *Mythos und Moderne. Begriff und Bild einer Rekonstruktion*, ed. Karl Heinz Bohrer, Frankfurt am Main 1983, 572–609.

1.3 Poetic Calculation and Political Critique: A Film-analytical Comparison — 39

Herr's novel *Dispatches* (1977) describes the cool-recording gaze of a war correspondent, the language of which does not seek to produce any emphatic relation to the events observed, but an almost tactile one. This language affects the characteristic style of the first-person monologue: the stunned astonishment that no expression of feeling can match. Finally, the double character in APOCALYPSE NOW is based on a type that belongs to the fixed ensemble of the Hollywood war film – the contentious relationship between the commanding officer and the soldier whose body is unconditionally subject to the officer's commanding will.

A shift of the central metaphor of *Heart of Darkness* crosses the novel's double character with the constellation of characters from the Hollywood genre. The river, which 'settles into the depths of the dark continent like a snake' in the story, now becomes an 'electrical cable' in APOCALYPSE NOW,[42] which connects Willard's body to his adversary's force of will.

We easily recognize Kurtz as the figure of absolute military authority; but he no longer conforms to the moral schema that the war film developed after the Second World War. He is not the technocrat commanding the battalion from the background, nor the patriarch who understands that soldiers have to be sacrificed; he is not the fatherly friend to his boys, sending them off to death with loving care; nor is he the cynical officer who replaces friendship with naked military authority and the commander's genius.

In the film staging of "Heart of Darkness," at the temple complex of a lost culture at the deepest point in the jungle, the commander becomes the acousmatic voice of a priestly and terrifying ruler. Whenever the gaze starts to contain him, his shape draws back into shadows, divulging the interior of darkness layer by layer – as if the meandering caves made of lighting grids and shadowy veils were grotesque outgrowths of his own uncontainable body. In the ornamental arrangement of the corpses, which are strewn like flowers and fruits about the walls, steps, and trees of the temple ruins, the despotism of the commander appears in the distorting mirror of the grotesque: an archaic father savoring his power in the ritual slaying of his children.

Conversely, the film shows Willard as the obedient soldier, whose eyes are opening more and more with each stage while at the same time he is drowning in the overflowing astonishment. The motif of the journey into the heart of darkness is carried out in stages that appear to be the unreal sequence of scenes in a nocturne, shaped ever more fantastically with every episode. There are stations of growing astonishment, of seeing that more and more becomes the hallucinatory vision of a medium. The astonished face becomes the expression being progressively seized

---

42 Cf. Elsaesser and Wedel, "The Hollow Heart of Hollywood."

by a foreign will, of an increasing paralysis of one's own powers, which – the goal of the journey – culminates in complete powerlessness. The commanding officer and the solider who sacrifices himself in obedience become one: one and the same body, a snake that bites its own tail, a force that circulates in itself.

The reevaluation of the genre's figures can thus be described as a narrative process in which preexisting metaphors and character types are successively reworked. But this reworking is not to be reconstructed at the level of the activity represented. Rather, the movement of the metaphors has to be produced by the spectators themselves. As much as the metaphorical movements of the film can be read as reflections of military authority – one finds one's way to this symbolism only by following the poetic logic that the spectators unlock as a specific shaping of a fictional world. The movement of the metaphor is carried out on the level of constructing an audiovisual image space, in which the perceiving, thinking, and feeling of the spectators has itself become the object of the film's calculations, of the aesthetic modulations of cinematic forms of experience. It emerges from the temporal arrangement of the percepts, affects, and actions that guide the dynamic of perceiving, feeling, and thinking that the spectators join in the process of viewing films.

In fact, APOCALYPSE NOW does not portray any action. Rather, it articulates a monologue throughout that is partly produced as a voiceover (in the diction of language from Michael Herr's novel), and partly at the level of what is represented (in the staging of what we can see and hear happening) as a subjective, "inner" speech. Indeed, every external event is defined in the astonished face of the protagonist as a subjective experience of perception: the outer world presented is always already given as a flow of sensations, thoughts, and feelings. Martin Sheen's astonished face functions like a converter that allows us to see the images of the external reality as those of an internal reality and vice versa. So, the journey downstream can be represented as the time in which a voice on an audiotape, a face on a photograph, the words in a letter, a dossier, the rumors and stories are concentrated into an outside subjectivity; a subjectivity that affects the sensation and thinking of the astonished person with such vehemence that his body can become the bearer of this outside will.

This strategy can be grasped at the level of the sound design. Indeed, Coppola is one of those directors of the New Hollywood who use the newly available techniques of surround sound as more than just a way to intensify the immersive qualities of cinema. Much more, he discovers in this immersion a new way to situate the spectator's perception in the image space of the film. This can be vividly demonstrated in the opening sequence of APOCALYPSE NOW.

At first there is nothing more than the rhythmic chopping of helicopter rotors in the darkened space of the cinema; then the screen gets brighter; we see the green of the jungle, the helicopters gliding over it like oversized insects. As if the jungle itself were exploding, the dense palms suddenly go up in blazing high flames. Napalm bombs. With this strike, a song starts up. Instead of detonation, we hear Jim Morrison's voice: "This is the end ..." As if the voice had escaped the bombarding, it becomes detached from the image of the exploding jungle, spreading out into the cinema carried by the musical arrangement. It gets closer and closer to the spectator's bodies, while the blazing flames on the screen seem to get oddly displaced; as if the image were wrested away from the infernal thunder of the jet fighters and detonating bombs, like sheet lightning from a faraway event from which no sound penetrates to us anymore. Whenever and wherever this explosion might have happened – what we see is pure vision, in which the film itself is presented as a kind of flashback.

Only the chopping of the rotors at the beginning maintains the connection between the screen image and the acoustic space; a wispy noise that flits from the left sound space to the right; or is it the other way around? The chopping forms a strictly rhythmic wall of sound from which the musical arrangement of the Doors song casually seems to emerge; it becomes the sound of a hallucinatory seeing. A sequence of visual dissolves begins; we see Willard's head on one side of the frame, on the other a statue vaguely refers to the temple ruins from the end of the film. But the question of whether we – the spectators – already see the end of APOCALYPSE NOW at its beginning is as difficult to decide as whether Willard's face is projected in reverse on the screen and the stature is visible in the correct vertical line. For beginning and end are as poorly suited to grasping the temporal structure of the cinematic arrangement as the geometrical orientation of over, under, front, and back can help us describe its spatial quality – even if we suddenly think we understand after repeated viewings: those are the last images of the film, Kurtz's empire going down in Napalm flames: "This is the end ..."

From this perspective, the ending of the film is highly ambivalent. Is the bombardment carrying out an order that Willard gave in case he did not return? We do in fact see him enthroned as the new ruler after having killed Kurtz. Viewed from the exposition of the film, this end seems like a flashback of the traumatized soldiers. Superimpositions link the vision of the burning jungle with Willard's face; the rotors of the helicopters become a ceiling fan. It is the view of a soldier lying on a hotel bed, looking at the ceiling and perhaps hearing the music that we also hear.

The musical arrangement fades into the background – an instrumental variation that is inserted between the verses that are sung – until the sound of the fan dominates. The monologue by the first-person narrator Willard begins. Sentences that could come from Michael Herr's *Dispatches* work their way into the musical arrangement, as if the even the monologue were one of the song's verses. Saigon,

Willard waits in his hotel to start a mission, the apocalyptic ending of which the spectator believes to have just seen. The song gets louder again. In a succession of fades of the drinking soldier we see him squatting on the ground naked, he dances, mimicking the movements of karate, finally falling on the ground, injuring his hand on a piece of broken glass and smearing the blood on his face, apathetic in his drunkenness, but dissolving into a fit of crying in the next moment.

In the character of Captain Willard, the exposition depicts the traumatized soldier who is tortured by memories that the film simulates as the story, still to be told, of a military special commando. And, at the same time, it turns the movie theater into the site of a present that is haunted by the insistent vision of a past horror, the past *as* horror. In this circular temporal structure, the exposition of APOCALYPSE NOW itself is composed like an audiovisual rock ballad in which the figurations of the war film genre are brought to a conclusive refrain. Instead of agony and death struggles, we see boozing, instead of the battle with the enemy we see the mimetic shadow dance of a drunken solider, instead of physical annihilation we see psychic breakdown, and instead of a grenade explosion we see the injury from a broken whiskey glass. Even the shell-shocked face has its counterpart in this arrangement. Two soldiers pick up Willard for his mission; they drag him into the shower to sober him up: his startled face when the water hits it, his cry ends the exposition: "This is the end ... My only friend, the end ..."

In APOCALYPSE NOW, neither the experience of the Vietnam War is described, nor is the war narrated as a past event; instead, modulations of the cinematic mode of experience are described that seem suited to relate the ever-present past war as an uncomprehended affective reality in the political community.

We can assume, at any rate, that new poetic concepts were necessary in the middle of the seventies to be able to relate to the feeling of crisis that American society must certainly have had at the time. The memory of the war, the circulating narratives and images of Vietnam might had been affect-laden in a way that can hardly be described or depicted. This might just be the reason that Coppola developed a new architecture of cinematic image spaces with APOCALYPSE NOW, new schemata of space and time. Indeed, the pathos-oriented models of the war film genre had to be fundamentally transformed in order to have any relation to the memory of the war as a collective reality that concerned the feelings and thinking of everyday, ordinary people.

Undeniably, these thoughts remain necessarily hypothetical. For even if I refer myself to my own memories of the cinema experience when I describe this film – as with all other previous films – the question of whether and to what degree the expressivity of the film can in fact affect its contemporary audience is still undecidable. By contrast, in film-analytical comparisons, it is possible at any time to reconstruct a poetic calculation and thus to make it evident that this calculation is not aimed at representing a past event, but at the insistent presence of this past in the breakdowns of the affective fabric of a political community.[43]

PLATOON: the melody of psychic consonance

By way of contrast, PLATOON can be described as an attempt to finally make it possible to narrate the experience of the Vietnam War as a past event.

Oliver Stone definitely builds on the altered forms of aesthetic representation in the Hollywood war film from the late seventies; but he leads them back to character constellations and melodramatic topoi that are much closer to classic narrative cinema before 1967. It is not necessary to perform any complex film analysis to see that the coarse opposition of types of communities – here the hash smoking black community, there the alcohol drinking rednecks, here the rock'n'rollers, there the country fans – revives a dramatic framework from the early days of the war film genre (the ethnically heterogeneous military community), which is only updated in its outward appearances: as if the film were an old war movie drama, revived in the setting, costumes, and acting style of the Vietnam War films of the late seventies. Consequently, a powerful narrating entity is necessary – a first-person narrator who is at once the voice of the protagonist, the voice of the author, and the voice of the eyewitness (Oliver Stone always

---

[43] In this respect, I do not in any way see the post-traumatic image of the sick war veteran as a metaphor that can accommodate breakdowns, as has been developed in a certain reading of the concept of trauma in cultural studies, but as a symptom of the crisis in the political community. Cf. Thomas Elsaesser, *Terror und Trauma. Zur Gewalt des Vergangenen in der BRD*, Berlin 2007; Hal Foster, "Obscene, Abject, Traumatic," in *October* 78, 1996, 106–124; Susannah Radstone, "Screening Trauma: Forrest Gump, Film and Memory," in *Memory and Methodology*, ed. Susannah Radstone, Oxford 2000, 79–110; Franz Kaltenbeck and Peter Weibel (eds.), *Trauma und Erinnerung / Trauma and Memory: Cross-Cultural Perspectives*, Wien 2000; Paul Antze and Michael Lambek (eds.), *Tense Past: Cultural Essays in Trauma and Memory*, New York/London 1996; Cathy Caruth, *Unclaimed Experience: Trauma, Narrative and History*, Baltimore 1996; Cathy Caruth (ed.), *Trauma: Explorations in Memory*, Baltimore 1992; Janet Walker, *Trauma Cinema: Documenting Incest and the Holocaust*, Berkeley, 2005. Cf. also the contributions to the section "Special Debate: Trauma and Screen Studies" in the Summer 2001 edition of the journal *Screen*: Susannah Radstone, "Trauma and Screen Studies: opening the debate," in *Screen* 42 (2), 2001, 188–193; Thomas Elsaesser, "Postmodernism as mourning work," in: *Screen* 42 (2), 2001, 193–201; E. Ann Kaplan, "Melodrama, cinema and trauma," in *Screen* 42 (2), 2001, 201–205; Maureen Turim, "The Trauma of History: Flashbacks Upon Flashbacks," in *Screen* 42 (2), 2001, 205–210; Janet Walker, "Trauma Cinema: False Memories and True Experience," in *Screen* 42 (2), 2001, 211–216.

emphasized his eyewitness quality as a Vietnam veteran) – in order to be able to maintain unswervingly that all war crimes, all betrayal, every death can be overcome in the coherence of the community.

In so saying, I am in no way getting into the question of whether PLATOON, with its poetic conception and directorial strategies, is at the top of its time, nor how it should be artistically evaluated. But if we describe the matter the other way around, it becomes clear that the moral ethos of the film is decided in the question of directorial strategies. PLATOON does indeed invoke the open conflict of a fragile sense of commonality by linking back to the representational models of earlier Vietnam War films; but only in order to translate them back into the homogeneous narrative perspective from the melodramatic model, which defined the genre in the late forties and fifties. These pathos-oriented models form the basis of staging PLATOON as a shared experience of mourning in a blockbuster format,[44] which promises its audience the therapeutic power of confessing guilt and remembering sorrow.

Here as well, the calculation can be grasped in the use of music. As if a worldwide feeling of sorrow had been reduced to a few musical phrases in a pop song, passages from Samuel Barber's "Adagio for Strings" is played over and over again; a piece of music that can be read as the 'naked expression of feeling.'[45] Due to the performance history of the piece – it is often used for state funerals of American presidents and mourning ceremonies of national rank – this feeling is established more unequivocally in its meaning than any term ever could be. The music sets the tone that defines the mood of the film staging as a whole. The pathos of the Vietnam film, the feeling of crisis, the common cause lost in argument, the guilt and the moral groundlessness – over and beyond all social fissures, the music ties a ribbon that holds together the mourning community. It literally defines the film as a funeral mass and the aesthetic experience as the unifying experience of shared grief.

One thinks – to make use of yet another comparison – of THE DEER HUNTER, of the small society of friends left behind in the local bar after the burial; how they stand with each other in the dark, closed bar because the funeral of a common friend had once again brought them all to this place; how they do not know how to behave, or what to say to each other; how one of them finally starts frying eggs for breakfast, another one sets the table, little by little each of them finds his place in the actions of everyday life that organize being together, eating, working

---

44 Cf. Robnik, *Kino, Krieg, Gedächtnis*.
45 http://www.npr.org/2010/03/09/124459453/barbers-adagio-naked-expression-of-emotion (January 21, 2016).

and talking. And then one of them starts to sing: humming quite slowly, quite softly the others hear the voice from the kitchen; in the end, they are all singing together: schoolchildren who finally remember a text they learned by heart after struggling to find the words: "America the Beautiful."

The cinematic scene is thoroughly comparable in its mood and compositional operation to the "Adagio for Strings"; only here it is not the piece of music, but the mise-en-scène, the shaping of the mode of cinematic experience, which sets the tone. The film shows us a grieving community that does not know what to do, what to say ... and they do what they have always done, time and time again at this place – they begin to sing together. The spectator remembers the afterwork meeting from the beginning of the film. They remember how Nick (Christopher Walken) exuberantly danced and sang along with the hit from the jukebox. Now they see that Nick is missing. It is this absence, which the staging of the film makes visible, that first causes the anthem to become a dirge for the survivors.

In PLATOON the music orchestrates a cinematic figuration of the sacrifice, the basic form of which was developed in the classical Hollywood war film genre. It is externally defined by iconographic references to Christian atoning death much like the feeling is defined by the performance history of the music piece that is played. One can see this very clearly in a third comparison: with John Ford's THEY WERE EXPENDABLE from 1945; a film that combined the basic forms of the newly emerging genre at the end of the war. Then one will realize that the pathos of commemorating the sacrifice is structured there by just that deep ambivalence that I sought to explain by means of the pathos formula of the *shell-shocked face*: the awareness of an irresolvable moral conflict that concerns the political community at its core and that cannot be assuaged by any sacrificial ritual. In Ford's film, the Christian burial ritual becomes the scene at which the helplessness of the protagonists, their moral confusion is represented and made visible. PLATOON answers this ambivalence with the authorial perspective of a coming-of-age story. From such a perspective, the conflict can be psychologically enclosed and grief can be staged as an individual emotion. This staging has the goal of experiencing collective psychic consonance, not any feeling for the community – and not at all any affective reality that has not been overcome.

Genre films as cultural practice

Perhaps it has become clear throughout the comparisons sketched out here how a change or consolidation of a specific perception of the common world can be achieved when the perceptual sensation itself becomes the object of modulation.

This is why Rorty's search for the boundaries of community, for the specific manner of inclusion and exclusion, is decided in the specific ways that the films are staged. The strategies of staging pathos are not merely aesthetic, as external as they may be; they always concern the feeling that links the forms of community, its political and social structure, with the thinking and sensing of real spectators, with their bodily experience. In the comparative analysis, the films' poetic proposals can be worked out in the ways they are staged, and can be described and qualified as a specific relationship between poetics and politics. In so saying, I do not in any way want to make the claim – which would be an endeavor for which one would have to proceed in a great deal more detail and using a great deal more material – to position the films in their social, political, economic and cultural relations in their contemporary contexts. Even if historiographic research completely sets the frames of reference in which the films are to be reconstructed as poetics. (Here by the way, at least in the case of the Hollywood war film, one has recourse to a very good state of the research.)

But the relationship between poetics and politics can in no way be reduced to an established functional or causal relationship between art or entertainment and society. The relationship between poetics and politics designates much more a field of contentious battles over the boundaries of the community, which is characterized by exclusionary maneuvers and attempts at naturalization, by redescriptions and reactionary overridings. The object of this battle are the media practices that refer to the feeling for the commonly shared world, the "sense of commonality" in Rorty's sense. In the following I will discuss poetic making in view of this field of practices.

In doing so, art and entertainment are not in any way meant to be seen as epiphenomena of social reality; rather as a social practice that is genuinely related to the task of questioning the boundaries of community. This practice is as much one of reception, of critique, and of theory as it is one of artistic and literary production.[46] For this reason, what is up for discussion is not the artistic dignity of the films (for instance the externality of the staging of PLATOON applied to the mere effect), nor their ideological subtext (the new conflicts are perpetually the old conflicts), but the way that pathos is restaged, which is what defines the Hollywood war film as a genre in the first place. In these stagings, practices in which a society seeks to see itself as a political community can be reconstructed as poetic conceptions.

In this respect, the films that I presented in the previous chapter are completely representative. In the way that SAVING PRIVATE RYAN, WINDTALKERS, and

---

[46] Cf. Streiter, "Die Frage der Gemeinschaft und die 'Theorie des Politischen.'"

THE THIN RED LINE re-stage and transform the image spaces, the narrative, and the characters of the genre, they target the pathos of a feeling for the communal. When they answer a crisis in this "sense of commonality," they only follow a fundamental tendency that defines the Hollywood war film genre as a whole. Indeed, the history of the genre can be described alongside the conjunctures in which phases of the disintegration of the democratic community alternate with those of integrating it, as a history of the crises and the renewal of the sense of commonality.

War films not only historically position the things that they represent, but also their spectators. They address a sense of commonality that is largely contingent and historically malleable. So not only can we read in the films the aesthetic strategies and poetic patterns that have the goal of embedding individual sensation in a socially shared feeling, a feeling for the community. They also unfold the historical transformations of this feeling of community. From mobilizing the will to fight through mourning commemoration of the sacrifices of war and on to wrathful judgment and guilty shame, the history of the Hollywood war film genre parades the history of these transformations along political events.

From this perspective, genre films can be understood as an exemplary poetic practice in the "history of making" that Rorty speaks of. It is equally exemplary for this history as the history of the Hollywood war film is exemplary for understanding what genre means at all in this context.

This brings in fundamental terms and relations that will be worked out further in the following chapters: community and the communal feeling, poetic making and history, genre and the sense of commonality. In doing so I will look into the question of the relationship between the things that we categorize – for more or less good reasons – as arts, literature, or entertainment media, and what has been discussed as the political in the last two decades.[47] What does political community mean? In what sense is this a question of feeling? And what is the connection of these feelings to the collective dynamics, the creation of which we ascribe to media and above all to visual media? The guideline by which I will seek to get to the bottom of this question is the history of the Hollywood war film genre. I would like to understand how the historical experiences and cultural phantasms of war are connected to the affective sensation of spectators in the poetic constructions of this genre, and what the relationship is between this affective sensation and the sense of commonality.

---

[47] Cf. Joseph Vogl, "Einleitung," in *Gemeinschaften. Positionen zu einer Philosophie des Politischen*, Frankfurt am Main 1994 7–27. Cf. also: Streiter, "Die Frage der Gemeinschaft und die 'Theorie des Politischen'"; Hebekus and Völker: *Neue Philosophien des Politischen zur Einführung*.

But what can the comparative analysis of war films, which are sensational Hollywood entertainment or slick propaganda, and often both at once, contribute to clarifying this question? Why discuss this relation between poetics and politics through examples from just this genre? Is it not merely a matter of ideology here? Why is it not enough, as Rorty suggests, simply no longer to make the distinction between the various discourses, construing all of them equally as competing descriptions of our world; a world whose only – if also politically highly significant – truth consists in being describable in infinitely multiplying perspectives? Why should we attribute special significance to the aesthetic modalities of experience when it comes to defining the relationship between poetics and politics more precisely?

The answer, which I develop in the following chapters, is basically quite simple. Because political communities cannot simply be detached and distinguished from the melange of religious, ritualist, and military forms of communitization. My expectation is that a theoretical perspective can be developed in the poetic practices that are associated with art, entertainment, and literature in a western context that would allow us to distinguish acts of subjectivization that relate individuals to the affective fabric of a politically grounded community from the forms of communitization mentioned above.

The task will thus be to identify and to conceptually understand aesthetic modalities of experience that relate to the community in a different way than is the case with cultic-ritual practices. The reconstruction through film analysis is thus fixed from the very beginning in the reading of philosophical texts that correlate the understanding of community or of the sense of commonality in different ways with the understanding of aesthetics. I would like to investigate genre cinema through the example of the war film as an ensemble of such modalities of experience.

By comparing two films that are externally utterly similar, but that could not be more different in their presentation of pathos, I hope to explain this problematic, my heuristic thesis, and my approach in an exemplary case study.

1.4 Propaganda, Avant-garde, and Genre Films

A comparative case study

In the following chapter I would like to conduct a comparative film analysis to show how two opposing principles of community can be comprehended in a double respect in each manner of staging – as antagonistic forces and as inner conflict. I would like to reconstruct the different film poetic concepts in one propaganda film from America and one from Nazi Germany, showing how the two refer to mutually exclusive ideas of communities. We can presume that the irreconcilable antagonism in its evidence is due to the circumstance that both films were designed as war propaganda. On the other hand, however, the conflicting principles of community denote a field of conflict that can be localized within the society in question. The American propaganda film explicitly formulates the absurdity of the undertaking of prescribing a media politics to a democratic political body with the goal of propagating the militarization of the population. This contradiction subsequently returns as a dramatic matrix of the newly forming war film genre.

Both aspects of this antagonism can be extracted and evaluated as a specific pathos of the films. For this reason, in the following argumentation I will concentrate on analyzing the concrete aesthetic procedures of these films and their affect-poetic conception. For the pathos of the films should be reconstructed in just these aesthetic procedures and staging strategies as a modality of experience that the spectators embody in their perceptual sensations as a relation to the world dominated by affects.[48]

In the media historical research, this level is often overlooked. Indeed, the war film is attributed a seemingly unlimited potential for the affective power to mobilize. But the question of poetic strategies and procedures of this mobilization is largely considered answered with reference to ideological function. The fact that war films want to mobilize patriotic feelings in the first place already defines their ideology – which relieves us of the task of investigating the differences. The ideological function of the war film makes them all the same. For instance, in a comprehensive study on the images of war in the twentieth century, which appeared in Germany some time ago, it is presented as such:

> After the Japanese attack on Pearl Harbor, the USA dramatically increased the production of documentary mobilizing films, for which, unlike in Germany, primarily fiction film directors were engaged. These films, compiled from newsreels and documentary footage, were above all meant to provide information about America's opponents and goals in the war. Among the most important of these productions were: Frank Capra's WHY WE FIGHT series (oriented to particular target groups, especially workers, people of color, and women, and which qualitatively differ very little from productions from Germany and Italy. They made ample use of racist imagery of the enemy, showed clips from the Soviet documentarist Roman Karmen, and were consciously inspired by Leni Riefenstahl's TRIUMPH OF THE WILL and Nazi compilation films such as THE CAMPAIGN IN POLAND and VICTORY IN THE WEST);

---

48 With this thesis I am drawing on a film-analytical model that I developed – in collaboration with others working on various research projects – following neophenomenology and Deleuze. Cf. Hermann Kappelhoff and Jan-Hendrik Bakels, "Das Zuschauergefühl: Möglichkeiten qualitativer Medienanalyse," in *Zeitschrift für Medienwissenschaft*, 5 (2), 2011, 78–96.

John Ford's Oscar-winning war documentary THE BATTLE OF MIDWAY and his DECEMBER 7TH; Lewis Milestone's air combat film THE PURPLE HEART (1944); Howard Hawks's film AIR FORCE (1944), produced with extensive special effects, as well as other combat movies.[49]

Now Capra's WHY WE FIGHT series was neither targeted at workers, nor in any special way at ethnic minorities, and at most very indirectly at housewives. The films were produced as informational material for recruits and only appeared in cinemas in exceptional cases and only in part. But this historical imprecision does not count for much if one compares it to the claim that Capra's works qualitatively (sic!) differ very little from German or Italian productions.

Whatever qualities this statement might refer to, to reduce the engagement with Riefenstahl's TRIUMPH DES WILLENS (1935) by the team around Capra in preparation for and during the course of the WHY WE FIGHT series to a basic common inspiration is pure nonsense. It not only contradicts Frank Capra's personal testimony, but also the state of knowledge of historical research. Already in 1993, Martin Loiperdinger published a study based on this research,[50] which presents the production history of the WHY WE FIGHT series. In fact, the idea was to make propaganda films exclusively from documentary material (be it adversarial propaganda, or be it that of one's own newsreels); the plan was – and expressly so in view of TRIUMPH DES WILLENS – to place the adversarial propaganda films qua montage into a new perspective in such a way as to cause them, in their representational forms and the representations, to testify against themselves. They were meant to be legible as images of that community whose triumph they propagated. The claim that Capra's films are qualitatively indistinguishable from the propaganda of the Axis powers not only overlooks this historical matter; it is completely blind to the poetic calculation of how film images are staged.

In the following I would like to compare Frank Capra's propaganda films with another film by Leni Riefenstahl, the address of which is very similar to that of Capra's works. TAG DER FREIHEIT – UNSERE WEHRMACHT [DAY OF FREEDOM – OUR ARMED FORCES] from 1935 is primarily directed at recruits. The method of the largest possible contrast is chosen as the experimental arrangement. For if the hypothesis is true that the question of the "sense of commonality," in Rorty's sense, is decided at the level of aesthetic processes and staging, then the staging concepts of Capra and Riefenstahl would have to be radically different.

---

49 Gerhard Paul, *Bilder des Krieges – Krieg der Bilder. Die Visualisierung des modernen Krieges*, Paderborn 2004, 255.
50 Martin Loiperdinger, "'Why We Fight' contra 'Triumph des Willens' – Feindbilder in der amerikanischen Gegenpropaganda," in *Widergänger. Faschismus und Antifaschismus im Film*, ed. Joachim Schmitt-Sasse, MAkS Publikationen, Münster 1993, 76–90.

It is not a matter of working out the fundamental difference in order to refute an obviously untenable thesis. Rather, the level can be gauged much more precisely against the backdrop of this thesis, a level on which the various qualities of the staging of the image correspond to highly opposing political intentions. Unless one were to claim in all seriousness that the films are based on a similar idea of society and politics.

TAG DER FREIHEIT: the media technology of fusion

Leni Riefenstahl's DAY OF FREEDOM – OUR ARMED FORCES was commissioned by the National Socialist German Workers Party on the occasion of reintroducing the draft. It is therefore, exactly like Capra's film series, directed at the recruits that were to be committed to the war effort. Both films unfold the ethos of belonging to the individual to the community, both target the pathos of self-sacrifice as the pledge of this belonging. And yet it is hard to imagine a greater contrast than that between their directorial methods.

Riefenstahl's film has a clear division. An epilogue shows a group of young men stripped to the waist at their morning wash (see Figure 5). We see laughing faces, youthful bodies, the joy of morning. This is followed by an interlude showing soldiers on foot and on horseback. Through highly stylized camera perspectives and artfully orchestrated mists, they have traded in their everyday corporality for uniforms, riding poses, and shots from below.

Following this we see the soldiers' deployment, marching into a kind of stadium rotunda; they march past the audience and the tribune of generals. The soldiers fall into the strict geometry of the Führer's review. This is followed by Hitler giving a speech to the newly recruited soldiers. In ornamental tirades, he continually varies the same metaphor. The young men can and should trade in their debased physical existences for their participation in a body that is as abstract as it is heroic – the newly re-established corps of German men, the armed forces of the fathers.

What then follows are the steps of just this transition, staged as the fusion of human material with technical material. Once again we see soldiers – faceless beneath their helmets – marching past the grandstand. This proves to be the opening of a maneuver: infantrymen throwing themselves onto the ground and shooting. Then, in a more or less strict escalation, we see soldiers on motorcycles, in cars with cannons attached, then light track vehicles, armored cars, and finally tanks.

The attentive gaze into the heavens by the Nazi elite announces the final stage: the aviators. Through the elaborated rhetoric of dynamic montage sequences, an image of strictly methodical annihilation appears: a kind of theatrically

Figure 5: Morning wash (TAG DER FREIHEIT).

fictionalized escalation according to the rules of a child's game – the cars outdo the men on motorcycles, the tanks outdo the track vehicles, and the aviators finally outdo the grenadiers still hidden within the tanks (see Figure 6).

The ordinary body introduced at the beginning of the film is the object of a ritual dressing that obliterates it in the end. This obliteration forms the basis for the life of the troops, the marching line, the battalion, the division, the army, the nation. But the pathos that attempts to tie the spectators – in this case the

Figure 6: The melding of man and technology.

soldiers themselves – to this community is based on a fundamental aesthetic mode of experience in the cinema: namely, the capacity to give a dynamic element to the spectator's space of perception and sensation, extending far beyond the scope of everyday perception. It is this use of media technology to unlock the perceptual faculty that is bound to a human body that the historical avant-garde so cherished. And the avant-garde already used metaphors of war to describe this unlocking.

> I am a kino-eye. I am a mechanical eye. I, the machine, show you the world as only I can see it. Now and forever, I free myself from human immobility. I am in constant motion, I draw near, then away from objects. I crawl under, I climb onto them. I move apace with the muzzle of a galloping horse. I plunge full speed into a crowd, I outstrip running soldiers, I fall on my back, I ascend with an airplane, I plunge and soar together with plunging and soaring bodies.[51]

---

[51] Dziga Vertov, *Kino-Eye: The Writings of Dziga Vertov*, trans. Kevin O'Brien, Berkeley/Los Angeles 1984, 17.

If Dziga Vertov celebrates the media technical mobilization of perception by cinema here using the metaphor of war technology, what it augurs is the reverse of the case with Riefenstahl. For Vertov, war technology can even become a utopian image in which all knowledge, all thinking and aspiration aims for a life lived to the fullest. The cinema itself here stands in for the illusion of an ego that effortlessly overcomes the spatio-temporal complexity of any explosion because the technology provides it with a body that has been infinitely expanded in its powers and possibilities.

Riefenstahl, on the other hand, stages weapons technology as a spectacle in which all the achievements of culture, all technology becomes the expression of the absolute power of the Führer. She ties into the aesthetic program that Walter Benjamin defined as fascist in 1930 on the occasion of a collection of essays brought out by Ernst Jünger. This program was fascist because, driven on by the historico-philosophical furor of German idealism, it describes war as a nation coming around, and the annihilation of everyday life as a necessary sacrifice in order to bring about the birth of a new heroic age:

> War, in the metaphysical abstraction in which the new nationalism believes, is nothing other than the attempt to redeem, mystically and without mediation, the secret of nature, understood idealistically, through technology. This secret, however, can also be used and illuminated via a technology mediated by the human scheme of things. "Fate" and "hero" occupy these authors' minds like Gog and Magog [...] Everything sober, unblemished, and naïve that has been considered regarding the improvement of human society ends up between the worn teeth of these Molochs, who react with the belches of 42-cm. mortars.[52]

Technology – for Benjamin the expression and form of a non-metaphysical thinking that moves in the immanence of the needs and demands of human cohabitation – becomes a poetic metaphor in the aesthetics of these fascists by which the "heroic features" of the new age take form: namely, in the ungovernable destructive forces of war.

"In this mystical theory of war," as Benjamin writes later, "the state naturally plays no role at all [...] Rather, what is demanded of the state is that its structure and its disposition adapt themselves to, and appear worthy of, the magical forces that the state itself must mobilize in the event of war."[53]

---

[52] Walter Benjamin, "Theories of German Fascism: On the Collection of Essays *War and Warriors*, edited by Ernst Jünger," in *Walter Benjamin: Selected Writings, Volume 2, 1927–1934*, Cambridge 1999, 312–321, here 319.
[53] Ibid., 319–20.

When we watch Riefenstahl's film, it is indeed astounding how self-evidently the avant-garde concept of a dynamic spatial image, decoupled from all ordinary perception, becomes the functional means by which to present this construction of the state and this stance. In TAG DER FREIHEIT, Hitler's position high above the military review on display beneath him, is transformed into an aesthetic experience for the cinema spectator. From this perspective, war itself becomes a spectacle of communitization. It is presented, if we follow Benjamin's analysis of the war metaphor in fascist thought, as the most efficient form of bureaucratic administrational technologies.

> In the person of the pilot of a single airplane full of gas bombs, such leadership embodies all the absolute power which, in peacetime, is distributed among thousands of office managers – power to cut off a citizen's light, air, and life. This simple bomber-pilot in his lofty solitude, alone with himself and his God, has power-of-attorney for his seriously stricken superior, the state; and where he puts his signature, the grass will cease to grow – and this is the "imperial" leader the authors have in mind.[54]

In Riefenstahl's TAG DER FREIHEIT the war spectacle is the expression of this absolute power, consisting in nothing other than in the possibility of total annihilation of the national people. The film stages the extinction of the everyday lives of ordinary people as a ceremonial experience of community, which the spectators take part in through their aesthetic pleasure.

Benjamin juxtaposes this pleasure with the "more sober children, who possess in technology not a fetish of doom but a key to happiness."[55] This 'happiness' is what Vertov means when he lauds the ego of the camera's eye using the metaphor of modern war technology, in which it is possible to imagine a subjectivity to which this technology opens up a completely different practice than that of war. Within action fantasy, the pleasure of such an ego has become a fundamental modality of genre cinema, an omnipresent phantasm of entertainment culture.

No war film that does not have a part in this aesthetic modality in one way or another. The question is what forms of affective collectivity are associated with this pleasure. What counts for Riefenstahl's TAG DER FREIHEIT at any rate, is what Benjamin wrote about the "theorists of fascism." What they decipher as "the heroic features" of a new national community are "the features of Hippocrates, the features of death."[56]

---

54 Ibid., 320.
55 Ibid., 321.
56 Ibid., 319.

Only a few years after the "Theories of Fascism," at the same time that Riefenstahl was producing her film, Benjamin was working on his most famous essay "The Work of Art in the Age of Its Technological Reproducibility." Against the backdrop of the advancing success of fascist media politics, he characterizes forms of taking aesthetic pleasure in death as follows: "Humankind, which once, in Homer, was an object of contemplation for the Olympian gods, has now become one for itself. Its self-annihilation has reached the point where it can experience its own annihilation as a supreme aesthetic pleasure."[57]

One can effortlessly relate these words to the stages of transformation of ordinary bodies into the military corpus, as TAG DER FREIHEIT stages it. They affect spectators who do not see themselves represented in such depictions, but who experience themselves as positioned in the scene as perceiving resonating bodies. In their shared aesthetic pleasure, they become that community that Hitler's addressed in his speech about the legacy of the fathers of the armed forces. They are unified in the celebration of a higher will, which is completed in the stages of annihilating their everyday creatural way of being.

PRELUDE TO WAR: "What put us in the uniform?"

The pathos sketched out above, which can be seen in the calculated staging of TAG DER FREIHEIT, also affects Riefenstahl's more famous film: TRIUMPH DES WILLENS [TRIUMPH OF THE WILL]. It led Capra to be convinced that film images could be turned against their creator.[58] The medial self-staging of the opponent had to show American soldiers what was so objectionable about this opponent, and to move them to respond to Riefenstahl's appeal to the sense of a national community with exactly the kind of harsh refutation that ultimately can represent the only reason to enter the war at all.

So Capra develops his own conception by studying the opponent's propaganda, and conceives the first and second episode of the WHY WE FIGHT project decidedly as a counter proposal to Leni Riefenstahl's Nuremberg Rally film, TRIUMPH OF THE WILL. He develops the montage of materials from newsreels,

---

[57] Walter Benjamin, "The Work of Art in the Age of Its Technological Reproducibility," in *Walter Benjamin: Selected Writings, Volume 4, 1938–1940*, Cambridge 2003, 270.

[58] "TRIUMPH OF THE WILL fired no gun, dropped no bombs. But as a psychological weapon aimed at destroying the will to resist, it was just as lethal [...] How could I mount a counter-attack against TRIUMPH OF THE WILL; keep alive our will to resist the master race." Frank Capra, *The Name Above the Title: An Autobiography*, New York 1971, 328.

documentaries, and the opponent's propaganda into a deconstructive process that could be compared with the strategies of the found-footage film. The films, even in their individual episodes, look like a cinematographic analysis of the socialization rituals of fascist societies.

In the following, I will concentrate on the first episode of the series, PRELUDE TO WAR. The film opens with the question: "Why are we Americans on the march? What put us into uniform?" First and foremost, this directly addresses the troops: the soldiers in the training camps and on their way in ships and planes that will take them to the most remote parts of the globe. Even if the rhetorical function of this question seems obvious, the answer can only be fully grasped at the end of the film.

At first the question is associated with the image of marching American soldiers: bright uniforms, music, casual marching, loose formations, and – recognizable in the medium shots despite helmets and uniforms – individual faces. Then, in a sharply polemical tone, which suggests that the question has actually been answered already, the film scans over possible answers.

The theaters of war around the world are called up. The recognizable images from newsreels and their geographic placement trace out a mental movement for the audience, which is promoted and structured by the off-screen voice: Is it because of Pearl Harbor…?! because of Poland, China, Russia? The montage thus formulates a stream of associations in which weapons technology is repeatedly placed in relation to images of destruction. Reinforced in the thundering of the noise of battle, the staging of the powers of weapons technology is related to its opposite: to images of wounded human bodies, killed and injured children, the faces of horrified, desperate women, oppressed men.

The staccato of the raging accusations is carried by a montage of pre-existing visual material, which is condensed into an affect-laden formula of pathos. Divided by the calls from off screen and the repeating explosions, the montage adds up, element for element, visual layer for visual layer, into a self-sufficient figuration of expression, an audiovisual movement image of rage. Its composition is based on the dense connection on various levels of movement according to a strictly implemented principle of combination. This seems to produce affect in the temporal form of an escalating tirade.

It is first: The opposition of light and dark sequences of perception on the level of the progression of the shots. Images of explosions, in which landscapes scatter in the flash, are answered by images of smoke billowing and darkening the light.

Second: The dissolve, the fluid transition, the fusion or layering of various images and levels of images. Tanks turning up dimly, rolling away over burning ruins or away from the rows of corpses and towards the spectators. Over the succeeding dissolves, they join up with flashes of the light of combat, the billows of smoke and flames into a figuration of movement that penetrates all other images as a continually morphing transition.

Third: the strictly organized alternation between oppositional directions within the shot (vertical, horizontal, diagonal, from the foreground to the background, or from the right to the left side, and then in reverse); these alternations translate the violence spoken of by the voice off screen into an audiovisual perceptual sensation of the constantly rising tension of mutually antagonistic dynamics.

Fourth: The temporal structuring achieved by building up symmetry and rhythm. The entire montage sequence is organized by the regular return of cannons aimed at the sky, which become visible to the left for a few seconds, then to the right, then exploding in a thunderous noise. They structure the sequence like a grammatical colon, which is then answered by the voice from off screen.

Like in a musical composition, the spectator's perceptual process itself is organized as a strictly divided sequence of opposing perceptual sensations. For the spectators, every moment of their perceptual sensation becomes a transitional moment of an expressive movement unfolding in time. And this in turn is woven together, at every moment, with the recognition of the visual motifs and motivic associations, the meaning of the speaker's words and the understanding of audiovisual formulas. The montage sequence forms an aesthetic experience of perception, which at every moment short-circuits the process of meaningful understanding with the affective sensual experience of the dynamic compositional patterns (see Figure 7).

What emerges is then the precious commodity that every propaganda film seeks to create: the impression that one could see, feel, and understand the world spoken of here in one and the same stroke; what emerges is evidence for the senses. The evidence that the world of which I am being told is visible there on the screen, and that everything that is visible there can be unlocked and assessed directly as an affective experience. It is this aesthetic evidence that gives the off-screen voice its power of persuasion.

In view of this method, Capra's film does not in fact differ from that of Leni Riefenstahl. But here, what is added into the cinematographic image is precisely that perspective that is cut out in Riefenstahl. The physical vulnerability of individual bodies forms the opposite pole to the destructive power of weapons technology. What is presented as the self-evident process of a power rising by stages in Riefenstahl can be experienced here by the spectator as the clash of completely unequal powers.

It is just this principle of the montage of opposing perspectives that also determines the entire construction of the film. For Capra introduces different cinematic modes of staging from sequence to sequence, of which the montage of association of the types described is only one variation.

Figure 7: The creation of sensuous evidence (PRELUDE TO WAR).

"What put us into uniform?" In what follows, repeated attempts to find an answer to the film's opening question will be made, and in ever new representational modes of the cinema.

The music changes to a spirited march. We see a typical cross-section montage, such as those we know from Ruttmann, or even the French avant-garde of the thirties. We see a play with movement and form, reproduced a hundred times, shimmering steel and endless columns of uniform objects: projectiles, airplanes, tanks.

The weapons industry's mass production becomes a metaphor for the power of American industrial production, and at the same time becomes an image for the change brought to society by the war. In analogy to the soldiers marching forward in their light-colored uniforms, what is reflected in the light play of movement of the glistening steel is the euphoric affirmation of world of civilians in the images of weapons geared for war. The display of weaponry is staged here as an expression of the country's economic power, not of state power.

Another change in the music brings in a sweet-lyrical motif that predisposes us to a representational modality that we know from genre cinema: "This is a fight between the free world and the slave world."

The Manichaeism turns the dramaturgical logic of melodrama into the backdrop to further argumentation. Within this logic, the world only knows two poles: here the world of good, there the realm of evil. America is the virtuous innocence that is threatened by the plainly villainous.

The world of freedom is first and foremost the freedom of religion: Moses, Muhammad, Confucius, Christ. But what links these communities of faith is that political power may not call on any of them as a higher legitimation if it seeks to guarantee the freedom of all.

In a very few shots, the founding act of America is called up. The monuments of the founding fathers are placed alongside historical paintings of the revolution – as is the architecture in which are presented the institutions that emerged from this founding. Even in its most venerable appearances, the state institution is claimed as a mere means to the end of political freedom.

The fact that this idea of the state is the diametrical opposite of that of the enemy emerges over the following sequence. The opening sequence is followed by a good ten minutes that are almost exclusively concerned with the 'world of slaves,' with Italy, Germany, and Japan.

The strategy is initially argumentative; the sequences speak of societies that do not seek to solve their social and economic problems by means of politics, instead subjugating themselves to a leader. Documentary footage from the twenties and early thirties is called upon to remind us of the great social crises before the film moves on to images of militarized socialization.

The parallel montage of the appearances of Il Duce, the Tenno, and the Führer shows us the masses themselves as a faceless body, responding to the ruler's theatrical speeches – "The head of the state is the voice of God" – with the same ritual of submission. The triumph of the will of the state is completed in the grandiose celebration of an ecstatic experience of community, with which every individual becomes a member of this body.

The next sequences spell out how this experience of community destroys the fundamental values of freedom. On the one hand, it is work. The propagandistic self-representation of a socio-political program of the Nazi state here becomes the image of immature dependence. On the other hand, it is religion. The hate for religion is represented as the hubris of state sovereignty, which turns the public space of politics into a stage on which the figure of the leader is presented as a divine force. In the end, this can be seen in child-rearing, in which the hubris of the state is represented most conspicuously. The state, the leader, the emperor lay claim to the entire lives of individuals, to their physical working powers, their beliefs, and their children. Politics becomes the means to redeem this claim. In place of politics, the force of the state appears, terror. In order to be able to grasp the opposition of terror and politics, Capra shifts the register of representation once again, drawing on yet another mode of genre cinema. The sequence could easily come from a gangster film from the thirties.

We might discount this as a rhetorical device to associate the Nazis with criminality. But what seems significant to me is less the moral subtext than the multiplication of perspectives through the alternating modes of representation.

For the spectators, the world of the gangster genre is structured by the opposition between the rule of law and violence, between the regulated enforcement of state power and terror as anarchistic-individual violence. So, the leaders of enemy states are denied any political legitimacy. They exercise violence, not power.

One can certainly designate the idea of individual freedom as an "empty signifier";[59] a metasign that only serves to structure the propagandistic discourse through the absolute opposition between the 'we' of the political community and the collectivity of others. This sign functions as a representative with which the founding act of the nation is positioned as a normative horizon before which every argument is derived from an uncircumventable difference: the difference between friendship and enmity. If this opposition is then rhetorically unfolded in metaphors of good and evil, what emerges is a Manichean image of the world, which necessarily imposes a reading informed by ideology critique.

And yet, one would miss the decisive difference if one were to reduce the films of Capra and Riefenstahl to the smallest common denominator of propagandistic rhetoric. In fact, on the level of verbally propounded political arguments, all that is established are merely a moral value and an ideological schema. For instance, when the freedom of religion is opposed to the disdain for this freedom on the side of the enemy. At the level of cinematic staging,

---

59 In Ernesto Laclau's sense. Cf. Ernesto Laclau, "Why do Empty Signifiers Matter to Politics?" in *Emancipation(s)*, London 1996, 36–46, here 37. Cf. also: Hebekus and Völker, *Neue Philosophien des Politischen zur Einführung*, 45–53.

however, the moral tenet does not correspond to any argument, but instead to the deconstruction of fascist self-representation as the hubris of state power. Enemy propaganda images are deciphered as testaments to a pseudo-religious ritual act that provokes a judgment of feeling awakened by one's own outlook. The state power of the enemy appears to be malicious and obscene because it obliterates the boundary between divine order and the order of the politically feasible. Against this backdrop, however, the freedom of religion no longer designates any abstract moral value. Much more, what now appears is the separation of politics and religion as a means, as a political strategy with the goal of historically realizing freedom. The ideal of freedom is related to the condition of its political feasibility. Indeed, to the same degree that it was politically possible to anchor the relation to God in the personality of individuals, this relation stripped political activity of its source of legitimation. Political power that infringes this principle turns into terror – an insight that Capra does not try to bring out as an argument, but as a judgment of feeling on the part of the spectator in the cinematic deconstruction of fascist self-fashioning. The idea that the freedom of the individual is ensured against the infringement of the communitarian exactly as much as individuality can be the exclusive refuge of transcendence is an analytical addendum to the affect-based judgment of an experience of film perception – which is to say, an addendum to an aesthetic judgment. Whether the real audience performs this or not is ultimately irrelevant to the intended effect.

PRELUDE TO WAR is also about differences in category between state terror and politics when it turns back to its own social life, once again to America. Stage for stage the ideal of freedom is compared to with the fascist principle of communitization. In place of the freedom of religion we see the idolization of the leader; in place of political difference of opinion we see the beauty of staging state power; in place of politics we see terror; and in place of the interactions of everyday life we see the militarization of social life. The fact that American virtue is crassly idealized will not have been overlooked, even in wartime. The question, then, is also not whether these representations sufficiently correspond to reality. What is much more important is what pathos is offered up here in contrast to the fascist national community, and what means are used to achieve this. Capra makes use of a genre that he was the undisputed master of at the time, proclaiming America's social ideal in the sentimental pathos of a family melodrama.

This sentimental pathos marks the fundamental difference between PRELUDE TO WAR and TAG DER FREIHEIT. It opposes the value of the everyday lives of ordinary people and their personal pursuit of happiness to the heroic pathos of war society. This difference forms the basis for Capra's strategy of decomposing the opponent's propaganda. It seeks to expose the imaginary core of the images, war as the ideal of fascist communitization, thus making the threat to any form of everyday cohabitation obvious.

It is quite astonishing how well Capra manages to turn Riefenstahl's visual staging against itself, and to make visible – in the faces of those who she had so dismissively relegated to the margins – the fear and indignation that these orgies of unification mean for individuals. "Let our boys hear the Nazis and the Japs shout out their own claims of master race crud – and our fighting men will know why they are in uniform."[60]

In fact, Capra's cinematographic analyses seem precisely to capture the idea of community that the pathos of Riefenstahl's films is based on. In continually new variations, they show how state power is founded on the ritual negation of the personal integrity of the individual. They show the formation of the masses into an ornamental representation of the power of their leader. They show the obliteration of the existence of the ordinary individual in favor of the military community. They show the military itself as a mode of fascist community building.

Capra and Riefenstahl each propagate an ideal of community, but they could not be more opposed. And this opposition can be grasped in the most diverse staging techniques. Riefenstahl uses the avant-garde art of montage to construct a homogenous perceptual perspective, which allows the spectator to take part in staging the power of the state. She lets the spectator share in the Führer's gaze, enthroned above at a vantage point from which he can enjoy the war below as spectacle and the annihilation of the person as the birth of a new ethnic community. Capra, on the other hand, multiplies the perspectives and standpoints by using montage to juxtapose highly heterogeneous modes of representation. Each of these modes has a different perspective, a different affective stance to the world: the montage of association, the cross-section montage, the mode of melodrama, and that of the gangster film.

This multiplication of perspectives confronts the heroic self-representation of the fascist state with the clash between opposing subjective stances and affective positionings – rage, pity, fear, indignation, horror. It deciphers this staging as a celebration of war that grounds the life forms of the fascist national community by negating any deviation that serves to individualize. Capra uses the representational modes of cinema to lay bare the ideal of community in the enemy's propaganda films. He challenges the judgment of his contemporaries in relation to this ideal, in order to mobilize the sense of community in them, the feeling of belonging to a completely different community.

---

60 Capra, *The Name Above the Title*, 331f.

Genre films and democracy

Riefenstahl's Nuremberg film is astonishing in its synthesis of entertainment cinema, artistic avant-gardism, and fascistic staging of masses. Capra's propaganda film attempts to respond at the level of this synthesis and to outdo the *Triumph of the Will* as avant-garde film poetics; he opposes the calculatedness of the Riefenstahl film with an analytical potential in cinema that lies in the generic heterogeneity of its formats, representational strategies, and poetic concepts themselves, and uses cinema's alternating modes and manners of representation to generate a variety of perspectives of mutually antagonistic positions and speech attitudes.

His film uses the various poetic modalities of genre films to spark a conflict in which these modalities themselves appear as different voices, stances, and rhetorical attitudes, which then respond to one another in polemical turns, unmasking what lies behind.

The multiplication of the representational modalities pulls the enemy's heroic self-fashioning out of the sky of high art and into the common reality of a multiplicity of voices – a heterogeneous juxtaposition of different points of view and affective evaluations, which Hollywood genre cinema ultimately appears to be. For Capra's cinematic world is not fixed by a systematic poetics that defines each genre by a specific subject matter with its own standard ensemble of characters, narratives, dramatic conflicts, and iconographic patterns.[61] Rather, it forms the system of a polyphonic speech, in which the various perspectives of experience and stances toward the world can be related to one another; the sense for the commonly inhabited world, the sense of commonality emerges in the interplay of reciprocal references and negations and in the appeal to agreement.

Capra's montage of the different modes of cinematic representation follows the ethos of a genre cinema that takes itself to be the medium of a democratic polity.[62] This ethos is the topic of the ludicrous story of Mr. Smith (James Stewart), who moves to Washington. In 1939 Frank Capra shot MR. SMITH GOES TO WASHINGTON (USA), which programmatically intertwined genre cinema and the democratic polity in the idea of unrestricted freedom of speech. The sentimental drama of the decent little Everyman who lands in the plots and intrigues of *realpolitik* is nothing other than a re-staging of the founding act of the American nation by means of cinema.

---

[61] Rancière associates this model of pre-modernist aesthetics with the classical narrative genre of Hollywood cinema. Cf. Jacques Rancière, *La Fable Cinématographique*, Paris 2001; and Jacques Rancière, *Film Fables*, London 2006.

[62] I will develop this theoretical position later with regard to the theories of Stanley Cavell.

Mr. Smith insists on his right to declaim his view of things in free, public speech. He uses the particular rule of the filibuster to get a hearing for this right, in an address that is not meant to end, and which gets more and more nonsensical the longer it lasts. He talks and talks for days on end, to the point of complete physical exhaustion; he exercises his right to speech for its own sake. In this literally pointless speech he in fact repeats the founding act of the democratic society by exceeding the boundaries of its institutional form. The whole country celebrates the freedom of the one, utterly ordinary individual whose interests are of no concern for any general public. For the only goal of democratic institutions is to guarantee freedom for those who wish to speak. Even if this speech itself is bereft of any other goal than to assert the speaking ego.

MR. SMITH GOES TO WASHINGTON seems somewhat like a Brechtian *Lehrstück* that works through this idea of community. The film re-stages the founding act of the nation, which is always already belated, always already constitutive in the re-enactment of a primal scene with which the political community is called to the stage of history.[63] WHY WE FIGHT positions itself in the sequence of such repetitions when one of his first attempts at answering the film's question, "What are we fighting for?" is to cite Abraham Lincoln, who held a famous speech at a cemetery after the Battle of Gettysburg, which in turn cited the founding statement of the United States: "That government of the people, by the people, for the people shall not perish from the earth."

The constitutive conflict

Nothing seems to run contrary to this ethos as much as the pathos of military communitization. War, as becomes clear in the first few minutes of PRELUDE TO WAR, negates everything that matters to the American Way of Life. This is the contradiction, embodied in the marching soldiers themselves, that begins PRELUDE TO WAR. It is the reason for the question that is posed right at the beginning of the film: "Why are we Americans on the march?"

Capra develops two lines of argumentation that run in contradictory directions. On the one hand, he appeals – equally convinced of the moral culpability of the enemy and the ideal of freedom of the American nation – to the sense of

---

[63] Cf. Jacques Derrida, "Otobiographies: The Teaching of Nietzsche and the Politics of the Proper Name," in *The Ear of the Other*, Lincoln 1985, 1–39; and Derrida, "Declaration of Independence," in *Negotiations: Interventions and Interviews 1971–2001*, ed. Elizabeth Rottenberg, Stanford 2002, 46–54.

community, the sense of commonality that connects a democratic community. He seeks to make it visible and obvious how much this sense of commonality even incorporates the enmity toward the fascist ideal of community. On the other hand, he propagates a restructuring of social life – marked by the militarization of civilian population – that is so similar to the how the enemy forms community that it could be mistaken for it. At any rate, the militarization of society represents releasing state power from its strict appropriation, which is accompanied by violating the basic values of the political community.

War is then the reversal of all civil circumstances, to the degree to which society now turns on its own citizens' pursuit of happiness, subordinating their private life plans to the interests of the state, as Caillois writes.[64] War is the state of exception in which state power reclaims its dominance. Instead of being subordinate to the protection of individual freedom, the state demands that its citizens focus their entire being on the necessity of protecting itself as the state. It requires nothing less than that every individual gives up exactly those rights, the defense of which defines the founding act of the nation.

This reversal becomes obvious in the uniformity of the marching soldiers.

"What put us into uniform?" The attempt to answer this question leads back time and again to the same paradox. On the one hand, Capra's film decodes the basic structure of the enemy's propaganda images, the geometrical and uniform depiction of the masses as the direct expression of fascist collectivization; on the other hand, it propagates exactly this uniformity in the battle against the enemy, against the world of slaves.

This paradox is embodied by the American soldier himself – both as American and as soldier. For indeed, he subjugates his bodily existence to carrying out an activity that robs him of his personal will. He merges into a corps, and its technological structure of bodies and media (media of movement, of perception, of communication, of transmission) is as far advanced as its ritual forms of communitization are archaic. Even when PRELUDE TO WAR seeks to make the American soldiers recognizable as individuals in the details – the march is less strict in comparison to the image from the enemy propaganda, the uniforms are lighter, and over and over again we look into the faces of ordinary people – it still formulates an irresolvable conflict. The soldiers have taken on the shape of those who they are diametrically opposed to – the slaves in the brown and black uniforms.

This conflict between the freedom of the individual and his self-abandonment in the military community is the basis for the specific pathos of the American war film genre: regardless of whether they are the gung-ho films of the mobilizing

---

[64] Roger Caillois, *Man and The Sacred*, Westport 1980, 165f.

phase or the films from the fifties and sixties that critically examined the military – one might think of FROM HERE TO ETERNITY, ATTACK! (Robert Aldrich, 1956, 1944) or THE THIN RED LINE (Andrew Marton, 1964) – whether they are films to commemorate heroes – like THE LONGEST DAY – or to settle accounts with a corrupt political leadership – like THE BRIDGE AT REMAGEN (John Guillermin, 1969).

The classic Hollywood war film is familiar with the euphoria of action cinema, the pleasure in phantasms of technologically breaking the boundaries of human perception; it knows what heroes have to go through, from their initiation and then glorious deeds down to their deaths and the elegiac ceremony of commemorating them; it knows the phantasm of an omnipotent, immortal collective body as well as it knows the sacrifice of the individual that nurtures this immortality – but such stagings are always contained within the melodramatic mode; it is in this mode that the Hollywood war film unfolds the subjective perspective of the powerlessly suffering ego: his desperation, his fear, his pain with regard to his obliteration in and for the military corps. The pathos of the genre targets the compassion for this ego's suffering, not its heroic transfiguration. It is the suffering of anonymous, ordinary individuals – such as those marching soldiers with which Capra's propaganda film begins; uniformed individuals who are threatened with disappearing in the community of the corps and who nonetheless maintain an individual ego in their suffering, an ego that does not merge into this community. Ultimately it is this conflict that defines and structures the genre, the irreconcilable opposition between the political and the military forms of community.

"Why are we Americans on the march, what put us into uniform?" With these questions, Capra names the conflict that was re-staged in innumerable war films. And if PRELUDE TO WAR time and again starts looking for an answer to this question, it is not so much to convince – the decision had already long been made. The discussion and argumentation is much more a goal in itself as a mode of participation. Capra's film is thus the attempt – against the coercion of factual circumstances – to keep open a space in which the procedure of public debate is still maintained for the soldiers as a fundamental medium that positions them within the political community. In this sense, the sequence where Capra uses montage to connect increasingly concise statements by the most diverse, most ordinary people (see Figure 8) designates the position of speech in which the film – quite in the sense of Christian Metz's impersonal enunciation[65] – itself sees itself placed: one stance among many different ones, which all have the same validity.

---

65 Christian Metz, "The Impersonal Enunciation, or the Site of Film," in *The Film Spectator: From Sign to Mind*, ed. Warren Buckland, Amsterdam 1995.

Figure 8: "In the event of war in Europe, I think we should stay out of it entirely." – "We should mind our own business." – „If my country calls, yes!‟"

In Capra's propaganda film, he restructures genre cinema in a way that allows him to refer to war as a political question that could still be argued over, even among soldiers. He stages the ethos of the democratic community as an image space of a plural conception of opposing perspectives, and even attempts in the cinema to create the space of public dispute in a place where this is not envisaged, namely, in the framework of a military community.

In reference to this space, even the soldiers remain civilian citizens, confirmed in all their political claims. From the perspective of PRELUDE TO WAR they are addressed as a political community that is defined by the plurality of the singular perspective of individuals, who can take on highly opposing attitudes toward the world. In this regard as well, Capra's attempt was much closer to the aesthetic avant-gardes than one might presume from a master of genre cinema. For him there were indeed certain political expectations tied to the cinema, which we tend to ascribe to a romantic understanding of art and to European auteur cinema. In this feature, as well, his works form the exact counterpart to Leni Riefenstahl's poetics. Like them, they take the cinema for a medium with which it seems to be possible to create completely new collectivities, to develop new forms of affective coupling of large masses of singular individualities, of variously perceiving, thinking, feeling bodies.

In contrast to these avant-garde poetics, however, which aim for new forms of collectivity and pursue the ideal of radical collectivization, Capra's propaganda films stress the tension between the individual claim to develop freely and the claims of political communities on individuals. This tension becomes manifest in the poetic construction of PRELUDE TO WAR as a constitutive conflict, an ultimately irresolvable contradiction. It manifests itself in the irreconcilable opposition of the militarized form of collectivization and the liberal ideal of political community, as the opposition between the individual pursuit of happiness and the demands of state authorities in a society at war.

Working out this difference as the distinct poetics of film by means of examples was the overriding goal of using film analysis to compare the propaganda films of Riefenstahl and Capra. What I wanted to make clear is that TAG DER FREIHEIT und PRELUDE TO WAR – for all their similarities in how they operate – pursue different poetic conceptions that each have the goal of relating their audience to the pathos of a community that could not be more opposed; although both, as I mentioned, completely pursue an idea of the opportunities of film, which was developed by the aesthetic avant-gardes in the twenties of the past century.

But the pathos, in which the audience experiences itself as part of a community, in a different one in Riefenstahl's TAG DER FREIHEIT than in PRELUDE TO WAR. It is through this pathos that determines how spectators situate themselves as sensing subjectivities and see themselves as related to a community. Both films configure the relation between poetics and politics in a particular way by developing a different directorial strategy in each case. Each one represents a specific attempt to establish the mode of aesthetic experience in the cinema as a mode of perception, of seeing and hearing the world. They can be described as utterly differently ways of installing the experiential mode of viewing films as a kind of perception that puts the audience in a particular relation to the common world, that is, it creates a relation between the audience and a specific sense of commonality.

Film analysis as a poetology of film

The conflict between the archaic forms of collectivizing in military societies and the communal ideal of liberal democracies comes to the fore – this was to be shown – on a different level than that of the arguments put forth or the contents represented in the films; it also cannot be fixed at the level of the all too obvious ideological schemata and mythopoetic patterns, which determine the argumentation as a hermeneutical deep structure. An analysis, however, that reads the films as texts representing thoughts, arguments, things, actions, persons, would put this argumentational structure into the focus. In fact, this is mostly how things go when speaking of war or propaganda films. The result of this is that "contents" are constructed in such film analyses that could be communicated just as well in other media and text forms – while the representational forms that we have been looking at as ways of staging become nothing more than an accidental ingredient from this perspective. Viewed as a stylistic or rhetorical instrument, they add expressive colorings and affective assessments to the contents represented, which are considered to be entirely external to these representations.[66]

From my point of view, the contents cannot be separated in any way from the pathos-laden forms of the cinema; and these in turn are not detachable from the concrete media couplings of spectator activities and moved projections that are put into effect as cinematic moving images. This is why films should not be analyzed as texts.

Certainly, in any film a wide variety of symbolic registers (whether they come from language, iconography, mythology, metaphor, or ideology) are called on and situationally activated as a complex of meaning. But these processes of giving meaning in film cannot be pinned down using textual theory. Much more, film thinking, according to the fundamental phenomenological assumption, is carried out in the process of embodiment. It is always carried out as a perception that realizes the expressive dimensions of audiovisual moving images directly as a process of bodily sensation, directly as a psychic, mental, physical activity of the spectator.

What we call film does not exist as a text or an image. Ultimately it is always only present in the process of coupling the moving image and the spectator's body; film cannot be separated from the event of its perception, feeling, and thinking, embodied in the spectators.

Correspondingly, film analysis is relegated to (re)constructing films as visual spaces in which the generation of film meaning can be described as an interaction

---

[66] Cf. Carl Plantinga, *Moving Viewers: American Film and the Spectator's Experience*, Berkeley 2009.

1.4 Propaganda, Avant-garde, and Genre Films — 71

between projected moving images and spectator activities. It will attempt to describe films as couplings of perceptual, affective, and conceptual operations, which belong in the same moment to both the register of the audiovisual image as well as that of spectator activity.[67] Films are to be reconstructed through analytical work as a medial installation of movements of perception, affect, and thought, which can only ever be conceived in concretely positioned interactions between spectator bodies and film images.

Any analysis that follows the theoretical premises outlined here will aim to explain the implicit construction of such installations in order quite literally to come to terms with it as a logics of poetic making. The preceding comparative study is meant to have clarified that such poetological reconstructions unlock historical meanings that are in no way consistent with the results of those analyses that refer to the issues represented by means of textual analysis.

In many regards – and working this out was the strategic interest of the comparative analysis – the poetic concept of the propaganda film PRELUDE TO WAR is genuinely connected with a specific understanding of the cinema. We can recap this connection in four points:

First, the political possibilities of audiovisual communication are not positioned within the perspective of an art of film, but in the plurality and heterogeneity of contemporary cinematic forms of expression. Instead of giving expression to the idea of the Führer state in the shaping of the film as a homogenous artwork, as in the case of Riefenstahl, in Capra the individual film segment is figured as a particular perspective in the many-voiced ensemble of interacting modes of expression and speaking positions of (genre) cinema.

Second, this heterogeneity of forms of expression is taken as a matrix of a many-voiced collectivity of a wide variety of perspectives. In utter contrast to avant-garde poetics, which seek to position film as a medium of producing a new subjectivity of mass society, for Capra cinema is a space in which the heterogeneous multiplicity of voices in the real polity can accentuate its oppositional, contradictory, or indeed highly opinionated approaches to the world.

Third, the modes of expression in genre cinema – melodrama, gangster movies, costume dramas – are introduced in order to generate affects and to submit them to a specific modeling. Viewpoints and opinions are articulated as affective reactions, adding up in how PRELUDE TO WAR is staged into an

---

67 Cf. Hermann Kappelhoff, "Der Bildraum des Kinos: Modulationen einer ästhetischen Erfahrungsform," in *Umwidmungen: architektonische und kinematographische Räume*, ed. Gertrud Koch, Berlin 2005, 138–149.

affect-dramaturgical continuous form. Compassion, fear, anger, injury, discouragement, or indignation form elements of a cascade of overlapping affective qualities, which are all in line with the rage as the formative affect figure of a poetics of mobilization.

Indeed, rage, at least in the western tradition, is considered the most powerful impulse in the mobilization to war. It is ultimately the decisive issue – as we are taught by the oldest war narrative in occidental tradition, the Iliad, which sings of the rage of Achilles – in the capacity for combat.

Finally, in the antagonism between the authoritarian forms of military collectivization and the liberal ideal of political community there is a schema of conflict worked out, which we may call melodramatic, and with good reason. Indeed, the melodramatic is defined by the fact that it opposes the archaic idea of the sacrifice, made by the individual for the community, to the subjective internal perspective of just such an individual: the suffering of a self that, not being bolstered by any higher meaning of life, falls into the void of a hopeless world.[68] The insistent questions "Who put us in the uniform? Why are we on the march?" already articulate doubt of the we-consciousness, which Capra's films themselves propagate. They already point to the suffering of a multifold self of the soldiers that takes form over innumerable war films in the pathos of the "shell-shocked face."

Seen in this way, all four of Capra's cinematic references mentioned here can be understood as the corner points of a poetics of genre that can be worked out step by step in the history of the Hollywood war film: 1. situating individual films in a space of plural speaking positions and modes of expression; 2. qualifying this space as the heterogeneous diversity of voices in a real polity; 3. constructing an affect dramaturgy of rage; 4. discovering a new melodramatic type, a new figure of pathos.

In fact, following Stanley Cavell, one might see a new type of individuality in the shell-shocked face, out of which a new genre is constituted.

---

68 Kappelhoff, *Matrix der Gefühle*, 182. Or also: Hermann Kappelhoff, "Artificial Emotions: Melodramatic Practices of Shared Interiority," in *Rethinking Emotion: Interiority and Exteriority in Pre-Modern, Modern, and Contemporary T hought*, ed. Rüdiger Campe and Julia Weber, Berlin/Boston 2014, 264–288.

2 The Poetology of Genre Films

2.1 Stanley Cavell's Genre Theory

When we speak of the soldier's suffering, we address the central pathos of war in the sense of a specific form of subjectification. In the following, it should become clear that what initially appears to be the description of a character can be seen as an intervening perspective on the commonly shared world. One approach to this is offered by the deliberate and specific appropriation of the terms medium, genre, and type in Stanley Cavell. He speaks of "type" in the sense of an unmistakable distinctiveness.[1]

This does not mean a typical characteristic that taxonomically combines a series of single units; it also does not mean a stereotype, in the sense of a conventional shorthand for significant characteristics with the goal of serial duplication or quick association. On the contrary, it means an unmistakable individuality, which is brought to bear on all social roles, cultural influences, and family resemblances; it means "typical" in the sense of an unmistakable characteristic, a behavioral pattern, gesture, or attitude, which is characteristic of a person, and which makes their individuality visible in any roles they might take on.

Types and individualities

The type designates the particular way in which a corporeally, socially, and culturally marked habitus is individually formed in each particular case. In this understanding of type, the double sense of the word, as both category and example, are strictly interrelated, which is closely linked with the term "person" in the western tradition. On the one hand this is the persona, the character masks of ancient tragedies, through which the living voices of a performer can be heard; and on the other hand, due to the unmistakability of his or her voice, the person can be heard and understood through the mask as a discrete, eccentric reality.

Cavell succinctly developed this definition of type in relation to STELLA DALLAS (1937).[2] It is not by chance that King Vidor's melodrama has become a

---

[1] Cavell describes this distinctiveness as "particular ways of inhabiting a social role." Stanley Cavell, *The World Viewed: Reflections on the Ontology of Film*, Enlarged Edition, Cambridge, M./London 1979, 33f.
[2] Stanley Cavell, "Stella's Taste: Reading Stella Dallas," in *Contesting Tears: The Hollywood Melodrama of the Unknown Woman*, Chicago/London 1996, 197–222.

widely-discussed reference in feminist film theory. STELLA DALLAS not only provided an impressive way to trace the repressive violence of the social habitus, it also gave rise to an argument about whether the film presents the character in her eccentric taste as an unrecognized individuality to be asserted; or whether it instead showed the character's failure as the taming of an intractable spirit. For Cavell, a new type of character in genre cinema is literally placed before our eyes in STELLA DALLAS. The conflict of a character that masters all registers of self-representation and yet sill fails in the demands of the game of social role-playing, presumably because she is lacking any sense of what is appropriate, causes us to understand the type as a specific representational form, which can be fundamentally distinguished from other forms of character representation – for instance in theater or literature. Stella's efforts to exert her eccentric taste almost define this form. Types are eccentric individualities who lay claim to being perceived and recognized as such. It is not difficult to recognize Rorty's idea here, that the new descriptions of a common world are always also creative presentations of self-image. Outrageous, unrecognized individuality designates the borderline case of the sense of commonality per se.

But the fact that Cavell develops his reflections in relation to the female characters in the melodrama contains yet another – and for us decisive – clue as to how to understand this 'type'. Although Cavell uses the term above all to point to the mutual relation of star and character in Hollywood cinema, it becomes clear when looking at the melodrama that individualities are exerted as a specific expressivity, a style of sensation, a stubborn pathos, in short, an affect type. But in melodrama this is always a question of how films are staged as a whole. In the following I would then also like to speak of individuality in the sense of a specific form of subjectification, a certain way of positioning the I-sensation in relation to the we-sensation of a commonly shared world. These forms of subjectification are not to be established solely, or even preferentially, in the character, the acting style, or the star type.

It is in this modification that the concept should be related to the pathos formula of the shell-shocked face, which we saw in the film analyses in the first chapter. I would now like to expand somewhat on these thoughts in terms of genre theory.

For Cavell, films are explorations of the socially and culturally marked appearances of our collective life. In these appearances they accentuate individuality as the particular per se, as "particular ways of inhabiting a social role."[3] Ultimately they pursue the goal of discovering new individualities. New individualities, however, allow cycles of films to arise in which the cinema can be differentiated into ever new genres.

---

[3] Cf. Cavell, *The World Viewed*, 33.

Against this backdrop, we can now argue that, with the shell-shocked face, the cinema brought out a new type of subjectification, which formed the starting point for such a cycle of films, which we should ultimately treat as the genre of war films.[4] The pathos formula of the shell-shocked face would then concern new individualities, new types of sensation and expressivity, even new types of pathos, which turn up at the boundaries of the common world. They turn up precisely where these boundaries become visible at all as a field of conflict. To this degree, new types of pathos constantly mark conflicts that concern the political community in its constitutional conflicts just like that spoken of in the first shots of PRELUDE TO WAR: "Why are we Americans on the march? What put us in the uniform?" What is true for genre cinema in general is also true for the war film in particular; when new individualities turn up, this is always part and parcel of a developing consciousness of the boundaries of the sense of commonality.

From this perspective, the form of suffering in the shell-shocked face could be understood paradigmatically as a generic form where we could see the following paradox: while it refers back to a constitutive conflict in the polity, it is only exposed in its fullness as a pathos formula in a series of films – thus only then gaining the status of a commonly shared reality in the first place.

Genres as media of a shared perception of the world

First we should give a cursory summary of the linguistic basis of Cavell's argumentation. Whether we are speaking, versifying, philosophizing, or formulating scholarly arguments – we use the same words and turn to the same grammatical rules that we use in everyday language. But we always do this in a concrete interaction, with highly variable intentions and the given conditions of a particular situation. Therefore, when we speak or write, we form our statements and descriptions not based on the fixed rules of any previous system, but we act and react in given situations.

Since we can in no way rely on a sure knowledge about the nature of reality, the question arises as to how we manage at all to relate to a common world in our interactions. How do we present a consistent common world at all – a world that we have to update anew from situation to situation? The answer is that the consistency of our idea of the world is tied to mutually acknowledging a wide variety of perspectives, approaches, and descriptions, which constitute reality as a commonly shared world.

---

4 Cf. ibid., 29ff.

Neither knowledge nor language in and of themselves can vouch for an intersubjective relation to the world; they merely provide the means to produce a commonly shared world by using words and grammatical rules. In this sense, ordinary language designates the reservoir of the tried and tested possibilities of successful interactions that are available for any concrete interaction. If we deviate from expected language usage in a given situation, an exceptional possibility of relating to the common world might arise, a new possibility of describing it; but it is equally possible for the interaction to fail. "This seems to me the moral of ordinary language philosophy as well, and of the practice of art. Put it this way: Grammar cannot, or ought not, of itself dictate what you mean, what is up to you to say."[5]

What does this imply for film? Just like language, film is also not a system for generating meaning. Just like language merely provides the conditions for us to develop manners of speaking and speech acts, film, as a media technology, merely presents the material basis with which to develop cinematic forms of expression. And just as every ordinary usage of language draws on a reservoir of tried and tested patterns of interaction in order to relate to a common world, films draw on a collection of tried and tested possibilities to generate acknowledged cinematic proposals of the world. To speak of these tried and tested possibilities, Cavell brings the term medium into play.

He designates such cinematic proposals of the world as media that appear in cyclical series over longer spans of time: "The first successful movies [...] were not applications of a medium that was defined by given possibilities, but the creation of a medium by their giving significance to specific possibilities."[6] This is exactly what defines a genre for Cavell.

Genres are thus defined by in their function as media that, over the course of a series of films, assert a specific perspective on the common world. The medium, however, and this is the point of Cavell's argument, is in no way identical to media technology. The latter just designates the material basis for creating films and genres of films as media. Genres are therefore media of discovering a new individuality, whose eccentric view of the world presses for general acknowledgment.

At this point it is necessary to define more precisely the relationship between film in its specific mediality as a particular register of poetic making and Rorty's idea of describing and redescribing the boundaries of the common world. For as obvious as it may be that Capra's poetic concept differs starkly from Riefenstahl's, it is just as obvious that literary and philosophical descriptions differ starkly from

---

[5] Stanley Cavell, *Themes out of School: Effects and Causes*, Chicago 1988, 45.
[6] Cavell, *The World Viewed*, 32.

those of film, of the performing or visual arts, or those of music and those of performance. Initially, the different arts and media designate nothing more than different modes of relating to the world. They are distinguished as particular perspectives on the world.

Such fundamental hypotheses correspond to a series of no less fundamental assumptions about film, genre cinema, and the historical dynamic of poetic making, which should be viewed more carefully. In order to do so I would like to start from Cavell's highly particular understanding of media. This opens up a way of understanding the poetics of genre that derives genres from generic forms of poetic making themselves, and not from the taxonomies of conventional classification systems.

This allows us to see a history of the film image that can be understood as part of a history of permanently changing the media "forms of sensory experience, of the perception of time"[7]: as part of a poetic making that generates the media forms that allow war to become a present or past event, one that is nearer or farther, and which, for the spectator, conforms to a commonly shared world.

The historicity of genre cinema

Such a history of the cinema is predicated on the idea that its historical development cannot be measured and assessed using pre-established terms. Correspondingly, films as audiovisual documents cannot simply be differentiated either from propagandistic manipulation or from fictional films, nor can they be differentiated from popular entertainment as reflective art. Is this an audiovisual document or a fiction? Propaganda or information? A ubiquitous genre fantasy or a poetic form of remembrance? Such questions can in no way be answered by referring to registers of taxonomic classification in which media and media formats, arts, and genres are differentiated and categorized by means of previously established correspondences between the contents represented and the form of media. Such an operation follows an understanding of categories based on rule-governed poetics, and its taxonomies are ultimately based on nothing more than conventional categories and representational correspondences.

In fact, there are more than a few research works that examine the relationship between the war film genre, the production of media images, and the politics of war. But they do so by following the schematics of rule-governed poetics, precisely in their critical impetus, when they define media formats and genres

---

[7] Jacques Rancière, *The Names of History: On the Poetics of Knowledge*, Minneapolis 1994, 101.

of representing war by means of the contents represented in them, and seek to assess them by comparing them to the reality of war: How is war represented in the media? How does media representation compare to the reality of war? And how is the one or the other question reflected in the fictional genre?[8] This analytic triad seems intuitively to arise from overwhelming evidence. But in fact it can only be meaningfully applied if we assume the undistorted, authentic audiovisual document as the Archimedean point of reference. We could call it the a priori of an ideal audiovisual image, which represents the reality of war with complete transparency.

But then the relation to be grasped in its dynamics and contingency is always already established. In what ways do films place spectators in relation to the political and historical reality of war? What spatio-temporal correlations get established between their bodies (their world of senses as a shared common world) and the acts of war? What is the relation of these correlations to the attempts of a society to relate to itself as a political community? And what kind of relation to the self as a political community becomes palpable in these correlations, which relate (more or less) peaceful spectators to a war which is that to decide the limits of this community?

It is not possible to get a clear view of the ramifications of such media references to, and perspectives on, the shared world, as long as we seek to establish a priori the distinctions between media formats, representational modes, and poetic concepts. These in fact refer back to the historically situated production of media with which a commonly shared perception of the world can be constructed. They refer back to the history of poetic making, which is a history of the permanent production of new perspectives and modes of describing the common world – a permanent production of media with which this world is created in the first place.

Without a theory of the history of poetic making, genre theory remains caught in the circular argumentation of taxonomic concepts.[9] We can thus emphatically support Altman's call, when he suggests that we reflect on the genre theoretical tradition, in order to break out of the circular reasoning that arises time and time

---

[8] This is still the case for many of the most fundamental current works on changing the forms of war, on the war film, and on the media reality of war. Cf. Rasmus Greiner, *Die neuen Kriege im Film: Jugoslawien – Zentralafrika – Irak – Afghanistan*, Marburg 2012, and Gerhard Paul, *Bilder des Krieges – Krieg der Bilder*.

[9] Thomas Sobchack, "Genre Film: A Classical Experience [1975]," in *Film Genre Reader IV*, ed. Barry Keith Grant, Austin 2012, 121–132; Jörg Schweinitz, "Genre und lebendiges Genrebewußtsein," in *montage a/v* 3 (2), 1994, 99–118; Markus Kuhn, et al., (eds.), *Filmwissenschaftliche Genreanalyse*, Berlin/Boston 2013.

again in relation to genre.[10] Where do genre films stand then in the history of poetic making, and what does this mean for an understanding of genre cinema in general and the war film in particular?

In order to elucidate this problematic more clearly and to position the Cavellian idea of media in its unlocking potential, it will be necessary briefly to discuss the theory of genre in film.

Why does a genre such as that of the Hollywood war film come into existence in the first place? What are the factors that lead to an ensemble of artistic representational types branching out to such a degree that they bring forth a new variety – let's call them combat films – of popular entertainment cinema? What led to the rise of a cycle of films that realized the media technological possibilities of cinema in a way that very quickly became perceived as characteristic of a genre? How is it possible at all that such a terrible historico-political experience as the Second World War became an object of entertainment art? These questions lead us into the core of the problem, which is closely tied to the theory of genre cinema itself.

In the following I would like to explain the relationship between the poetics of genre cinema and the historical configurations of how political communities are proposed, which was the topic of the first part of this book. How did the media technological possibilities in these films become the condition for a new description of the common world? The perspective that we could develop in relation to Cavell might give a first clue as to the direction I would like to pursue in this question. Can combat films be understood as a new medium of configuring a common perception of the world?

My primary concern in the following is not how to understand the war film as a genre in Hollywood cinema. Even the question of the relation between this genre and the history and presence of war is only of indirect interest. Within the framework of this book, the point is to gain basic insights into the relation between genre poetics and politics. In view of this relation, I certainly hold that the correlation between poetic forms of representing war and the political ways that the violence of war appears are paradigmatic. For this reason – and this follows a point by Steve Neale[11] – the war film allows us to realign the fundamental problems of genre theory in terms of poetology.

---

10 It is surely not by chance that Altman is one of the few theorists of genre cinema who manages to sketch out an approach in the dialects of the semantic and syntactic dimension of genre that describes the historical dynamic of genre poetics in a way that avoids taxonomic schematism. Cf. Altman, *Film/Genre*, 207–226.
11 Steve Neale, *Genre and Hollywood*, London/New York 2000, 121ff.

2.2 On the Critique of the Poetics of Genre

From this perspective, the mutual relations between the different formats of representing war as a medium of art and entertainment, information and public policy can be viewed. We can learn very little about the relation between genre cinema and politics if we do not examine the interaction between the various media that realize the possibilities of film as media technology in their own special ways. Genres, in and of themselves, are defined by the interplay of a wide variety of representational forms and should be viewed as elements of a system of genre poetics.[12] It is only possible to define a single genre when taking account of the dynamic of the historical transformations of such a system.[13]

Classical and post-classical

In relation to this dynamic the widely abused distinction between classical and post-classical genre cinema is plainly too general. I also find it highly dubious to claim that the latter is reflexive about its somewhat naïve, straight-forwardly narrative predecessors.[14] This thesis hypothesizes a single aspect of historical reflexivity, which is ultimately typical of every genre-poetic form. The ironic reflection

---

[12] In the debates about genre theory, this claim has been raised over and over again since Frederic Jameson, without changing much in the circumstances that research in genre poetics usually only deals with a single genre.

[13] Genres cannot be examined apart from their historical context. Cf. Michael Wedel's genre-theoretical work at the beginning of his monograph on the German music film: "The basic revision of the term genre in film studies since the 1990s can be demonstrated in two tendencies that have recently marked the field well beyond the question of genre. On the one hand we can speak of a 'historical turn' in genre research, which – under the effects of 'cultural 'studies' as well as inspired by the principles of the 'New Film History' – goes back to the careful cultural contextualization of aesthetic phenomena of genres as well as to the historical situatedness and explanation of generic processes of constitution, stabilization, exhaustion, and reformation." Michael Wedel, *Der deutsche Musikfilm: Archäologie eines Genres 1914 – 1945*, Munich 2007, 32.

[14] In this sense, Thomas Schatz takes a predetermined understanding of genre as the basis for his historically influenced observations, according to which genres always follow an evolutionary schema: "A genre's progression from transparency to opacity – from straightforward storytelling to self-conscious formalism – involves its concerted effort to explain itself, to address and evaluate its very status as a popular form." Following this formalistic conception, even newly emerging genres would have to run through an internal evolutionary process, independent of developments in other genres, a process that is nonetheless oriented to a system of historical relations. Thomas Schatz, *Hollywood Genres: Formulas, Filmmaking, and the Studio System*, Philadelphia 1981, 38.

that is claimed for post-classical genre is only one of a large number of relations to the history of poetic making that can be distinguished for each poetic form. Indeed, they are always defined by a relation to the present, which is located in the tension between tradition and innovation. Ultimately, every act of poetic making positions itself in such reflexivity in the history of this making.

Practically every film is tied into the history of the poetics of film and that of the other arts (*téchne*) of poetic making by such reflective relations. In this respect, classical Hollywood cinema cannot be distinguished from the New Hollywood nor from post-classical genre cinema.[15]

A similar misunderstanding lies at the basis of the talk about the end of the war film genre. Today this idea is vehemently put forth in view of films about the war in Iraq[16] – much like the Vietnam film was being discussed as a genre after the end of the classical war film thirty years ago. Of course the representational forms of the war film genre have changed; and certainly these changes are consistent with the new forms of warfare that we observe with each new war – and certainly the media technologies of this observation have also changed, in which the western media even bothers to observe a war in the first place.

The fact that recent films about the Iraq War thematize the changed media spatio-temporal circumstances of the "new wars" is obvious. It would be highly alienating if they did not do so. And it is equally obvious that they interact with the media forms that create the visibility of the war in the first place. But even this is ultimately true for all films. Being media of perception, they realize the changed conditions of the media technology of audiovisual images in each case. This, however, is in no way an indicator of the end of genre films; rather it refers

---

15 Cf. Barry Langford, *Film Genre: Hollywood and Beyond*, Edinburgh 2005. In the first chapter of the book, "Who needs Genre?" Langford problematizes the understanding of genre in film studies from a variety of angles. He writes a short history of genre research in film studies by means of the questions and difficulties that it finds itself confronting: "Problems of Definition," "Problems of Meaning," "Problems of History" are the names of the subsections. In the last there is a critical discussion of the 'evolutionary' model, as Schatz uses it, assuming that genre films in a 'classical' period are more naïve and unreflective than in a 'mature' or 'revisionist' period.
16 Dennis Conrad and Burkhard Röwekamp, "Krieg ohne Krieg: Zur Dramatik der Ereignislosigkeit in Jarhead," in *All Quiet on the Genre Front: Zur Praxis und Theorie des Kriegsfilms*, eds. Heinz B. Heller, et al., Marburg 2007, 194–207; Garrett Stewart, "Digital Fatigue: Imaging War in Recent American Film," in *Film Quarterly* 62 (4), 2009, 45–55. Rasmus Greiner does not speak of the end of the war film genre, but of a radical incompatibility with conventionally defined ideas of genre: "The processes of denationalization and transgressing borders have become so enduringly inscribed in film representations of the new wars that they can hardly be brought in line any more with a classical, organistic understanding of genre." Greiner, *Die neuen Kriege im Film*, 464.

to the historical dynamic of the genre poetic system itself. Where else should we look for this dynamic if not in ever new poetic proposals of audiovisual image spaces, which reflect the changes to our world as changes in our perception of the world? Precisely the fact that the new war films – be they Vietnam War films or Iraq War films – provide us with a way to understand the changed media conditions of the visibility of war as a changed perception of the common world puts them in line with the history of the poetics of the Hollywood war film.

The Hollywood war film has taken the changed forms of warfare, as well as the changed media representations of war, as the object of its presentation at every point in time. If this were the decisive factor in the continuity and break in the genre, then it would have periodically come to its end. The idea is interesting. But this ultimately refers back to a fundamental misunderstanding. Namely the idea that genres are defined by the constancy of the objects they represent. The representation of new forms of warfare, taken by itself, is no reason to infer that we are dealing with a new kind of film. Nor do new forms of warfare as such give any indication of whether we are once again on the front lines of old colonial wars. The relation of individual films to the history of systems of poetic genres cannot be decided at the level of the objects represented or of their contents.

Taxonomies of rule-governed poetics

Certainly, most approaches to genre theory in film studies are marked by just this idea. When genre cinema is discussed theoretically, this generally happens with the expectation that genres can be defined in their representational forms by a formal relation to the issues represented. This is the case whether we take the object of representation as the decisive criterion by which genres can be taxonomically arranged; or whether we conceive the issues represented as the objects of a discursive treatment, defining the social function of the genre in this.[17] Usually the

---

[17] The distinction between the "mythos/ritual" approach to genre theory and the approach of ideological criticism is perhaps interesting: "Yet in general myth is, as Neale observes, ideological criticism minus the criticism: that is, whereas writers such as Judith Hess Wright ([1974] 1995) identify genre's ideological dimension with its provision of imaginary and bogus resolutions to the actual contradictions of lived experience under capitalism, proponents of genre as myth tend to a more neutral descriptive account of how genres satisfy the needs and answer the questions of their audiences. In other words, they do not stigmatize such satisfactions as delusion designed to maintain individuals and communities in acquiescent ignorance of the real conditions of their oppression. Moreover, the dialectical nature of the Lévi-Straussian schema implies that underlying social contradictions are less resolved away than repeatedly re-enacted and thus – at least in

one is connected to the other and genre cinema is developed as a taxonomy that practically functions as a cartography of social or cultural fields of conflict.[18] So theoretical engagement with genre cinema is completely guided by the idea that it is precisely the genre film that can provide insight into the network of social conflict zones, "a privileged insight into 'how to understand the life of films in the social.'"[19]

In fact, such ideas follow the taxonomic schematism of old genre theories from rule-governed poetics, which Altman justifiably thinks that we must take into account in order precisely not to perpetuate their aporias and normative sets.[20] Certainly this warning is mostly ignored, so that the theoretical abbreviation of arguments from rule-governed poetics has carried through into current discussions about genre cinema.

As a rule, the discussion of genre in film studies ignores this condition anyway because genre poetics – ignoring literary traditions – is often understood as a phenomenon of modern popular culture; as if genres were an invention of the age of the entertainment industry.[21] With the effect that not a few of the sufficiently familiar aporias of genre theory are based on the argumentative alignment with a taxonomic logics, the foundation of which remains largely uncritically in the darkness of tradition.[22] The obvious aporias of genre concepts in film theory are often due to this blind spot. This is often the case even for the definitions of genre themselves.

---

principle – exposed by their mythical articulations." (Langford, *Film Genre*, 21. Refers to: Judith Hess Wright, "Genre Films and the Status Quo [1974]," in *Film Genre Reader II*, ed. Barry Keith Grant, Austin 1995, 41–49.)

18 Thomas Schatz, for instance, assumes that specific problems are treated in each specific genre, "key American ideas and dilemmas," as Langford writes (Langford, *Film Genre*, 20; Barry Langford, "Film Genre," in *Film Genre Reader II*, ed. Barry Keith Grant, Austin 1995, 41–49). Schatz's basic thesis runs: "In so far as these problems are discrete, each genre has its own specific set of concerns and performs a particular kind of cultural work; in so far as these issues are generally relevant to American life, the system of Hollywood genres as a whole enables a kind of ongoing national conversation about such issues." (ibid. Langford, *Film Genre*) The classical Hollywood studio system would be particularly suited to sustain this kind of national self-image because it can produce large quantities of genre movies, dominating the "American popular imagination" (ibid.; Langford, *Film Genre*).

19 Christine Gledhill, "Rethinking Genre," in *Reinventing Film Studies*, ed. Christine Gledhill and Linda Williams, London/New York 2000, 221–243, here 221.

20 Altman, *Film/Genre*, 1.

21 In Germany, for instance, a relatively strict separation of the usage of the terms category (*Gattung*) and genre (*Genre*) has become established, with category being reserved for the old poetics and genre being used for modern media culture.

22 Most essays on genre movies understand genre as a concept associated with modern entertainment culture and its basis in industrial production. If anything else is considered at all, it is the traditions from the 19th century, mediated by the concept of the melodramatic mode (Brooks)

Well into the eighteenth century, genre poetics could claim a transcendental order to justify the taxonomy of their systems through a regulated connection between form and contents. The idea of such a regularity necessarily leads to a circular justification when arbitrary convention appears in place of a transcendental order. Bordwell and Thompson write: "Genres are based on a tacit agreement among filmmakers, reviewers, and audiences. What gives the films some common identity are shared *genre conventions*."[23]

If we follow this definition, we would initially define the genre of Hollywood war movies as a body of films arising from so-called *combat movies*. Their identifying features are compiled like a profile that, on the one hand, qualifies a film as belonging to this body – and, on the other, constitutes the genre as a taxonomical schema in the first place. Jeanine Basinger's "anatomy" represents the most exhaustive mapping of classical war movies in this sense.[24] The elements of this mapping are in turn conveyed on the level of the action represented. For instance, the specific social composition of a group, the intentions and goals collectively ascribed to the members of this group, the diverse iconographic signs of warfare it is equipped with, a certain number of narrative episodes that the group goes through over the course of the film.[25] As a result, narrative or dramatic stereotypes are identified that function as a list of common characteristics. Using this list one can distinguish the combat film from all other genres in the Hollywood system on the one hand; and on the other they can function as a taxonomic schema with which random films can be identified as representatives of this genre.

Christine Gledhill summarized this procedure as follows:

> Each genre represented a body of rules and expectations, shared by filmmaker and audience, which governed its particular generic 'world' and by which any new entrant was constructed and operated. The task of the genre critic was to survey the terrain of this world, identify its *dramatis personae*, iconography, locations, and plot possibilities, and establishing the rules of narrative engagement and permutation.[26]

---

or by theories of literary genres like the Romance (Frey, Jameson). The tradition of poetics itself is virtually never brought to bear in this context. Cf. Peter Brooks, *The Melodramatic Imagination: Balzac, Henry James, Melodrama, and the Mode of Excess*, New Haven/London 1976; Northrop Frye, *Anatomy of Criticism: Four Essays*, Princeton 1957; Fredric Jameson, "Magical Narratives: On the Dialectical Use of Genre Criticism," in *The Political Unconscious: Narrative as a Socially Symbolic Act*, London 1981, 103–150.

23 David Bordwell and Kristin Thompson, "Film Genres," in *Film Art: An Introduction*, New York 2010, 328–348, here 330.
24 Jeanine Basinger, *The World War II Combat Film: Anatomy of a Genre*, Middletown 2003.
25 Cf. Jeanine Basinger, *The World War II Combat Film*, 56ff. and 67ff.
26 Gledhill, "Rethinking Genre," 223.

When genre cinema is discussed, the argumentation most likely implicitly or explicitly follows this schema. And yet every attempt to ground the taxonomic order of a genre system in the logic of conventional systems of meaning necessarily leads to the very same circular logic.

A mode of industrial production

On the other hand, genre taxonomy can easily be described as an arbitrary designation system of studio production, of marketing, and of criticism, which seeks to reconcile the expectations of producers, spectators, and critics. Research on genre cinema in film studies can then distinguish between various definitions that could be the object of genre research. On the one hand, these are the approaches that start from the contents represented and analyze genre films as cultural discourses ("mode of representation"). On the other hand, this includes those that refer the genre system to the industrial mechanisms of production and marketing ("mode of production"). And, finally, there are theories that see genre cinema as an aesthetic practice structured by different "modes of experience."[27]

The first register, that of the "mode of representation," is attributed to discourse analyses based on ideology critique, mythology, or cultural criticism; in the second, the "mode of production," the economic mechanisms of entertainment culture are historiographically examined; finally, in the third, the technological possibilities of film are investigated as a mode of aesthetic experience.

Film theory – under the sign of the New Historicism – has above all attempted to ground the taxonomic approach empirically in view of the "mode of production." And in fact, one can reconstruct a conventional designation system at the level of production and marketing. Here the basic operations of studying historical sources can be applied, for instance to reconstruct a taxonomic practice of designation from trade journals, studio files, court papers, censorship documents, and scripts from the film industry. Supplemented by the typical sources of contemporary historical research – newspapers, distribution and press materials – the expectations of the spectators and the audience's knowledge of the genre can be empirically reconstructed. As a result, a precisely located understanding of genre cinema can be reconstructed and related to the films as a contemporary context.[28]

---

[27] See ibid., 222.
[28] Cf. John Belton, "American Cinema and Film History," in *American Cinema and Hollywood*, and John Hill and Pamela Church Gibson, Oxford/New York 2000, 1–11, here 9. Audience expectations which are attributed to reception and constitution of genres are not only attached to film here.

This research does allow us to get a full overview of the highly dynamic development of single genres and the genre system as a whole. But it remains unclear how this dynamic should be modeled theoretically and dealt with analytically. One answer to this question could first and foremost be determined by cultural function. But even the organizational structure of the economic basis of entertainment productions itself does not allow for any statements about the cultural function of the systems of genre poetics. Unless one simply assumes a need for entertainment as a market demand, which industrial genre production then responds to – defined solely by the goal of economic success.[29] Such an approach is obviously unsatisfactory, if only because it cannot say anything about the need for entertainment itself, which is supposed to be given by nature. Definitions of the cultural function of systems of genre poetics based on this are only possible as a speculatively formulated, theoretical outlook.[30] These outlooks then once again refer back to cultural representations, to the discourse of genre cinema.

A mode of representation

At any rate, the discussion about genre cinema based in cultural studies seeks to answer the question of cultural function primarily in terms of discourse analysis. Whether these discourses are examined, depending on the theoretical approach taken, as forms of mythological knowledge, ideological schemata, patterns of cultural identity, formations of normative evaluation, or the treatment of social conflicts – as constitutive objects by which genres can be differentiated, they are

---

Neale therefore also no longer links genre categories to the films themselves. He joins with Alan Williams, which called for genre studies under historical points of view. Neale writes: "He [Williams] says, three things: '(1) starting with a genre's pre-history, its roots in other media; (2) studying all films, regardless of perceived quality; and (3) going beyond film content to study advertising, the star system, studio policy, and so on in relation to the production of films.'" (Steve Neale, "Questions of Genre," in *Film Genre Reader III*, ed. Barry Keith Grant, Austin 2003, 160–184, here 180f. Refers to: Alan Williams, "Is a Radical Genre Criticism Possible?," in *Quarterly Review of Film Studies* 9 (2), 1984, 121–125).

29 In view of this function, genre-poetic subdivisions can in no way be traced back to any classification system that studio production and its marketing organizes. Cf. Altman, *Film/Genre*, 15ff./ 90ff./ 113ff.

30 Neale's examinations of the transformation of the western genre on the basis of distribution and press materials lead him to conclude that genre can only be understood as a continual "process" (Neale, "Questions of Genre," 167–172). But how this process is to be conceived remains a theoretical problem – albeit a clearly formulated one.

always considered only in relation to the contents represented.[31] This is also and especially the case for the genre of the war film.[32]

"War" in the war film is always more than just a narrative storyline. There are always the actual historical experiences connected to it as a cache of media images of personal and collective memories, and at the same time highly phantasmatic elements. Military initiation rites, tragic guilt and the heroic act, the sacrifice of the individual for the life of the community, the confrontation with the awareness of one's own death, the social state of emergency that destroys all forms of civic life or forces them under a terrorist order – the singular narrative of

---

31 Langford's objections are as follows: Genres as such are not as consistently and clearly separated from one another as Schatz claims; there have always been mix forms for which it is not so easy to say which concerns that treat. In many genre films it is also not at all possible to recognize that they struggle with some social problems – and in reverse not all films of a genre that do the same thing struggle with the same problems. Langford therefore accuses Schatz of a too strong tendency toward generalization. Furthermore, as Schatz himself concedes in his 1983 book, his arguments are much more difficult to apply to New Hollywood than to classical Hollywood, since the former is characterized by "diversified entertainment markets and [a] weaker generic landscape" (Langford, *Film Genre*, 20).

32 There is a broad range of literature to cite here for the war film. Cf. for example: Michael Anderegg (ed.), *Inventing Vietnam: The War in Film and Television*, Philadelphia 1991; Linda Dittmar and Gene Michaud, *From Hanoi to Hollywood: The Vietnam War in American film*, New Brunswick 1997; Jeremy M. Devine, *Vietnam at 24 Frames a Second: A Critical and Thematic Analysis of over 400 Films about the Vietnam War*, Austin 1999; Winfried Fluck, "The 'Imperfect Past': Vietnam According to the Movies," in *The Merits of Memory: Concepts, Contexts, Debates*, eds. Hans-Jürgen Grabbe and Sabine Schindler, Heidelberg 2008, 353–385; John Hellmann, "Vietnam and the Hollywood Genre Film: Inversions of American Mythology in the Deer Hunter and Apocalypse Now," in: *American Quarterly* 34 (4), 1982, 418–439; Gebhard Hölzl and Matthias Peipp, *Fahr zur Hölle, Charlie! Der Vietnamkrieg im amerikanischen Film*, Munich 1991; Stefan Reinecke, *Hollywood goes Vietnam: Der Vietnamkrieg im US-amerikanischen Film*, Marburg 1993; Julian Smith, *Looking Away: Hollywood and Vietnam*, New York 1975; Jason Katzman, "From Outcast to Cliché: How Film Shaped, Warped and Developed the Image of the Vietnam Veteran," 1967–1990, in *Journal of American Culture* 16, 1993, 7–24; Mark Walker, *Vietnam Veteran Films*, Lanham 1991; Brian J. Woodman, "Represented in the Margins. Images of African American Soldiers in Vietnam War Combat Films," in *The War Film*, ed. Robert Eberwein, Brunswick N.J. 2005, 90–114; Michael Paris (ed.), *The First World War and Popular Cinema: 1914 to the Present*, Edinburgh 1999; John Whiteclay Chambers II, "'All Quiet on the Western Front' (1930): The Anti-War Film and the Image of the First World War," in *Historical Journal of Film, Radio and Television* 14 (4), 1994, 377–411; Bruce Chadwick, *Reel Civil War: Mythmaking in American Film*, London 2002; Seeßlen, "Von Stahlgewittern zur Dschungelkampfmaschine: Veränderungen des Krieges und des Kriegsfilms"; Auster: "'Saving Private Ryan' and American Triumphalism"; Basinger, *The World War II Combat Film*; Greiner, *Die neuen Kriege im Film*.

this storyline stakes out the whole course of a mythological complex. We might call this the "cultural fantasy" of war.[33]

Now as a rule this narrative is reconstructed as discourses which in film are represented by a completely different medium. If we take a cursory glance through the large number of cultural-historical essays about war films, we cannot shake the impression that we are reading interpretations of literary works. The mythological, phantasmatic, or ideological complexes of meaning might be clearly recognizable at the level of cinematic representation; ultimately they maintain a completely indifferent stance toward the mode of media representation.[34]

This blind spot in the research is all the more astounding since it is not uncommon–even in the same studies – to find photography, films, the audiovisual image emphatically being claimed as independent source materials for cultural-historical research. In fact, audiovisual media do extend cultural-historical discourses with new material, but at the same time they leave them completely untouched. As a kind of media arrangement they seem to be easily removable from the real object of analysis – the 'mythical oration,' the 'ideological schema,' the 'cultural discourse,' the 'social negotiation' – as easy as it would be to remove a plastic wrapper from a book containing everything written on the discourse

---

[33] This also includes the relationship of war and war rhetoric to a racist discourse of nation and history as described by Michel Foucault (Cf. Foucault, *Society must be defended*) or the ritual figuration of war as a form of social state of exception in Roger Caillois (Cf. *Man and the Sacred*).

[34] Cf. on this point, for example: Brenda M. Boyle, *Masculinity in Vietnam War Narratives: A Critical Study of Fiction, Films, and Nonfiction Writings*, Jefferson, NC 2009; Mark Heberle (ed.), *Thirty Years After: New Essays on Vietnam War Literature, Film, and Art*, Newcastle upon Tyne 2009; John Carlos Rowe and Rick Berg (ed.), *The Vietnam War and American Culture*, New York 1991; Daniel Hallin, *The Uncensored War: The Media and Vietnam*, New York 1986; Bernie Cook, "Over My Dead Body: The Ideological Use of Dead Bodies in Network News Coverage of Vietnam," in *Quarterly Review of Film and Video* 18 (2), 2001, 203–216; Richard Godfrey and Simon Lilley, "Visual Consumption, Collective Memory and the Representation of War," in *Consumption Markets & Culture* 12 (4), 2009, 275–300; Guy Westwell, "Accidental Napalm Attack and Hegemonic Visions of America's War in Vietnam," in *Critical Studies in Media Communication* 28 (5), 2011, 407–423; Rick Worland, "The Other Living-Room War: Prime Time Combat Series, 1962–1975," in *Journal of Film and Video* 50 (3), 1998, 3–23; Thomas Schatz, "World War II and the Hollywood 'War Film,' " in *Refiguring American Film Genres: History and Theory*, ed. Nick Browne, Los Angeles/London 1998, 89–128; Philippa Gates, "'Fighting the Good Fight': The Real and the Moral in the Contemporary Hollywood Combat Film," in *Quarterly Review of Film and Video* 22 (4), 2005, 297–310; Leo Braudy, "Flags of Our Fathers/Letters from Iwo Jima," in *Film Quarterly* 60 (4), 2007, 16–23; Clayton R. Koppes and Gregory D. Black, *Hollywood Goes to War: Patriotism, Movies and the Second World War from Ninotchka to Mrs. Miniver*, London/New York 1988; Martin Barker, "*A Toxic Genre*": *The Iraq War Films*, London 2011.

of war films. The medial mode of film, which we have sought to grasp earlier as a shared perception of the world, following the work of Cavell, is usually not reflected at all in discourse-analytical studies.

In an attempt to define the war film genre taxonomically, Basinger brings a third factor into play. She establishes that war films, first, convey particular attitudes toward the acts of war; second, that they resort to historical information that the spectators possess.[35] And third, she adds: "The tools of the cinema are employed to manipulate viewers into various emotional, cultural, and intellectual attitudes, and to help achieve all the other goals."[36]

Here she attributes an independent dimension of effect to the level of cinematic representation. Certainly, to equate it with the "tools of manipulation" is highly insufficient. Indeed, it is a matter of the forms of media experience of film itself. This mode can neither be described as a relation between manipulating agents and manipulated spectators, nor can the media technological conditions of film be understood as a toolbox for aesthetic effects. Both would assume an objective reality of the historical events, which could then be represented as such.

And yet, these reflections do raise a question that might lead us out of the aporias of genre theory: In what way are historical experiences and cultural phantasms in the cinematic mode of experience connected to a perception of the world on the part of the spectators? Ultimately this question is asking to define the function of genre cinema, which can no longer be located at the level of the social or cultural discourses represented in the films. Rather, it concerns the films as media of a shared perception of the world. This allows us to see the media technological basis as a condition for a specific mode of aesthetic experience.

A mode of aesthetic experience

As problematic as Basinger's terminology might seem from a theoretical standpoint, the choice of words is quite instructive: "the various emotional, cultural, and intellectual attitudes"; these words imply – much like the talk of manipulation – an affective dimension, which provides some perspective on the events represented as an evaluative entity, without being accessible on the level of the "knowledge" represented; they imply just that desire for "acknowledgment" that we know from Cavell as the decisive factor for success in any communicative interaction.

---

35 Basinger, *The World War II Combat Film*, 57.
36 Ibid.

Having said this, we can sharpen the question as to how the phantasms of war (the myths, ideologemes, propagandistic narratives), along with the historical events, can be connected in the mode of film experience to a spectator experience. Indeed, this can be formulated – this was one of the concerns of the first part of the book – as a question for the boundaries of a sense of commonality. How do films manage to relate an audience of singular spectators to the feeling of belonging to a common world? How do the boundaries of this commonly shared world come into view? In what form are these boundaries extendable by new types of subjectification? And – concretely related to war propaganda – how can such an abstract principle as that of connectedness to a political community be so deeply anchored in spectators' affectivity that they defer the basic impulse to self-preservation?

From this perspective – and this is precisely what becomes clear in the films shot during and shortly after the Second World War – the function of the war film genre is not to be conceived as manipulating any moral attitude toward war. Rather, the films literally try to found the feeling for the communal, the sense of commonality, anew. They aim to acknowledge a relation between the individual and the society, which runs completely against the interests of the individual. While this may also be articulated as a propagandistic directive in narratives and arguments – we might think of the voice-over in Capra's PRELUDE TO WAR for instance – the acknowledgment of the relationship is determined by the question of a shared feeling for the common world; it is determined by the film's mode of aesthetic experience.[37]

The war film can then only become a medium of mobilization if it happens in the living bodies of subjects as an affective reality of a kind of militaristic common sense; if it allows this sense of commonality to be grasped by the senses as a perception of the world, at the same time bringing to bear a concrete feeling for this world. This entanglement of the subjective reality of the sense of self with a common sensing of the world designates the seam at which war and genre cinema come together.

On the one hand, this means that film is defined as a media technology that provides the opportunities to link the cultural, political, and mythological narratives, as the conditions of a common world, with the corporeally-bound reality of sensation in concrete individuals.[38] On the other hand, the representations of the

---

[37] As we stated above: as a mode of the subject's split perception, which in one and same moment produces the visibility and the audibility that the subject as spectator confronts as an utterly meaningful world, to which he or she precisely does not belong.

[38] The film differs from other modes of poetic thinking in that both of these elements constantly merge in its conceptions of the world. Cf. the definition above developed in relation to Cavell.

war film itself are brought in as the conditions of constructing a common world, a feeling for the communal. The world of the films represents neither the myths of cultural fantasy nor an actual historical event; it views these as the concrete conditions of a community to relate to itself as a political community in a given historical constellation.

The knowledge of these conditions can be represented in taxonomical orders. Indeed, this knowledge of orders itself is only a further aspect, an extension of the material basis of poetic making.[39] Even if every historically-situated poetic making is necessarily embedded in economic, social, and cultural conditions, these conditions are still in no way identical to the poetic logic of this making.

2.3 Modes and Modalities (Gledhill)

Christine Gledhill took the mode of aesthetic experience in film as the starting point for her fundamental revision of genre theory in the cinema. She was guided in this by a concept that sees melodrama as a paradigmatic mode of representation (the "mode of excess," as Brooks conceived it for literature) of modern entertainment. From this perspective, genre cinema appears to be a system within the culture of entertainment, which is structured by the dynamic mutual relations of a variety of aesthetic modalities ("the concept of modality as the sustaining medium in which the genre system operates"[40]):

> The notion of modality, like register in socio-linguistics, defines a specific mode of aesthetic articulation adaptable across a range of genres, across decades, and across national cultures. It provides the genre system with a mechanism of 'double articulation', capable of generating specific and distinctively different generic formulae in particular historical conjunctures, while also providing a medium of interchange and overlap between genres.[41]

This dynamic principle can be described in an exemplary way in reference to the melodrama. Looking back from today to the now forty-year discussion about film melodrama,[42] we can see that, in this case, basic theoretical objections to

---

39 This would correspond in its main features to Foucault's use of the term technology.
40 Gledhill, "Rethinking Genre," 223.
41 Ibid., 229.
42 Cf. Hermann Kappelhoff, "Melodrama and War in Hollywood Genre Cinema," in *After the Tears: New Perspectives on the Politics of Victimhood*, eds. Scott Loren and Jörg Metelmann, Amsterdam 2016 .

a conventional understanding have become accepted. Hardly anyone would attempt to define melodrama as a specific genre through its storyline; even less would we be able to come to any agreement as to which groups of films could be ascribed to such storylines taxonomically. As Christine Gledhill puts it: "Melodrama is not nor ever was a singular genre."[43] Rather, it designates a "culturally conditioned mode of perception and aesthetic circulation," which has historically unfolded as a "genre-producing machine."[44] From this perspective, the melodramatic appears as a basic mode of entertainment cinema, and of western entertainment culture in general, which can structure a wide variety of genre systems and genres. It describes – following Gledhill and others – the mode of aesthetic experience of modern entertainment per se.[45]

Initially this means the way in which a fictional world becomes a medium to perceive a world for a concrete reader/spectator. Gledhill summarizes the essential criteria, which Peter Brooks had already defined for the "mode of excess." On the one hand, there is the strictly polarized world in which everything that appears becomes the expression of a battle between opposing moral forces (Manichaeism); on the other hand is the visceral and affective addressing of the spectator by just this expressive excess.[46] The hyperbolic expressivity of the melodramatic performance is aimed at affecting the spectators in order to press them into a morally assessing stance.

In the culture of modern entertainment – at least in the period from the second half of the nineteenth century to the first half of the twentieth – the melodramatic mode was certainly one of the basic modes of aesthetic experience. But I would not go so far as to equate melodrama with entertainment. Rather, the melodramatic – as I have already pointed out – should be distinguished as a specific pathos of individualized suffering both historically from older forms of pathos (such as the Christian Passion or the historical succession of the interpretations of tragedy) as well as from other modalities of genre poetics in entertainment (such as the modalities of comedy, of horror, of action, of the thriller).[47]

Although I do not follow the thesis that modern entertainment is to be defined by the melodramatic mode without reservations, I do find a fundamentally new

---

[43] Gledhill, "Rethinking Genre," 227.
[44] Ibid.
[45] For instance in the sense of the 'mode' of Neale or Singer. Neale, *Genre and Hollywood*; Ben Singer, *Melodrama and Modernity*, New York 2001.
[46] Cf. Gledhill, "Rethinking Genre," 228f.
[47] In view of this (incomplete) list of the aesthetic modalities of genre cinema, I myself have attempted to reconstruct the melodramatic as sentimental enjoyment. Cf. Kappelhoff, *Matrix der Gefühle*.

understanding of modern genre poetics sketched out in Gledhill's argument. The generic principle that she calls "a genre-producing machine" is diametrically opposed to the taxonomical logic of conventional genre theory. Indeed, it looks to a historical dynamic of genre-poetic making, which is necessarily beyond the scope of taxonomical order. We only need to see it as the dynamic principle of genre poetics per se, in which the melodramatic is still added as a paradigmatic modality.

Beyond the taxonomies of rule-governed poetics

This allows us to localize the modality of experience in modern genre poetics in the term 'melodrama' in a way that becomes instantly comprehensible in its political functionality:

> As a genre-producing machine, melodrama is forged from the convergence of two broad-based cultural traditions: one, excluded from official culture, which contained a mix of folk and new urban *entertainment* forms, and another, more formally coherent, deriving from an increasingly influential middle-class fiction and *theatre of sentimental* drama and comedy.[48]

In fact, the break in cultural history between the traditions of court culture, steeped in rule-governed poetics, and the culture of modern entertainment, is manifest in melodrama. The generic principle of the melodramatic mode designates precisely the historical fracture in its difference to the taxonomic principle of the orders of rule-governed poetics.[49]

In the schema of rule-governed poetics the taxonomy of genres was founded on a divinely ordained order of nature. Only the transcendental motivation made it possible to set down rules about which object is to be represented through which forms. Certainly the rules directly followed from a political aim. The taxonomic schema – as can be claimed in light of French classicism[50] – served the perpetual repetition of the political power structure of state order on all levels of representation. In the system of rules of poetics, it was established who was

---

48 Gledhill, "Rethinking Genre," 227, [my italics, H.K.].
49 I would continue to maintain that melodrama, for the purposes of this book, should be taken as paradigmatic because it signifies the appearance of a new pathos form of the sacrifice. For this reason, however, we should also distinguish it as mode of aesthetic experience from other modalities of experience. Cf. Kappelhoff, *Matrix der Gefühle*.
50 Michael Lück presented this quite convincingly in the lecture series "Genre und Gemeinsinn" at the Institute for Theater Studies at the Freie Universität Berlin on May 7, 2013.

allowed to speak in the strictly hierarchized world of the state, from which place, and in which way, which statements were representative at all and which were excluded from the realm of representation as a matter of principle.

Against this backdrop, the melodramatic mode becomes historically legible as a break in the rules, in which the logic of modern genre poetics is grounded – namely as a different configuration of the poetic and the political. The poetological break in the rules is immediately politically legible:

> As a genre machine, however, melodrama brought into play a major cultural boundary of modern society, between a mass culture of content and affect-defined genres and the formally defined artistic kinds of high cultural classification. [...] melodrama had been used to unite audiences.[51]

With the new configuration of the relation between poetics and politics, the plurality of individualized perspectives and ways of sensing turn up as heterogeneous modes of speech and expression. These are all principally located on one and the same level of representation, which no longer represents any hierarchization of a previous order. In principle, this means that it has become possible to think and represent worlds that are structured by speech from many, equal voices. Gledhill has explained these ideas in an illuminating comparison of Bakhtin's concept of polyphony in the modern novel and the logic of the melodramatic mode.

> Mikhail Bakhtin suggests that the novel's distinction lies in its capacity to reproduce all other modes of speech and writing. It is a genre of active heteroglossia, capable of drawing into itself all languages and cultural forms, high and low, literary and vernacular, past and present.[52]

Such a poetics is to be understood to be principally unlimited in its possible combinations, mixtures, and crossings, and not through any taxonomical schema.

If modern genre theories nonetheless seek to illustrate the generic dynamic of poetic making in a taxonomic schema, they reproduce they old principles of rule-governed poetics. With the difference only that nature, as the guarantor of a transcendentally grounded order, is replaced with mere convention. The taxonomic

---

51 Gledhill, "Rethinking Genre," 230.
52 Ibid., 234. Still, unlike Gledhill, I would locate melodrama and the modern novel on the same plane. When she writes "melodrama might be thought as doing the same in reverse direction, drawing social, popular, and high-art cultures and discourses into its orbit," her argument once again winds up in the aporias of genre taxonomies. The opposition of high and popular culture conceals the circumstance that melodrama and the modern novel (in Bakhtin's sense) are due to the same epistemological break in poetological thinking.

order no longer fulfills the purpose of representing an absolute power structure. But it does subject the dynamic heterogeneity of the practice of genre poetics to a homogenizing model patterned after the economic calculations of the entertainment industry. It is obvious that taxonomic logics would accommodate these calculations. Indeed, in this way the economic principles of socialization are found in the category distinctions of poetic making. Except that the economic calculations say as little about the logic of modern genre poetics as does the common sense of an audience that is more or less steeped in tradition.[53] The difference between modern poetological thinking and the representational system of rule-governed poetics is thus made unrecognizable.

No matter how poetic making is inserted into the economic, social, and cultural conditions of a political community, these conditions in no way define the logic of its historical dynamic. Instead modern genre poetics should be related to the configuration of the understanding of politics and poetics that it is based on. Then it would be possible to see that power as a law of nature has been replaced by the historical contingency of political action. This experience of contingency is even bound to the awareness that every commonly shared world assumes the poetic practice of its fabrication and construction. The dynamic of the taxonomic ramifications of modern genre poetics should be understood from this historical state of awareness.[54]

From this perspective, genres can be grasped as a dynamic interplay between a wide variety of modalities of aesthetic experience. They can no longer be related to a fixed schema of categories. Rather, they should be reconstructed as a poetic practice that is carried out in the dynamic mutual relations between generic modalities, and the designation of its political function must always first be conceived in terms of media history, as a historically situated mode of aesthetic

---

[53] One might bring to bear this common sense as a general genre knowledge on the part of the audience. Then one would capture exactly that part of the history of poetic making on which the economic calculations of the entertainment industry are based (Sobchack, Tudor, Carroll). Indeed, we can assume that the entertainment industry always proceeds opportunistically in relation to the audience, and has combined elements from different genres at all times. Cf. Sobchack, "Genre Film: A Classical Experience"; Andrew Tudor, "Genre [1973]," in *Film Genre Reader IV*, ed. Barry Keith Grant, Austin 2012, 3–11; Noël Carroll, "Film, Emotion, and Genre," in *Passionate Views: Film, Cognition, and Emotion*, eds. Carl Plantinga and Greg M. Smith, Baltimore 1999, 21–47; Richard Maltby, *Hollywood Cinema*, Oxford 2003.
[54] The research never tires of thematizing this dynamic. In fact, however, there are only a few consistent attempts to link the taxonomic logic with the historical dynamic. Along with Christine Gledhill and her term mode, we could also name Rick Altman's semantic-syntactic essay, which we have already mentioned.

experience. That is, genres are always only to be observed historically as a specific figuration, transformation, ramification, and fusion of a variety of modes of poetic making.[55]

Genre and affect dramaturgy

In this question as well, Gledhill's understanding of the melodramatic mode can provide us with an approach: "Thus action and sentiment, pathos and spectacle, presumed today to appeal to differently gendered audiences, are drawn into a composite aesthetic and dramatic modality, capable of different emphases and generic offshoots."[56] Between the poles of action and sentimentality, and gauged according to degrees of the intensity of dramatic or lyric expressivity,[57] a spectrum of unlimited combinatorics emerges. Instead of singular genres, generic modes within a system of genre poetics can be distinguished as specific expressivities and affect-generating modalities (the sentimental sadness of the melodrama, the laughing of the comedy, the scariness of the horror genre, the suspense of the thriller).[58]

From my point of view, modern genre poetics itself is described here as a combinatorics of affect modalities. This provides the possibility for a wide variety of affect-dramaturgical schemata, which in turn can be related to a wide variety of media technologies and techniques of poetic presentation.

But this also calls up the most prominent of all definitions of the function of genre poetics. In his famous statement on tragedy in his poetics, Aristotle defined it in terms of affect dramaturgy as "catharsis." The modalities of representation would thus have to be arranged and carried out in such a way that the cathartic effect was produced as the sensation of the spectators: the purification of their

---

55 Cf. Wedel, *Der deutsche Musikfilm*.
56 Gledhill, "Rethinking Genre," 230.
57 Ibid., 234.
58 The concept of body genres as formulated by Linda Williams remains exemplary in this regard. Cf. Linda Williams, "Film Bodies: Gender, Genre, and Excess," in *Film Genre Reader III*, ed. Barry Keith Grant, Austin 2003, 141–159. Also Altman's concept of the ritualistic function of genres, which starts from the assumption that genre films give the audience a space to experience their fears, wishes, and desires, offers a suitable starting point. Altman takes various viewpoints into account in relation to the function of genre and consolidates them. On the one hand, he describes the *ritualistic function* of genre (living out fears, wishes, and desires), on the other the *ideological function* (confirming ideologies, manifesting power structures). Cf. Altman, *Film/Genre*, 26ff.

feelings or the purification of their feeling.[59] Aristotle understands this effect as the specific pleasure of the spectators, their enjoyment. In the manner of this enjoyment, tragedy should be distinguished from other modes of mimesis, from other genres of poetic making.

Up to present day discussions of genre poetics, the model of catharsis has shaped innumerable attempts to determine the relationship between poetics and politics. Even Gledhill's reflections can be categorized among these attempts. Genre films would then be understood as interventions in the dynamic of affective connections, in the affect economy of a polity.

From this perspective the different modes of experience, affect modalities, and speaking perspectives of modern genre poetics can be related to the affective basis of political communities. They can be – still quite in keeping with the Aristotelian idea of tragedy – subdivided into a variety of modes of enjoyments, according to the manner of pleasure.[60] The modes of genre cinema would then designate these differing forms of aesthetic enjoyment. Genre cinema would then be understood at this level as a system of differing expressive modalities, which address the spectator's affectivity in order to position it in a commonly shared world of sensation – and in these modulations, the individual sensation of the spectator could always be understood in its interwovenness with a collective world of feeling.

Seen in this way, genre films provide us with the experience by which we are affectively interwoven with the world in highly variable ways – and with those who share this world with us. Sentimental enjoyment, horror, thrill are such affective relations to the world, each developing a different figuration of the relation between "I," "we," and the "others."

Even if these modes can be arranged as ideal types into certain genres, this circumstance should not keep us from thinking that it is always an issue of heterogeneous combinations of modes of aesthetic experience. The modalities of horror obviously belong to the crime film or the melodrama, as do those of the sentimental to the western or the gangster movie, those of the comic to the action film and the action mode to each of these genres. Even the so-called classic genre cinema should be understood as a dynamic process of permanently reconfiguring these modalities, and in no way as a rule-governed poetic system.

---

[59] Cf. Martin Vöhler, "Reinigung in der griechischen Kultur," in *Un/Reinheit: Konzepte und Praktiken im Kulturvergleich*, eds. Angelika Malinar and Martin Vöhler, Paderborn 2008, 169–185.
[60] Cf. Aristotle, *Poetics*, ed. Anthony Kenny, Oxford 2013, 22–26.

We should also view the aesthetic mode of genre cinema itself in a double aspect: on the one hand as a modality of heterogeneous modes of expression and speaking perspectives; on the other as different modes of aesthetic enjoyment. The former refers to the film images itself as a material of expression, the latter to the affect-economic function of poetic making.

Such a definition should not be confused with psychologically grounded reception aesthetics, such as those developed in cognitive film theory. Taxonomies that emphasize aesthetic effects merely replace the arbitrary convention with a naturalistic order. Only that this naturalism is now grounded in cognitive or evolutionary psychology and no longer in metaphysics.[61] The dynamic of historically diverging modes of poetic making avoids the one approach as much as it does the other. Instead of describing systems of genre poetics as taxonomies, which construct regular relations between objects, the modes of representation, and the intended effects, these systems should be viewed as the interplay of a variety of modes and modalities of embodied being-in-the-world.

From Cavell's perspective they can be understood as the interplay of a variety of media with which this being-in-the-world is reflexively made accessible to us as a commonly shared form of perceiving, feeling, and thinking.

The historical dynamic of poetic making

In our cursory reconstruction of the term genre in film theory it should now have become clear that neither the level of production nor that of the objects represented are a suitable basis for modes of aesthetic experience (modes of aesthetic enjoyment). Indeed, these modes cannot be traced back to either one. Nonetheless, they do name theoretical fields of reference that thematize fundamental aspects of the practice of the poetics of genre. We must thus distinguish between two registers to which we might refer the theoretical definition of genre. These are the "mode of production" and the "mode of representation" on the one hand; on the other hand, they are the "modes of experience" which can be divided into modes of aesthetic experience, speaking perspectives, and heterogeneous modalities of expression. But these distinctions cannot be read taxonomically.

---

61 Cf. alongside Plantinga (Plantinga, *Moving Viewers*) also Ed S. Tan, *Emotion and the Structure of Narrative Film: Film as an Emotion Machine*, Mahwah, NJ 1996; Murray Smith, *Engaging Characters: Fiction, Emotion, and the Cinema*, Oxford 1995; Torben K. Grodal, *Embodied Visions: Evolution, Emotion, Culture, and Film*, Oxford 2009; Torben K. Grodal, *Moving Pictures: A New Theory of Film Genres, Feelings and Cognition*, Oxford 1997.

Each of the distinctions named does more to illuminate certain aspects, certain conditions of poetic making, without any of them subsuming the other. Each of them designates a genuine field of inquiry, and only their relations to one another allow us to reconstruct the history of poetic making.

I will summarize: systems of genre poetics, if we wish to speak, for instance, of Hollywood cinema as one such system, are historically-situated, dynamically behaving ensembles of generic speaking perspectives, modalities of expression, and modes of aesthetic experience. These ensembles are to be positioned on the same level as the media technological conditions and possibilities of film as well as the production conditions of the film industry.

Something similar can be said about the mythological, ideological, cultural critical, or socio-psychological narratives that are represented in genre films. Their representation in no way defines the cultural function of film, although the historical conditions do become concrete it them. This allows certain conflicts in a community to become perceptible as constitutive conflicts of a political community – while others remain invisible.

Genres are media of the communal fabrication of a common world. They form that heterogeneous ensemble of affect perspectives, attitudes and stances, which Capra calls on in PRELUDE TO WAR as the expressive modalities and speaking perspectives of the cinema of his time. For him, the cinema in fact provides the possibility of generating affects in which cinematic images and human bodies are joined into new collectivities. When he embeds this distinct possibility in the experiential space of contemporary genre cinema, which provides a multitude of such possibilities, then this is exactly what designates the political positioning of his poetics.

We might recognize the specific configuration of the relation between poetic making and politics in the Hollywood cinema of the years between the two world wars. This configuration itself is structured by the intractable contradiction between the new media forms of propagandistic mobilizing efforts and the multi-voiced world of the old genre cinema.

From this perspective, however, even the term 'genre system' itself becomes dubious – or at least highly unclear. Indeed, the term suggests the idea that genre – like language or myth – can be addressed as a fixed symbolic order in the sense of structuralism. The dynamic of ramification in genre cinema, however, can only be understood from the logic and the history of poetic making – as a permanent process of relating poetic making to its own history. This making cannot be traced back to any law, any convention, any representational order, according to which genres could be built or distinguished. It can only be reconstructed historically along the criteria named as media of producing a perception of a common world.

When Cavell attempts to grasp the cycle of a genre by using the term 'family resemblance,' then he is singling out the junctions of an expanding network of references that is ultimately unlimited. In a certain sense, current poetic making crisscrosses the entire field of historically specific configurations of genre as media of perceiving the world in its multiple reflexivity. The reconstruction of such a network of reflexivities is not equal to the spectator's reception. Nor is it possible to ascribe its construction as the whole to an author. The history of the media, arts, and genres of poetic making is contained in every poetic proposal, just as the history of information technology is contained in the computer program that I use to design my kitchen.

Instead of continuing to construct conventional arrangements of genre, this historically existing genre systems should be analyzed as different perspectives on the history of poetic making, which represent the common ground of current poetic making. They themselves, in their poetic rules and concepts – and this is the basic assumption here – stand in a constitutive relationship to the given political order. They establish the boundaries of a common world as much as they interrogate them. A poetological understanding of genre must refer this system, as media of producing the perception of a common world, to the contingent historical configuration of poetics and politics. This is exactly what I mean when I speak of the poetology of the war film genre.

At any rate, when speaking of war films in the following, I am referring to media for perceiving the world, through which a political community ensures itself a shared experiential horizon of values, relations to the world, belongings, and exclusions.[62] Genre films do this in poetic proposals of every new spaces of aesthetic experience, in which they refer to themselves as a political community. It should have become clear that, in this self-relation, something else is meant than the representation of social conflicts or historical events or their negotiation. The relevance of genre for the experience of social facts and their relation to social reality is decided at the level of the historical transformations of the genre system to be described, of the emerging and transforming poetics of affect in genre cinema in which concrete configurations of modes of aesthetic experience are fixed as positionings of aesthetic enjoyment.

---

62 Even if the individual genre of the war film is the focus of this book, my research is less directed at defining individual genres than in positioning them within a system of artistic entertainment, as well as at the question of their function within the network of art, entertainment, and information media. A genre system is always an ensemble of expressive forms and ways of functioning that behaves dynamically, which join together as historical variable modes of representation, and which behave in a complementary way toward one another. It is thus part of a sphere of social communication in which heterogeneous events within social reality are made accessible and become transformed as aesthetic experience of living together.

The reconstruction of historical genres – or genre systems – always implies a (deconstructive) perspective on the history of thinking genre theory, as Altman has called for. It equally concerns the contingent configurations of the relation between the poetics of genre and politics and the interplay of different formats of media representation (genres), modes of aesthetic experience, and affective modalities.

The Hollywood war film as a paradigmatic object

Tracing the emergence of a new genre, like the Hollywood war film, is just such a perspectival construction; it can be used like a burning glass to focus the relations that define the dynamic of these ramifications. We can easily correlate this dynamic with other phenomena in which comparable developments occur. The gangster film becomes film noir, the women's film becomes the family melodrama, and the western becomes the psychological drama. The external indicators of a change are indicated in this, which – and this is very much the common sense of the research on genre cinema – concerns much more than the transformation of a more or less definable genre system. The emergence of the war film genre is directly tied to the triumph of that mode of affective mobilization of collective power of agency that we sought to trace by comparing Capra's PRELUDE TO WAR and Riefenstahl's TAG DER FREIHEIT.

This qualifies the Hollywood war film genre as a paradigmatic object. Thinking about genre poetics for western culture in the twentieth century can be concentrated into a paradigmatic configuration of the poetics of genre and politics, much as was possible for melodrama in the eighteenth century. What with melodrama was the interiority of the subject and the history of its poetic making is now the examination of collective affectivity, in which this interiority is already inserted – an examination that is doubtlessly linked to the largest excesses of destruction in human history.

2.4 What is a Poetics of Affect?

More than any other Hollywood genre, the war film is linked with the idea that film or cinema might manipulate its spectators and be in the service of greater goals and ideological interests. Nonetheless, when it comes to thematizing the media presentation of war, one predominantly comes across studies using discourse analysis. If feelings are spoken of after all, this is usually related to the scenes represented or the iconographic motif, without taking the mediality of the film image into account. But how can such abstract things as political, national, or military interests be entwined with the affective processes of individual spectators? In the film analyses so far, we have spoken time and again of affect poetics, affect dramaturgy, and affect economy in view of these questions. But what exactly does all of that mean?

In a certain way it is quite simple to answer this question, indeed it even seems almost redundant after the excursus on genre theory. One can merely point out one way that affect appears, one that stands at the beginning of all reflection on genre poetics in the western tradition – namely laughing and crying.

Both forms of expressive behavior seem to have fundamental cultural practices tied to them, which have formed two paradigmatic objects of the formation of poetic theory in tragedy and comedy.

Today we can no longer uncritically follow along when one – like Helmuth Plessner – maintains that we can take laughing and crying to be a decisive criterion for differentiating the human species;[63] indeed, laughing as well as crying are now considered a reliable indicator of affective belonging and bonding with a social community. Laughing and crying may thus not be recognizable outside the horizon of our own species simply because we do not belong, just as we most likely still have big problems identifying practices that thoroughly fulfill comparable affect-economic functions in other cultures besides those marked by the western tradition, such as the poetics of the comic and the tragic. At any rate, however, laughing is intuitively available to us as an expression of belonging and sociality; even where it occurs at the cost of others, it is both the expression of and the motivation for processes of socialization. Crying – at least tendentially – can be considered an appeal by the individual, who experiences him or herself excluded, separated, and debased by such communities. Whatever the case may be, not only do we have the foundational text of poetic thinking in Aristotle's theory of tragedy; poetic theory, at its core, is at the same time proposed as a poetics of affect. Indeed, Aristotelian catharsis designates the most prominent model of media affect modulation. It can be distinguished from other artistic operations of emotionalization in the fact that it implies a specific dynamic of developing affect.[64] According to tragic literature, the goal of reaching a successive increase

---

63 Helmuth Plessner, *Lachen und Weinen: Eine Untersuchung nach den Grenzen des menschlichen Verhaltens*, Munich 1950.
64 Cf. Martin Vöhler, "katharsis/Katharsis," in *Aristoteles-Lexikon*, ed. Otfried Höffe, Stuttgart 2005, 304–306; as well as Dirck Linck and Martin Vöhler, "Zur Einführung" in *Grenzen der Katharsis in den modernen Künsten: Transformationen des aristotelischen Modells seit Bernays, Nietzsche und Freud*, eds. Dirck Linck and Martin Vöhler Berlin/Boston 2009, IX–VIV.

in the arousal of "tragic feelings" ("fear and pity") through the dramaturgical arrangement of its sequence of scenes must be precisely defined in the rhetorical calculation of the kind, the dose, and the gradation of affects. Affects are aroused in order to be deliberately dismantled (discharged, purified).[65]

This is the aim of the term *affect poetics*, which, alongside the performing arts, can be related to all forms of audiovisual moving images. It encompasses on the one hand dramaturgy, the design and arrangement of the complex of scenes, which follow the calculation in order to shape a particular course of feeling in the spectators' process of perceiving what is represented; on the other hand, it includes the rhetorical strategies to provoke and to model specific emotional reactions by introducing techniques of calculated affecting. The term *affect dramaturgy* is aimed at the circumstance that individual scenes can be assigned to specific qualities of affect with particular expressive patterns of pathos and staging strategies, and that these qualities, in and of themselves and in their succession, follow a calculation to affect the spectator. While *affect rhetoric* means a calculation of representation, which is capable of introducing expressive modalities of the film image compliant with the standards of a particular intention to affect. Finally, the *affect-economic function* of media practices is included in this, that is what is defined in Aristotle's famous essay on tragedy as catharsis: "Tragedy is a representation *(mímesis)* of an action *(práxis)* of a superior kind – grand, and complete in itself – presented in embellished language *(lógos)*, in distinct forms in different parts, performed by actors rather than told by a narrator, effecting, through pity *(éleos)* and fear *(phóbos)*, the purification *(kátharsis)* of such emotions."[66]

Purification here does not mean the psychic condition of the individual spectator, but the affect economy of the political community, the polity.[67] It is thus not possible to offhandedly bring in modern psychology's understanding of emotion and feeling for affect poetics. The "purification of such emotions" cannot be broken down into a schema of impulse-reaction between the spectator and the object of representation (familiar from reception aesthetics). Just as little as can the sense of commonality be equated with the feelings and bonds, tendencies, and belongings that individual persons develop in concrete social relationships.

---

65 Cf. ibid.
66 Cf. Aristotle, *Poetics*, 23.
67 This becomes particularly clear by placing Aristotelian "poetics" as the objection to Plato. Cf. Linck and Völher, "Zur Einführung," IXf. as well as Bernd Seidensticke and Martin Völher, "Zur Einführung. Katharsiskonzeptionen vor Aristoteles," in *Katharsiskonzeptionen vor Aristoteles*, eds. Bernd Seidensticke and Martin Völher, Berlin/Boston 2007.

On the other hand, affect poetics are always also to be conceived and introduced rhetorically, that is, in terms of aesthetic effects. Ultimately, the pathos of the Hollywood war film cannot be separated from media technologies and the operations of aesthetically modulating spectators' emotions.

Approaches from cognitive psychology: appraisal

Within the research literature in film studies on spectator emotions, the dominant essays can be located in the field of cognitive film theory.[68] Inherent to this line of research is an indirect relation to empiricism. What is common to these works is a transfer of theories, terms, and models from cognitive psychology into a film studies context. These theories themselves, in turn, are closely linked to a continuing empirical review, falsification, and updating within experimental psychology.

Despite the close proximity of cognitive film theory to experimental psychology and to neuropsychology, most of the relevant proposals dispense with any connection whatsoever to empirical research. As a rule, theoretical theses and hypotheses from cognitive psychology are transferred into models of how to understand film reception, which never leave the realm of theoretical reflection.[69]

---

[68] Cf. Grodal, *Moving Pictures*; Grodal, *Embodied Visions*; Carl Plantinga and Greg M. Smith (eds.), *Passionate Views: Film, Cognition and Emotion*, Baltimore, MD 1999; Plantinga, *Moving Viewers*; Greg M. Smith, *Film Structure and the Emotion System*, Cambridge 2003; Smith, *Engaging Characters*; Tan, *Emotion and the Structure of Narrative Film*.

[69] Cf. Nico H. Frijda, *The Emotions*, Cambridge 1986; Nico H. Frijda, "Emotions, Cognitive Structure and Action Tendency," in *Cognition and Emotion* 1, 1987, 115–144; Klaus R. Scherer, "What are emotions? And how can they be measured?," in *Social Science Information* 44 (4), 2005, 693–727; Valentijn T. Fisch and Ed S. Tan, "Categorizing Moving Objects into Film Genres: The Effect of Animacy Attribution, Emotional Response, and the Deviation from Non-Fiction," in *Cognition* 110, 2009, 265–272.

The same goes quite generally for recent experimental research on film, which is restricted to a large degree to measuring the effect of media contents using social science methods or physiological and neurophysiological methods. Indeed, a handful of essays have been developed in recent years within neuropsychology to model the affective dimension of aesthetically-organized perceptual sensations as neuronal processes. How the models are to be conceptualized specifically with regard to audiovisual media and their contents, however, remains unclear. Cf. Helmut Leder, et al., "A Model of Aesthetic Appreciation and Aesthetic Judgements," in *British Journal of Psychology* 95, 2004, 489–508.

The experimental examination of neuronal correlates of film affectation at the current time is based on an understanding of film that seek to grasp this merely as an emotionally classified stimulus material, on the basis of behavioral methods. This means that films or film scenes and

A significant exception to this are the works of Ed S. Tan, which also provide a decisive impulse research on film emotions based on cognitive psychology. Admittedly, it would perhaps be better to call these works psychology informed by film theory.[70]

Tan's distinction between so-called *fiction emotion* and *artifact emotion* remains the standard for a whole series of film-analytical approaches to the emotionalization of the spectator.[71] At the same time, Tan provides influential postulates for cognitive media studies. He takes his theoretical approach to the term 'emotion' from the works of the psychologist Nico Frijda,[72] formulating: "An emotion may be defined as a change in action readiness as a result of the subject's appraisal of the situation or event."[73]

What is clearly undertaken here is the *first* influential postulate for cognitive film theory. According to this understanding, emotion is always tied to the idea of a cognitive 'appraisal' specific to the situation. This draws a sharp dividing line from concepts like atmosphere, mood, mixed emotions, and affective processes that are not object-focused, but temporally extended, which would be highly significant for the experiential modality of film.[74]

The transfer of this idea of emotion into a media context turns out to be problematic. For Frijda it represents an essential requirement that the feeling subject a) appraises the object of emotion as real and b) sees his or her own options for action affected by this. Neither seems to be the case for the film spectator.[75]

---

other audiovisual media contents here primarily have the function of reliably unfolding certain affective effects first of all across a large number of subjects, so that it becomes possible to examine these affects by means of statistic methods. Cf. Israel C. Christie and Bruce H. Friedman, "Autonomic Specificity of Discrete Emotion and Dimensions of Affective Space: A Multivariate Approach," in *International Journal of Psychophysiology* 51, 2004, 143–153; Philippe R. Goldin, et al., "The Neural Bases of Amusement and Sadness: A Comparison of Block Contrast and Subject-Specific Emotion Intensity Regression Approaches," in *NeuroImage* 27, 2005, 26–36; Philippe R. Goldin, et al., "The Neural Bases of Emotion Regulation: Reappraisal and Suppression of Negative Emotion," in *Biological Psychatry* 63 (6), 2008, 577–586; James J. Gross and Robert W. Levenson, "Emotion Elicitation Using Films," in *Cognition and Emotion* 9 (1), 1995, 87–108.

70 Cf. Tan, *Emotion and the Structure of Narrative Film*.
71 Cf. Jens Eder, *Die Figur im Film: Grundlagen der Figurenanalyse*, Marburg 2008; Hans J. Wulff, "Empathie als Dimension des Filmverstehens: Ein Thesenpapier," in *montage a/v* 12 (1), 2003, 136–161.
72 Cf. Frijda, *The Emotions*; Frijda, "Emotions, Cognitive Structure and Action Tendency"; Frijda, *The Laws of Emotion*, Mahwah, NJ 2006.
73 Tan, *Emotion and the Structure of Narrative Film*, 46.
74 See in this book: II.4.3. Emotion, Feeling, Affect.
75 Cf. Tan, *Emotion and the Structure of Narrative Film*, 233.

This problem is resolved according to Tan's conception by the link between an illusionary presence and the impossibility of interactively intervening that is typical for film perception.[76] Spectators might sense the fictional world as real, but they can only be emotionally moved by the events on the screen by associating their own issues and preferences with the fictional characters. Sympathy and strategies of guiding it thus become the foundation of emotional sensation in film. The same can therefore be extracted by film analysis using the appraisal of constellations of action and characters with regard to characters marked as sympathetic.[77]

This analytical perspective turns out to be the *second* influential postulate for cognitive film theory. Even if it is occasionally assumed that spectators imagine themselves in the place of the fictional characters through mental simulation in the sense of the *Theory of Mind* (TOM),[78] or if the transfer of the character's emotions to the spectators is modeled as a psychological chain of reaction forced in mimesis[79] – the bond between spectator emotion and fictional character functions as practically axiomatic consensus in cognitive film theory.

By on the one hand establishing a concept of emotion tied to the situation and to appraisal, which cannot take complex mixed emotional states or those not related to objects into account, or can only take them into account as an accidental value, while on the other hand nonetheless linking the relation of the object assumed by this concept of emotion to the fictional character, cognitive film theory performs a significant reduction, which blocks access to any idea of the modes of aesthetic experience and the affective dimensions of expressive modalities in film.

Mood cues

An approach to cognitive psychology that does take the mode of aesthetic experience into account has been developed by Greg M. Smith in the *Mood Cue* approach.[80] Smith also assumes a model of understanding taken from cognitive and neuro-cognitive psychology. But he does not choose fictional events and characters,[81] but the aesthetic-figurative of film as the central reference point for

---

76 Cf. ibid., 232ff.
77 Ibid., 248; See also: ibid., 196.
78 Cf. Grodal, *Embodied Visions*, 181–204; Grodal, *Moving Pictures*.
79 Cf. Carl Plantinga, "Die Szene der Empathie und das menschliche Gesicht im Film," in *montage a/v* 13 (2), 2004, 6–27.
80 Cf. Smith, *Film Structure and the Emotion System*.
81 Cf. ibid., 65–81.

his cognitive-theoretical concept of spectator emotion. In doing so he manages to extend the idea of emotion that emphasizes the temporality of the film experience. According to this, emotions would not necessarily be tied to an object; rather, they would stand in the context of an associative network, in which a wide variety of components, such as memories, thoughts, tendencies toward action, psychological reactions, and vocalizations, are associatively linked – and in which the emotions function to a certain extent as the knots that hold the networks together.[82] A quite specific temporal dynamic emerges from this for film reception. Several parts of one and the same associative network, which merge in the total or in their succession, could favor the formation of one emotional disposition, for which Smith chooses the term mood.[83] This would mean that emotion and mood maintain a double mutual relation: the continuous, repeated sensation of a certain emotion would lead to the formation of a mood consistent with this emotion; in reverse, the mood – as an emotional disposition – would subsequently favor coherent emotional reactions. Accordingly, the interplay of mood and emotion would have its own dynamic, the result of which would represent sustained emotion episodes:

> An emotion episode is a series of emotions that are perceived to be a structured coherent unit having a beginning, a middle, and an end. When we remember being angry for a significant period of time, we are usually remembering an emotion episode. An emotion episode is an emotional transaction between a person and his or her environment, a transaction composed of several subevents but that is perceived to have an internal consistency.[84]

The emotion episode is thus essentially distinguished by forming a closed temporal form, which at the same time is related to the comprehensive entirety of a basic mood. Smith therefore answers the question of the degree to which films can have an intersubjective emotional effect beyond the highly diverse emotional dispositions of concrete spectators. Namely, to the degree to which the arrangement of the formal elements – at the most diverse levels of design such as camerawork, montage, lighting, music, or dialogue – is coherently unfolded in its quality of emotional expression as the experience of a temporally fixed emotion episode.[85]

As instructive as these reflections are, they nonetheless remain caught in the psychologistic reduction to a model from reception aesthetics. The modes of media experience are subsumed to the individual psychological conception of the subject.

---

82 Cf. ibid., 29.
83 Ibid., 39.
84 Ibid.
85 Cf. ibid., 41.

If we wish to take account of the modes of film experience, it is necessary that the term 'affect' is not developed from generalizing and abstract psychological principles; at any rate not if we assume overlapping and mutually determining configurations of media technological processes and human actors as the basis of all cultural activities. This is why it is necessary to take the media theoretical definitions of film explained in the previous chapters seriously, and then to ask how films can be described as acts of viewing films, in which they are embodied as processes of sensing and thinking in spectators.

Emotion, feeling, affect

At this point, then, a small excursus is necessary to define the usage of the terms affect, feeling, and emotion. In fact, most treatments in which the relationship between media and emotions is thematized start from a psychological definition of the term. In general, emotions, feelings, and affects are more or less ascribed to clearly identifiable personal agents who then are modulated or coded "by the media" (this formulation usually means cultural practices that are identifiable through particular media technologies). What are called emotions here are usually affective evaluations of the world of objects, which are attributed to consistent subjects as psychologically-grounded processes.

If, however, we start from a relational affectivity, then the focus is on those media practices in which affects can be observed as effects of particular media formats, media practices, and forms of media communication. From this perspective, it does not seem possible to trace affective dynamics back to individually attributable emotions, but on the contrary they themselves point back to processes of subjectification. The "I" of "I feel" is always a media effect of becoming-affected, which has found its form of symbolic expression. For its part, this stirs up discursively created, epistemic regimes and media practices, whether they be artistically (aesthetic pleasure), socially (e.g. upbringing), or religiously (rituals) motivated, aimed at entertainment and pleasure, the practice of affective habitus, or the creation of belonging. In such practices, positions get established from which an "I feel" can be experienced and formulated in the first place. It should always be conceived as an effect of subjectification, which refers back to historical discourses, cultural practices, and technologies of power and domination, structured by media in each case.

From Aristotelian tragedy to Hollywood cinema and entertainment television, the problem of affects turns up in the area of conflict between formation of political community, media practices, and human agents. From this perspective, representations and representational forms, contents and technologies of media usage themselves should be understood as part of the operations in which processes of affecting and becoming-affected are molded into a shared world of feelings.

Based on the reflections outlined here, I find it necessary to counter the typical usages of the terms as synonyms and to distinguish clearly between affect, emotion, and feeling. I speak of *emotions* as purely situational, affective assessments, with which individuals position themselves in the world of objects surrounding them. This means the instantaneous, largely involuntary affective self-positioning of concrete individuals in current situations. *Affects*, on the other hand, concern the fundamental dynamic in which bodies are connected to one another through the faculty of affecting and becoming affected as living bodies (that is, the capacity to affect intentionally and to respond reflexively to becoming-affected).[86] *Feeling* designates the basic affective embedding in a given environment, defined from the standpoint of a reflecting subject. The term aims at subjective sensation, seeing oneself affectively connected to the world in a multitude of ways. This implies both long-term affective attitudes, that "being-in-the-world" ("*être au monde*") from phenomenology[87] and the "belonging" to collective feelings.[88] But it also means the temporary moods[89] and atmospheres in currently given situations (social constellations, spaces of experience and landscapes, artistic experiences, entertainment, play), in which the former can be updated, mobilized, or modulated.[90] The processes of this embedding are always formed by symbolic and media practices.

---

[86] Cf. Deleuze, *The Movement Image*, 87; Brian Massumi, *Ontopower: war, powers, and the state of perception*, London 2015; Brian Massumi, "Navigating Movements," in *Hope: New Philosophies for Change*, ed. Mary Zournazi, New York 2003, 210–243.

[87] Cf. Maurice Merleau-Ponty, *Phenomenology of Perception*, London 2013; Jan Slaby, et al., (eds.), *Affektive Intentionalität. Beiträge zur welterschließenden Funktion der menschlichen Gefühle*, Paderborn 2011; Thomas Fuchs, *Leib, Raum, Person: Entwurf einer phänomenologischen Anthropologie*, Stuttgart 2000; Hilge Landweer, *Scham und Macht: Phänomenologische Untersuchungen zur Sozialität eines Gefühls*, Tübingen 1999.

[88] Belonging is often conceived as strongly spatial, and is highly associated as an emotional structure with the principle of positioning (Cf. Elspeth Probyn, *Outside Belongings*, New York/London 1996; bell hooks, *Belonging: A Culture of Place*, New York 2009; Nira Yuval-Davis, *The Politics of Belonging: Intersectional Contestations*, Los Angeles/London/New Dehli/Singapore/Washington DC 2011; Guibernau Montserrat, *Belongin: Solidarity and Division in Modern Societies*, Cambridge 2013.

[89] 'Mood' in Damasio (Cf. Antonio Damasio, *The Feeling of what happens: Body and Emotion in the Making of Consciousness*, New York, 1999, 341f., endnote 10) and 'mood cues' in cognitive film studies.

[90] One example is the nostalgia that allows the temporal dimension to appear as an aspect of spatiality – which is not necessarily fixed to the past (cf. on this Svetlana Boym, *The Future of Nostalgia*, New York 2001; Alison Blunt, *Domicile and Diaspora: Anglo-Indian Women and the Spatial Politics of*

The feeling, therefore, is the binding link between emotional processes from an individual psychological perspective and the concept of a constitutive inter-affectivity as postulated by affect theory. Viewed in this way, feelings are to be understood as processes in which a situationally given dynamic of affective assessments of the surrounding world are correlated and aligned with the basic affective embedding of the individual (his or her feeling for the common world).[91] This implies both the permanent reflexive monitoring of current affective changes in clear situations ("feeling" in Damasio's sense[92]) and the feedback to symbolic forms and media operations of emotional embedding, of the basic correlations between individual and surroundings.

A reflexive feeling (Dewey)

In this understanding I am following John Dewey's concept of aesthetic experience. For Dewey, the specific character of an experience is given in perception, with which its singular elements of sensation can be conceived as a complex entanglement of a self-contained temporal unit. Feeling means the conception, the grasping of a unit as a temporal form of mutually entangled elements of sensation. The feeling is the form in which an experience steps out of the stream of everyday sensation as an integral temporal form.

This is exactly why for Dewey experience per se is aesthetic – the attribute of the aesthetic is the capacity to "round out an experience into completeness and unity as emotional" – and the 'capacity of the aesthetic' per se is a feeling.[93]

From Dewey's perspective there is therefore only a gradual, and no categorical distinction between everyday and aesthetic perception. For him, perception only exists in its full sense when it has become experience, that is, when is has become aesthetic:

> There is [...] no such thing in perception as seeing or hearing *plus* emotion. The perceived object or scene is emotionally pervaded throughout. When an aroused emotion does not permeate the material that is perceived or thought of, it is either preliminary or pathological.[94]

Home, Oxford 2005). This relation to time and space seems to keep the concept open to adaptation; nonetheless the occasionally implied link back to a feeling individual is not unproblematic.
91 In addition Hauke Lehmann, *Affektpoetiken des New Hollywood: Suspense, Paranoia und Melancholie*, Berlin/Boston 2016.
92 Cf. Damasio, *The Feeling of What Happens*.
93 „I have spoken of the esthetic quality that rounds out an experience into completeness and unity as emotional." John Dewey, *Art as Experience*, New York 1980, 41.
94 Ibid., 53.

2.4 What is a Poetics of Affect? — 111

Artistic treatment, like the perception of art objects, belongs to the cultural practices in which perception, thinking, and making are intentionally decoupled from everyday activity in order for the sensation of perception, in all its temporal extension, dynamics, and intense connectedness with the perceived object, to become the object of aesthetic enjoyment as a feeling. The enjoyment of experience consists in the self-perception of one's own sensation of feeling as intense connectedness with a realm of objects (the process of sensing an object, the object as occurrence).

This means nothing more than that a general becoming-affected is transferred into the reflexive form of one's own being-in-the-world; experience then, in contrast to temporary sensation, awareness, and recognition, means an affective relation of exchange, in which the perceiving subject connects with the sensed world.

Such an understanding of aesthetic experience has the advantage of being as open as possible, since it neither concerns a categorical distinction between everyday and aesthetic experience, nor does it claim any a priori territorial definition of realms of art in distinction to entertainment, information, kitsch, etc. At the same time, the understanding of feeling as an interaffective penetration of the world and the subject is genuinely linked with that of aesthetic experience. Feeling "provides unity in and through the varied parts of an experience."[95] So the understanding of aesthetic experience not only allows for the largest possible internal differentiation between modalities of artistic treated forms of experiencing various media and media formats, genres, and generic modes. It also retains, in the complementary understanding of aesthetic enjoyment, indeterminacy in relation to each concrete episode of feeling, in which experience emerges as an effect of subjectification and can in no way be ascribed to a given subject a priori: "Emotion is the moving and cementing force. It selects what is congruous and dyes what is selected its color, thereby giving qualitative unity to materials externally disparate and dissimilar."[96]

As I see it, however, feelings should be as fundamentally distinguished from the reflex of an assessing emotional relation to the object as the incoherent or temporarily manipulated impulse to the senses is from the temporal shape of the process of subjectification, which Dewey links to the term aesthetic experience.[97]

Obviously, he is attempting to get the free play of the powers of recognition – which for Kant is a transcendental condition of the possibility of making and

---

95 Ibid. 44.
96 Ibid. 44.
97 Cf. ibid., 52 and 58.

aesthetic judgment, a judgment of taste – as a phenomenon that is directly accessible to everyday experience. The idea that experience is linked to the complete affective penetration of all the subject/object relations given in a situation (that is, the heterogeneous elements of sensation), which find their temporal unity in feeling, is ultimately the attempt to shift the becoming self-aware of the subject's faculties into the realm of everyday experience. But to what degree is it possible to convey what I enjoy as the experience of my capacity to experience to others, and for them to be able to reproduce it? How can there be an aesthetic judgment about which one can speak? Dewey tries to solve the problem by proposing the judgment of taste as an act of communication between artist and art recipient. The former gives an experience expression in the creation of an art object, the latter enjoys the deliberate createdness of an artistically constructed context for all the elements of sensation: "The aesthetic sensation is thus considered to be bound to the sensation in its essential core."[98]

One might see this idea merely as a more complicated variation on the question of the artist's intentions; but the "sensation of creating" is in no way all that the author wants to tell us. Rather, the idea of an internally divided sensation of perception, articulated in the process of creating a feeling for the world and made current in a process of perception in which every 'sensation element,' has become the expression of a creative process, is highly instructive for film theory. Indeed, it leads us back to the phenomenological "expression of experience by experience," with which the film image was defined as a mode of experience:

> In a search for rules and principles governing cinematic expression, most of the descriptions and reflections of classical and contemporary film theory have not fully addressed the cinema as life expressing life, as experience expressing experience. Nor have they explored the mutual possession of this experience of perception and its expression by filmmaker, film, and spectator – all *viewers viewing*, engaged as participants in dynamically and directionally reversible acts that reflexively and reflectively constitute the *perception of expression* and the *expression of perception*. Indeed, it is this mutual capacity for and possession of experience through common structures of embodied existence, through similar modes of being-in-the-world, that provide the *intersubjective* basis of objective cinematic communication.[99]

The film image per se is understood as a moving image, which, intentionally aimed, articulates an affective stance toward the world and at the same time is grasped by spectators as a sensation of perception, which appears as the perception of a different "I."

---

[98] Ibid., 62. This sentence is not included in the English translation.
[99] Vivian Sobchack, *The Address of the Eye: A Phenomenology of Film Experience*, Princeton 1992, 5.

If we look into the feeling of viewing films, then first and foremost it concerns the temporal form of perception divided in itself. Neither the actors in their talented performances, nor the characters in their actions, neither the social spaces in which figures are located, nor their relationships are given per se as representations in film images. Rather, they are to be understood as a product of the spectator's perception, feeling, and thinking in the act of viewing films. The tie that binds the screen image and the spectator body is neither the storyline nor the action, but the faculty of affecting other bodies and of being affected by other bodies. In order to understand the interaffective structure in which technological and human, artistic and organic bodies are intertwined with one another, it is necessary to make sure of the material in which both of them are grounded; and that is – at least we can say this for all cinematic appearances of audiovisual images – movement itself.

Spectator feeling

If we follow Vivian Sobchack,[100] even movement ultimately unfolds outside the physical film material, aside from the screen. The movement generated in the medium of film images takes on a different, physical reality in the perceiving body of the spectator as the physical, sensory experience of being-affected. The movement of the film image materializes as the physical sensation of the spectators, is *embodied* by them[101] – spectator perception and film expressivity are directly intertwined in movement.[102]

The movement of the film image thus concerns discrete but adjacent dynamics, which are carried out at highly varied levels. For one this is the external movement of the body in space (the movement of the objects and bodies represented in a space, which we assume as the homogeneous spatiality of our ordinary world); for another it is the inner movement of the audiovisual image, the combination of different dynamics of framing, montage, reframing, moving shots, etc., which allow the film's visual space to arise for the spectator; and last but not least it is the affecting of the perceiving body, the dynamic of sense impressions, emotional development, and mental operations, in which this visual space becomes a way of perceiving the world embodied by the spectators, a world of someone

---

100 Cf. ibid.
101 Ibid., 9.
102 Ibid., 13.

other than one's own subjectivity.[103] The film image encompasses the movement of bodies in space and the dynamics of the embodying perceptual process of the spectator in the movement of a visual space that unfolds and changes in the time of the film.[104]

In this sense, then, the film image is to be understood as a form of media experience that has a direct effect on the movement of affect and incorporates it. Eisenstein called such an overall movement the 'fourth dimension' of film; he laconically noted that this would be time itself. He gave a concrete quality to the temporality of film images through the aesthetic operation of montage, which starts at different levels of visual staging (namely light, camera movement/framing, editing and montage, acting style; we could also add sound, music, and dialogue) and is in no way limited to editing and the concatenation of visual segments. Every level of the shaping of film movement has a part in the operations in which the external movement of bodies is separated from the homogeneous space of ordinary perception, in order to become linked to the affective dynamic of viewing films and to anticipate a thinking of affected bodies of an undefined, infinitely expandable subjectivity of the collective.[105] From this perspective, the film image itself becomes the "fourth dimension" of a space of perception in which all the dimensions of movement (movement in space, the movement of the film itself, and the affective dynamic of viewing films) can be referred back to one another and can be generated from one another. It can also be formulated the other way around: Since film montage, understood in the broadest sense, refers to the affective dynamics of spectators in its own movement on the one hand, and to spatial movement in a given space on the other, the film image emerges as the fourth dimension of a space in which cuts, separations, and couplings can be experienced between the different dimensions of movement as shaped time, as a temporal form.

The compositional shape of the moving images – one might, following Eisenstein, speak of the montage of a multidimensional moving image – marks the interface between the movement of the image on screen and the processes of embodiment in the spectators' perceptual sensations. In this theoretical model, the episodic unfolding of a complex montage of movement can be described as the compositional shaping of the modulation of the spectator's affective sensations.[106]

---

[103] Kappelhoff, *Matrix der Gefühle*, 21f.
[104] Cf. Kappelhoff and Bakels, "Das Zuschauergefühl"; Sergej Eisenstein, *Das dynamische Quadrat: Schriften zum Film*, Cologne 1988, 90–108.
[105] Cf. Hermann Kappelhoff, *Realismus: Das Kino und die Politik des Ästhetischen*, Berlin 2008, 21ff.
[106] Cf. Sobchack, *The Address of the Eye*.

It is precisely in this dimension of movement that Sobchack sees the intersubjective dimension of cinema. Spectators realize the film image as a specific perspective and way of perceiving the world. They realize it as a specific way of being-in-the-world, which is unfolded in the process of cinematic staging. Spectator feeling is then grounded in the temporal form of this unfolding. This means, to speak with Dewey, the reflexive sensation of a feeling in the created and shaped unity of its temporal unfolding.[107]

But how can the interaffective structure of the film image be described in the ways it concretely appears, and analyzed in its function of generating meaning?

2.5 Expressive Movement: A Methodological Concept

In one research group[108] we tried to identify rhetorical and dramaturgical strategies of mobilizing affect in comprehensive comparative film-analytical studies.[109]

---

107 Cf. Dewey, *Art as Experience*, 43.
108 This work was done within the project "Affektmobilisierung und mediale Kriegsinszenierung," carried out in the context of the Excellence Cluster "Languages of Emotion" (director: Hermann Kappelhoff; research associates: Jan-Hendrik Bakels, Hye-Jeung Chung, David Gaertner, Sarah Greifenstein, Matthias Grotkopp, Michael Lück, Christian Pischel, Franziska Seewald, Anna Steininger) and the successor project funded by the DFG, "Inszenierungen des Bildes vom Krieg als Medialität des Gemeinschaftserlebens" (director: Hermann Kappelhoff; project members: Tobias Haupts, David Gaertner, Danny Gronmaier, Cilli Pogodda, Eileen Rositzka; associated researchers: Jan-Hendrik Bakels, Matthias Grotkopp, Christian Pischel).
109 Within the several projects conducted at the Freie Universität under my direction, this approach forms a research focus and is also used for other genres. For a more precise derivation of this approach as well as examples of analyses, see the materials collected at www.empirische-medienaesthetik.fu-berlin.de. The basis of the research work in all the participating projects is an IT-supported analysis method that was developed as part of the research project "Affektmobilisierung und mediale Kriegsinszenierung" at the Excellence Cluster "Languages of Emotion" at the Freie Universität in Berlin. The *eMAEX* system (*electronically based media analysis of expressional movement images*) combines a film-analytical procedure with a web-based infrastructure, facilitating a multimedia processing of analytical studies. The focus lies on the temporal structure of compositional movement figurations and dramaturgical arrangements in audiovisual representations. The goal of this approach is to make it possible to trace the affect-modeling function of such representations in an analytical description – as affect dramaturgy in relation to the entire film, as expressive movement in relation to the expressive progressive form, which are perceivable as units within the film. A wide variety of net-based audiovisual applications make it possible to bring analytical identifications and descriptions of such compositional patterns into a systematic sequence and to give public access to their results as a complex multimedia presentation. For a thorough presentation of the eMAEX system cf. Hermann Kappelhoff

The focus of our work was the Hollywood war film. The methodological gains of our research consisted in developing a film-analytical model that – supported by audiovisual forms of representation in net-based media – were aimed at describing compositional figurations of movement in great detail.[110]

The model was based on the idea that audiovisual images, in their compositional movement – that is, the construction and arrangement of moving images – structure the temporal matrix of affective and perceptive processes of viewing films. The dynamic course of shaping cinematic images, that is, moving images, model the temporal structure of the spectator's bodily sensations which is performed by film perception. The audiovisual moving image structures this affective sensation in its temporal shape.

We thus make the methodological assumption that moving film images can be grasped in their compositional structure and connection as temporal gestalt units, which correspond to the "elements of sensation" that Dewey brings to bear on the unity of aesthetic experience. The shaped temporal figurations, as "experiential material," as "elements of an aesthetic experience" in Dewey's sense[111] – and this is the fundamental hypothesis of our research on genre cinema – found a complex emotional sensation, which is itself genuinely grounded in the aesthetic form of the film; in its reflexive shape as a unit of experience the process of affecting can be distinguished qualitatively from the individual emotional reactions with which spectators respond to what is being represented and the forms of that representation. Even though this process might ultimately be composed of single emotive reflexes, which are identical with ordinary emotional reaction patterns, in our descriptive analyses of genre films we assume that the temporal dynamic of aesthetically modeled spectators' affects specifically shaped over the course of the film is more than the sum of its parts. As a temporal form, it grounds the rhythm and the tempi of an emerging, unfolding, and transforming spectator feeling (that is, the reflexive feeling of perceiving and being-affected by the film images).

We therefore view neither the spectator's emotional process nor the modalities of film expression as accidental aspects of stylistic, formal, or aesthetic

---

et al.: eMAEX: Ansätze und Potentiale einer systematisierten Methode zur Untersuchung filmischer Ausdrucksqualitäten, in http://www.empirische-medienaesthetik.fu-berlin.de/media/emaex_methode_deutsch/eMAEX-_-Ansaetze-und-Potentiale-einer-systematisierten-Methode-zur-Untersuchung-filmischer-Ausdrucksqualitaeten.pdf?1401464494, (December 5, 2015).

110 These analyses can be found at: http://www.empirische-medienaesthetik.fu-berlin.de/emaex-system/affektdatenmatrix/index.html (December 5, 2015).

111 Cf. Dewey, *Art as Experience*, 49f. and 245.

additions to a given narration or representation, but as a foundation that precedes all embodying constitution of meaning in the film as mode of experience.[112]

The processes of *meaning making* cannot be detached from the affecting power of the forms of cinematic expressivity.[113] Film analyses that refer directly to the actions, characters, or contents represented mask exactly the temporal structures of viewing films that representation, as a product of this process, is based on in the first place: the constitution of a visual space in which things, bodies, and powers are positioned in relation to one another and react with each other in a way that is fundamentally different from what we assume as the shared everyday world. The fact that, for genre cinema, all representation and all meaning making is preceded by a feeling for the world in which interacting bodies can be grasped in their sensual intentionality may already be indicated in the circumstance that pleasure, aesthetic enjoyment, is essentially determined – and this is clearly seen in the modes of suspense, horror, and thriller – through the specific temporality of various dramaturgies of affect.[114]

On the basis of the theoretical assumptions outlined here, our comparative analyses understand the film image as a dynamically unfolding arranging and rhythmization of spectator feeling, which can be grasped on the various levels of shaping the modalities of film expression as the compositional unity of moving images.[115]

---

112 As a rule, such an approach is developed by means of the term style. This brings into play aspects of film expressivity that closely resemble the aesthetic modalities mentioned above. Carl Plantinga writes, for instance: "Particular stylistic choices in editing and camera movement, for example, might be 'exciting' or 'energetic'. An audiovisual combination of languid tracking shot and music may be experienced as peaceful and relaxing." Plantinga, *Moving Viewers*, 141.

It seems as if this is also a matter of the aesthetic expressive modalities of the cinema. But if Plantinga is connecting style to affective resonances, both are still being subordinated to the function of representation. In the term style, expressive modality as well as spectator feeling become an accidental bonus of a per se representing image. Following a cognitivist conception of aesthetic effects, style merely adds the trigger of affective response to the action represented. For instance, Plantinga says about a scene from Hitchcock: "It is the filmic narration that guides the film's intended elicitation of affect." Ibid.

113 Hermann Kappelhoff and Cornelia Müller: "Embodied Meaning Construction: Multimodal Metaphor and Expressive Movement in Speech, Gesture, and Feature Film," in *Metaphor and the Social World* 1 (2), 2011, 121–153.

114 On the temporality of suspense, see for instance Lehmann, *Affektpoetiken des New Hollywood*, and Sarah Greifenstein and Hauke Lehmann, "Manipulation der Sinne im Modus des Suspense," in: *Cinema* 58, 2013, 102–112.

115 On the model of film expressivity as well as the term of spectator feeling, see: Kappelhoff: *Matrix der Gefühle*; Hermann Kappelhoff: "Unerreichbar, unberührbar, zu spät... Das Gesicht als kinematografische Form der Erfahrung," in: *montage a/v* 13 (2), 2004, 29–53; Kappelhoff and

In our film-analytical model we therefore attempted to describe compositional structures as a specific progression and shaping of audiovisual movement patterns. In this undertaking we found the term 'expressive movement' very useful. Indeed, by using this term we can formulate the various theoretical reflections on the embodiment processes of film perception and the technological conditions of media as a film-analytical model, which I have presented in the previous chapters. I have already dealt extensively with the concept of spectator feeling and expressive movement in another text; I will therefore only explain the main feature of the argument in the following.[116]

Expressive movement as temporal form

The film-analytical concept of expressive movement was developed by examining melodramatic representation in theater, film, and music theater.[117] The guiding thesis here was that media and art forms (stage, acting, dance, film) develop aesthetic operations and poetics of affect that are aimed at activating and shaping the affective processes of a broad and anonymous audience.

The objectives associated with these cultural practices of shaping emotional sensations through aesthetics are indeed each different – since these practices are tied to different media, artistic operations, and material. But in the history of sentimental art and entertainment we can indeed point to certain basic poetic strategies of shaping emotion that are grounded in highly divergent media presuppositions. Among the significant operations that can be widely observed is the shaping of figurations of movement as a specific form of expressivity. This can mean the gestural shaping of the acting, but also the design of the set as an image that transforms within itself, it can mean performance of dance or pantomime or also the interplay of declamation and musical composition; finally, it can also mean the compositions of film movement in the sense outlined above.

Bakels: Das Zuschauergefühl; Thomas Scherer, et al., Expressive Movement in Audio-Visuals: Modulating Affective Experience, in: *Body – Language – Communication: An International Handbook on Multimodality in Human Interaction*, Handbooks of Linguistics and Communication Science 38.2., eds. Cornelia Müller, et al., Berlin/Boston 2014, 2081–2092.

116 For a positioning of this approach in current and historical theories of the emotional effect of moving images, cf. Kappelhoff/Bakels: Das Zuschauergefühl; the interrelation of expressive movement and the affective grounding of meaning making has been elaborated in Kappelhoff/Müller: Embodied Meaning Construction. For a systematic and historical analysis of the term 'expressive movement,' see Kappelhoff: *Matrix der Gefühle*.

117 Cf. ibid.

2.5 Expressive Movement: A Methodological Concept

The term 'expressive movement' seeks to grasp these dynamic figurations as a temporal form. The term, however, should in no way be used – following conventional usage – to trace the forms of artistic representation back to an intentional expressive desire; rather, expressive movement, much like the strategies of affect rhetoric in Aristotelian tragedy, is geared toward affecting the body of the viewer, spectator, or reader.

If we understand affects, as summed up in the project, in the broadest sense as the faculty of bodies to affect (to initiate affect dynamics of other bodies) and to be affected, expression is not to be understood as an innersubjective relation (an external movement in which an interiority of feelings is expressed). Expression therefore precisely does not mean the intrapsychic correlation between physical movement and affective dynamics, but shifts the focus to the relationality of affect, to the affect itself as relationality.[118]

The theoretical framework of these reflections is formed on the one hand by the psychological, linguistic, and anthropological theories of expressive movement, which were formulated in the first third of the last century by Wilhelm Wundt, Karl Bühler, and Helmuth Plessner.[119] On the other hand, we should mention the concepts of expressive movement from aesthetic philosophy and art theory – for instance in Georg Simmel and Konrad Fiedler.[120]

Expressive movement in this context should be understood as a category of interaffectivity; it does not refer back to a feeling, but generates the feeling in the affective resonance of interacting bodies. Such an understanding of expressive movement is succinctly formulated by Plessner.[121] For him expressive movement is not any distinct *type* of movement, but a specific *dimension* of movement, which is grounded in the perception of temporal *shape*:

---

[118] In developing the methodological approach to classical theories of the expressive, we have been guided by Plessner and Bühler as well as by Gadamer and Merleau-Ponty and on up to Deleuze and Massumi.

[119] Cf. Karl Bühler, *Ausdruckstheorie: Das System an der Geschichte aufgezeigt*, Jena 1933; Helmuth Plessner, "Die Deutung des mimischen Ausdrucks: Ein Beitrag zur Lehre vom Bewußtsein des anderen Ichs [1925]," in *Gesammelte Schriften VII*, Frankfurt am Main 1982, 67–130; Wilhelm Wundt, *Grundzüge der physiologischen Psychologie*, Bd. 2, Leipzig 1880, 418ff; Wilhelm Wundt, *Grundriss der Psychologie*, Leipzig 1896, 198ff.

[120] Konrad Fiedler, "Moderner Naturalismus und künstlerische Wahrheit [1881]," in *Schriften zur Kunst I*, Munich 1991, 82–110; Konrad Fiedler, "Über den Ursprung der Künstlerischen Tätigkeit [1887]," in *Schriften zur Kunst I*, Munich 1991, 112–220; Georg Simmel, "Aesthetik des Porträts [1905]," in *Aufsätze und Abhandlungen 1901–1908* (Bd. I), Frankfurt am Main 1995, 321–332; Georg Simmel, "Die ästhetische Bedeutung des Gesichts [1901]," in *Aufsätze und Abhandlungen 1901–1908* (Bd. I), Frankfurt am Main 1995, 36–42.

[121] Cf. Plessner, "Die Deutung des mimischen Ausdrucks," 67ff.

> Wherever movements appear in the realm of the organic, they proceed according to a unified rhythm, they exhibit a dynamic shape that can even be verified through experiment. They do not unwind piece by piece, as if the succession of their phases could be associated with the individual elements; they do not form a mosaic in time, but instead evince a certain wholeness, within which the individual curves of movement are variable.[122]

The essential quality of expressive movement consists in its temporal gestalt ("a certain wholeness"), which is realized at every point of its course.[123] The temporal form, however, does not refer to the feeling of an intentionally directed body, but to the body's capacity to affect other bodies when its movement takes on a visual [bildhaft] character for others. Plessner speaks – generalizing the switch from intentional action to the visual character for others – of "movement image(s)."[124] Movement images do not exist on their own terms, but are only formulated in the affective resonance of a perceiving body. From this perspective, feeling appears bound to a temporal, even dramatic structure, which encompasses the affecting and affected body.

Expressive movement thus means the potentiality of a constellation of affect, which on the one side (that of the perceived, affecting body) is seen as an intentionally directed movement, while on the other (that of the perceiving, affected body) it responds as a feeling for another's sense of self. In a certain way it designates the transition from one configuration of affectively interconnected bodies to another, without being existent for itself at any particular point of this transition.[125] The peculiar ontological status of the expressive movement corresponds to what Peirce classified in his semiotics as "firstness," using the example of perceiving color.[126] For Plessner this becomes palpable in a special way in laughing

---

122 Ibid., 77. My translation. The German original reads: "Wo immer im Reich des Organischen Bewegungen erscheinen, verlaufen sie nach einheitlichem Rhythmus, zeigen sie eine, wohl auch experimentell nachweisbare, dynamische Gestalt. Sie rollen nicht stückhaft ab, als ob ihre Phasenfolge aus einzelnen Elementen assoziiert worden wäre, bilden kein Zeitmosaik, sondern eine gewisse Ganzheit ist vorgegeben, innerhalb deren die einzelnen Bewegungskurven variierbar sind."
123 For a historical and systematic unfolding of the term expressive movement cf. Kappelhoff, *Matrix der Gefühle*.
124 Plessner, "Die Deutung des mimischen Ausdrucks," 77.
125 Cf. Hermann Kappelhoff: "Das Wunderbare der Filmkunst: Die Illusion des lebendigen Ausdrucks," in *...kraft der Illusion: Illusion und Filmästhetik*, eds. Gertrud Koch and Christiane Voss, Munich 2006, 175–189; Hermann Kappelhoff, "Ausdrucksbewegung und Zuschauerempfinden: Eisensteins Konzept des Bewegungsbildes," in *Synchronisierung der Künste*, ed. Robin Curtis, et al., Munich 2012, 73–84 as well as Scherer, et al., "Expressive movement in audio-visuals."
126 Cf. Deleuze, *The Movement-Image*, 95 ff.

and crying.[127] Indeed, laughing or crying subjects can be understood as movement images, which give expression to something by allowing their own bodies, in their affective resonance with other bodies and in the interaffective entanglement with the world surrounding them, to emerge as the ground on which all commonality is based.

From this perspective, the term could become a central reference point both for film theory, both classical and modern. It thus determines various concepts such as Kurtz's *poetics of expressionist film,* Eisenstein's idea of a *fourth dimension* of film, Béla Balázs's notion of the film image as a *chord of feeling*[128] or Münsterberg's film theory which is informed by the psychology of perception.[129] Like the psychological, linguistic, and art-theoretical approaches to expressive movement, film theory also assumes gesture and facial expression to be the paradigmatic form of movement. It includes, however, all the levels of shaping the film image as elements of a dynamic figuration of expression: along with acting also color, light values, creating space, music, montage, etc. – the film image itself is viewed in its temporal dynamic in analogy to the expressivity of physical movements and micro movements.

In modern film theory, this idea has been pursued in a variety of ways. The most prominent essays can be ascribed to the term of *time-image or of affection-image* on the one hand,[130] and to the works in film and media studies on *embodiment* and *immersion* on the other.[131] Viewed as a whole, all the positions named here pursue the idea that the special quality of the mode of film experience should be sought out in the connection between the movement image generated by media technology and affective dynamics. At the same time, however, it should have become perfectly clear

---

127 Cf. Hermann Kappelhoff, et al., (eds.), *Blick – Macht – Gesicht*, Berlin 2001.
128 Cf. Balázs, *Early Film Theory: Visible Man and The Spirit of Film;* Sergej Eisenstein, "The Filmic Fourth Dimension" in *Film Form: Essays in Film Theory,* ed. Jay Leyda, New York 1977, 64–71; Rudolf Kurtz, *Expressionismus und Film*, Berlin 1926.
129 Cf. Hugo Münsterberg, *The Photoplay: A Psychological Study*, New York/London 1916. Already in 1916 Münsterberg had already declared the entanglement of movement as it unfolds in time and individual emotional sensations as the affective dimension of cinema. He was thus already transforming the idea of expressive movement into a category of inter-affectivity organized by media.
130 Cf. Raymond Bellour, "*Le déplides émotions,*" in *Trafic* 42, P.O.L., 2002, 93–128.; Gilles Deleuze, *Cinema 2: The Time-Image*, London 1989. Petra Löffler, *Affektbilder: Eine Mediengeschichte der Mimik*, Bielefeld 2004; David Rodowick, *Gilles Deleuze's Time Machine*, Durham 1997.
131 Cf. Robnik, *Kino, Krieg, Gedächtnis*; Steven Shaviro, *The Cinematic Body*, Minneapolis 1993; Sobchack, *The Address of the Eye*; Vivian Sobchack, *Carnal Thoughts: Embodiment and Moving Image Culture*, Berkeley/Los Angeles 2004; Williams, "Film Bodies."

that expressive movement is fundamentally different from what Smith calls "emotion episode." Both are indeed defined as a unit of temporal figuration; in Smith, however, this unit arises from the coherence of distinct elements, while the expressive movement itself achieves the expressive quality in its temporality.

In relation to the film image, expressive movement cannot be grasped as a temporal form at the level of the individual means of representation; neither can it be ascribed to the (gestural-facial) movements of the actor in the image nor to the rhythm of the montage, neither to the changing light values and color compositions nor to sound design per se. The different modalities of expression of the audiovisual image become comprehensive as expressive movement within the context of the space of perception, which is only produced in the first place in the act of viewing. They are introduced in every detail into the temporal structure of emergence and permanent modulation of the entire visual space of film. In the modulation of the visual space of film the patterns of expressive movement (expressive movement units) and diverse modalities of expression of audiovisual images are inextricably interwoven in their expressive qualities. In their interplay, the film image is manifest as the time in which a visual space arises, alters, and persists as a distinct spatio-temporal construction in the spectator's perception.[132]

The various units of expressive movement can then also not be evaluated and qualified individually and in isolation. They should be grasped in their interplay as a dynamic shape of mutually merging expressive movements, which are continually reapportioned and branch out, fuse and couple, repel and diverge, become concentrated or overlap. The expressive movement in film should be conceived as "audiovisual rhythm,"[133] which includes all levels of representation. Related to the position of the spectator, this rhythm appears as a physically affecting force that constantly alters in its intensity. One might speak of a film affect,[134]

---

[132] The term 'visual space' does not refer to a space that is constituted in the same way as everyday perception. Here as well, it is not addressing the illusion of homogeneously sensed spaces, created by classical narrative means (for instance, as space of plot or narration). Rather, 'visual space' refers to the emergence of a space as the film unfolds over time, which only happens in the act of viewing, and which can be described as a modulation of forms of aesthetic experience. Cf. Kappelhoff, "Der Bildraum des Kinos."

[133] The dissertation by Jan-Hendrik Bakels clearly shows that the term can by no means be applied metaphorically. Cf. Jan-Hendrik Bakels, *Audiovisuelle Rhythmen: Filmmusik, Bewegungskomposition und die dynamische Affizierung des Zuschauers*, Berlin/Boston 2016.

[134] Cf. the term 'affection' in Deleuze, *The Movement-Image*, 87. as well as Gilles Deleuze and Felix Guattari, *A Thousand Plateaus: Capitalism and Schizophrenia*, London/New York 2008, and Deleuze and Guattari, *What is Philosophy?*.

which branches out in the bodies of sensing, feeling, and thinking spectators in order to cause the visual space of a film to emerge in the articulation of their perceptual sensations. That is – if we follow the theoretical positions sketched out – the space of experiencing another way of experiencing the world. This is exactly why one cannot distinguish between stylization and narrative function. In every detail, the way a film is shaped, the directorial style concerns the temporal form of the film world becoming visible and becoming audible over the duration of perceiving a film.

The temporal patterns that thus arise in order to merge immediately into other temporal formations thoroughly correspond to the subjective experience that we know as emotional states. Tense expectation or monotonous waiting, waking up and drifting off into sleep, paying attention and sinking into scattered absence are examples of such experiences of subjective, sensed time. They are neither represented as the characters' sensations nor described in their actions. Rather, they occur in the continuous modulations of the visual space of the film as a feeling of awakening or drifting off, paying attention or sagging, extending or constricting the perceiving body in the physical presence of the spectators. For them the temporal shaping, the rhythm of a film's visual space becoming visual and audible, its successive coming-into-appearance and altering becomes a sensation of the self that belongs to another self.

Every ascription of meaning, every understanding of film is always already grounded in the joining of the film images with the perceiving body of the spectator in audiovisual rhythm. This becomes palpable wherever the dramaturgy of tension refers to the succession of the action represented. Even thrill and suspense emerge from the rhythm of the transformations in the visual space and not at all from the course of the action represented.[135]

The war film and the historical dynamic of genre cinema

The affect poetics of genre cinema in general, and the war film in particular, are based on such rhythmic use of film's visual spaces (the entirety of what is visible and audible).[136] We should once again take up Gledhill's instructive distinction between the modes and modalities of aesthetic experience from this perspective, and specify its application to the theories of expression. Mode would then mean

---

135 Cf. Greifenstein and Lehmann, "Manipulation der Sinne im Modus des Suspense."
136 All of this is linked to the idea of an absolute change in movement, its opening up to time. See Deleuze, *The Movement-Image*, 1ff. and Deleuze, *The Time-Image*, 34 ff.

the specific model of aesthetically organizing media structures, in which different ways to experience space and time, bodies, language games, and relations between social forces are realized and form a certain stability (the melodramatic mode, the mode of horror, of action movies, etc.);[137] the modes of aesthetic experience can be determined and realized in different medial constellations. Modalities, on the other hand, designate the diverse aesthetic forms of expression of a specific media technology and their affective quality, which can turn up in a wide variety of generic figurations (for instance, the patterns of cinematic expressive movement, which can be sensed as sentimental-sad, elegiac, horrifying, uplifting, frightening, joyous, comic, euphoric, sexually exciting). The expressive modalities mark out the field of the generic forms of a specific media technology in each historical-cultural media practice ("the concept of modality as the sustaining medium in which the genre system operates"[138]); while the modes of aesthetic experience branch out and are differentiated in a wide variety of media practices.

The concrete modalities of aesthetic expression are thus in no way genuine elements of the war film genre; and even the set of narratives and the degree to which iconographic motifs have an originary relation of belonging to the films that are ultimately perceived as a genre is very minimal. In fact, all possible expressive modalities can be found in these films. Narratives and iconographies are linked to them that, on closer inspection, turn out to be hybrid forms, which we know from a variety of genres. Even in terms of modes of aesthetic experience, the Hollywood war film as a whole turns out to be a hybrid formation, which – as we have seen – combines and reconfigures different affect-dramaturgical patterns.

Thus, in all Hollywood war films we can detect expressive modalities aimed at destabilizing perception, for instance by evoking an invisible threat outside the field of vision or by using diffuse visual backgrounds in which clearly defined shapes dissolve in dynamic metamorphoses. These aesthetic modalities are intuitively linked with feelings of fear. They play with the paradoxical pleasure that the threats represented in the film practically become embodied in the subjective perspective as one's own sense of fear – "I am helplessly at the mercy of impermeable natural forces!", "I am shattered by the superiority of weapons technology!" – but at the same time belong to a world that, in the visual space of a perception that has been internally split, is radically separated from that of

---

137 Cf. in more detail: Matthias Grotkopp and Hermann Kappelhoff, "Film Genre and Modality: The Incestuous Nature of Genre Exemplified by the War Film," in *In Praise of Cinematic Bastardy*, eds. Sebastien Léfait and Philippe Ortoli, Newcastle upon Tyne 2012, 29–39.
138 Gledhill, "Rethinking Genre," 223.

the spectator. Another expressive modality that regularly turns up in war films is aimed precisely at the opposite pole in the affect spectrum of genre cinema: the ecstasy of the medial transgression of space, time, bodies, and objects in the kinesthesia of montage and of the intensification of movement. Here, what is staged is the thrill, the pleasure of overcoming all physical limitations, and the phantasmatic suspending of the everyday in the presentation of the violence of exploding weapons or vehicles zipping through space. The pleasure in fear associated with the horror film and the energetic exceeding of ordinary perception in the phantasms of the action movie point to two opposing modes of aesthetic experience, the polar arrangement of which is a fundamental element of the affect poetics of the war film genre.

Something similar could be said about the melodramatic mode, which – as we have seen – has fundamentally structured the films of the genre.[139] The subjective sensation of a helpless suffering, which is articulated in the excessive expressivity on all levels of cinematic representation, designates the generic form from which numerous expressive modalities spring.[140] In the war film the subjective sensation of the soldier is articulated in the expressive modalities of melodrama: his deprivation, his agony.[141] The films stage his individual suffering as the sentimental interior perspective of an ego. Their opposing pole is found in the objective definition of this suffering as the sacrifice of the individual for the community. The expressive modalities associated with this cannot be attributed in any unambiguous way to a mode of film experience. Usually they are associated with the western. Here, like in the war film, the relation of the individual to the political community is grounded in a mythologizing recourse to historical events, to the talk of the birth and rebirth of the nation by overcoming injustice, violence, and the terror of war. The staging of commemorating the sacrifice here is aimed at a suffering, a pain that no longer belongs to any individual, but relates the individual in its affectivity to a feeling for the political community.[142]

In order to grasp and describe the dynamic of the constant ramifications and recombinations of the modes and modalities of genre cinema in their historical valence, we will have to construct the historical moment itself as an observatory level. This is the sense in which we understand the emergence of genre as an originary constellation in our research on the Hollywood war film. We have labeled the mobilization of the population for war, their moral fortification during the

---

139 Ibid., 227.
140 Cf. ibid. as well as Brooks, *The Melodramatic Imagination*, 204.
141 Cf. ibid. as well as Kappelhoff, *Matrix der Gefühle*.
142 Cf. Basinger, *The World War II Combat Film*, 239.

war, and the commemoration of the sacrifices after the war as the basic functional dimensions within this affect poetics, which initiate a fundamental transformation of the genre.

In the following I will attempt to develop and specify such an originary constellation in concrete studies in film analysis. At first, however, I would like to present the methodological tools that have allowed us to grasp the films of this genre structurally in their affect-dramaturgical construction, to compare them with one another, and to define them as genre in their historical-political dynamic.

In contemporary research, the war film genre of classical Hollywood cinema is described by a relatively manageable number of stereotypical constellations of plot and character.[143] The object of these standard scenes can on the one hand be assigned to relatively clearly distinguishable affect areas – the death scene corresponds to mourning, the battle scene to fear, heroic deeds imply figurations of rage; on the other hand, however, the scenes are characterized by compositional patterns that aim to affect the spectators without it being possible to assign them per se to any particular quality of affect. We will be speaking of such assignations as "pathos scenes."

It is no accident that the term "pathos scene" is reminiscent of Aby Warburg's term "pathos formula."[144] The link between affective effect and the establishment of forms and modalities of expression represents a common point of reference; the pathos scene differs from Warburg's concept, however, in that it does not bind the affective dimension to the historical sediment of aesthetic prototypes of the human sensation of affect, but in each case to the specific compositional execution of genre-poetic expressive modalities as affect-modeling audiovisual moving images.[145] The temporal assignment of pathos scenes shapes the macrostructure of the audiovisual rhythm, which we have used to define spectator feeling. When we speak of *affect dramaturgy*, we mean these arrangements.

The specific operational form of alternating and interweaving emotional values in each case – pugnacity, rage, fear, mourning – ultimately also designates the level referred to by the affective integration of the spectator into a commonly

---

[143] Cf. ibid. and Bronfen, *Specters of War*.
[144] Cf. Aby Warburg, "Dürer und die italienische Antike," in *Werke in einem Band*, eds. Martin Treml, et al., Berlin 2010, 176–184 as well as Aby Warburg, "Einleitung zum Mnemosyne-Atlas (1929)," in *Der Bilderatlas Mnemosyne. Gesammelte Schriften*, Vol. II 1.2, Berlin 2008, 3–6.
[145] When I named the shell-shocked face as a pathos formula in the introduction, this was exactly not to address it as the crystallization of an anthropological constant, but as a generic form on which the historically and culturally situated modalities of expression in a genre of poetic making are based.

shared feeling and a feeling for the communal. The staging of commemorating the sacrifice, the shared remembrance on the suffering, communal mourning, but also rage, is grounded on such operational forms of accentuated affect alteration and transformations, which only emerge in their temporal shaping over the course of the entire film as the experience of cinematic time. In the descriptive reconstructions of the affect-dramaturgical model and the expressive modulations of individual scenes, it can become tangible how a feeling for the communal emerges as a feeling of the spectator and comes into effect in social and political processes.

Pathos scenes: The affect-dramaturgical framework of the Hollywood war film

In a large number of comparative studies on Hollywood genre cinema we attempted to define the dramaturgy of the war film in eight categories, each representing a different type of such pathos scenes.[146] Other divisions could certainly also be named. We settled on these since they provided a useful tool for us to make a comparative analysis.

The division of pathos scenes allowed us to conceptualize the visual and representation units of war films as discrete modulating steps in the process of the audiovisual shaping of a continually unfolding sensation of perception, and to qualify them in terms of the rhetoric of affect. It was not in any way meant to define narrative stereotypes.

Instead, the goal of our research was to identify vertices that act as vectorial forces of affect in the process of film perception. This is why we tried to define clearly distinguishable pathos figurations that aim for a spectator feeling that unfolds over the duration of film perception. The basis for classification was formed by detailed descriptive film analyses in an extensive body of films, which can easily claim empirical validity.[147] As a result, an analytical instrument emerges that, on the one hand, made it possible to compare the affect-dramaturgical structure of a wide variety of audiovisual representations of war (that is, not only feature films and documentaries, but also television news reports, video clips, etc.);

---

[146] Cf. the research project "Affektmobilisierung und mediale Kriegsinszenierung": http://www.empirische-medienaesthetik.fu-berlin.de/affektmobilisierung/abgeschlossene projekte/projekt_affektmobilisierung/index.html (December 5, 2015) and especially the idea of pathos categories: http://www.empirische-medienaesthetik.fu-berlin.de/emaex-system/affektdatenmatrix/kategorien/index.html (December 5, 2015).
[147] On the methodological proceedings, cf. Kappelhoff, et al.: eMAEX: Ansätze und Potentiale.

on the other hand, on this basis it became possible to describe and compare the specific expressive modalities of individual scenes, which were worked out for the war film as particular dramatic spheres of conflict, and to qualify them in terms of affect poetics.

It was clear in all of this that, on the one hand, the scenes can be qualified in their affective dimension through the hybrid combinatorics of the modes of aesthetic experience in genre cinema (melodrama, horror, action, western), and on the other through the specific shaping of the expressivity of the film images (the micro level of expressive movement). The individual pathos scenes can therefore in no way be assigned to particular feelings, but instead designate a span of conflict, which can cover highly opposing affect values.

We summarized the pathos scenes in each case as opposing pairs in four fundamental dramatic spheres of conflict. Each could be assigned certain affect qualities, so that as a result we had at our disposal a complex descriptive system that remained dynamic within itself. This allowed us to conceive, describe, and compare widely divergent representations of war in audiovisual media as affect dramaturgies.

The following is a brief outline of the pathos scenes.

I. **The first sphere of conflict concerns the opposition between civilian and military community.**

   I. (1) *Transition between two social systems*: **the pain of parting / a sense of community**

   The pathos scenes shift our focus to the difference between the ordinary sociality of civilian life and that of the military community. They thematize the appearances of dissolution in society in the exceptional state of war, the disintegration of social ties, and the initiation into an archaic communal form. What we see is the appearances this dissolution takes, the transitions and the reconfiguration of all social relations. The stark opposition between civilian and military communal forms takes the foreground. The affects that emerge in this concern separation and the loss of trusted bonds. The main focus of this is the separation of men from women.

   From the point of view of films, the military community appears to find its original driving force in the strict division of the sexes. The scenes show how the prospective soldiers are separated from their wives, girlfriends, and families, sometimes elegiacally, sometimes skeptically, sometimes with a patriotic tinge. They show them becoming detached from all models of civilian relationships and inducted into the community of the military. What is emphasized in these scenes is exactly the "in between," the threshold phase after being detached from previous relationships and before being integrated into the new community. These pathos scenes gain their affective potential primarily from the staging of the collapse of forms of civilian communality, the agent of which is the heterosexual couple; to various degrees, aspects of initiation blend into a new communal form.

This allows separation anxiety (like in BATAAN or THEY WERE EXPANDABLE) to become the focus; but it can also foreground the pride in the community to which one will soon belong (like in GUNG HO!); it can be decisive for the newly won feelings of self-worth (GUNG HO! is also an example of this), but it can also emphasize abasement and submission (FROM HERE TO ETERNITY).

I. (2) *The formation of a group body (corps)*: **loss of the self (fear)/exaggerated self-esteem**

The final phase of the initiation process is the (re)integration into the army. Here the relationship of the individual to the military body is staged in all its variations. On the one hand, the way such scenes are presented emphasizes the individual corporeality that is explicitly distinguished from the uniformed body, which joins into the military corps and can merge into it. The staging of the individual body is in contrast to the innumerable rituals of transformation – from haircuts, getting a uniform and entering the barracks to military drills and the submission to a radical hierarchy of command – in which the individual soldiers become members of a functional chain of complex military operations that combine their bodily actions with technical procedures, allowing them to become seamlessly integrated. The individual bodies are converted into a group body of the military community, which is also staged as physically concrete. The merging is itself staged as a dramatic process, the outcome of which is pressure on the individual – for instance in configurations of physically pressing constriction – often in order to find its goal in geometrically emphasized figurations of the group body – for instance in the presentation of drills. The affective potential of these pathos scenes is based on the one hand on fear-oriented experiences of ego-loss, and on the other on pleasure-oriented experience of bodily consolidation, of belonging and participating in a communal body that overrides the limitations of the individual body.

II. **The second field of conflict concerns the primary actions of the military community, combat and battle.**
This field can also be described by means of two opposing pathos scenes. One of them stages the force of arms of battleships, airplanes, cannons, bombs, and guns in order euphorically to confirm the combat strength of the military corps in the modalities of action movies. The other focuses on staging nature as a metaphorical complex in which the intangible threat of the enemy can be expressed.

II. (1) *Battle and technology*: **feelings of (omni)potence/impotence**

The staging of arms technology is aimed at the experience of participating in an overpowering and invulnerable life of the military community. In the stunningly acted-out destructive work of the missiles, flame throwers, and grenades, the fantasy of unrestricted self-agency is realized. The basic audiovisual motif of the staging of such fantasies of grandeur is the explosion; it forms the stuff of highly dynamic expressive movements, in which the individual bodies meld with the troop, the landscape, the munitions, even with the enemy in ornamental moving images.

In the image of the triumphant melding of organic bodies with the devices and weapons of the war machine, of human and mechanical bodies into the physical unity of a combat unit, we can see the central phantasm and the fundamental affect of mobilization films at the time of the Second World War. The latter concerns both the battle sensation represented as well as the aesthetic sensation of the spectator. In the foreground is a specific enjoyment of the spectator, which we associate with the mode of aesthetic experience in action films – which we have already discussed.

The mode of experience that is featured here conveys to the spectator the illusion of a gaze that leaves behind all the temporal-spatial restrictions of the human body. The spectator can effortlessly traverse the spaces of perception and sensation in a filmed act of war without even getting a scratch. This shifts the focus to the special relationship between weapons technology and the media technology of the cinema. Action movies give us everything called for by modern weapons technology as an image space: a seeing and hearing that traverses spaces that can only be described in their dynamics by using mathematical formulas. The flip side of this sensation consists in scenes of individual bodies becoming overpowered by the violence of the weapons. The affective dimension of these scenes lies in the illusionary power of action movies, the illusion of the protagonist and of the spectator that the acts of war can be enjoyed as a cinematic image of the joy of triumphant melding. But the fantasy of omnipotence constantly threatens to turn over into an image of overpowering and helplessness in view of the violence of the weapons, exceeding all human measure.

II. (2) *Battle and nature*: **horror (fear)/enmity**

The violence of the enemy is indeed represented less in the destructive power of technical weapons than in the appearances of a demonic and hostile nature. Nature itself appears as a faceless enemy, who cannot be pinned down anywhere, and yet is present everywhere; in these scenes it is staged as a menacing force inherent to everything visible, but remaining invisible itself – up to the point at which it exposes its concealed shape in a deathly attack.

The impenetrable jungle, the encounter with oversized killing machines that move like fantastic primeval animals, the ground that separates beneath one's own feet: these are the manifestations of an uncanny life of matter, in which the platoon finds itself enclosed.

Nature becomes a hostile chaos, which undermines the perception and the orientation of the individual as well as the efforts of the corps to maintain the order that its ability to act is based on. This panic is met with endurance, the courage of desperation, and the aggressive self-assertion of the military sense of order.

The soldiers therefore often appear as battling against nature, which they try to subjugate or destroy. The decisive escalation of the chaotic power of nature is then its destruction by the force of weapons. Its explosive metamorphosis gives the threat a face of terror.

In the expressive modalities of the horror genre, the films put an experience of fear on display that attempts to attack the perception of spectators and protagonists alike in the moment of a sudden appearance of terror.[148] The acoustic space that encloses the soldiers as well as the audience is filled with noises and musical motifs that portend something menacing. A permanent frightened tension characterizes the fundamental affect of all pathos scenes in which nature is unfolded as a metaphoric complex of the faceless enemy.

Even the deep ambivalence itself is part of the horror; it is seen not least in the fact that the soldiers align themselves with nature for their

---

148 Elsaesser and Wedel have worked out the links between the genre modality of horror and the composition of the acoustic space in connection with the presentation of the jungle in APOCALYPSE NOW. Cf. Elsaesser and Wedel: "The Hollow Heart of Hollywood."

own protection and camouflage, to hide themselves in it and to be kept safe by it. On the other hand, precisely in this process of aligning human bodies and nature, all the threat of the uncanny finds its point of crystallization (in BATAAN this ambivalence became the dramatic motivation for the entire film staging): the fog from which the enemy bursts forth (THE THIN RED LINE), the tiger that suddenly lunges at the soldiers (APOCALYPSE NOW), the open grave that the soldiers lean over while the camera shows their faces from the perspective of the dead (THE STEEL HELMET) ... In these scenes nature also always appears as an enticement to give oneself over completely to the exhaustion of one's own body in order finally to finally become one with nature. Ultimately, the nature of the faceless enemy is staged as the consciousness of one's own mortality.

The melodramatic theme of all war films – the experience of being a vulnerable body that is coming to a sure death – becomes the representation of a paranoid perception of the world, realized in the visual spaces familiar from the horror genre: the uncanny uncertainty about what one is seeing or hearing; the fear of being abandoned; the panic over the amorphous chaos that threatens to swallow up everything.

III. **The third field of conflict concerns the sensitivity to one's own individual existence.**

Here the conflict targets the becoming-aware of one's own subjectivity and individual corporeality—as a process of disillusionment about the communal feeling of participating in the power of the military bond. The corresponding pathos scenes are thoroughly characterized by the expressive modalities of the melodramatic mode of experience. That is, the object of staging here is always subjective experience, the suffering of an individual protagonist.

III. (1) *Homeland, woman, home*: **feeling of comfort/pain of loss (homesickness)**

These pathos scenes focus on what is external to the military community, on the possibility of eventually leaving it and returning to the ties of civilian cohabitation. For one thing, this can be the actual discharge from the military community, the return to civilian life. Here the focus is on the burdensome memory of the experience of war and – often linked with this – the painful consciousness of having lost the ties to the community back home. What is presented much more frequently than a temporary or permanent discharge from the military order of war are encounters with women or the memories of such encounters. As a whole, these memories have a special status;

they are often marked by media references to social and cultural life before the war – for instance photographs or music on the radio. The affective potential is therefore also mostly qualified as a consoling or painful longing for community beyond the war, as a homesickness for the lost ordinariness of civilian life.

III. (2) *Suffering / victim / sacrifice*: **agony/grief**

Here the focus is on the experience of the soldier's bodily pain, vulnerability, and death. The euphoria of taking part in the military community follows the collapse into the powerlessness of physical existence, the abandonment of the individual, who becomes aware of a vulnerable, mortal body. The extreme expression for this powerlessness is the image of the soldier left on the battlefield, or in the jungle – the image of his abandonment staged in the expressive modalities of the melodrama.

In the melodrama of classical Hollywood cinema it is the woman who falls from the illusion of love into the consciousness of being abandoned; in the war film it is the soldier, broken by the illusion of an omnipotent masculinity. The spectator, who had just taken part in the illusion of a perceiving body that no force of arms can harm, is now placed into relation to the collapse of a disillusioned consciousness, which is experienced in its physical existence as threatened, abandoned, vulnerable, and mortal.

The staging of suffering appears in three variations: as a victim, as a sacrifice, and as a scene of suffering. In the image of the victim the sudden consciousness of radical contingency takes the foreground, which is usually realized in the staging of an unmediated moment of death. In the sacrifice, the death of the soldier is charged with a higher meaning, usually tied to the ideal of the army and the nation. The sacrificial death becomes a heroic death; often by linking death or burial with the idea of the renewal of the community. In the center of these pathos scenes is a staging of the subjective experience of the suffering soldier; the interior view of an irresolvable, irreconcilable experience of suffering marks the pathos of the Hollywood war film as a whole.

IV. **The fourth field of conflict concerns the renewal of civilian society beyond military communitization, the shared memory of war, but also the moral critique of warfare and the military.**

IV. (1) *Injustice and humiliation/moral self-assertion*: **rage/feelings of guilt**

The successive unfolding of a film image, which is equally the melodramatic representation of suffering and the pathos form of commemorating the sacrifice, designates the driving principle of the dramaturgy of the Hollywood war film during and immediately after the Second World War.

But very soon characters are already turning up that expand the affect-dramaturgical scope by a renewed disillusion: the indignation of the soldier who experiences even the commemoration of the sacrifice and the forms of military community as deception, abasement, or betrayal, and who therefore snaps or runs amok when he returns home. The soldier's return to a morally evaluating ego-position is seen in the reaction to the injustice and abasement experienced within military structures, either as a figuration of rage or of a sense of guilt. The way these figurations are presented makes it possible to grasp a specific sensitivity that articulates an individual, subjective ego-experience as a moralistic relationship to the social forms of the military and the nation. The affective dimension of these pathos scenes is on the one hand rage turning over from a moral judgment into the pleasure of the corporeal, which comes to a head in furor, rebellion, and the explosive rage of the one going berserk. On the other hand, it is the sense of guilt as a consequence for one's joint responsibility for the suffering inflicted, in which collective identity and group membership is emphasized. The return to an independent, individual self-assertion is also characterized by the defiant or accusatory exit from the military social form.

IV. (2) *Sense of community as a shared filmic remembrance of shared suffering: sense of community*

In these scenes there is a direct reference to the feeling for the collective history of the spectators, in which the films explicitly refer to the film images of war and the memory of these images.

At first glance these pathos scenes are merely defined by the use of documentary material in fiction films. This can include widely familiar film material from newsreels and combat reports, images of the aftermath of battle, the wounded and the dead, but also the rituals of drilling, of ordinary military life. The documentary or testifying character of the film images – we will be able to trace this by analyzing WITH THE MARINES AT TARAWA – creates a specific affective relation between film and spectator. In the memory of the news images during the war years, the corresponding scenes relate the fictional film to a present, shared memory of a past experience of suffering, in which the basis for a new communal feeling is sought out.

The documentary material that is edited in breaks through the horizon of the fictional world of the film and becomes an appeal to the spectator's memory. But these scenes do not simply hold up a mode of facticity or authenticity to fiction. Instead they create a reference of the staged events to these documentary images, which in turn become charged with fictionality. Oftentimes the fictional characters themselves are staged as spectators or witnesses. In their behavior and their reactions, they provide a kind of frame for the inconceivable aspects of the film images of war, bestowing them, at the level of sentimental memories, with a terror and fear that are no longer real.

Genre history and history

We have identified pathos scenes as a generic form of the affect poetics of the Hollywood war film. They can be described and compared in their temporal arrangement in individual films as a specific dramaturgy of affect in each case. The war film sets up a course of affects that the spectators run through, from initiation and melding into a community through the intoxicating sense of omnipotence, horror, and fear on to suffering and wrath. This creates a film image on which something as abstract as a political community can be made concrete as a field of references for individual feelings.

Indeed, the individual scenes can in no way be attributed to distinct affects; but they can easily be described in their compositional patterns as audiovisual expressive movements, to which one can attribute certain modes of genre. Essentially, this applies to the western, the melodrama, the action movie, and the horror film. Each of these genres marks a specific affect domain and the expressive modalities and staging strategies associated with it.

The initiation of the military community is attributed to the affect area of pleasure in the state of exception, the anarchist negation of social ties, but also the oppressive fear of ego-loss; it includes the pride in belonging and the euphoric lust for battle as well as the abasement of the subjugated. The expressive modalities can be grouped around the ways male physical strength is presented, which are familiar from the western, the adventure movie, and the athletic film. In their expressive modalities, the battle scenes defined by weapons technology vary the affective tension of the action mode – between the thrill of the omnipotent power of destruction and the powerlessness in the face of the destructive powers of technology. The representation of nature as an invisible enemy and an impalpable threat borrows its expressive modalities from the subjectifying figurations of fear from the horror genre. While the experience of suffering in the monopathic expressive modalities of sentimental melodrama are brought to figure, the staging of mourning and the transformation of the image of suffering link the melodramatic mode in a figuration of sacrifice with expressive modalities that belong to the western.

On the basis of this immanent field of reference of Hollywood genre cinema, the pathos scenes can be described in their concrete expressive modalities and audiovisually-shaped, temporal dynamics and qualified as modulation of spectator emotion. Based on such film analyses it should therefore be possible to explain how the cultural phantasms of war and the knowledge of historical acts of war can be linked through media to the affectivity of spectators in order to become a kind of a priori object[149] of a sense of commonality as a film image. For films can only become a medium for participating in a feeling for the communal when this feeling occurs as a physical "I sense." But such an "I sense" is not identical with the emotional reaction of spectators, nor it is represented in the film's characters. It is the affective basis of the film's visual space itself, a split feeling for the world, which allows the visual space of war films to emerge from the interaffectivity of cinematic movement image and affected perceiving bodies. But then the affect-poetic description model can serve to reconstruct the historical ramifications of film formats and expressive modalities, genre, and generic modes themselves as a history of the sense of commonality.

Using the methodological model sketched out here, the war film genre can be worked out in its historical development using concrete examples of mutually-related, "family-like" films.[150] The dramaturgical framework of the pathos scenes forms the layer of a two-fold inscription of concrete historical-social constellations. On the one hand, by comparing the pathos scenes, their accumulation and arrangement, as well as the concrete ways they are staged, it is possible to describe the transformations of the genre; on the other hand, the various historical-political constellations can be seen in these transformations. The films made during the war, for instance, emphasize the complex of initiation and the military community, the films made immediately after the war are aimed at the apotheosis of the figurations of mourning and sacrifice, the films of the fifties emphasize the moral indignation, the unresolved conflict.

Speaking schematically, the war film genre can be represented as a permanent reconfiguration of the modes of aesthetic experience and the expressive

---

[149] On the term "a priori object of feeling," cf. Hermann Kappelhoff, "Apriorische Gegenstände des Gefühls: Recherchen zur Bildtheorie des Films," in *Bildtheorie und Film*, eds. Thomas Koebner, et al., Munich 2006, 404–421.

[150] On the term "cycle," cf. Cavell, *The World Viewed*, 29ff.; on family likeness, cf. Stanley Cavell, *Pursuits of Happiness: The Hollywood Comedy of Remarriage*, Cambridge 1997, 29.

modalities of Hollywood cinema. It is obvious that terms like citation, hybridizing, and self-referentiality are inadequate if we are trying to grasp the reconfigurations of the generic modes of Hollywood cinema in such a historical perspective. Indeed, this would mean taking what is basically the norm as a significant exception. For genre systems – and we are discussing the question based on Cavell's theoretical proposal – always have to be conceived as a continual process of historically reconfiguring their modes and modalities of aesthetic experience.

One might, following the thesis that I raised in the first part of this book for the films around the turn of the millennium, understand this reconfiguration itself as a response of Hollywood cinema to a historical crisis of the feeling for community in American society. It can be linked as much to the question of the entry into war and the heavy losses in the war in the Pacific as to the sacrifices and aftereffects of a victorious military campaign. If the mobilization films are to be understood as a response to the question of how national-political and military interests can be linked to the affective attitudes of individuals, one can propose that later films seek to answer the question of how the pathos of the sacrifice must be understood when the community that this sacrifice is made for is defined by an ethos granting unqualified primacy to the happiness of the individual.

In this sense, the "emergence of the genre" itself is still a theoretical construct. With this construct, a level of projection is meant to be inserted into the dynamic of the history of poetic making, a level at which fundamental aspects of this dynamic – in this case the historical transformations of the Hollywood genre system – can be reconstructed. This does nothing to alter the condition that we cannot conceive of this dynamic as having been brought to rest at any point. It is an originary construction.[151] It attempts to sketch out lines from a history of political thought that cannot be separated from the history of poetic making, which – without any definable beginning, direction, or goal – continues on in ever new ramifications.

Following this, the history of Hollywood genre cinema can be represented as ramifications and differentiations of various modes of film experience in which different realms of experiencing a shared reality are proposed, tested, and recalibrated. Seen as a whole, genres per se are nothing other than specific arrangements of a wide variety of modes of experience and modalities of expression,

---

151 Here I am following a methodological model that Theo Girshausen developed for the history of theories of tragedy. Theo Girshausen, *Ursprungszeiten des Theaters: Das Theater der Antike*, Berlin 1999.

which should always be understood as reconfigurations, that is, as shifts and breaks in the established media forms of poetic making.[152]

From this perspective, the history of cinema as a whole means the interplay of a wide variety of media formats, arts, and modes of experiencing the filmic; it means the dynamic interactions between the poetics of a wide variety of *téchne* of film communication, its genres and subgenres. Nowhere can such an interplay be observed better than in 1940s American cinema.

When Hollywood's most successful directors (Ford, Capra, Wyler) put their services at the disposal of the government, the army, or the secret service at the time, this was done to mobilize a population that was anything but excited about entering the war. Indeed, in the summer of 1939, still 95% of US citizens were of the opinion that the best thing would be for the USA to stay out of the war.[153] Hollywood's leading forces, who were able to move an audience of millions with their works, applied their tried and tested abilities to change the mood in the country fundamentally. Hollywood literally entered into the propaganda offensive with its entire know-how about spectator feeling. The new genre came out of a media offensive with which a country was meant to be moved from resisting the war to entering it.

We should not lose sight of the fact that this process was carried out at all levels of genre-poetic differentiations. In the cinema the media technology of film was developed into the dominant media practice of the war years; it unfolded in different speaking positions: those of documentary, newsreel, educational films, and of course the fictional entertainment movie. Each of these media formats rests on a number of different affective modalities of expression, which in turn point back to the history of cinema from the twenties and thirties. The media practice that emerged in this way was structured by a basic conflict between the demands of militarized collectivization and the tradition of a liberal democratic polity. Ultimately, it formed modes of aesthetic enjoyment marking the new genre in its specific pathos and placing it into relation with other modes of aesthetic experience: be they those of genre cinema or those of western entertainment culture.

The reconstruction of the emergence of the Hollywood war film should therefore convey an idea of the dynamic of poetic making in its relation to political thought.

---

152 In exactly the sense that Gledhill describes the dynamic of modalities: "The notion of modality, like register in socio-linguistics, defines a specific mode of aesthetic articulation adaptable across a range of genres, across decades, and across national cultures. It provides the genre system with a mechanism of 'double articulation', capable of generating specific and distinctively different generic formulae in particular historical conjunctures, while also providing a medium of interchange and overlap between genres." Gledhill, "Rethinking Genre," 229.
153 William P. Hansen, et al., (eds.), *The Gallup Poll. Public Opinion 1935–1971*, Volume 1, 1935–1948, New York 1972.

3 The Emergence of the War Film Genre: A Construction of its Poetological Origins

3.1 Genre and Film Document

When the bow doors of the Allied landing boats opened on the coast in northern France on June 6, 1944, it was not just thousands of soldiers that were discharged into the battle over Normandy. The doors also released small 35 mm cameras, which had been installed on the boats, and which were turned on when the doors opened by an automatic mechanism.[1] A total of 400 cameramen took part in the invasion, meant to document the event with photographs and film.[2] The person in charge of the footage at Omaha Beach was Hollywood director John Ford, who was active as Chief of the Field of the OSS Photographic Branch, and who had a whole staff of cameraman at almost all fronts of the Second World War to gather military intelligence.[3]

Found footage

The material generated at Omaha Beach then disappeared into the secret archives of the US military, where it remained for 54 years. While the coming decades saw no end to the debates about the authenticity of representations of war on film, these film images, which were hardly to be outdone in terms of authenticity as it is commonly conceived, were hidden in basements in secret archives.[4] The fact

---

[1] In his biography of John Ford, Andrew Sinclair speaks of 500 cameras attached to the landing boats, which each shot four minutes of the invasion by means of an automatic triggering device. Cf. Andrew Sinclair, "John Ford's War," in *Sight and Sound* 48 (2), 1979, 99–104, here 102. Over the course of his research, however, Thomas Doherty came to the conclusion that it must have been more like 50 cameras, of which 47 were destroyed. He also assumes that the cameras on the landing boats were manually started. Cf. Thomas Doherty, *Projections of War: Hollywood, American Culture, and World War II*, New York 1993, 242.
[2] Cf. ibid., 242.
[3] Cf. Sinclair, "John Ford's War," 102.
[4] The historian Douglas Brinkley traces the lengthy research work that eventually led to the fact that the film material, mostly shot in color, was only found in 1997/98 in the National Archives in College Park. Cf. Douglas Brinkley, "The Color of War: John Ford stormed to the Beach at Normandy on D-Day, armed with Full-Color Film. What happened to the Footage he shot?" in *New Yorker* 74 (20), 1998, 34–36, here 35f. Brinkley, who took part in the preservation of the film

Figure 9: John Ford's D-Day.

that the film images were the work of a master of genre cinema is only one of the points in the history of the fate of this film material (see Figure 9).

When looking at the images for the first time, what is surprising is their melancholy mood. There is a tendency to link their elegiac effect with the soldiers' faces. They strike the viewer in a way that always seems to be bound to an aspect of the photographic image that comes up all too often. Roland Barthes, for instance, analyzed this effect in *Camera Lucida* as the specific diegetic gesture of photography: the mode of "that-has-been."[5] Undoubtedly, those men were part

---

material as director of the Eisenhower Center at the University of New Orleans, concedes that the entirety of the material could not be found.

5 "I call "photographic referent" not the *optionally* real thing to which an image or a sign refers but the *necessarily* real thing which has been placed before the lens, without which there would be no photograph. Painting can feign reality without having seen it. Discourse combines signs which have no referents, of course, but these referents can be and are most often "chimeras." Contrary to these imitations, in Photography I can never deny that *the thing has been there*. There is a superimposition here: of reality and of the past. And since this constraint exists only for Photography, we must consider it, by reduction, as the very essence, the *noeme* of Photography. What I intentionalize in a photograph (we are not jet speaking of film) is neither Art nor Communication, it is Reference, which is the founding order of Photography. The name

of the largest military operation of the Second World War. Undoubtedly, they got into the boats in just this way; undoubtedly, they saw the movement of these clouds, this sky, the blue of this sea.

In fact, it is this particular blue that we mostly find ourselves moved by. But the soldiers themselves never saw just this blue. For it can be traced back to the special color technology of the film material. Peculiarly, it might move us because it results from a color film technology that we are not very familiar with. Even American moviegoers were only able to experience this elegiac tone of the color in these film images for a short time. For this exact color process was rarely used in entertainment movies.[6]

The film material from the archives, however, was only seen in the cinema briefly, and then only in part. In February 1945, advertisements announced the film BEACHHEAD TO BERLIN (1944) as part of the movie program. The film, produced by the Navy, was twenty-one minutes long and contained the majority of the color material that has by now become familiar. After this indication of its screening, the film was considered lost for a very long time.

"The Color of War" was the name of the article in which Douglas Brinkley disclosed the spectacular findings in the *New Yorker* in 1998. He reported on the lengthy archival research and the lost material. His article suddenly makes clear how much and how enduringly film images influence the memory of such events that are considered part of the fateful hours of the nation: "Most Americans today think that the Second World War happened in black-and-white. That's how it was filmed for newsreels and government archives,"[7] reads the article's first

---

of Photography's *noeme* will therefore be: "That-has-been," or again: the Intractable." Roland Barthes, *Camera Lucida*, New York 1981, 76f.

[6] The pigment content of the three base colors on the Kodachrome color film of the original footage (single strip) was developed in the lab on three separate film strips and then copied for the 35mm used for the cinema. The patented process was carried out by the firm Technicolor. The colors that resulted from this had a similar effect to those of the three-strip Technicolor process in which footage was shot on three separate 35mm films. This caused the base colors red, blue, and green to be perceived especially intensively. This process was not commonly used for documentary purposes until the entry of the USA into the Second World War, since previously (and also afterwards as well) black-and-white material was usually used for footage of current events. To this point, moviegoers were familiar with this color scheme primarily from "escapist" productions, in which the excessive effect of the three strip Technicolor process was considered abstract and as a special attraction; for instance THE ADVENTURES OF ROBIN HOOD (1938), GONE WITH THE WIND (1939) and various animation films by Disney from the 1930s and 1940s. Cf. Cf. Thomas Doherty, "Documenting the 1940s," in *Boom and Bust: The American Cinema in the 1940s*, ed. Thomas Schatz, Berkeley/Los Angeles 1997, 397–421, here 411.
[7] Brinkley, "The Color of War," 34.

sentences. In fact, they bear witness to something that is easy to formulate theoretically, but that goes decisively against our ordinary understanding: namely, the fact that even personal memories are marked by media configurations in which we secure for ourselves our commonly shared world.

What becomes clear in the report, however, is how closely the fate of these film images is bound to the history of Hollywood genre cinema. We can assume that, were it not for the speculation that we might find documentary images in the secret archives that had come from the hand of one of America's most famous directors, the lost material might never have become the occasion for such meticulous research. At any rate, the findings in this article were announced with the headline: "John Ford stormed the beach at Normandy on D-Day, armed with full-color film. What happened to the footage he shot?"[8]

At least equally significant, however, is the circumstance that another famous director had dealt with this material:

> As soon as Paisley had the surviving reels in hand (some are still missing), he was eager for someone to produce a full-color documentary – an epic, he hoped, not unlike the one that Ford had hoped to make. He is now in the process of donating a copy of the film to the Eisenhower Center at the University of New Orleans, of which I am the director. The center, which is the home of the largest oral history of Second World War veterans, is now working with the director Steven Spielberg and others to preserve the color film. (Spielberg's own Second World War epic, *Saving Private Ryan*, is set for release this month.)[9]

This identifies another point that influences the fate of the film images from D-Day: namely, the circumstances under which the film material came to light for the public the second time. In this case, it is a public that is not at all comparable to that other moviegoing publics during the war years. Indeed, this public is made up of spectators of movies from the American entertainment industry from the end of the last century, an industry with global operations. Spielberg even used the found film material as a significant reference in one of the biggest blockbuster successes of the end of the century. The famous opening sequence in SAVING PRIVATE RYAN (1998) is in fact created from completely fictional footage. But it is staged – I spoke about this in the first part of this book – to give the impression of a reenactment; the fictional recreation then also does not so much concern the invasion of Normandy itself as it does the work of documenting it on film. What is recreated is the work of shooting the film footage on D-Day.

---

8 Ibid.
9 Ibid., 36.

Ostensibly such a staging concept itself might be aimed at reaching the highest possible level of authenticity. The impression of being a filmed document gives the fictional film an aura of certified witness. This is why, in reviews and academic articles, there is no end to claiming that no film could be more realistic than the landing sequence at the beginning of SAVING PRIVATE RYAN.[10] Even the accusation of it being a falsifying representation of war, because it is trivialized by genre conventions, ultimately refers to the same effect.[11]

But anyone who knows the original footage from D-Day from the programming loops of the history channels on television networks knows that the landing sequence from SAVING PRIVATE RYAN does not at all attempt to recreate the found footage material. The blue has become an artfully prepared greyish blue, and we imagine that we can see it fading. And while on television we never get to see much of the battles of the landing in Normandy, Spielberg presents us with an effect-laden perceptual spectacle that presents to us what might have been visible using the possibilities of modern cinema technology, if fifty cameras with today's film technology had been thrown into the battle. The focus – as I have already described in detail – is to stage being-in-the-thick-of-it, being-there.[12] The montage sequences do not simply mimic the unretouched technical reproduction of what the cameras recorded. Instead, they delegate what the cameras recorded to a sentient and thinking body, to that body's perceiving gaze. This is why these images have become much more widely accepted in their historical reference than the original footage has, footage that got incomparably less attention when it was presented publicly.[13]

Only in the opening sequence of Spielberg's blockbuster does the production of the cameras at Omaha Beach on June 6, 1944 become a historical event for a global audience: in the experiential space of genre cinema. In this respect,

---

10 Neal Ascherson, "Missing in Action," in *The Observer*, September 6, 1998, 7; and Toby Haggith, "D-Day Filming for Real: A Comparison of 'Truth' and 'Reality' in *Saving Private Ryan* and Combat Film by the British Army's Film and Photographic Unit," in *Film History* 14, 2002, 332–353.
11 Hermann Kappelhoff, "Sense of Community: Die filmische Komposition eines moralischen Gefühls," in *Repräsentationen des Krieges: Emotionalisierungsstrategien in der Literatur und in den audiovisuellen Medien vom 18. bis zum 21. Jahrhundert*, eds. Søren R. Fauth, et al., Göttingen 2012, 43–57.
12 Cf. also Thomas Elsaesser: "*Saving Private Ryan*: Retrospektion, Überlebensschuld und affektives Gedächtnis," in *Mobilisierung der Sinne: Der Hollywood-Kriegsfilm zwischen Genrekino und Historie*, eds. Hermann Kappelhoff, et al., Berlin 2013, 61–87.
13 Footage that was shot over the course of the invasion, but which does not show the actual storming of the beaches, can be found in the British TV series THE SECOND WORLD WAR IN COLOUR (1999). More material can be found in THE PERILOUS FIGHT: AMERICA'S WORLD WAR II IN COLOR (2003), Episode: WRATH – D-DAY-V-E-DAY, and above all in D-DAY IN COLOUR (2004).

SAVING PRIVATE RYAN is no different than a possible re-release of the film BEACH-HEAD TO BERLIN (1944). Both films allow for a world to emerge in the seeing and hearing of the spectator that belongs to an absolute past. Only that in one case it happens in the fiction of a highly successful blockbuster, and in the other in the mode of a film-historical retrospective. One is about the concrete attempt to relate a contemporary audience to a common history. The other would be an appeal to undertake such an attempt.

With the opening sequence of SAVING PRIVATE RYAN the fate of the filmed war document, its production, its being forgotten, and its rediscovery becomes an object of reflection through the possibility of experiencing history in film images. The numerous essays, academic treatments, and critiques that have appeared on this subject since the end of the nineties are a significant testimony to this.[14] Spielberg thus restored the documentary film material quite literally to a form of reception that is of great significance for the reflection to follow here. In the experiential space of the blockbuster movie, the found film images become a globally shared sensation of history.[15] In this space one of the most fundamental possibilities of the media technology of film is staged as an experiential mode of a present-time being-there. The film images of the historical event become a perceptual event in the present of a global audience; they become the aesthetic experience of an audience that senses these images as both physical sensation of the self and

---

14 On SAVING PRIVATE RYAN: Auster, "'Saving Private Ryan' and American Triumphalism"; Robin Curtis: "Embedded Images: Der Kriegsfilm als Viszerale Erfahrung," in *Nach dem Film* 7 ["Kamera-Kriege"], 2005, http://www.nachdemfilm.de/content/embedded-images (July 24, 2015); Jan Distelmeyer, "Transparente Zeichen: Hollywood, Vietnam, Krieg," in *Nach dem Film* 7 ["Kamera-Kriege"], 2005, http://www.nachdemfilm.de/content/transparente-zeichen, (24. Juli 2015); Catherine Gunther Kodat, "Saving Private Property: Steven Spielberg´s American Dream-Works," in *Representations* 71, 2000, 77–105; Paul Hammond, "Some Smothering Dreams: The Combat Film in Contemporary Hollywood," in *Genre and Contemporary Hollywood*, ed. Steve Neale, London 2002, 62–79; Hermann Kappelhoff, "Shell shocked face: Einige Überlegungen zur rituellen Funktion des US-amerikanischen Kriegsfilms," in *Nach dem Film* 7 ["Kamera-Kriege"], 2005, http://www.nachdemfilm.de/content/shell-shocked-face, (July 24, 2017); Polan, "Auteurism and War-teurism"; Robnik, *Kino, Krieg, Gedächtnis*; Georg Seeßlen, *Steven Spielberg und seine Filme*, Marburg 2001, 148, 150.

On Eastwood: Braudy, "Flags of Our Fathers / Letters from Iwo Jima"; Tania Modleski, "Clint Eastwood and Male Weepies," in *American Literary History* 22 (1), 2010, 136–158; Rikke Schubart and Anne Gjelsvik (eds.), *Eastwood's Iwo Jima: Critical Engagement With Flags of Our Fathers and Letters From Iwo Jima*, New York 2013; Robert Burgoyne, "Generational Memory and Affect in Letters from Iwo Jima," in *A Companion to the Historical Film*, eds. Robert A. Rosenstone and Constantin Parvulescu, Malden 2013, 349–364.

15 Robert Burgoyne, *Film Nation: Hollywood Looks at U.S. History*, Minneapolis 2010.

as the sensorial world of an utterly different subject, of an ego that is absolutely separated from them in time and space.¹⁶

One might take the enjoyment of such an audience for a symptom and understand the entertainment value of history in the blockbuster movie as expressing a culture, a history that has become a kind of drug in the aesthetic sensation of media presentations as a way to help us get over the loss of authentic experience. The experience of the war film becomes a prosthesis for a society that can only still relate to the semblance of its own history, and thus to itself as a political community.¹⁷ But such a thesis presumes that authentically experiencing history might be carried out in some other possible way than as a poetic construction of a common world in which a society seeks to understand itself as a present between yesterday and tomorrow. If we do not wish to follow this notion, we would have to concede that historical experience is always also a question of aesthetic experience. The particularity is merely covered up by the strong perspective taken in each specific case. This is what Rorty means when he says that every construction of a common world is inevitably ethnocentric.

But then we would have to correct the claim cited above that the Second World War entered the memory of the American population in black-and-white, because newsreels and documentaries of the war first became visible in this way. In the "today" of a community, the color of yesterday as the history of the political community is always being decided anew. Even the simple fact that many color documentaries of the events of the war were shown quite successfully in American cinemas during wartime demonstrates that the black-and-white war was a decision made in the media aesthetics of the present, which perceived black-and-white as more realistic than color footage.

How little the atmospheric coloring is determined by the mere existence of real visual documents might be clarified by the fact that two of the three films that I will present in the following – because they are considered extremely prominent examples of the documentary presentation of combat action during the Second World War – are shown in a blue similar to that from BEACHHEAD TO BERLIN, a blue that affects the viewer even more oddly when he or she encounters the film images of Omaha Beach as electronic color signals on television or laptop monitors.

---

16 Cf. Sobchack, *The Address of the Eye*; Robnik, *Kino, Krieg, Gedächtnis*; Kappelhoff and Bakels, "Das Zuschauergefühl".
17 Robnik, *Kino, Krieg, Gedächtnis*, 333ff. In this use of the term "political community," Robnik is referring to Rancière.

There is therefore authentic found footage from D-Day, the production of which was organized by one of the leading directors in Hollywood, and there is fictional material that a no less leading director circulated by restaging the production of film material as a grand movie spectacle.

In the fate of these film images, the creation, their disappearance and rediscovery, their reconstructions and restagings, we can note the media's intersections of collective perceiving and feeling. Thus, a temporality of feeling and perceiving can be described that can neither be traced back to individual memories nor to the facticity of historical events. Rather, the history of the film footage of D-Day teaches us that even the undirected production of cinematic images, because it is not explicitly edited and addressed, can facilitate the emergence of virtual perceptual events that are realized in the sensing, feeling, and thinking of bodies which belong to completely different time/space configurations than does the production of the footage itself – unrelated to the question of whether this footage was at all directed to any perceiving body (and if so, to which body). In the contingent bifurcations of film images, history can be described as a history of forms of perception and modes of sensation, which allow the basis of a commonly shared sensed reality, a communal world, to emerge in the first place.

Between installing cameras on the bow doors of the landing boats at Omaha Beach and Spielberg's reenactment of this event in the experiential space of the contemporary blockbuster movie lies the history of the Hollywood war film genre. Looking at the history of this genre we should be able to clarify the question of how the film documents of war relate to the historical self-perception of a community; and how the cinema of the last century played its part in the formation of such collective self-perceptions and self-imaginings. What forms of collectivity are associated with this? And how do they relate to the history of a century that was defined by the horrors of totalitarian forms of political community as much as it was by the experience of total war?

The experiential space of war films

Initially, one can refer back to the very well documented facts of production economy and history to trace the development of the Hollywood war film. One can show how the genre evolved in the interplay of war documentation and propaganda, from the commissioned works of the Hollywood studios and from the hiring of a number of renowned directors whose abilities were put to the service of government offices and military institutions.[18] The historical research over

---

18 Cf. Doherty, *Projections of War*.

the last few decades has compiled innumerable details about the collaboration between the entertainment industry and state institutions, military and publicity agents, cultural-sociological think tanks, administrative steering committees, and Hollywood's artistic personnel.[19] With the outbreak of the Second World War all available knowledge was sought out to mobilize the possibilities of mass media communication. It was no accident that Hollywood took on a key position in this alliance of media and politics. No other social, economic, or political institution had any comparable knowledge at their disposal to organize the affects, thoughts, and ways that modern mass society perceived by means of media. It was the poetological knowledge about the possibilities of entertainment cinema to take up affects in their collective appearances and to model them as individual feelings that provided the hope for concrete directions in making successful propaganda.

When the question was how a democratic community could be reshaped into a war society, this presumably followed ideas about cinema's effect on the masses very similar to those of the film avant-gardes in Europe during the twenties and early thirties. It was no accident that among the experts activated in this context were theorists like Kracauer and Bernays,[20] who were quite familiar with the aesthetic theories of the avant-gardes and film avant-gardes.

---

[19] Cf. David Culbert (ed.), *Film and Propaganda in America: A Documentary History, Volume II, World War II Part 1*, New York/Westport/London 1990; David Culbert (ed.), *Film and Propaganda in America: A Documentary History, Volume III, World War II Part 2*, New York/Westport/London 1990; David Gaertner, "Mit allen Mitteln: Hollywoods Propagandafilme am Beispiel von Frank Capras Why We Fight-Reihe," in *Mobilisierung der Sinne: Der Hollywood-Kriegsfilm zwischen Genrekino und Historie*, eds. Hermann Kappelhoff, et al., Berlin 2013, 307–344; Brett Gary, *The Nervous Liberals: Propaganda Anxieties from World War I to the Cold War*, New York 1999; Brett Gary, "Communication Research, the Rockefeller Foundation, and Mobilization for the War on Words, 1938–1944," in *Journal of Communication* 46 (3), 1996, 124–148; Claudia Schreiner-Seip, *Film- und Informationspolitik als Mittel der Nationalen Verteidigung in den USA, 1939–1941*, Frankfurt am Main/Bern/New York 1985; J. Michael Sproule, *Propaganda and Democracy: The American Experience of Media and Mass Persuasion*, Cambridge, UK 1997.

[20] This list could also be extended to include the writer Archibald MacLeish, who directed the Defense Ministry's Office of Facts and Figures and the Library of Congress during the war, the political scientist and propaganda theorist Harold D. Lasswell, the sociologist Paul Lazarsfeld, and the pollster Hadley Cantril. Of those named here, Lasswell must certainly have been familiar with the theories of the avant-garde, since he had thoroughly absorbed Walter Lippmann, who, in his work *Public Opinion* (1922) – which Dewey criticized – made a contribution to the theory of masses in the communication age that was as significant as it was controversial. Bernays also often referred to Lippmann in his publications. Cf. David Gaertner, *Tickets to War: Propaganda,*

The genre films produced before 1940 by Capra, Ford, Wyler, and others testify to the idea that cinema provides the possibility of creating forms of political community.[21] In this regard, the concepts of genre and poetics among Hollywood directors are no different than the poetic proposals of Vertov or Eisenstein, to name two of the protagonists of the European avant-garde. Only that in contrast to them, the positions in Hollywood were hardly ever formulated programmatically. As a general rule, the poetology of genre cinema is implicit as the form in which poetic making appears. It was as inherent to the operations of studio production as it was to the routines of individual producers and production teams, the technologies of staging, composing, narrating, acting, photographing, designing sets, and lighting, as it was to the capabilities of aligning these diverse technologies to one another, so that in the end films emerged that could affect a highly heterogeneous audience in the same targeted way.

As I have already mentioned, within media history all of this is well-worn terrain.[22] For this reason I will limit myself to emphasizing a few aspects that are of strategic significance to the arguments here.

The production of films significant for the emerging war film genre can be roughly subdivided into four groups. The first of these are the training and educational films for the soldiers.[23] Their production became more and more professional as the need increased. For instance, John Ford produced a training film about sexual hygiene in 1942 on the Fox studio lot (SEX HYGIENE).

The second category is the "newsreels" that the film industry produced in a wide variety of forms. They represented one of the most significant informational media during the war years, which could always be sure of finding great public interest. Their production was itself a fixed component of the military mission. The documentary film and photo material was produced by the cinematographers of the US Army Signal Corps or the Navy Photographic Unit. If civilian cinematographers were involved in these productions, they were also subordinate to military regulations. The material always had to be cleared by the war ministry's censorship office. In the programming loops at cinemas, even the most banal entertainment movies were embedded in film images that reminded the spectators of an omnipresent war.

Kino und Mobilisierung in den USA von 1939–1945, dissertation manuscript, Freie Universität Berlin, unpublished.
21 Cf. Capra, *The Name Above the Title*.
22 Cf. Doherty, *Projections of War*.
23 The vice president of Twentieth Century Fox, Darryl F. Zanuck, was responsible for distributing commissions to the film studios at the same time in his function at the Army Pictorial Service.

Thirdly, there are the informational and documentary films, the "orientation films" and "combat reports." It was above all in this genre that those directors who had most decisively influenced Hollywood filmmaking at the time produced films which then became the starting point for a new genre cycle. The four most important names to mention here are: Frank Capra, a major in the Signal Corps at the time. He not only made the seven-part series WHY WE FIGHT[24] (USA 1943–1945), the first part of which, PRELUDE TO WAR, I have already dealt with extensively, but also produced the film TUNISIAN VICTORY (USA 1943). George Stevens, also in the service of the US Army Signal Corps. He led a unit of "combat photographers" that accompanied the Allied troops from Normandy to Paris. William Wyler, who initially joined the Signal Corps as a civilian. He became involved in the information film THE NEGRO SOLDIER (USA 1944). The film – in analogy to the WHY WE FIGHT project – stood under the central question: "Why it was also a black man's war." The project failed, clearly due to everyday racism, which Wyler's team encountered during shooting and which – following the wishes of the commissioning body – was not allowed to be addressed in the film.[25] Later, after having been sworn in as a major in the US Air Force, Wyler put together a film team that was supposed to shoot a documentary about the 8th Air Force in England: THE MEMPHIS BELLE: A STORY OF A FLYING FORTRESS (USA 1944). It is one of the most commercially successful documentaries of this type; a kind of latecomer appeared in the immediate post-war period: THUNDERBOLT (USA 1947). Finally, there is John Ford, who – as we know today – commanded his own group of cinematographers from Pearl Harbor to Omaha Beach in the service of the US Secret Service. With the films DECEMBER 7TH (USA 1943) and THE BATTLE OF MIDWAY (USA 1942) he worked out some of the fundamental aspects of the new film genre.

Last but not least we should mention the genre films in a stricter sense. They initially turned up as mobilization movies, fictional action films that addressed a young audience to get them excited about the adventure of war and the communal aspects of the military.

Unlike during the First World War, the restrictions made by the military censorship bodies did not primarily intervene during the production of film and still photo material, but during their evaluation. Whether they were civilians or members of the Army or Navy, the cinematographers wore uniforms and were strictly incorporated into the military order. All film material had to be surrendered to the appropriate military offices, so that any form of public reporting on

---

24 Cf. Capra, *The Name Above the Title*, 311, 314.
25 Cf. Axel Madsen, *William Wyler: The Authorized Biography*, New York 1973, 227.

the war was relegated to a pool of approved material.²⁶ The great majority of the material was in fact not released and later disappeared into secret archives.

The censoring bodies were also the ones to fix a first perspective onto the endless succession of film footage from the war – Ford's DECEMBER 7TH is a telling example of this. The scarcity of the film material produced allowed for series of selected film scenes to turn up over and over again in various parts of the cinema programs at the time; they circulated between reports from the front, newsreels, and mobilization films, while other images were rendered invisible. The interplay of military film production, censorship, journalistic editing and artistic treatment, all organized by the military, allows for a seemingly unending stream of film documents of the war, which branched out in the viewing venues all over the country into a referential network of reciprocal self-referencing between information, educational, entertainment, and mobilization movies.

American cinema in the later thirties and forties thus allows us to outline the field of media practice in an exemplary way, a field where a wide variety of perceptual politics intersect.²⁷ At the time, films ran in so-called 'staple programs,' which served the pedagogical and logistical aims of the military, together with propaganda pieces commissioned by governmental authorities and various news formats: newsreels, war reports, and documentaries. Here the entertainment movies of the old style encountered a new type of genre film that also blatantly exposed its goal – mobilizing the population – whenever it was not expressly authorized by military or state institutions.²⁸

In the network of the wide variety of formats of cinematic media technology, the aesthetic calculation of the entertainment industry, the political public, state propaganda, and military warfare were inseparably intertwined with one another. Feature fiction films sometimes appeared showing the audience at home the victory of the Allies over the course of the very same production process as that of newsreel material that did not reveal anything about the outcome of the campaign that the film production was part of.²⁹ The interweaving of a wide variety of modes of film images caused contemporary cinema to become an experiential space in which the war became an event for the American population according to precisely established perspectives and selected aesthetic modalities,

---

26 Cf. Doherty, *Projections of War*, 233f.
27 Cf. David Gaertner, "World War II in American Movie Theatres from 1942–45: On Images of Civilian and Military Casualties and the Negotiation of a Shared Experience," in *mediaesthetics* [online study], 2016, http://www.mediaesthetics.org/index.php/mae/article/view/50.
28 Cf. Gaertner, *Tickets to War*; Doherty, *Documenting the 1940s*.
29 These films were released in the cinemas in 1943 with very little delay. They include, for instance, Billy Wilder's FIVE GRAVES TO CAIRO (1943) or John M. Stahl's IMMORTAL SERGEANT (1943).

an event that could be positioned in the socially shared world. It can be grasped as the interplay of a variety of perceptual politics in which perspectives are established and aesthetic modalities are defined, which allowed even the most remote military theaters and most horrifying incidents in the war to appear as a native domain. The war had become – beyond all personal fears and experiences of suffering – an understandable incident for every citizen, male or female, in a socially shared reality. (One can see certain traits of television prefigured in the experiential space of American war films. It served to relocate the space of this world-making into the intimacy of the private home.)

This is why it is not surprising that a fundamental transformation within the network of contemporary cinema went along with the media-historical constellation outlined here. It is seen most clearly in the emergence of a new genre of Hollywood cinema, the 'classical war film,' the "combat movie."[30] It goes without saying that there were war films before this; but it is only in the forties that the war film becomes a genre designating a distinct position within Hollywood's entertainment cinema. This position was marked through the western. Starting in 1942, the mobilization films literally took its place. They occupied its slot in Hollywood's genre-poetic system and in certain sense have not left it to this day. The western itself largely disappeared from cinema programs for the duration of the war, in order then to return in a transformed shape[31] and to occupy a different place in Hollywood cinema's economy of affect, which lies much closer to the sentimental pleasure of the melodrama than to that of cinematographic history.

The traditional western falls back on pre-cinematic objects in which the experience of history is conveyed; they are historical and literary narratives, paintings and photographs, which refer to the history of the Indian Wars, the conquest of the West, the birth of the nation, and so on. When the war film took over the Hollywood format of great histories after the Second World War, it resorted to the audiovisual image production of very recent or just ending events of war.

Unlike the Western, the war film therefore does not refer to an image of the past molded by the poetics of mythology, but adapts the audiovisual documents

---

30 John Whiteclay Chambers II, *World War II: Film and History*, New York 1996; Basinger, *The World War II Combat Film*.

31 Bazin was very early to describe this fundamental transformation, and John Ford himself, after years of wartime production, shot the model example of a Western with MY DARLING CLEMENTINE, which can in no way still be called 'classical.' André Bazin, "Evolution du Western," in *Cahiers du cinéma* 9 (54), 1955, 22–26; English translation: André Bazin, "The Evolution of the Western," in *What is Cinema? Vol. 2*, Berkeley/Los Angeles 2004, 149–157 . Cf. also John G. Cawelti, *The Six-Gun Mystique Sequel*, Bowling Green 1999, here 91–98. Further film examples would be THE OX-BOW INCIDENT (1943), DUEL IN THE SUN (1946), and RED RIVER (1948).

of the very recent past into the iconography – that is, the landscapes, scenes, characters, and pathos formulas – of an image of history. In the war film, the cinematic image of history is dissected out of the audiovisual document; even better: the audiovisual document is carved out as a film image of history. This is why the history of the genre is inseparably linked to the history of changing media technologies, which are both technologies of war and of its perceivability.

The topography of the new genre can therefore already be seen in the referential network of the movie house programs during the war, even before it can be treated as a genre at all. Its basic pathos and dramatic patterns are also already developed in those combat reports and orientation films that were produced by directors such as Ford, Capra, and Wyler.

The genre of the Hollywood war film thus emerges in a historical constellation that has inscribed itself into the genre as a mixture of different perceptual politics. In the war film genre, the aesthetic strategies of propaganda and information films, of audiovisual and photographic documents, are transferred into a genuine pathos system that is characterized by certain speaking perspectives, expressive modalities, and affect-dramaturgical patterns. It essentially transferred these perceptual politics into a specific affect poetics.

It is exactly this transformation that I would like to examine in the following chapters. I would like to describe it as poetic making that is aimed at shaping forms of film perception and modes of experience allowing war to become visible as an event in the common world. (One can call this an "aesthetics of politics," to borrow a term from Jacques Rancière.[32])

From this perspective, the war film genre is fairly clear where Hollywood cinema encounters its own image production as the forms of describing and redescribing the limits of the political community. Genre films themselves very quickly become media of circulating and repeating audiovisual war documents; whether it be – exactly like the battle description in SAVING PRIVATE RYAN – by restaging widely familiar film material; whether it be by editing this material into the fictional world as found footage. Viewed in this way, the footage of the landing of the American troops at Omaha Beach on June 6, 1944, is only one telling example to which countless others could be added (this also goes for early mobilization movies such as GUNG HO!).[33]

---

[32] Cf. Jacques Rancière, *The Emancipated Spectator*, London 2009, 74.
[33] GUNG HO! (1943): scene "End of training and transport" (00:26:48:17–00:30:06:17); GUADALCANAL DIARY (1943): scenes "Landing" (00:16:44–00:23:43:05); "The great offensive" (01:19:57:06–01:27:18:17); SANDS OF IWO JIMA (1949): scene "Invading Tarawa" (00:36:20:24–00:48:59:05). These are all other scenes mentioned in the following can be found at

With these films, the area of conflict in which the war film emerges as a genre of Hollywood cinema becomes clear. On the one hand, there is the perceptual politics of war, and, on the other, there are the staging strategies and the poetics of genre films; on the one hand more or less militarily initiated media practices that establish the aesthetic conditions, perspectives, and experiential modalities of the visibility of war; on the other poetic concepts in which the cinema is proposed as an experiential space in which these perceptual politics become accessible as histories of our perceiving, feeling, and thinking.

What is the relation between the image documents and the fictional forms of representation? How are they adapted and what poetic logics or what strategies in terms of aesthetic effects are expressed in them? And the other way around: What function do the aesthetic strategies, patterns, and formulas that emerge in the context of entertainment movies take on within a representation of war that aims to inform, document, and instruct? These questions will be the focus of the following film analyses.

3.2 Document and Propaganda

A different film, a different fate for documentary film footage: DECEMBER 7TH from 1943. The film, for which John Ford is signed as responsible, along with Gregg Toland, seems particularly steeped in the tensions and contradictions of crisscrossing perceptual politics. On the one hand, it is discussed to this day as a prime example of propagandistic deceptive maneuvering, claiming as documentary material what are in fact re-enacted and staged scenes; on the other hand, it is presented, and no less insistently, as a victim of censorship, which sought to eliminate the inconvenient criticism of the lack of defense capabilities in the run-up to the attack on Pearl Harbor, and which did not want to see any mention of the situation among Americans of Japanese descent.[34] On the one hand, DECEMBER 7TH received the Oscar for Best Documentary Short; on the other, it was only released for screening in a significantly shortened version. On the one hand, the film is considered a John Ford production; on the other, it is the commissioning body itself that is presented to the audience in the first sentences spoken: "Your War and Navy

---

http://empirische-medienaesthetik.fu-berlin.de/emaex-system/affektdatenmatrix/filme/index.html (last viewed on July 7, 2017).
34 Cf. James M. Skinner, "December 7: Filmic Myth Masquerading as Historical Fact," in *The Journal of Military History* 55 (4), 1991, 507–516, here 513ff; Greg Wilsbacher, "Al Brick: The Forgotten Newsreel Man at Pearl Harbor," in *The Moving Image* 10 (2), 2010, 30–59, here 41.

Departments present DECEMBER 7TH."[35] Ford and Toland, two filmmakers highly respected in their field, remain unmentioned. The credits at the end name "The US Navy Photographers" as the producers. Finally, the semi-documentary character of the film itself attests to a fundamental ambivalence in such film productions. DECEMBER 7TH shows re-enacted, elaborately staged battle scenes on the one hand, combined with documentary footage on the other.

DECEMBER 7TH

Shortly after the attack on Pearl Harbor Ford was commissioned by the military center to shoot a documentary about the event. He himself, in turn, put Gregg Toland in charge of directing the documentary. The two initially worked together, after they arrived at the scene of the Japanese attack in the spring of 1942. They spoke about the various possibilities of re-enacting the enemy attack in a series of fictional scenes, staged the battle scenes on the airfield, and filmed the activities at the airport as well as the many rescue and recovery operations. Ford left the shoot for his deployment to Midway Island, where another Japanese attack was expected. In case of an attack, the experienced Hollywood director was supposed to have everything ready to get useable film material;[36] as for Toland, he went back to Hollywood and shot the majority of scenes at the studios of Twentieth Century Fox, which are missing from the final version of DECEMBER 7TH.[37] By the time a first rough cut was prepared in November 1942, the problems had already begun. The film's impression was clearly not convincing enough. It was the rambling fictional scenes in particular that caused the trouble, presenting a sleepy-lethargic Uncle Sam in long-winded dialogues as a not very subtle allegory for the lack of defense readiness conditions in the USA.[38] By December the discussion had obviously even reached the White House.[39]

As a result, the roughly eighty-minute film that Toland had produced was not released in cinemas and was kept under wraps until John Ford made an attempt, after his return, to reconstruct the film that had been roughly drafted at the site of the attack. He had the film edited into a thirty-minute version, cutting it back

---

35 Cf. DECEMBER 7TH – RESTORED VERSION; scene "Vorspann [*opening credits*]" (00:00:00:00–00:00:54:00).
36 Wilsbacher, "Al Brick," 40.
37 Skinner, "December 7," 510.
38 Ibid., 513.
39 Wilsbacher, "Al Brick," 41.

to its core sequences, "[...] shorn of all but the raids and the salvage footage."⁴⁰ This version won the Oscar for best documentary film on March 2, 1944, so it had to have been finished by December 1943 at the latest. Although even the final version did not get a regular run in cinemas, it is assumed that DECEMBER 7TH was seen by millions of people in special screenings for workers in the war industry.⁴¹

The affect-dramaturgical concept

But back to the film itself: When John Ford got to Pearl Harbor with his production team, all that was left for him to find were the silent witnesses of the destruction that the attack had left behind. The very first shot of DECEMBER 7TH shows this quite plainly: burned-out airplane hangars, bomber planes that had been shot down. The staging concept made clear in this exposition defines the film as a whole. The camera's gaze lingers on a spot on the ground, a dried-up puddle, a sailor's cap right next to the spot – underscored first with dramatic-suspenseful, and then gloomy-elegiac musical motifs, giving off the impression of tragic significance. But it is not only the music, every detail of the visual staging follows the melodramatic rhetoric of Hollywood genre movies, almost as if the film were formulating the audiovisual phrase: 'Look, here are the traces of our dead.'

At the end of DECEMBER 7TH, in one of the last sentences, the visual staging is in fact translated into words. The commentator's voice-over is rhetorically directed to the enemy: "You spilled our blood."⁴² The eventual response to the melodramatic elegy of the opening scene is a gesture of rage. The menacing gesture is directed toward a future that demands gratification, even revenge. The cinematic arrangement at the opening, however, leads into the present of a calamitous event that is not quite past, that is just now passing. The sequences that follow aim to restage the just past event of the first military battle of this war on American soil as the present of the spectators' sense of perception in the act of film viewing itself. DECEMBER 7TH allows the event to emerge as a past that reaches into the physical present of the film spectators, that persists in the present of their sense activity. With the concluding menacing gesture, a present of the spectator's feeling and thinking is opened up to an uncertain future. Only from there, from that future, can the sense of the act of war represented in the film be decided.

---

40 Skinner, "December 7," 515.
41 Wilsbacher, "Al Brick," 41.
42 DECEMBER 7TH – RESTORED VERSION; scene "A people's war" (01:09:27:12–01:15:43:26).

On the basis of this time construction, DECEMBER 7TH develops a dramaturgical schema that was then played out in countless genre films. Like a simple three-act play, the film can be divided into the sequence before, during, and after the attack; only that each of these parts develops its own audiovisual expressivity, which the spectators realize in their sense of perception as alternating layers of affect, as alternating affective modes (see Figure 10).

At first we see a man sleeping in a rocking chair; the friendly off-screen voice speaks to him as a living allegory; Uncle Sam, who has every reason to be tired after so much disturbing news in the year that was just coming to a close.[43] We see the beauty of the morning sun, rising up with the camera over the hills of a tropical island. This is followed by images of the waking city: soldiers idling in the beauty of the morning light or casually going about their morning exercises. They could be taken for college students. Then a field mass, Marines in dress uniform, a priest speaks about Christmas approaching. The waking city, the soldiers at the Hickam Field Airbase, the field mass in the open air. The exposition leads us into a Sunday morning on a paradisiac island, showing us a picture-perfect illustration of eternal peace. Only the voice-over breaks up the lyrical arrangement, when idyllic Hawaii, which, even immediately before the attack still imagines itself to be safe and secure under the protection of the Pacific fleet, is metonymically addressed as the image for the illusory peace that reigns throughout the country.

The sequence that follows shows the attack by the Japanese on the American Pacific fleet. It contains, to a not insignificant degree, film material that was shot for Fox newsreels during the battles. Today we know that this footage was shot by various cinematographers who were present at the theater of war during the attack.[44] The combat footage – precisely in its reminiscence of familiar newsreel images – forms a basic reference point within the sequence of the montage. It has a counterpart in the elaborately staged scenes with which the combat action is presented, using the mode of action movies, as a dramatic event taking place directly before the spectators' eyes. Is this a sign of deception? Or is it precisely

---

[43] DECEMBER 7TH – RESTORED VERSION; scene "Vor dem Angriff [*before the attack*]" (00:39:26:29–00:43:25:00).

[44] Wilsbacher mentions Al Brick from Fox Movietone News and Captain Eric Hakansson, Skinner, however, names C. Daugherty and Lt. Commander Edward Young as the photographers of the documentary footage. Brick's stay in Hawaii is mentioned in an article from the time ("Filming Pearl Harbor(s)," in *Motion Picture Herald* 146 (7), February 14, 1942, 9) and is supported by the film material for which he himself had created documentation. As for Hakansson, Wilsbacher refers to the archival holding of a 35mm film that is held at the National Archives and which is attributed to him (cf. Wilsbacher, "Al Brick," 58, fn. 40). Skinner gives no sources for his information.

Figure 10: Changing affect layers (DECEMBER 7TH).

the "Masquerading as Historical Fact" – as James M. Skinner entitled his essay on the subject – which conveys to us basic insights about the fate of the footage from DECEMBER 7TH?[45]

---

[45] The idea goes well beyond Skinner's article. Skinner's title is referring more to a strict understanding of propaganda, in that he implicitly prefers Ford's "purified version" to

Staged reminiscence rather than historical document

Today, any internet user can compare the scenes shot during the attack by the Japanese with the corresponding scenes edited into the film in every detail. The history of the combat footage includes the fact that since 2013 it can be viewed as a web video on YouTube, on the very same internet platform where one can also see both versions of DECEMBER 7TH. While watching the web videos, it quickly becomes clear that, without any precise knowledge of the location, hardly any idea at all can be made of the concrete operations. The combat footage remains hermetic.[46] Even more, this footage eludes the perspective that is the central point of the montage sequence in DECEMBER 7TH: the perspective of the soldiers, surprised in their sleep, in their cabins, at the field mass, at their early morning exercise; they die as they are still trying to find their weapons, hit by bullets, sinking down behind their machine guns, or are quickly being felled by a shot in the back. In the way these scenes are arranged, they are no less imaginary than a scene of a noble hero dying in a western. Indeed, they do not leave us in any doubt whatsoever as to their character as staged melodramatic or action genre scenes. The dying and fighting takes place in a representational mode that is perfectly familiar to the contemporary audience from pathos-laden westerns – not least those shot by John Ford himself.

Toland's: "Amid all the contemporary criticism of Toland's work, little was said, or perhaps could be said, about its major flaw as a piece of propaganda, to wit, its fence-sitting and its inconsistency. Effective screen propaganda polarizes, reinforces concepts, and deepens prejudices if these harmonize with official policy; or, alternatively, it changes minds and alters consciousness when the public mood is not in tune with the perceived goals if the nation's leadership. Those aims are not achieved by providing a forum for reasoned debate or attempting to reach a general consensus, as are commonplace media procedures in time of peace. On the contrary, propaganda must be confrontational, factually selective, deliberately omissive when necessary, allowing no room for doubt, compassion, or the self-examination of issues. On the screen, such an approach demands clarity of exposition no less than in print. Given that *December 7* was originally intended for a select, targeted audience of servicemen and workers in war industries, the need was for a picture that would confront people who might not be otherwise motivated to watch it on their own accord, and elicit the conditioned responses of hatred for Japan and all things Japanese, as well as pride in the accomplishments of those who had literally salvaged much from the disaster that was Pearl Harbor." Skinner, "December 7," 515.

46 These sequences were published on the internet in 2013 by the curator of the Fox Movietone News Collection, Moving Image Research Collections, University of South Carolina, Greg Wilsbacher:http://www.youtube.com/watch?v=MKBNBADbXCY (March 12, 2017).

Even if the cameramen present are supposed to have managed to film the fighting, fear, and death of individual soldiers over the course of the attack, this footage would have been rejected, and not just for reasons of piety. They would have been as hermetic as the other original footage – but unlike them the hermeticism would have been the expression of an undefinable horror. The mode of fiction works as a gesture full of piety, which not only disguises the horror that is represented in the history books by the number of 2403 dead and 1178 wounded. It also seeks to give the events of war a form that integrates them into the common world of senses in the first place. If we can correctly assume that footage of real dying could be consumed on today's web video platforms as pure spectacle – albeit with greater popularity than the genre scenes from DECEMBER 7TH – this merely points out the dynamic in which what we seek to fix as the socially shared world has changed dramatically.

In fact, no reconstruction guides us into the world of the contemporary spectator; for us, the boundaries of its sensibility can only be read on the films. But it is difficult to imagine an audience that would let themselves be deceived by these scenes or that would have felt deceived by them. The temporal construction that is started from the beginning of DECEMBER 7TH includes the subjunctive irrealis, in which the film lets the spectator commiserate with the fate of the fighting soldiers. The function of the combat footage that is added is actually to construct this subjunctive tense within the staging. It calls on feelings and knowledge that, for the spectator, are linked with these images: 'This is how we would have seen it if we had been here at this place when the film footage was taken, which we know from the newsreels.'

Even before the pre-existing film images of the obsequies are arranged as a visual image of 'after the attacks,' the film turns to the graves of fallen soldiers.[47] The camera's gaze dwells on a fresh grave. The voice of the commentator focuses on the dead, asking them to introduce themselves. An off-screen voice answers, giving the name, rank, and hometown of an individual soldier, like at roll call; we see photographs of the dead, footage of their parents, of the wife, of a child. They come from every corner of the country. The different hometowns and regions have taken the place of ethnic background (we no longer say: "He's a Jew," we say: "He comes from Brooklyn.") In the end the commentator asks the dead why they all speak with one and the same voice. The answer is obvious, they say: "We are all alike. We are all Americans."

---

[47] DECEMBER 7TH –RESTORED VERSION; scene "Die Toten sprechen [*the dead speak*]" (00:59:19:12– 01:01:27:00).

The irresolvable conflict that we spelled out in relation to Capra's film finds a highly peculiar solution here. War is the time in which the dead teach the living that all Americans speak with one voice, no matter where they and their families might come from. The staging of the film is directed at the sole voice from this community, at the feeling of unity, of the commonality between dead Americans and living ones. The appeal to the sense of commonality needs no film documents testifying to an event, the reality of which no one doubts. It is based on the pathos forms of film that allow the cinema to become a medium for a new form of affective collectivity: a communality based on a media practice that is much more like religious ritual than political discourse.

The only eyewitnesses that DECEMBER 7TH explicitly calls on come at the end of Gregg Toland's long version. Once again we are confronted with a dead soldier, but this time not as a photograph, but as a sailor in dress uniform, played by an actor.[48] He turns directly to the audience, looking into the camera: "So that's the story of Pearl Harbor, before, during and after the infamous attack on December 7th. It's all true. You can take my word for it, because I know. I was there. I died there." A second soldier in an entirely different uniform joins him, a veteran from the First World War. Both turn away; they begin walking through the Arlington National Cemetery. We watch the two ghostly apparitions, the newly arrived and the long-established resident of the cemetery. Then the camera follows them at a suitable distance. While the two stroll among the soldiers' graves, we hear them disputing: Would this war be the last? Is it a war for democracy? Or is it just defending the rights of those who have decided to live in a democracy?

At the very latest at the epilogue of the long version, it becomes clear that the massive cuts that Ford had made to this version were not only made in deference to the military censorship bodies. At a time in which lives lost were being reported daily, the closing sequence must have appeared highly macabre and somewhat insipid. Even more so since the film, in its arrangement of the main part, in the 'before, during, and after the attack' had already found a succinct dramaturgical form and a precise closing; we see how the war turned a paradisiac island into a place that would be radically changed by the various defense measures. Finally, the off-screen voice that, as we have mentioned, makes its lament about the compulsory state of war as a tangible threat to the enemy: "You spilled our blood."

---

[48] DECEMBER 7TH – RESTORED VERSION; scene "Gespräch zweier toter Soldaten [*conversation of two dead soldiers*]" (01:15:46:26–01:21:29:18).

In view of this film ending, which can be seen in the final version, the epilogue of the longer version seems quite superfluous. If I am thematizing it here nonetheless, it is because the clumsy allegory clearly presents a fundamental motif of the war film, exposing its ambivalence to the glaring light of day. While the ghosts are walking thorough the Arlington Cemetery, the answer to the question "Why are we on the march?" is worked through as an answer that the dead soldiers give their future dead comrades.

The unity of the community, which is summoned up in the dispute between the dead soldiers, therefore ultimately turns out to be the bond between the living soldiers and the dead. Once again we encounter the archaic principle of military collectivization, which we find obscenely displayed by Riefenstahl, and thematized as an irresolvable contradiction by Capra. The transformation of the political community by military forms of collectivization is the neuralgic wound that never stops hurting in the history of the American war film genre.

The face of the invisible enemy

One of the other cuts concerns the prologue, which is marked by a comparable allegorical construction. The sleeping Uncle Sam, who we saw at the beginning of the short version, is completely exhausted because he has held up his end of an intricate conversation in the good half an hour that was edited out. A shrewd devil's advocate confronted his credulous optimism with arguments of a veritable demonic ambiguity. At the center of the dispute is the sense of commonality. But now its limits are in question. Could it be that not all Americans are loyal Americans? As if it were an educational film being shot to instruct soldiers in order to give them behavioral rules for dealing with enemy-minded populations in occupied territories, the ever-present dangers of espionage and sabotage are presented. In short scenes, which Toland obvious had shot in a Hollywood studio, the film graphically plays through the possibilities of betrayal in the everyday lives of ordinary people. As for those of Japanese descent, which accounted for one third of the inhabitants of Hawaii, one should be on the lookout for disloyalty. Particularly – the film here provides plenty of space for the arguments – those whose religion pledges them to the Japanese emperor as a political leader. The patriotic discussion in which a representative of this group emphatically ensures that, in the case of war, even the Japanese population will work for a political life-form "for which other Americans have lived and fought and died," only illustrates – against the backdrop of the ever-present dangers being presented for all to see – Uncle Sam's naïveté.

The prologue thwarts the sense of commonality that the photographs of fallen soldiers calls on when they speak with one voice despite all ethnic differences. With the ethnic discrimination, which can hardly be surpassed in directness, a certain ambivalence finds its way into the film, which can obviously not be equilibrated. An any rate it is incompatible with the credo of the voice of America, which overcomes all differences in war: "We are all alike. We are all Americans."

A last element of the poetics of the war film genre comes from intersecting perceptual politics. If the cuts that Ford had made to the long version ultimately execute an act of censorship, then it is in view of the schema of the rhetoric and dramaturgy of affect, which we have outlined above. In comparison to the long version, all images that might give the enemy an ordinary face are removed in the final cinema version. The long version's numerous shots in which Americans of Japanese descent could be seen as ordinary people are completely missing. The enemy has become faceless. The only thing that remains of the many everyday faces of those of Japanese descent is a grotesque figure showing Asiatic facial features. It is no coincidence that it turns up as part of an animated sequence. We see a map of the Pacific region, on which the plan for Japanese expansion is represented in animated motion. Radio towers grow up from the map, sending out radio signals that spread out all over it. A voice, in English but with a strong Japanese accent, announces the successes of the military operation.

In succinct metonymy, the animation figures propaganda itself as part of warfare. The commentator's voice-over interrupts the victory announcements and responds to the voice of the invisible enemy in the same way as it had to the voice of the dead before; only that in place of photographs of fallen soldiers, the oversized mask that I mentioned appears in a dissolve. The numerous plain faces of the American soldiers, which had reported on their various ethnic backgrounds in one and the same voice, are countered with a demonic grimace through which the voice of the enemy protrudes. All human traits have been removed from it. All that remains of the ambivalent presentation of everyday life and the problematic situation of Hawaii's Japanese population, which had been thematized in the long version, is one short scene. In this scene, we see Japanese characters and names on the advertising signs and billboards for cafés, restaurants, and businesses painted over or replaced with American markings.

In how the enemy is represented in DECEMBER 7TH, another fundamental modality is foreshadowed that will become formative for the war film. The phantasm of an invisible, faceless enemy is closely associated with the expressive modality of the horror genre. In the affect dramaturgy of the Hollywood war film, horror becomes a constitutive element that can be traced on up to the Vietnam War movie.

Contradictory perceptual politics

Viewing the reconstructed long version of DECEMBER 7TH, we can study how far apart the different perceptual politics were from one another at the point of the entry into war, and how they collided in their goal setting. They employ a poetic logic of contradictory propositions, which obviously were only reconciled little by little.

The censored opening section is conceived like a training film for local troops operating in enemy territories. On the one hand, it addresses the local population as taking part in war, and on the other it treats Hawaii like foreign turf, one third occupied by potential enemies. The epilogue dabbles in militaristic mobilization propaganda. Finally, the centerpiece, the representation of the events surrounding December 7, 1941, turns to the audience at home. In the long version, as well, it is identifiably the self-contained main part to which only insignificant changes were made for the short version. These basically concern those passages in which the film seeks to explain the ambivalent stance toward Hawaiian inhabitants of Japanese descent.

On closer inspection, in fact, even the main part is structured in a contradictory way. On the one hand, like a newsreel report it installs a speaking perspective that refers to a concrete event in the shared world (a perspective which does not in any way need to be verified through authentic footage). On the other hand, the representation of the events follows a strictly dramaturgical buildup for calculated rhetorical effect.

The sequence of scenes allows for a temporal succession of the sensation of perception to emerge in the changing expressive modalities, which follows a calculated strategy to generate and shape affect. Seen as a whole, in their opposing expressive qualities the scenes already articulate the fundamental affect-dramaturgical schema of the Hollywood war film genre: the peaceful world at the beginning; the emerging threat; the plight and the vain fighting of the soldiers surprised by the enemy's superiority; the actions of fighting back; the mourning of the dead; the euphoria of resistance and the threat of revenge. Each of these scenes follows different expressive modalities. In their precisely calculated succession, they make up a script of alternating qualities of sensation, which the spectator experiences as stages of an emerging and transforming feeling in his or her own bodily sensation.

Much like Capra's PRELUDE TO WAR, DECEMBER 7TH alternates between sentimental passages and others emphasizing fear, threat, and terror. It also focuses on rage in a similar way. But the rage – much more than it is represented in the film – is required of the spectators themselves as an individual feeling, directly linked with the sense of commonality. The last sentence, "You spilled our blood," requires rage as a genuine contribution from the spectator. In the cascade of alternating affects, the short version turns out to be almost a blueprint for the rhetoric and dramaturgy of the Hollywood war film. The representation of war here is very much calculated toward the affective assessment of the spectators. This may be rage or animosity, pity or shame, mourning or horror – but the events represented always demand a judging feeling from the spectators, with which they position themselves in a community.[49]

The appeal to the sense of commonality relies as little on the evidentiary value of authentic film footage as it does on the spectator's belief that the dead are directly speaking to them. Rather, the found footage – much like the gravestones and the photographs – are the occasion for the speech that pretends to be a unified voice in which the film images speak of attack, of the ruins, graves, and photographs of the dead. "We are all alike. We are all Americans." Already in the earliest war documentaries we come across a way of using combat footage that will form a fundamental element in the affect poetics of later genre films. The recurring images of war films from former times become, in the present of a later genre cinema, the media of the feeling for a commonly shared memory.

3.3 The Media Practice of Military Collectivization

Obviously, John Ford had very quickly handed over work on DECEMBER 7TH to Gregg Toland in order to be flown to Midway. An attack by the Japanese was expected there. And this time it was meant to be filmed on location by Ford's camera team. Already in the credits at the beginning of the report, THE BATTLE OF MIDWAY[50] (1942) expressly points out that what follows are "authentic scenes." Nonetheless, the arrangement of the scenes follows the affect-rhetorical schema that we have already encountered in its main features in DECEMBER 7TH. In terms of its production history, it is the other way around; the experience with the production of THE BATTLE OF MIDWAY forms the backdrop for the revisions of DECEMBER 7TH.

The affect rhetoric of THE BATTLE OF MIDWAY

A significant aspect of the poetic construction of the film is the fact that it was shot on Technicolor. In the first shot, a landing at Midway, the island comes into

---

[49] In short, it concerns the register of feelings, which in emotion theory are differentiated from basic emotions as social feelings. In the perspective developed here it is a matter of collectivities created by means of affects.

[50] I am referring to a version reconstructed in 2012. It can be found at: https://www.youtube.com/watch?v=MW8tQ_6dqS8 (July 28, 2015).

view as an arrangement of color. It appears as a color scale, ranging from the pale colors of the sand and the greyish brown of the buildings and facilities of the military base through the dark grey of the war machinery, dissolving almost into the abstract: a sand-colored strip, reaching out into the expanse of blue, which ranges from the deepest sea blue through the bright sky to the pastel blue tones that shimmer through white veils of clouds. The aerial shots, with which the film gauges this bright expanse, establish an endless space with the first shots. The combat action is then later staged as an increasing darkening of this brightness, up to the edge of black, which absorbs all color.

The affect-rhetorical pattern of the staging is also established right from the beginning. It can be succinctly grasped in the usage of music, which structures the scene changes in the opening sequence, a film beginning that seems like a potpourri of militarily-tinged mood music. Together with the credits, the music starts up immediately with a triumphant intonation of "My Country 'Tis of Thee"; only very briefly, when the title of the film appears, do we hear a pathos-laden and heavy motif in the style of a studio intro. When an explanatory intertitle appears, the film turns back to a staider version of the anthem. The last sentence in the text is: "The following authentic scenes were made by US. Navy Photographers."[51]

A map shows Midway; it marks the middle of the Pacific between Japan and the USA; the music changes with this shot to a cheerful, exhilarating motif in vaudeville style with large orchestral instrumentation and dominant horns. From the viewpoint of a cockpit we see another airplane flying in parallel: "A Navy Patrol Plane." The off-screen voice is introduced in the curtest of diction. It explains the view from the plane to the island, then to the pilot in his plane: "A routine control. Only behind every cloud may be an enemy." The sentence of the off-screen voice and the view to the pilot, peering tensely into the clouds, give the exhilarating music a dramatic undertone.

Midway Island is presented, just a strip of sand, but an important outpost. The commentator addresses the spectators directly: "Your front yard." This will continue to happen often. Then we find ourselves on the island, we see battleships, army buildings, a plane that has just landed on the water. We observe young men jumping into the water and pulling the plane onto the landing bridge – as if it were a scene of young people enjoying a day at the beach. At least that is what is suggested by a shift in the music to a jolly, almost manically fast version of the famous children's song "Pop! Goes the Weasel." Only a few seconds, then the scene and the music change again. We hear a cheerful, proud orchestral version

---

51 THE BATTLE OF MIDWAY; scene "Ankunft im 'Vorgarten' Midway [*arriving at the 'front yard' Midway*]" (00:00:00:00–00:02:05:26).

of the U.S. Marine Corps anthem, in the same instrumentation as that of the vaudeville motif from before: marching soldiers, battleships in the background, flags waving in front of the bright blue sky.

This is followed by an abrupt change in the music, a hectic, fluttering, melodic motif: quick chromatic sequences of notes that alternate going up and down accompanied by an alarmingly repetitive, slow half step ("little second").[52] We see seabirds flying every which way; an unsettling shot that leaves the spectator somewhat disoriented. The dramatic insertion is kept short, much like the children's song interrupting the orchestra earlier. It is enough to establish the birds flying in the sky as a metaphor for disquieting tension, before an equally short and thoroughly opposing atmospheric motif is associated with them. Now we see the seabirds awkwardly waddling on the ground. A staid, rhythmic horn motif imitates the lumbering motions of the birds in a Mickey Mouse style. The commentary presents them as the "natives of Midway," who the soldiers have sworn to liberate. Later, after the sequence that shows the air attack, the motif will be picked up once again. A bird, disheveled and mangled by the grime, is asked if the Marines had kept their promise. There is an abrupt mood change from highly dramatic tension to the relief of comedy. Already in the short insertion during the exposition the expressive modality of dramatic tension is associated with relief by comedy – and vice versa. The middle section breaks off, once again we see birds in the sky: "The birds seem nervous." The comedic scene is immediately linked with the unsettling image of birds flying away as a metaphor for a diffuse threat and fear.

Once again a radical change in mood is introduced. A slow accordion motif begins, its wistful, melancholic melody seems to conjure up homesickness; the star-spangled banner comes into the frame. There is a cut from the birds in the blue sky to a scenario that is equally picturesque and gloomy. We see the silhouette of soldiers in the dark back-lit shots, shadowing figures in front of the evening horizon; we see them smoking, playing accordion; then we see into their faces – mute, serious, tired, lost in their thoughts in the reddish light of the setting sun.

Primed by the musical atmospheric painting, the shots of the setting sun become the expression of longing and melancholy; the voice-over links this expressive figuration as well to a diffuse sense of fear. "Something" is hidden behind the setting sun; something that one can sense so much that even the birds are anxious. The rumbling of an approaching storm mixes in with the sentimental

---

[52] THE BATTLE OF MIDWAY; scene "Die Ruhe vor dem Sturm [the quiet before the storm]" (00:02:05:26–00:03:24:26).

sounds of the accordion. The setting sun designates the site where the enemy is lurking, waiting to attack at some point. The evening sky suddenly seems dramatically clouded, the movements of the lookout patrol seem tense – like in mimetic alignment with the anxiously fluttering birds shortly before. In a few seconds the scenario of sentimentally attuned sociability has been transformed into an image of gloomy expectation of the coming battle: sentries backlit by the setting sun, weapons put on display, the rumbling of the thunder (see Figure 11).

Figure 11: Opening sequence of THE BATTLE OF MIDWAY.

When we see the briefing and the preparations for the expected attack in the following sequence, which might be the next day, we can always observe the birds in the background as they flit around in the sky. Their anxious movement seems to keep the alarming tone, which had been used to introduce them, present as a visible threat.

The opening sequence described here articulates a succession of opposing expressive figurations in just a few minutes. These can be summed up as atmospheric images by means of the musical motifs: from the triumphant anthems and the mild dramatics of joyful pop music played by a large orchestra through the exhilarating self-satisfaction of marching Marines, the brief allusions to relaxed childhood joy and whimsical comedy, to the sentimental night music, underscored by rolling thunder. Much as the aerial shots at the beginning had established the space of the film world as gradations of color values, the changing expressive figurations of the exposition map out a scale of differentiating affect values, which can be completely understood as the spectrum of everyday emotional life: of the seriousness of work, of the joy of comradery, of the euphoria in experiencing common strengths, through the comedic sides of creatural existence and the span of fear, pain, and mourning inherent to the awareness of separation, parting, and death. In the continual modulation by the changing expressive qualities of the film staging, the threat of the enemy who lives in the darkness beyond the setting sun and behind every cloud can suddenly erupt, related to a subjective sense of the self between the ordinary lust for life and a no less ordinary awareness of one's own mortality.

Sentimental pathos versus military pathos

In the short opening sequence, all the appearances of nature – the light, the colors, the times of the day, the birds, even the island itself – assemble into an expressive ensemble that is realized in the spectators' perception as a scale of sensation in their own, ordinary corporeality. For them, the silhouette of the patrolling soldiers backlit by the setting sun literally becomes the projection surface of an ego that they endow with the sensations of their own embodied perceptual experiences. In this process the film staging perfectly matches the sentimental mode of the melodrama.

Correspondingly, the sequences that now follow are shaped according to all the rules of the rhetorics of melodramatic affect. From here on, the spectator's perception is guided by a second off-screen voice, the maternal speech of a woman. The voice initially shows itself to be impressed by the efforts of the military leadership to protect the island; but in the very next moment it turns to the young men with maternal concern. The voice does not represent the anxieties and fears of the contemporary spectator; it provides an affective perspective to the position of spectating itself. Even before the audience is shown the images of the battle over Midway, the soldiers, in their subjective sensation and their individual particularity, have become the decisive reference point in this perspective. The staging is thoroughly aimed at bringing them as close as possible to the spectators as individuals, presenting them as the spectators' own sons. The commentary once again speaks directly to the audience: "Men and women of America: here come your neighbor sons home from the day's work."[53]

Then follows the attack. At first, instead of the birds, all we see are the dark grey enemy airplanes in the blue sky; the defensive weapons shoot black balls of smoke into the bright blue sky. Then finally the bombs explode: the dirt flies up as the bombs hit, flames blaze, and thick, black clouds of smoke appear. We see the embattled soldiers, entrenched and barricaded behind heaps of sand sacks; we see the earth breaking open beneath their feet, the detonation of the bombs jarring the camera and forcing the exposure negatives to jump the frame; we sense the chaos reigning around the camera team when buildings collapse. War machinery, depots, and fuel tanks are engulfed by brightly blazing flames, sending swaths of black smoke into the air and stretching out over the island, as if they were trying to squelch any hope for a good outcome that the daylight might bring. Fire breaks out everywhere, the destruction mounts, swaths of smoke waft up into the air (see Figure 12).

Until the moment that, in a western movie, we would hear the cavalry's fanfares; in THE BATTLE OF MIDWAY it is the voice of the commentator, laconically announcing that the Japanese fighter planes start to retreat when the American battle ships turn up. The film dwells for a while in the action mode and lets the spectators see a bit of the US Navy's fire power, only shortly thereafter to switch back from the heroic pathos of the battle scene to the sentimental pathos of the melodrama, back to presenting the "neighbor sons."

Like in roll call, they are presented to us after the successful battle, each one with his name and his individual face. At first the returning pilots are welcomed by the camera and the off-screen voice after a job well done. Then those still on duty, searching for missing soldiers who had crashed into the sea with their machines; finally, the rescued soldiers are presented, recovered alive after nine days, ten days, eleven days. The ordinary faces of young men, sometimes beaming with joy, sometimes smiling in fatigue, sometimes serious and concerned, sometimes relieved and exhausted. The maternal voice, who had not spoken at all during

---

[53] THE BATTLE OF MIDWAY; scene "Gute Arbeit! [*Good work!*]" (00:11:31:20–00:13:06:03).

Figure 12: Attack scene from THE BATTLE OF MIDWAY.

the combat operations, urgently chimes back in: "Get those boys to the hospital, please do, quickly."[54]

Once again the sky shines bright blue. The black clouds of smoke have disappeared. We see the destroyed military base, even the hospital lies in smoldering ruins. Like in DECEMBER 7TH the presentation of the destruction follows a rhetoric of affect that appeals to the spectator's rage; here in THE BATTLE OF MIDWAY, as well, the denouncement is followed by a funeral service, going to great pains to present the fallen soldiers.[55] The melodramatic atmosphere is once again transposed when a tragic-heroic pathos takes the place of maudlin sentimentalism in the scenes of the burial rituals. It is thus clearly connoted as military-paternal, just as melodramatic sequences are marked by the maternal voice. In the somber tone of the military ritual the commentator presents some of the officers attending the burial.

---

[54] THE BATTLE OF MIDWAY; scene "Verwundete Helden [*wounded heroes*]" (00:13:06:03–00:15:20:26).
[55] THE BATTLE OF MIDWAY; scene "Ehre den Toten [*honor to the dead*]" (00:15:20:26–00:17:17:28).

Feigning and falsifying: historical knowledge

It is exactly here that Ford makes a considerable falsification. He edits footage of President Roosevelt's son into the row of soldiers who are bidding farewell to their dead in a ritual of mourning (see Figure 13), although the footage was shot thousands of miles away.[56] The question of whether Ford used a gimmick to win

Figure 13: Roosevelt's son.

---

56 The fact that James Roosevelt, the son of the current president, was not on the Midway Atoll at the time was first pointed out by Michael Kloft in his television documentary HOLLYWOOD UND DER KRIEG: WIE STARREGISSEUR JOHN FORD DEN D-DAY DREHTE (HOLLYWOOD AND WAR: HOW STAR DIRECTOR JOHN FORD SHOT D-DAY, 1998). According to his research in archival holdings at the National Archives in Washington, DC, Kloft indicates that the origin of the material with James Roosevelt was reconstructed. The material was presumably shot during a parade on an airfield two thousand miles from Midway. This had not yet been recognized in the English-language research literature. Even as late as 2014, the film journalist Mark Harris, in his book *Five Came Back: A Story of Hollywood and the Second World War*, maintained: "It has never been determined whether James Roosevelt was actually present on Midway." Mark Harris, *Five Came Back: A Story of Hollywood and the Second World War*, New York 2014, 158.

favor for his film with the authorities and in this way to get around the censorship boards and into the cinemas, or whether he was merely trying to win the population over to the political leadership in the country is ultimately beside the point. Either way, THE BATTLE OF MIDWAY seems to grossly violate the ethos of the documentary.[57]

This may seem strange, given that there can be no doubt that the President's sons were in fact in action as Navy officers during the Pacific War. The moral reproach is thus not so much aimed at the falsification of historical facts. Rather, Ford's actions raise a fundamental doubt that concerns film itself as a medium for conveying historical knowledge.

Does a film represent what actually happened, or is the objectivity of film images not itself a propagandistic effect that should be mistrusted in principle? Whenever Hollywood war films or the engagement of the American film industry in the Second World War is discussed, the arguments very quickly run along these lines. (Exceptions to this confirm the rule.[58])

Usually in these discussions, two categorically different questions get mixed up. The first question concerns the moral-political evaluation of war: Is the moral reprehensibility of its horrors adequately represented? This question is as counterproductive as it is common. In general, it is presumed that the horror of war is unfathomable, and representation, whatever the form might be, is outmatched by the reality of suffering. At the same time, however, the representation is supposed to be suitable and appropriate. The aporias of the discussion about the anti-war film are based on this contradiction.[59] The second question concerns film as a medium of history: Does what we see factually correspond to the facts

---

[57] The editor of THE BATTLE OF MIDWAY, Robert Parrish, protested when Ford asked him to add the material showing James Roosevelt after the film had been completed and shortly before a screening THE BATTLE OF MIDWAY at the White House. According to Parrish, the material was too different from the rest of the film in its visual and sound qualities. Even he had no knowledge that James Roosevelt had not been present at Midway. Afterwards, Ford attempted to diffuse Parrish's reservations. Cf. Robert Parrish, *Growing Up in Hollywood*, New York 1976, 150f and Harris, *Five Came Back*, 154f.

[58] For exceptions (for example the engagement of the American film industry during the Second World War) cf. Doherty, *Projections of War*, especially the section on THE BATTLE OF MIDWAY: 252 f., on Capra's WHY WE FIGHT: 74. Cf. also Bill Nichols, *Representing Reality: Issues and Concepts in Documentary*, Bloomington 1991. Here especially Nichols's writing on John Huston's THE BATTLE OF SAN PIETRO (1945), 26–27, 34–38, 129. On the current dichotomy, cf. Paul, *Bilder des Krieges – Krieg der Bilder*, 255–257.

[59] Cf. the articles in Søren R. Fauth, et al., (eds.), *Repräsentationen des Krieges: Emotionalisierungsstrategien in der Literatur und in den audiovisuellen Medien vom 18. bis zum 21. Jahrhundert*, Göttingen 2012.

as they occurred at a particular place and a particular time in our shared world? Or is the film material given a particular perspective and falsified? The discussion about the relation between representing war in the media and the history of war can largely be traced back to a pro and con of one or the other of these questions. This is actually surprising. For the implicit assumptions contained in these questions do not at all correspond to the current state of media-theoretical discourse.

Both questions presume a highly schematic understanding of the representational mode of film documents; they imply a premise that concerns the state of film images and their relation to (historical) reality: namely that the media technology of film per se – that is, on the basis of its technological conditions – does indeed have the possibility of faithfully representing reality.

In the debates about the war film, this idea stubbornly returns. It may have its roots in the idea of the ontological realism of film images, that is, in the theory that sees a relation to reality warranted in the technological automatism of film photography itself, which is supposed to keep it free from subjectivist reshaping.[60] But the privileged relation to reality – and film theory has been working on this for a long time – is also only a "reality effect" of media.[61] This effect in fact points back to the specific possibilities and technological conditions of the medium of film, but it should not be understood as a given representational relation between the media image and reality in the technology itself. For it is only at the level of producing a film image that we can decide in which perspectives and experiential modalities a relation to a shared reality arises.

If the authenticity of film documents is spoken of time and time again as soon as there are debates about the war film, it is ultimately about this effect. The skepticism over the moral and historical dignity of film images of war in fact concerns the dubious – because imaginary – structure of film's reality effect. And it is precisely propaganda films, as we have seen, that emphatically aim at this effect; they suggest the evidence of being an eyewitness, which takes on a physical reality in the here and now of the film spectator's sense activity. And yet, authenticity is always an effect of particular staging strategies.

---

60 It is no accident that this idea is maintained by the film theory of the post-war period. Indeed, it is aimed against the constructivist emphasis with which avant-garde film poetics seemed to be seamlessly extended into the propagandistic concept of the war years. On this idea, cf. Bazin, "The Ontology of the Photographic Image," in *What is Cinema?*, Vol. 1., Berkeley/Los Angeles 2005, and Siegfried Kracauer, *Theory of Film: The Redemption of Physical Reality*, New York 1960, 88.

61 A term that Metz developed to capture the idea that film lets us see full reality as an aesthetic mode of cinema. Cf. Christian Metz, "On the Impression of Reality in the Cinema," in *Film Language: A Semiotics of the Cinema*, Chicago 1991, 3–15.

Sentiment versus document

This concerns more than just the edit which brought the president's son to the funeral service at Midway. The sequence that explicitly takes its value as a visual document from the idea that the camera is placed in the middle of the battle action also does not in any way follow the idea of representing the truth of reality. Even the effects of authenticity are subject to the affect-rhetorical regime that we have already examined in DECEMBER 7TH. They are due to a staging that has the goal of linking the feeling and thinking of physically present spectators with a commonly shared feeling for the historical event represented here.

The filmstrip jumping the frame suggests authenticity. At the same time, however, the American flag is hoisted up by soldiers in the middle of fire and black smoke, following all the rules of the art of directing, and is thus stylized into an iconic formula (see Figure 14). Not that I want to claim that the commentator's voice is lying when it comments on the action with a somber voice: "Yes, this really happens." Certainly, at some point while the combat was raging and a few flags were burned along with the buildings destroyed, someone hoisted the Stars and Stripes. Most likely, the director had also observed something similar. Nonetheless, it is clear that the scene forms a perfectly arranged icon: the men

Figure 14: Stylization of the American flag into an iconic formula.

battling against the black smoke, standing their ground at the flagpole; the camera's framing that follows the flag as it is hoisted up through the darkness; the fluttering red-white that shines in front of the ice-blue background; finally the Stars and Stripes, seen in a long shot, hoisted up on a pole that seems to reach to the heavens – it blows in the wind, positioned in the upper third of the frame in which the blue holds its own against the black clouds.[62]

This setting will be staged over and over again in later war films, on up until the arrangement congeals into a pathos formula with Joe Rosenthal's famous photo "Raising the Flag on Iwo Jima," then becoming the subject of films, monuments, and postage stamps as a formulaic icon – before New York firefighters would erect the icon in this arrangement on September 11, 2001, for a new form of war, and Clint Eastwood would turn it into the topic of a kind of meta-film about the media image of the war film in his diptych FLAGS OF OUR FATHERS and LETTERS FROM IWO JIMA.

We can assume that it was not only the war photographer Joe Rosenthal – as seen in Eastwood's film – who was looking for a photographable arrangement of the scene and thus had the moment when the US flag was hoisted at Iwo Jima recreated. John Ford was also on the lookout for the parameters of a successful visual arrangement. Ultimately, it is hardly possible to distinguish whether there ever was a battle in the Second World War in which the Star Spangled Banner was raised over the clouds of dust made by the still raging battle, without thinking of the script from a scene from a Hollywood movie.

But how can films like THE BATTLE OF MIDWAY or DECEMBER 7TH be understood as documents at all if we do not require facticity from what they represent as events? How can their ethos be evaluated in terms of morality and politics, how can their representations be historically verified, if they obviously follow no other goal than to mobilize all social forces for the war?

In view of the falsification that Ford conducted in his film, the answer seems simple. The editing-in of the President's son complies with an ideological schema that not only defines these propaganda films, but American war propaganda per se: from government authorities in Washington to simple soldiers, from managers and engineers to workers back home and in the army, from military film crews in the service of war to moviegoers in the smallest provincial towns – the whole country found itself in a war in which every individual had to take his or her

---

62 Scene "Ehre den Toten [*honor to the dead*]" (00:15:20:26–00:17:17:28). The hoisting of the flag is not seen in this version, the description given here is based on a digitally restored version available on YouTube. https://www.youtube.com/watch?v=MW8tQ_6dqS8 (starting at 06:33 min., July 28, 2017).

place and had work to do; regardless of social position, military rank, individual freedom. As a description of social realities, this would be an expected ideological scheme, which could not be considered very persuasive. It looks different when we take the pathos form in the films itself as the message. Then we see that, for instance, THE BATTLE OF MIDWAY or DECEMBER 7TH try to become a medium of a sense of commonality, which precisely no longer corresponds to that of a liberal democracy. They generate the communal feeling of a society at war.

The sentence preceding the film as a signature of authorship calls on just such a feeling: "The following authentic scenes were made by U.S. Navy Photographers."[63] It wants to say: 'We, the Navy photographers, are letting you, the spectators, participate as eyewitnesses in the battles of your sons.' The promise of authenticity does not concern the facticity of the events, but the feeling of inviolable connectedness in a society, which is no longer a political bond, but a military one. When films like THE BATTLE OF MIDWAY enlist authenticity, they do so in view of the affect-rhetorical demands that allow cinema to become a medium of such a transformation.

What does the film document document?

How can films like THE BATTLE OF MIDWAY or DECEMBER 7TH be codified as historical documents if this codification can neither be oriented toward the standard of faithfully representing factual events, nor toward evaluating them morally and politically? Beyond the dichotomy of objective representation and deception, the question could be formulated somewhat differently: What kind of world is it that emerges as a common world for the spectator in the staging of the events of war? What are its particularities? How does it relate to the shared world from which – and this is not an insignificant aspect of propaganda films – we are banished without question as soon as a society has transformed itself into a society at war?

Hollywood war films prove to be wholly indifferent to the idea that it is the role of film images to represent the reality of the events of war. So just as Ford artfully stages the funeral service for the fallen soldiers in THE BATTLE OF MIDWAY, William Wyler has the soldiers, whose triumphal process through Italy he documented on film, appear like extras turning up for morning washing on the set of a history film. The site of perception, however, that such stagings refer to, is always

---

63 THE BATTLE OF MIDWAY; scene "Ankunft im 'Vorgarten' Midway [*arriving at the 'front yard' Midway*]".

designated by a concrete subjective standpoint. It is always a particular location in a principally unlimited field of other perspectives.

The effects of the authentic are part of staging a mode of aesthetic experience, which I attempted above to conceive as the illusion of being-in-the-middle, of being-there. This emphasizes one of the possibilities of film technology which has been realized much more extensively in the aesthetic pleasure of genre cinema than in the film document. The illusion of being-in-the-middle forms the basis for all the expressive modalities of the action film; of a genre that we grant no power whatsoever to guarantee reality or authenticity in the historical sense.

The feeling of taking part in an event with one's own eyes, of sensing it in the physical presence of bodily sense activity, represents the essential condition for an aesthetic pleasure based on the illusion of a sensation of the world that can leave behind all the limits of what is possible for sense and action. From my viewpoint, such a pleasure defines – I already spoke of this in the analysis of the Riefenstahl film – why we enjoy action movies.

In THE BATTLE OF MIDWAY, the modalities of action films are added to the melodramatic affect rhetoric sketched out above. Which means nothing more than that the effects of being-in-the-middle are framed and embedded in the melodramatic staging of a subjective sensation of the world; the effects of an impossible participation in combat events already appear in the mirroring of subjective reflection.

When the film asserts a claim of presenting "authentic scenes" to the spectators, this is in no way meant to vouch for the objectivity of what is represented; rather, it requires us to acknowledge a subjective sensation of this reality. The reference to authenticity functions – much like the maternal voice that is concerned for the soldiers' well-being – as a fundamental orientation of the spectator's perceptual sense. It sets the genus, quasi its mode, in which the pathos pattern of melodramatic staging inscribes itself. It asserts a claim for acknowledgment as such, as a world of subjective experience.[64]

The poetic logic of film documents such as THE BATTLE OF MIDWAY is much more defined by the ethos of subjective opinion than that it allows for the film image to take on a special possibility of vouching for the reality of events. The reality that is thematized in these films is ultimately that of a subjective sensation, against which every media representation remains deficient; the reality referred to by films such as THE BATTLE OF MIDWAY cannot be detached from the

---

64 It is thus no accident when directors of Hollywood war films, from John Ford and Sam Fuller to Oliver Stone and John Irvin, make claims, time and time again, of subjective witness. Obviously, this claim is then articulated again as a persistent proof of the realism of film images.

'I sense,' 'I think,' 'I feel' of a concrete, physical-sensory being-in-the-world. It means the awareness of an incommensurable experience of horror and suffering. In the American war film genre, this is always the suffering of the (fallen) soldier.

But witnessing, as a sympathetic view of this suffering, is delegated to the spectators themselves. The voice of maternal concern that Ford introduces in BATTLE OF MIDWAY describes exactly the function of the melodramatic mode in the war film genre. Only in the perception established by the voice does the soldiers' suffering become palpable – not in the representation of the events, but as a feeling for a world shared with the soldiers. In the melodramatic mode, this feeling becomes a feeling for the communal. The melodramatic genus of the mode of perception, of sympathizing and commiserating, is the appeal that calls on the sense of commonality. The reality that is meant to become a physical reality in the spectator's sense activities is the feeling for the communal.

3.4 Affective Mobilization

Military mobilization is deeply intermingled with the media mobilization of the senses of perception at all levels. This can be considered a truism of media theory at least since Virilio's *War and Cinema*.[65] In fact, there seems to be evidence that modern wars are decided above all by media technologies, which make it possible to represent and manage a weapons technology that can provide access to all conceivable dimensions of space and time. Tracking down, projecting, making visible and conceivable becomes a direct component of destructive power. In its capacity to solidify the correspondence between multiple, dynamically changing perceptual spaces, which can only be grasped in reality as mathematical formulae, modern war technology accords with media technology.[66] The aesthetic experience that allows spectators to project impossible spaces in their physical seeing

---

[65] Virilio, *War and Cinema*.
[66] Friedrich Kittler writes: "The history of the movie camera thus coincides with the history of automatic weapons. The transport of pictures only repeats the transport of bullets. In order to focus on and fix objects moving through space, such as people, there are two procedures: to shoot and to film. In the principle of cinema resides mechanized death as it was invented in the nineteenth century: the death no longer of one's immediate opponent but of serial nonhumans.... With the chronophotographic gung, mechanized death was perfected: its transmission coincided with its storage. What the machine gun annihilated the camera made immortal." Friedrich Kittler, *Grammophone Film Typewriter*, Stanford 1999, 124.

and hearing refers back to an illusion that is genuinely linked to the media technology of cinema. As the illusion of a gaze that overcomes the spatio-temporal-complexity of any explosion, it is one fundamental trait of aesthetic pleasure and the agent of action cinema.

Affect dramaturgies in the range of action and melodrama

It is not by chance that the action film, from FIRST BLOOD to TERMINATOR 3, celebrates the phantasm of an indestructible body in relation to the war film. Regardless of whether this happens under the cloak of science fiction, ancient gladiator battles, the Middle Ages of fantasy films, or in the décor of the historical war film: what is staged is always the phantasmatic potential of media technology itself, the capacity of cinema to mobilize the spectator's space of perception and sensation. The Hollywood war film, however, ultimately deals with quite different conditions of visibility than does the action film.

Whether at a landing in the African desert, at Normandy, or in Italy, whether in the War in the Pacific at Guadalcanal or Saipan: the protagonist of the classical Hollywood war film is the reconnaissance patrol or the assault detachment, the smallest part of the troop that operates, in close proximity to the events of war, as the eyes, ears, and nose. To the degree that they become the sense organs of a military body, the individual soldiers lose their own sense of things. What they do no longer conforms to the action radius of the individual body, but to the hierarchy of command. This perception of the foot soldier, always operating at the edge of blindness, is the basic audiovisual motif of the classical war film. Be it the invisible enemy, concealed in the night, in the jungle, or in tunnels and caves underground, be it the chaos of curtain fire, the colorful clouds of smoke from bombs, the flash of an exploding grenade: the reconnaissance patrol is the epic ego, which is wholly enclosed in an event without itself having any way to get a view of this whole. The Hollywood war film is much more often about this experience of being blinded by the glare than about the feelings of triumph common in action films, the illusion of overview. In no way does it follow the stereotype of the classical hero's tale. Quite often the action does indeed establish a young hero who is transformed into a man used to suffering; but the goal of this is not the same one that we know from the psychological coming-of-age novel [*Entwicklungsroman*].

For the character of the soldier, the war takes place as an objective event, ruled over by a will, a law, that is not accessible to him, that always remains mysterious, secretive. For him, war is always meaningless slaughter, an impenetrable chaos of sensations. The soldier himself is only one appearance in an intentionally directed event that concerns him without revealing itself: he is its object.[67] The films describe this event as a process of transforming his bodily sense of self and his desire. The first stage is represented as a rite of initiation, the passage from an insufficient individual to a participant in the symbols of a fully valid, male subject power; the second stage denotes just this phantasm of unlimited subject power; the third stage shows the reversal of the process, the experience of being thrown back to the vulnerability and helplessness of an individual body. It shows physical suffering from the perspective of the sensitive individual.

From the collectivization in the drill, the euphoric intoxication of destruction in the armed military community, to the experience of the abandoned and once again individual body, the subjective sensation of the individual forms the basic point of reference for the film staging. The interior view of the sensitive subject, on which an action is carried out that it can merely suffer, and cannot actively dictate, designates the pathos of the Hollywood war film; it is its overriding reference point. This is also the case for those films tirelessly claimed to be somehow completely different from the old genre, the films about the so-called new wars in Iraq and elsewhere. Focusing on the representational perspective of the subject in the film staging allows the hero's suffering to become a form of melodramatic pathos; it could be called the melodramatic core of the war film genre.

GUNG HO!: The mobilization film

I would first like to explicate this thesis using a film that starts urging on its addressees already in the title: Ray Enright's GUNG HO! from 1943.[68] This mobilization film brought a new word into the English language – "Gung ho" henceforth meant raw rah-rah patriotism.

---

[67] The epic mode of speaking constitutes a world that exists independently of the narrative itself, as an outside to this speech. "Plot" then means an entanglement of various objective forces which are completed independently of the narrator's perspective, also independently of the agents enclosed within the plot. "Poetry develops these sculptural pictures for our imagination by presenting them as determined by the action of gods and men, so that everything that happens either proceeds from morally self-subsistent divine or human powers or else is a reaction to external hindrances, and in its external mode of appearance becomes an *event* in which the thing at issue goes ahead on its own account while the poet retires. To describe such events in their wholeness is the task of *epic* poetry which reports poetically in the form of the broad flow of events an action complete in itself and the characters who produce it, either as one substantive worth or as adventurously intermixed with external accidents. In this way it presents what is itself objective in its objectivity." Georg Wilhelm Friedrich Hegel, *Aesthetics: Lectures on Fine Art*, Vol. 2, Oxford 1975, 1037.
[68] The full title reads: 'GUNG HO!': THE STORY OF CARLSON'S MAKIN ISLAND RAIDERS.

The dramaturgical structure could not be simpler. At the beginning the prospective soldiers are introduced as more or less unhappy individuals.[69] The army recruitment officers are representatives of the idea of the good father, gathering together the country's prodigal sons. In the application interview the young men not only reveal their squalid backgrounds and their precarious situation in life, but also their insufficiency in morals and practical life matters. Then we see the general's address, promising the fresh recruits on screen and in front of the screen a new life in the fighting community of the army.[70] In their military leader they will find stability and paternal protection, they will learn composure and discipline in the athletic drills, strength and a sense of something higher in the pledged fighting community. The next sequence shows us the young recruits exercising enthusiastically, underscored by cheerful music.[71] We see the half-naked bodies shouting as they train, their movements looking more and more like those of an overall group body (see Figure 15). And we recognize film material that comes from newsreels. (SANDS OF IWO JIMA and other films will also use this material.)

Finally, we see the seriousness of war staged like the play of a well-trained football team, which can barely be distinguished in its concrete action from the moves of an actual match – only that, from case to case, a player has to be retired because he has met with enemy fire.[72] A short mourning anthem seals the victim's fate before the film turns back to the events of battle. We see the perfect interplay of a highly efficient group body, following the course of the game, which is interrupted time and again by the short minor phrases of a sacrificial scene (see Figure 16).

At first glance, GUNG HO! follows the quite simple schema of a heroic epic. But even if the image of the enemy is simplistic in its racism, the image of suffering heroicized, the war euphemistically prettified, the mobilization film is not merely about representing and propagating hostility and pugnacity. Instead, GUNG HO! traces out an affective course that is pursued ever further in countless later war films.

This course aims to stage things in a calculated way in which opposing affective qualities – which one can technically classify as certain feelings such as pugnacity and fear, euphoria and mourning, we-feeling and hostility – can be mutually interrelated in the sequence of scenes. For the spectator, what emerges

---

[69] GUNG HO!; scene "Recruitment selection" (00:02:22:16–00:13:18:07).
[70] GUNG HO!; scene "Address 2" (00:13:18:07–00:15:53:21).
[71] GUNG HO!; scene "Drill and merging" (00:15:53:21–00:19:59:01).
[72] GUNG HO!; scene "Jungle battle and the machine gun nest" (00:51:57:11–01:00:18:13).

Figure 15: Formation of the group body in GUNG HO!

over the course of the scenes is a variety of affect qualities that in no way need to be semantically defined ahead of time, a continual process of affection that only becomes palpable as a feeling in the form of its continuity. The process of affection is crisscrossed and interwoven in a variety of ways with the dramaturgical development of the course of action. The dramaturgical schema of the calculated alteration of visual constellations defined by opposing affect qualities

Figure 16: Battle action and sacrifice.

already carries within itself all the conflicts and ambivalences of the mobilization film, which will only be foregrounded and worked out in later films.

The transformation of needy individuals into soldiers

The starting point – and in this the films are no different than Riefenstahl's propaganda – is about taking pleasure in sensing one's own individual corporeality. There is hardly a war film that does without scenes of half-naked soldiers in the morning, cleaning up at washtubs and under improvised showers in the great outdoors. We see young soldiers frolicking about. It is these scenes that give the group its social contour, where funny bits and short dialogues let us see the individual types: the joker, the roughneck, the quiet type, the dullard, the nice guy, the coarse redneck, and the scrupulous city boy. Or we see joking, fresh-faced boys who have just turned up at the front, startled by the gloomily frowning, taciturn men. At the end of the film they are either dead or at least have become just as quiet and withdrawn. Hardly any war film does not reproduce this schema in its plot in one way or another. Its hero is the innocent-naïve youth at the beginning of an actual or imaginary journey, at the end of which stands either the man with experience, or death and a commemoration of the sacrifice. In between we see the hero as a cog in the wheel of the war machinery.

What is presented at the beginning are the realistic, ordinary bodies of young men, more or less vulnerable, more or less unhappy, more or less inadequate. At the zenith is the fantasy of triumphant virility, the intoxicating heights of a super-ego in the fighting community. At the end is the agony of the soldiers who had sacrificed themselves for the community and the rituals of mourning. This summarizes the ideal dramaturgical line of the mobilization film.

Hollywood war films during and in the first few years after the Second World War stage the steps of this transformation as a process in which the ordinary qualities of individual bodies' sensations, which we find staged in scenes like that of the ritual washing up in the morning, are converted into a lust for battle and valor unto death. This is why rituals of self-transgression in military training and in the collective battle experience are the focal points of these films. This is why the young men in GUNG HO! are introduced in their inadequate and needy individuality. This is the reason for the long montage sequences representing how insufficient individuals are transformed by drill and training into effective battle troops. This is the reason for the sense of sportsmanship dominating the battle scenes. These scenes stage the melding of ordinary bodies into the armed corps, the military collective, as elation. The image that emerges is one of euphoric participation in a collective body with nearly insurmountable forces.

From the last encounters with the pretty girls to whom they bid farewell so as to share the memory of the image of the woman as a community-forming power, to the hard training, the physical drills, to the euphoria of a battle that is completed as the perfect interlocking of weapons, machinery, and human bodies, GUNG HO! traces the stages of this process in great detail. The highlight of the film is the staging of rescuing the almost already lost fighter by using war technology.

In fact, in one way or another, nearly every later Hollywood war film describes the procedure by which individual bodies are converted into a military corps, into an arrangement of symbolic, technological, and biological material. We are familiar with the euphoria that is staged in the representation of this process, already from the maneuvering scenes from the Riefenstahl film and the war metaphor that Vertov uses to celebrate the power of cinema. In fact, it is also true for the Hollywood war film that, in the interplay of weapons technology, the power of human bodies, and team spirit, they activate above all a fundamental mode of genre cinema that links them with the adventure genre and with action movies. In the unity of the military corps, forces emerge that surmount all the physical limitations of individual bodies; forces that are turned into the spectator's sensations in the cinematic staging of battle, of the force of arms, of the skill of the individual, and the platoon's teamwork.[73]

Peripety: switching from action to melodrama

In GUNG HO! the action mode defines the numerous battles scenes in which the interplay of the platoon and weapons technology is always presented anew. The film thus turns out to be an advertisement for the army, focusing over and over again on the individual achievements of the recruits, as if the successful interplay of groups of men and weapons technology were above all due to the esprit and the athletic prowess of individuals: for instance, the scene in which the enemy fighter-bomber is redirected to its own posts by a deceptive maneuver that could have been thought up by a schoolboy (unnoticed, a Japanese post is redecorated by the soldiers gathered there as a US base).

In the expressive modalities of action cinema, the imaginary melding of the physical ego with an inviolable, armed body of the military unit is carried out as the completely harmonic interlocking of all the elements of the military corps. Mobilization films like GUNG HO! therefore seem to adhere to an equally simple and transparent ideology of patriarchal initiation. For the representation of the feelings described designates intersections at which the sensations of the hero, and the hero himself, are transformed: step by step, in order to become a fighting, killing, suffering, and raging soldier. Using this schema, the mobilization film during the war years describes the individual assimilation to the cultural imagination of masculinity per se, the community of soldiers.

At second glance, we recognize that even in the films from the mobilization phase, the dramaturgical line is crisscrossed time and again by experiences of fear, discouragement, and pain. Even if GUNG HO! flattens all contradictions, it shows us the deep ambivalence associated with this transformation. Indeed, the film consistently maintains the perspective of the individual going through this process. In the drill and in battle, we sense not only delight, but also the fear that goes along with it, bereft of any self-determination to become a mere function in

---

73 In view of Linda Williams's work, one might look at the implementation of the action mode as one of the generic forms of the body genre. Thomas Elsaesser and Michael Wedel have understood the specificity of the post-classical war film under this theoretical topos. Cf. Linda Williams, "Film Bodies: Gender, Genre, and Excess," in *Film Quarterly*, Vol. 44, No. 4, 1991, 2–13. Also: Thomas Elsaesser and Michael Wedel, *Körper, Tod und Technik: Metamorphosen des Kriegsfilms*, Konstanz 2016.

an operational chain, the course of which is radically deprived of any actual individual perspective. It is the fear of those who experience themselves as a cog in the machinery in which the human body is inserted as a functional component.

GUNG HO! stages this ambivalent experience in a specific setting by representing the passage from training camp to battlefield as a long submarine ride. We see sweaty bodies crammed in together, enclosed in the belly of the heaving machine. The film shows us the passage as a dismal image of physical hardship: as if the spectators themselves could taste the stifling air of the soldiers' quarters, sense the panic of the shortage of breath that one can be overcome by in such claustrophobic constriction (see Figure 17).

As much as GUNG HO! represents the euphoria of an overwhelming frenzy of power in the athletic competition, in the off-screen voice, in the image of the powerful armaments, it also compresses the experience of fear and of the horror of ego-death in the submarine sequences into a highly effective image. It draws its basic dramatic tension from the opposition between the euphoria of exuberant power and the fearful experience of ego-loss. The submarine passage gives expression to the nightmarish sensation of relinquishing control of one's own body to an external entity.

These scenes do not simply represent an action, but literally stage a feeling, a subjective sensation. The sequence unfolds an indirect subjective experience in which a sensation becomes palpable that, despite all integration into a group body, is articulated as an individual, subjective sense of self.

The film stages a sense of self that suddenly becomes aware of its precarious situation and of being a member of a collective body, a member that has no influence on the body's action and movements, on its will. *I am no longer master of my own body, my senses, my will, I am completely enclosed, penned in, completely and utterly fused with the boat and the other bodies.*

For the spectator in the space of the cinema, it is precisely this sense of self that becomes a direct sensation of perception.[74] Namely, when the officer walks back and forth between his men, we see neither officer nor men. Rather, we see an odd connection of body fragments arranged in space; above, below, and on all sides, we see faces, hands, arms, shoulders pressed against one another and structured by the bracing of the berths. We might identify this spatial arrangement as the interior space of a machine, saying about the abstract structures: "Okay, maybe this is what a submarine looks like." But what we actually see is a montage of fragmented human body parts, as if they were disassembled into their parts, in order to be recombined into a new body in the interior of a machine.

---

74 GUNG HO!; scene "Confinement in the submarine" (00:30:06:17–00:34:56:13).

Figure 17: Breathlessness.

In the following scenes, this is intensified.[75] The doors are closed. The officer that had been speaking with his recruits now speaks to the enclosed men from outside through a loudspeaker. The voice that addresses the men in the interior of the

---

75 GUNG HO!; scenes "Group body in the submarine" (00:34:56:13–00:37:32:23) and "Briefing in the submarine" (00:37:32:23–00:41:13:07).

machine lets the commanding will that embodies the authority and knowledge of the situation become palpable as a radically separate exterior to personal physical sensation. Now, at the latest, the densely packed faces and intertwined bodies become an expressive figuration in which subjective experience, the panic in the face of the constriction, and the shortage of breath are articulated. The passage in the submarine becomes a temporal form in the film staging that allows for a feeling to arise for the spectators in a process of permanent affectation, so that they ascribe this feeling to the faces on the screen as fear.

As unrepresentative as the transport of large military units over large stretches of ocean by submarine is, a metaphorical field of references is strikingly employed in the staging of the visual space: young men who are enclosed within the belly of a heaving machine, only to be reborn after days of panicky constriction in the depths of the ocean as a military troop under the thundering of cannonry, discharged onto land, where they finally become transformed into a fighting machine. In the image of the men enclosed in the most constricted of spaces, who anxiously wait to see if the torpedoes fired at their ship will tear it apart in the next moment, deep ambivalence finds its expression, which is linked with the transformation in the process of military communitization itself.

GUNG HO! stages a sensation of perception in which the increasing panic is conveyed to the spectators as a subjective sensation that they embody in the activity of their own senses: the physical sensation of a quite external will, a voice from the outside, which has taken the place of my ego. The euphoria of a sense of community carries within itself the panic of ego-loss. In the cinematic expressive figuration, this ambivalence becomes an aesthetic sensation to the spectators themselves. For GUNG HO! stages this in a way that compresses and manipulates expressive qualities with which the film image directly affects the spectators' bodies.

In cinematic visual spaces like that of the submarine passage, a staging strategy is already inscribed in the prototype of the mobilization film which then decisively marks the war film genre: an indirect subjective speech in which the flip side of the military body is asserted, the perspective of the individual, which gives validity to the higher will of the military community in its physical suffering. For all the rah-rah patriotism, the experience of fear that is associated with the loss of ego is put on screen as a subjective sensation.

The action mode – the melding of organic bodies and arms technologies in the dynamic perceptual mode of the cinema – always marks the peripety in the war film, the radical turn from one affect quality to another. The rise into the heights of an ideal community, the triumphant feeling of being part of an insurmountable force, only prepares the plunge into the depths of physical suffering of a mortal individual, who in his suffering perhaps becomes a hero, perhaps a sacrifice.

At each moment, the cinematic staging of battle by the armed military unit can jump over into the perspective of a single soldier who, wounded, abandoned, overburdened, paralyzed by fear, or overcome by pain, sees himself confronting death; at each moment, the euphoria can switch over into the experience of helplessness, forsakenness, and physical weakness; at each moment, the scene from action cinema can become a horror film threatening annihilation by enemy forces or a melodrama of the suffering individual. If the object of the staging was still just participating in the power of a military unit, it has now become the experience of the incongruity of the human body in the face of the coercive force of arms and the threat of the invisible enemy.

Michael Wedel has described this switch as follows:

> This situation is found in nearly every modern war film, but it is only partially described by characterizing it as the plot device of the "last stand" (of the last bastion that all too often turns out to be of lost posts, cf. King 2006: 298 ff.). A unit is isolated and exposed to enemy fire; the radio equipment doesn't work or there is none. The chain of command breaks down, the strategy comes to nothing. Reinforcements never arrive, there is never any rescue commando anywhere: the opponent's traps snap shut. A group of scattered soldiers is left to its own resources, the only thing left is mere survival, for many that lay dying the paramedic (if there is one) becomes the most popular man.
>
> Following Deleuze (1989: 275ff.) we might describe these moments as situations in which the narrative vector of the action-image – and with it the sensory-motor agency of the individual to act – falls into crisis, and in its place appears the modeling of an affection-image, which acts at and between bodies.[76]

This switch from action mode into an affection-image can occur in the expressive modalities of the horror film or in the sentimental modalities of the melodrama.

Fighting spirit and the willingness to suffer: a dramaturgical comparison

In mobilization films such as GUNG HO! the switch from action scenes into melodramatic expression is barely played out. In the short repeated elegiac trumpet motif, the horror is reduced, with little subtlety, to something perceived on the aesthetic margins. Even the threatening face of a demonically animated nature is played through in the casualness of a scenic stereotype. When the soldiers

---

[76] Wedel, "Körper, Tod und Technik," 88. Wedel refers to Geoff King, "Seriously Spectacular: 'Authenticity' and 'Art' in the War Epic," in *Hollywood and War: The Film Reader*, ed. J. D. Slocum, New York/London 2006, 287–301 and Deleuze, *The Movement Image*.

move through the palm forest of the South Seas island, the enemy is in fact lurking behind every hill and in every tree top. But not much more is implied by this than the setting of the previously established rules of the game. The agony as well as the fear of the soldier is realized and framed by the battle scenes in the action mode. GUNG HO! thus diminishes precisely that subjectification of the relations of perception that determine later war films. This can be seen very easily by comparing the dramaturgical structure of GUNG HO! with Tay Garnett's film BATAAN (1943).

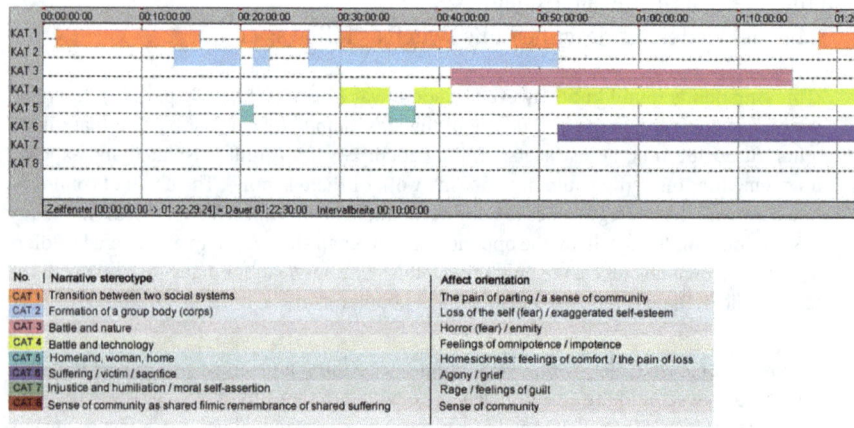

Figure 18: Diagram showing the temporal arrangement of pathos scenes in GUNG HO! (Ray Enright, USA 1943).

The first efforts toward developing the dramaturgical line of the war film as a prototypical three-act structure can be recognized in GUNG HO! (see Figure 18). In the first fifteen minutes we find scenes that present the disentanglement from civil society (pathos category 1); then, in the next thirty minutes, the initiation into the military community (pathos category 2) and its contrast to civil society (pathos category 2 with references to pathos category 3). The battle action (pathos category 4 between minute 30 and minute 42) is completely referred to the process of initiation in these scenes of the submarine passage; the force of arms is an invisible threat, only acoustically underlying the image of panic. Starting with minute 40, the film changes into the action mode in order to shift the focus in the last twenty-five minutes to the presentation of weapons technology and the soldiers' own fighting power. It is consistently accompanied by short sentences about suffering and death, without the melodramatic expressive modalities ever replacing the staging of the soldiers' fighting power. In the first act the disentanglement from civil society is presented, in the second the formation of the military community, in the third their fighting power. The staging of nature as a horrifying threat takes a back seat, as does the melodramatic presentation of the victim.

The dramaturgical structure of BATAAN is quite different. An air raid hits the nearly endless flow of people fleeing: broken figures, children, women, the wounded, carrying with them what little they could manage to save.[77] The representation of the flow of people describes a society that has already been destroyed in the exceptional state of war, an improvised community of the afflicted made of Philippine civilians and the heavily battered American military. Even when the distinctions in the movements of the marching soldiers and the civilians arduously inching forward is exhibited, the regular rhythm of the sound, the framing, and, above all, the same vectorial directionality of the two groups links them into a unified movement that incorporates everything. The attack of the Japanese fighter pilots shatters the unity of the stream of people fleeing; they are dispersed in the same eccentric movement as the ground exploding beneath them. Anyone who did not find cover in the adjacent jungle, the cars and the buildings, remains lying on the open streets. As the noise of the enemy planes fades, the shots become longer again, the previously bustling streets show a battlefield, dead and wounded bodies mark the way. Here and there a wounded person arduously moves, dying impulses in the midst of destruction and chaos. The flow of people fleeing, the improvised community of war victims, is scattered in every direction …

From the films about the First World War to the films about Vietnam, the Hollywood war film has been marked by two fundamental ways of staging space: the explosive dissociation of perception spaces in the representation of a literally detonating ground and – corresponding to this – an acoustic tableau that overrides the boundary between image and spectator, enclosing the spectator in the space of the representation. In BATAAN, the staging of such a visual space occurs at the beginning of the film. The explosion practically captures the inner texture of the audiovisual composition itself: smoke, scattered earth, fire and the smoke of gunshots cause the visual field itself to come apart, visual segments are torn off, objects and bodies filled up, warped, and tattered until finally the concreteness of the film image as a whole has become deformed into an abstract arrangement.

---

[77] BATAAN; scene "Attack on the refugee trek" (00:01:16:14–00:04:53:12). On the following, cf. the analytical description of the composition and expressive movements in this scene by Sarah Greifenstein in our data matrix: http://www.empirische-medienaesthetik.fu-berlin.de/en/emaex-system/affektdatenmatrix/filme/bataan/01_angriff_auf_den_fluechtlingstreck/index.html (July 7, 2017)

BATAAN: the pathos of the victim in military collectivization

The film begins, like many other war films, with the breakdown of civilian society. Except that in BATAAN the end is already being represented in it. The battle over the Philippines has been lost for the American troops at this point in the chronology of the Pacific War.

The film tells of the suicide mission of a platoon trying to the last man to stop the enemy from crossing a bridge. The soldiers fight for the time that would allow the American troops to reorganize in an orderly retreat after having been decimated in the Philippines.

The destructive power of weaponry is completely attributed to the enemy. And this enemy is absolutely invisible. Nonetheless, an overwhelming presence is developed in the sound of the airplanes, the bomb explosions, and the rounds of gunshots. As the explosion is conveyed to the spectators almost as the destruction of the audiovisual composition, the noise of the battle action forms an acoustic space that the spectators share in their perceptual sensations with the characters on screen. The enemy remains in the shadows. He becomes visible – and this will only change in the last quarter of the film – in the effect of deadly shots, exploding bombs, and rounds of machine gun fire from the low flying planes. The arms technology of war has become an unpredictable power from above, which can strike and decimate at any time.

At no point is the recourse to arms, repeating at regular intervals, associated with the euphoric feelings of triumph that we find presented in the battle scenes in GUNG HO! and other mobilization films. The soldiers in BATAAN no longer stand under the protective shield of the heavy guns of the war ships and airplanes. Left quite to their own resources, exposed in their vulnerable bodies, they are surrendered helpless to the enemy attacks. And if in the battle any excitement among the men is represented that seems like the euphoric sense of power, then we link this much more with the bitter rage of those who have already fallen; they can no longer defeat their tormentors, but they can add one last sting at the price of their own destruction.

The weapons that the soldiers still have available to them – we see this right at the beginning when a badly wounded G.I. is lifted into an emergency vehicle, still convulsively holding onto his gun when they try to take it from him – are their most personal possessions; they are signs of the devotion and self-sacrifice to the military community, without being linked to any sense of power anymore.

In the small military community, which has been abandoned as a separated part of the troops from the reorganized army, the individual, the singular personality, seems to return. We can see this in the scene in which the scattered troops are brought together again by Sergeant Dane (Robert Taylor) into a new battle unit immediately following the attack.[78]

Audiovisual composition and the affective dynamic

In analyzing the following scenes in great detail, I am attempting to get to the affect dynamics that are grounded in the composition of the expressive movements.

The complexity of the scene emphasizes the separation of the soldiers and makes it possible to see what is being negotiated at the level of dialogue – between sergeant and captain: the breakdown of the troop into individuals who no longer form a combat unit. At the level of the staging, an overriding movement is attributed to the sergeant – the long, drawn-out pan, the presence of his voice. It is contrasted with the emphatic isolation of the scattered activities of the individual soldiers in the framing of different courses of movement separated from one another. With Dane's appearance the individual actions of the soldiers, ordinary individual activities (washing, putting away the dishes, loafing around) lose any dynamic of their own. The soldiers are still carrying out the last hand movements before they turn their gaze to him, then their movements become slower. Step by step, through the choreography of their lethargic movements and circular pans, all the other characters focus on the sergeant (expressive movement unit (EMU) 1).

The result is an image of strict geometrical proportions, which encloses the group as it forms into a single framing. The geometrical order is then heightened by the editing, which sews up the sergeant and the individual troop members into a unit by the constant repetition of similar shot/reverse shot and question/answer schemes (EMU 2).

The affective dimension is shown in the opposition between military communitization and individual activities, staged in the summarizing movement that incorporates the commander and the initially scattered individual activities of the soldiers. Their individual body movements give way to unified directions in gaze and movement, which find their center in the sergeant. The strict geometry of the group image succinctly expresses the successful melding of the military unit

---

[78] BATAAN; scene "The Sergeant and his squad" (00:10:11:18–00:15:41:27). On the following, cf. the analytical description of the composition and expressive movements in this scene by Sarah Greifenstein in our data matrix: http://www.empirische-medienaesthetik.fu-berlin.de/en/emaex-system/affektdatenmatrix/filme/bataan/03_der_sgt_und_seine_truppe/index.html (July 7, 2017).

Figure 19: Military communitization in BATAAN.

(see Figure 19). The film then also consistently maintains this tension, constantly contrasting the compelling force of the military call with the stubbornness of individual activities, which results in thoroughly comedic effects – as if the military unit had to be formed time and again from the ordinary gathering of men, only to sink back into the loose connection of single ordinary activities shortly thereafter.

The film constantly refers its audience to the experience of a dissolving community, the platoon is constantly reorganized as a military community, and there

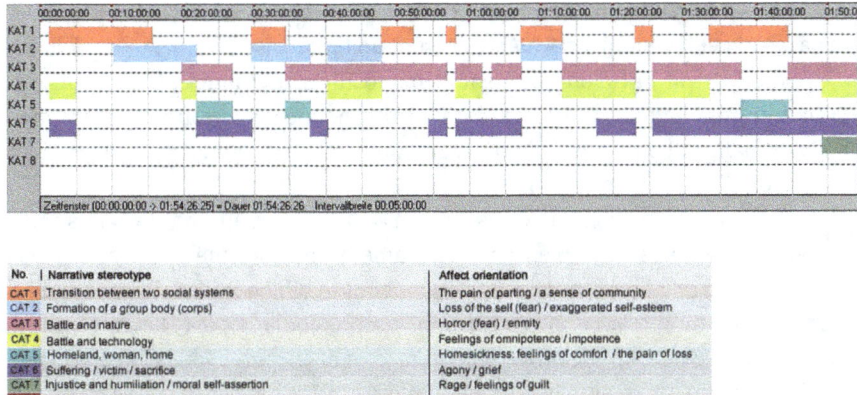

Figure 20: Diagram showing the temporal arrangement of pathos scenes in BATAAN (Tay Garnett, USA 1943).

are constantly more or less short battle actions that end with the staging of the sacrifices, their suffering, their death. Instead of the stages of the mobilization film, as seen prototypically in GUNG HO!, in BATAAN the alternation between the different pathos complexes (dissolution of the civilian community and formation of the military one, the staging of battle and of death, of mourning and the figure of the sacrifice) is staged in ever new cycles (see Figure 20). With each grave and each new cross the cycle starts over again from the beginning; only the scenes of agony, the pathos-laden representation of the sacrifice, expand ever further, as the graves define the visual space little by little.

Almost from the very beginning (starting with minute 20), the representation of nature dominates how the film is presented. Except for the exposition and the first minutes in which the platoon is formed, all scenes are positioned in the twilight of the jungle. In its picturesque iconography it is similar to an enchanted forest, hiding the defenseless soldiers in its darkness, keeping the enemy from getting hold of them, providing them with a precarious abode shut off from the enemy's eyes. At the same time, however, in the ornamental pattern of the interlocking shrubbery, the shadowing and layers of the jungle's trunks, branches, and leaves are shown as a visual space in which the enemy is permanently present as an invisible threat. He gets his sinister face in the forms of nature.

The platoon's camp hidden in the jungle melds into the tangle of dark palms, bushes, underbrush, and fallen trees, as if, despite all adversity, it could offer the shelter necessary to improvise a family setting in enemy territory. In fact, time and again there appears an ordinary community with familial role distribution, which lets the camp become a little pocket of home for a short time.

This can be described quite tellingly in a sequence in which a young soldier manages to get reception on an American radio broadcast.[79]

In the interplay of montage, visual composition, and music, the slow transformation from anxious tension in light of the menacing surroundings, through the joy at a direct connection to home, and on to relaxed comradery is staged as a succession of spatial figurations.

Initially, the film stages anxious tension (EMU 1). Two alternating shots show soldiers whose gazes are fixed past the camera and into the off-screen space. That is, on the one hand there is a medium shot in which Private Eeps (Kenneth Spencer), standing still behind a machine gun, is looking past the camera into the off-screen space, on the other a medium shot of Corporal Todd (Lloyd Nolan), standing next to a tree and also looking into the off-screen space. This gives rise to a dissociated visual space that is not linked to any consistent space of action, neither through the visual composition nor the montage. The staging leaves everything at a dissociated spatial figuration that stands in contrast to the space of action to come (EMU 2).

The gazes looking past the camera and into the off-screen space directly associate the indeterminate space with danger. On the one hand, the expressive quality is heightened on the level of visual composition by the light values. Both shots are discreetly lit in the center of the image, while they get darker toward the margins of the frame. This allows for the visual space to transition fluidly into an undefined black. On the other hand, a temporal dynamic is introduced by the soldiers' repeated appearances. In the alternation from stillness to movement, a metric pattern is developed that lends the scene of tense observation an internal time, gives it duration. Finally, the expression of tense observation is staged, also at the level of mimic-gestural movements of expression. The soldiers crouch through the image slowly and steadily; both the background noises emphasized at the beginning of the scene – rustling leaves, the rattling of weapons, footsteps – and the soldiers speaking only with muffled voices create a stillness that lends the visual space as a whole the expression of tense-anxious expectation. Finally, the noise of radio searching for a station announces the radical alternation of the expressive framework.

A cut leads to a completely different scene. In a long shot, clearly defined in the visual composition, we see the soldiers gathered around a radio. The previously

---

[79] BATAAN, scene "Sounds from the radio" (00:34:25:21–00:37:54:23). On the following, cf. the analytical description of the composition and expressive movements in this scene by Jan-Hendrik Bakels in our data matrix: http://www.empirische-medienaesthetik.fu-berlin.de/en/emaex-system/affekt-datenmatrix/filme/bataan/09_radioklaenge/index.html (July 7, 2017).

indeterminate space (EMU 1) gives way to a now clearly outlined space of action. The transition between wide shots, medium shots, and close ups follows the conventions of a spatially oriented montage. The fact that the borders of the frame in the long shots coincide with those of the interior space represented gives the scene a stage-like character; the now clear lighting makes it possible to visually orient oneself in the whole (see Figure 21).

Figure 21: Alternating figurations of space.

The dynamic within the visual composition and the transforming facial expressions of the protagonists are organized in time by diegetic music. The drum solo that sets in marks a turning point in the choreography – from the protagonists indeterminately scattered through the space in the beginning to a group image concentrically staged around the radio. With the brass coming in at the end of the piece the music finally finds a motoric echo in Ramirez's (Desi Arnaz) movements, his fingers drumming along and the rhythmic movements of his shoulders. In the interplay of music and gestural-facial movement, a dynamic expressivity arises that articulates an affect of increasing, joyful excitement; in the sharp contrast to the dissociated spaces of anxious tension, an interior space of civil sociability emerges.

A new shift in the spatial presentation now connects both spatial figurations. A common meal in the open air; once again there are two disparate spaces; now, however, both are linked with the interior space by means of the music from the radio into an overarching expressive arrangement (EMU 3). All tension has eased, the jungle itself now seems to have become the interior of a sociable gathering of civilians.

The scene is a prelude to a further round in the circular process of dissolving a civilian community and (re)organizing it into a military one, including a renewed staging of sacrifice. But the perspective on the events has changed over the course of the three spatial figurations. While the jungle, nature, had consistently been associated to this point with the threat of the enemy, which is confronted by the military alliance, this dichotomy is now broken up. In the succession of tension, joy, and relaxed sociability, an indirect subjective perspective is articulated in which the personal individuality of the soldiers is at work. It is, as it were, the interior view of their sensitivity. The scenes of joyfully relaxed sociability are as diametrically opposed to the military fighting community as it is to the feeling of the permanent presence of the enemy. The dialogue then also puts them in direct relation to the memories of a past civilian life at home.

Like a beat, the skirmishes that return in regular intervals divide the basic temporal structure of the film, in which the eerie omnipresence of the enemy can be made out little by little in the twilight of the jungle, becoming a shape of overwhelming terror. Initially, it is just the bang of isolated shots and short skirmishes, which quickly tear apart the illusion of the forest offering the soldiers any protection that would allow something like ordinary social life to emerge in their camp.

In the anxious expectation of what the forest twilight is hiding, which can be seen in the soldiers' tense faces, reflected almost imperceptibly in the background music, the idea of the enemy unfolds for the spectator as an eerie presence that belongs to the jungle itself, and that takes on a visible shape little by little. The film stages the subjective consciousness of implacably approaching death in the expressive modalities of the horror film. After almost an hour and a half of cycle running through over and over again (between relaxed sociability, tense expectation, armed conflict, scenes of death and mourning), it is in fact the scene of a horror film in which the soldiers find themselves directly face to face with the enemy for the first time.[80] The guard can't believe his eyes – did the trees and bushes right behind him just move toward him? The first skirmish in which

---

[80] BATAAN, scene "Close combat" (01:25:29:20–01:33:30:04). On the following, cf. the analytical description of the composition and expressive movements in this scene by Matthias Grotkopp

the G.I.s finally get to see the enemy begins with a grotesque scenario. In their camouflage, the enemy soldiers themselves have become the plants in the forest, as if the trees and bushes were now themselves coming after the Americans as ghostly fighters.

The apotheosis: fusion of separated visual spaces

In the first part of the scene the topic of anxious expectation is once again established. The staging is structured by two antagonistic visual spaces, with an anticipation of their explosive collision. The tension, with its stress on anxiety, is created by an interplay of extradiegetic music – a variation of stereotypical horror motifs – and a montage in which the two spaces are related to one another in their opposition in such a way that the collision seems inevitable.

The acoustic horror motif, with clanking fata morgana sound surfaces and the tolling of bells, synaesthetically merges with the static long shots of the primal forest: the flat-ornamental iconography of branches, bushes, trees, their background lost in surfaces of light and dark shuffling in and out of one another. In a repeating reverse shot they are referred to the guarding soldier Leonard "Sailor" Purckett (Robert Walker), entrenched behind the sandbag barriers. In the stiff repetition of the shot, the primitive shapes of moving trees and bushes stand out little by little against the background; their movement toward the foreground only becomes really palpable with the marked synchronous stop at the end of the shot. The fantastic scenario in fact only gets its contour in the stunned gaze of the soldier. He pauses in disbelief, questioningly tilting his head to one side – underscored by the tolling of bells – until he finally believes his own eyes. In the end we can clearly see how a troop of enemy soldiers, camouflaged with shrubbery and bushes, advances ever more quickly toward the only loosely enclosed encampment.

On one hand the visual space is defined by a movement from the depths, which reconfigures it in its ornamental structure; in the reverse shot a comparable reconfiguration is carried out by the pointed repetition of the geometrically arranged group image that we saw at the beginning, when this group of scattered individual soldiers coalesced into a troop. Sailor signals the alarm to his sergeant, the American soldiers gather together at the provisional defense barrier. Pressed close together they form a line body by body, just above the sand sacks, which takes up the lower surface of the image. The alternation of shot/reverse shot

---

in our data matrix: http://www.empirische-medienaesthetik.fu-berlin.de/en/emaex-system/affektdatenmatrix/filme/bataan/23_nahkampf/index.html (July 7, 2017).

between the two such opposing spatial configurations raises the expectation of a clash. In the shots to follow, the isolated faces of the soldiers come into focus, the background and the barrels become blurred. The two-dimensional shots of the softly illuminated faces stand in opposition to the now highly contrasting lines and textures of the ornamental forest landscape moving out of the depths. The cuts from the individual faces back to the long shot are accelerated, the grotesque shapes come ever closer. At the same time the even duration of the long shots creates a calm that, in relation to the accelerated frequency of the close ups, heightens the eerie effect even more. The doom, the clash of the separated visual spaces adamantly comes nearer and nearer. The tension rises, but the soldiers obey the order to stay quiet until the very last moment. The close ups are spaced out in such a way that every movement of individual faces is related to the figure of the commanding sergeant. All the individualization from the previous scenes is withdrawn, the platoon confronts the eerie terror as an unfaltering military body. The tension in the soldiers' faces rises further, until the sergeant's command has an almost liberating effect. One last anticipatory moment: "Alright, on the count …" – the music stops, absolute quiet (EMU 2).

What follows can be described as a process of fusion. After the scene was initially structured by the sharp separation of antagonistic visual spaces, now both visual spaces are combined into one shot. We see the platoon assembled in a line, the forest with its moving tree figures in the upper part of the image. The sand sacks delineate a horizontal line in the image that keeps the two visual spaces separated from one another as precisely defined frontline.

With the sergeant's command, the volleying begins. The thick wall of sound, the clouds of smoke from the muzzle flashes blur the frontlines. Close ups show soldiers shooting, their guns aimed directly at the camera. Illuminated by the rhythmic flashes of light from the muzzles, the faces become expressive surfaces in which we can now perceive – instead of tense anticipation – unleashed fury, furious solemnity, or wild resolve, but also wanton excitement and self-indulgent pleasure. The visual spaces are still separated, the montage still suggests two dynamic spatial constructs, clashing head on. But now they are related to one another and combined into an inseparable action. On the one hand, there are the figurations of audiovisual boundary breaking, rhythmically chanted shots, flashes, faces, smoke – and on the other the destructive effects of this explosion of armed violence. For a short period of time the platoon seems to be able to take part in the euphoric lust for power in the force of arms after all, if only in the desperate courage of the last stand. The chaos of the simultaneously exploding firearms is followed by short episodes in which the battle operations are increasingly taken apart into a variety of patterns of action and reaction. The clear division into two visual spaces starts to dissolve (see Figure 22).

Figure 22: The fusion of separate image spaces.

The previously antagonistically opposed spaces are now unified into a single visual space. This is followed by stages of reconfiguring it, which can be described as an affective modulation:
1. At first it is the image of an emphatically fighting military unit. The soldiers lunge at a commando in the formless depths of the visual space. Thick wafts of fog have definitively transformed the thicket of the primal forest into a fantasy image of fear. In long shots we observe how more and more enemy

soldiers come out of the depths of the image, emerging from the fog, while the individual actions of the group are shown from behind so that we initially do not see any individual agents, but the unfaltering military body that had been formed at the beginning of the scene.
2. This is followed by the representation of the smooth, virtuoso dexterity of the individual soldiers, which we perceive as the lust of battle in their actions. The space is hostile in itself, the attacks come from all sides, the group acts in all directions. Now it is the perfectly synchronized timing that combines the individual agents into a fighting unit – the relish of one's own destructive power. In the overview, however, with which the complicated and unclear actions finally get combined into a space of action, the turnover is already announced. For this gaze is attributed to an enemy machine gun stand in the treetops.
3. Exhaustion gets the upper hand; after the endless variations of battling and killing, weakness and vulnerability become manifest, the timing of the actions loses its precision, the movement to save takes too much time, just a moment, a strike, and the comrade is dead ...

   In BATAAN the agony is staged less in the dying of the individual than in the slow exhaustion of the group's fighting power; it is not formed so much in the physical death throes – this practically takes its sublimated form in the feverish death of the Californian Felix Ramirez (Desi Arnaz), afflicted with malaria – but much more in the mourning rituals of the recurring burials and the ever increasing graves. Toward the end, in the burial mounds and the crosses that spread out over the fog, the encampment that provided temporary shelter and protection to the soldiers is completely absorbed in a visual space that from the very beginning showed the war in the décor of Gothic horror.

With each new circulation, BATAAN shows the switch from the action mode into an affection-image – whether in the expressive modality of the horror film or in the sentimental modality of the melodrama. Each time this forms the starting point for staging the mourning of the fallen soldier; with each switch the film as a whole unfolds little by little into an audiovisual image that itself seeks to become the medium of commemorating the sacrificial victim. In a certain sense, this simultaneously designates the climax and the conclusion of the affect-dramatic course of the Hollywood war film from the first years after the Second World War. This course aims for a cinematic image that lets us see how ordinary bodies are caused to disappear in the formation of a military community in order then to return in the transfiguration of the sacrifice as a pathos form. The pathos of commemorating the sacrifice forms the core of the films in which the genre was formed and expanded in the first years following the war. Afterwards figures increasingly appear that expand the affect-dramaturgical schema even further:

the disillusioned soldier, his moral indignation and his rage, the soldier gone berserk, and the ex-soldier back home and running amok.

The emergence of the genre from the perception politics of war films

The analyses of DECEMBER 7TH, THE BATTLE OF MIDWAY, GUNG HO! and BATAAN have shown that the films should be reconstructed as poetics that each establish the cinema in its own way as a space of aesthetic experiencing commonly shared relations to the world. In aesthetic modes and affective modalities they determine the conditions under which war is visible, perceivable as a state of this world. The modes of aesthetic experience and expressive modalities of this cinema are thus strictly subordinated to a setting of political goals that is aimed at fundamentally reshaping all areas of social life.[81] In this sense, the films can be situated historically in a network of agents (military, entertainment industry, government), media technologies, and aesthetic practices, which are aimed at controlling the perceptibility of war. This means controlling the sensations, affects, and slogans that circulate in the visual and audiovisual representation of war.

This is seen particularly clearly in the black bars in DECEMBER 7TH ostentatiously covering the image and tagged as "censored." The fact that the censorship is so explicit appeals to the acquiescence with the regime of authoritarian collectivization. This appeal is no less constitutive for the aesthetic calculation of military perceptual politics than is the stubborn attempts to include the personal perspective of the American soldiers, each one suffering for himself, into the mass deaths of war.

The perceptual politics of Hollywood cinema during the war years was on the one hand related to the soldiers themselves. It may primarily have been a matter of schooling the troops and strengthening their readiness for combat. In fact, the films address all aspects of their physical and psychic existence in order to subject them to a new principle of collectivization: sexuality, hygiene, ordinary behavior patterns – all aspects of the elementary sense of self become the object of psycho-physical reorganization in the films. The films themselves are military

---

[81] "War well represents a paroxysm in the life of modern society. It constitutes a total phenomenon that exalts and transforms modern society in its entirety, cutting with terrible contrast into the calm routine of peacetime. It is a phase of extreme tension in collective life, a great mobilization of masses and effort. Each individual is torn from his profession, his home, his habits, and lastly, his leisure. War brutally destroys the circle of liberty that everyone preserves for his own pleasure and respects in his neighbor." (Caillois, *Man and the Sacred*, 165).

exercises that insert the individual soldiers in their whole bodily action radius and their individual forms of expression into the network of the military community. They refer the individual soldiers to their deployment locations, which they present to them as complex chains of activity, the rationality of which entirely eludes them in the emergency of the combat mission. They present the individual soldiers with the highly specialized functions of intermingling technical, medial, and physiological processes in military operations, which they can only very rarely examine in their intentionally defined formation. For the soldiers the films themselves function as training, inserting them into the functioning process in which human and technological material, physiologically and technologically determined processes are intermingled in a way that is nearly unimaginable outside the mobilization of war. The mobilization films of the early war years, no less than the training films, are to be understood in this sense as military practices. They seek to create the anthropo-technoid collectivity of the military (the corps) to the same degree that they allow this collectivity to become the object of aesthetic pleasure as monumentally expanded physical strength in the mode of action cinema. The staging of these films modulates the military practices, the drills, that compel the individual body into the collective action formations of the military – almost linking archaic rituals and modern sports training – as the pleasurable experience of the genre audience.

On the other hand, this perceptual politics is aimed at the 'home front.' I have attempted to show that the focus on information, political discourse, or ideological coordination is only superficial. Certainly, there was an attempt to allow for the needs of the population to understand and get a grasp on the war situation through newsreels and informational films. But in the interplay of informational, entertainment, and propaganda films, it becomes clear that aesthetic strategies were above all focused on consolidating both the armed forces and the civilian population into the unity of a military community. The unity of such a community finds its pathos in the images of the sacrificed soldier and the melodramatic modalities of compassionate spectators (BATAAN).

In view of the multiply overlapping perceptual politics, hardly any meaningful distinction can be made between the media strategies and technologies of warfare and those of war propaganda. Even less distinction can be made between war policy and the media representation of war in art or journalism. The audiovisual document is as central for the analysis, planning, and implementation of military operations as the staging strategies of entertainment cinema are for mobilizing a society geared up for war. Warfare, war correspondence, war propaganda, and entertaining war films are inextricably intertwined. They cannot be removed from the events that are represented in them. This is the reason for the highly ambivalent character that is always attributed to film documents of war.

Regardless of whether the films are teaching recruits about sexual hygiene and sexual behavior in enemy territory, or are aimed at mobilizing and informing the armed forces internally; whether they are describing the situation to the population at home in newsreels or war documentaries; or are addressed once again to the soldiers as fellow citizens in the political field, only to show them the necessity of militarizing their lives – the circulation of film images between different media formats and genres turns the contemporary cinema into the site at which the unity of the nation sworn to war is produced as a shared perceptual world. In relation to this world, the films are historical documents of a poetic making that seeks to reconfigure the social world of a democratic polity into the world of a military community. What Cavell claimed about the relation of the film world to reality in general applies to this site in particular: It always only allows us to perceive those aspects of the reality of war that have become a commonly shared world in a given media constellation.[82]

War films do not convey to us any image of the reality of war; they convey the world of war as a specific mode of perception, of feeling and thinking. This, however, following Cavell, is no claim of validity that could be aimed at knowledge about the war, but at the recognition of an experiential perspective. This claim to recognition neither seeks to be sanctioned by higher authorities, nor does it wish to assert itself as non-partisan and general. It always concerns a subjective experiential perspective that seeks to be perceived and recognized as such in the aesthetic construction of a cinematic seeing and hearing. Neither media technology nor historical knowledge supply us with the opportunity to assess whether the representation of facts has been falsified, heroically exaggerated, told from a single partisan perspective, ubiquitous only in the imagination. We should always understand these representations as perspectives that determine the way these facts are or should be perceived by the spectators. Their historical critique and their analysis always concerns the arrangement of the modes of aesthetic experience of cinema itself. This is the sense in which I understand the Hollywood war film as part of an "aesthetics of politics,"[83] which recalibrates the field of what can be perceived and said in the commonly shared world.

This is equally the case for films that are beholden in their poetic concept to the documentary and to the historical report, rather than those that we attribute to fictional genre cinema. Each representation of historical war events in audiovisual mass media is part of a politics of perception forms that determine the media conditions of the perceptibility of war; each one can thus also become the

---

[82] Cf. Cavell, *The World Viewed*, 29–32.
[83] Rancière, *The Emancipated Spectator*, 74.

object of poetic reconstructions of these conditions. Each one is part of the production and transformation of forms of sensing our common world. In fact, in this sense it should be possible to describe, assess, and historically situate all films that propose an image of war as working on the sense of commonality, even if few of them can provide informative results.

Producing, censoring, evaluating, circulating, and archiving film images of war create the media-technological conditions of a cinema that could become the site of a specific experience of temporality and history in a world whose territorial borders have been radically challenged, a world mobilized to war. The massive amounts of film documents have not only supplied the iconographic matrix of the Hollywood war film; they have literally created the material basis for cultural work in fantasy and memory; for Hollywood's war films very quickly presented themselves as such, as cultural work in memory in the mode of genre cinema. The genre did not arise because the Second World War as a historical fact became the subject of narratives about the history of the United States; it arose because the mobilization of all the possibilities of media by war brought forth new conditions of experiencing historical time and global space.

In order to define this context further, one last film-analytical study will be made on the history of the emergence of the genre.

3.5 On the Historicity of Film Images

The Hollywood war film genre cannot be understood without the evidentiary value attributed to the film material in relation to a historical event. It is not conceivable without the emphatic emphasis laid upon the documentary function of photography and film. Of course, films such as THE BATTLE OF MIDWAY or DECEMBER 7TH are perceived differently than fictional genre productions like GUNG HO! or BATAAN – even if the latter are meant to maintain strict precision in their reference to the same historical events – but they follow a poetic logic that develops a specific form of the film material's perspective toward the common world.[84]

The documentary, the essay film, the propaganda film, the news item can be distinguished in their specific speaking perspectives from forms of fictional film representation. They refer to a concrete fact in a common world, which is

---

[84] Cf. Francois Niney, *Die Wirklichkeit des Dokumentarfilms: 50 Fragen zur Theorie und Praxis des Dokumentarischen*, Marburg 2012, particularly chapter 13: "Die Rekonstruktion: dokumentarisch oder fiktional?," 63–69, or chapter 15: "Wo beginnt die Inszenierung, wo endet das Dokumentarische?," 72–76.

unquestionably assumed to be a generally shared world. The diegetic worlds of fictional films, on the other hand, hermetically seal themselves up – and here I am following Cavell – from the ordinary world in their poetic principles. Even if they correspond in every detail and every singularity to the phenomena of the ordinary world, they are still always based on a construction that can only be related to our common world in its entirety, in the logic of its poetic conception.

Fictional films allow for all representations to enter into relation with one another solely through the logic of their poetic concepts. They propose worlds in which things and bodies, animate and inanimate material, technical and physiological procedures, intentional and non-intentional movements are placed in relation to one another in a way that is completely intelligible in its cohesion. Indeed, the cohesion of all elements is utterly created, devised, constructed. The world of fictional films always follows a law that, in principle, can be reconstructed as the implicit poetic logic – as the blueprint for an arbitrary proposal of the world.

Exactly this is what is not the case for the documentary genre. These films always relate to the world from a distinct perspective, a world that is assumed as a commonly shared everyday world, almost in blind trust as to its existence. The everyday world itself can neither be measured nor represented. In its many facets with many perspectives, it designates nothing other than the culturally and historically given order of our sensibility. We can indeed unlock it theoretically as the a priori condition of our feeling and perceiving, but cannot perceive it itself. In the perspectivized unfolding of the fictional and documentary relation to reality we can see a level of ramification in the field of poetic making in the medium of film, a first, fundamental differentiation of the generic modes of film images.

When the film document encounters the spectator in the cinematic mode of experience of an actual being-there, as is the case for the war films of the 1940s, it is no different than an illusion created by media technology, such as we know from action cinema. But the authenticity effect here clearly has a different impact than in genre cinema.

Today, we tend to associate comparable effects with different audiovisual media: the repeating loops of the news stations reporting on terror attacks or showing how soldiers are lynched by an angry mob; internet videos in which executions and torture are documented. Mere knowledge about these events could never have such a heavy impact as these audiovisual documents do. This is particularly the case for the experiential mode of cinema. We might try to get away from the pestering feeling of being a living, present witness of crimes and violent acts by reflecting on the media setting. But even then the affect would be quicker and more powerful. We might attempt to prove that the images are constructed, but by that time our bodies have already long reacted to them and have experienced themselves positioned as eyewitnesses in the scene of another present. The horror consists in the fact that our bodies participate in this scene of another present as affected bodies.

This becomes obvious if we remember the phenomenological definition of the cinematic mode of a present being-there. Spectators that provide the film image with a corporeal present in the real sense activities of their own sensation of cinematic perceiving experience themselves as direct witnesses of the events being represented, even if their presence is solely due to the illusionary reality effect[85] of media technology. There is no distinction among films in this point; it makes no difference whether their speaking perspectives are documentary, reporting, or fictionalizing. In the documentary, however, the particular event in each case is experienced by the spectator as a fact of the always already given, common world of their everyday existence – without calling into question this common world itself in its constitutive structure.

To the degree to which spectators of documentary films take the film viewpoint as the entirety of their everyday world, film images can unfold a chill that has nothing to do with the horror of fictional films.

A succession of automatic world projections (Cavell once again)

Stanley Cavell saw this reality effect as the decisive aspect of the film image. For him, here is where we can find the answer to how the conditions and possibilities of film, as opposed to language, are created. "What conditions of movie-making are to be explored? What 'possibilities' of the medium of movies are now given significance?" The answer to this question has achieved a certain notoriety: "The material basis of the media of movies [...] is [...] a *succession of automatic world projections.*"[86]

Now the ontological aspects of this thesis have been sufficiently discussed, and Cavell – for good reason – has been read in the tradition of the cinematic realism of Bazin or Kracauer. Admittedly, there is a certain danger associated with such a reading, which gives media technology itself a kind of exclusive access to reality. This is why an ontological reading can hardly be made compatible with the "moral of ordinary language" philosophy. Film as media technology has

---

[85] Cf. Metz, "On the Impression of Reality in the Cinema" as well as Gertrud Koch, "Müssen wir glauben, was wir sehen?," in *...kraft der Illusion: Illusion und Filmästhetik*, eds. Gertrud Koch and Christiane Voss, Munich 2006, 53–70, and Kappelhoff, "Das Wunderbare der Filmkunst."
[86] Cavell, *The World Viewed*, 72.

specific possibilities at hand to construct a world; but these are in no way more realistic, closer to reality, than is language, for instance. It is merely a matter of different possibilities, a different *téchne*, for proposing media of perceiving the world.

In fact, however, there are other aspects of what we call reality that come to play here. The world of cinematic world projections means nothing other than that aspect of reality that is given to us in moving visibilities and dynamic audibilities; 'World' is always what is left over from reality under the specific conditions, regards, and perspectives of a medium of poetic making.

In the case of film, then, these conditions would be the following:

1. "succession": This means the linear movement of film, the mechanical procedures in the camera and projector. These mechanical procedures are the condition that movement can emerge as a meaning-generating factor at all; they are the condition for each shot in its duration, each camera movement, each gestural movement within the shots to come into relation with the previous and following shots and courses of movement, taking on meaning as a point in time within a rhythmically subdivided whole.

2. "automatic," on the other hand, means the arbitrariness of a directionless sequence of shots in which an intentionally undefined seeing and hearing is unhinged frame by frame from the unlimited possibilities of the perceptible. The succession of these automatic incisions taken in themselves form an indistinctive aggregation of radically contingent and thus also absolutely distinct moments of being-affected and becoming-affected for chance configurations of bodies. Of these configurations, the chain of interpenetrating human and technical procedures that range from turning on the camera to projection are still the smallest part. They can be seen as visual matter that moves in itself, producing an unending mass of distinct visibilities and audibilities through an arbitrary sequence of serial incisions. It is in this visual matter that lines of perspective can first be registered. This defines the third term.

3. "world projections": Initially, these are nothing more than the viewpoints from which the visual matter is apportioned and divided in series of expressivities and sense impulses. Only in this line of perspective do the sequences of projections come together into a spatio-temporal unit of the film image, into a cinematic visual space. Only here does a perceivable world arise, the projections of which are arranged according to a distinct point, from which the film as a projection of the entirety of a world can be seen and heard.

In film theory this viewpoint has been the central object of theoretical debates. It has been conceived as the illusion of an all-seeing ego, as the embodying, immersive, empathetic spectator-ego that identifies with the image or the character;

when it has not simply been equated with the empirical spectator, who cognitively unlocks or decodes films according to previous knowledge banks or symbolic systems.[87] What is common to these highly contradictory film-theoretical approaches is that they assume the spectator to be a given entity, who, supplied with various attributes, interacts with the film in one way or another. The spectator is conceived as an agent that travels through all embodiments, immersions, empathetic or cognitive processes – or however else one has conceived the mode of film experience – as an unflappable ego. He is proposed as an ego that precedes every interaction, that is always already the same, and that remains the same in perpetuity through any and all interactions.[88] Due to its self-certitude, this spectator is protected from just that experience that Cavell describes as constitutive for film media.

The split in perception in the act of viewing films

For Cavell, the media technology of film can be distinguished in the fact that it facilitates world projections in which the worst fears of skepticism seem to be fulfilled:

> Film is a moving image of skepticism: not only is there a reasonable possibility, it is a fact that here our normal senses are satisfied of reality while reality does not exist – even, alarmingly, because it does not exist, because viewing is all it takes. [...] The basis of film's drama [...] lies in its persistent demonstration that we do not know what our conviction in reality turns upon.[89]

---

[87] As a classical example of some of the aspects of the first variant, see: Jean-Louis Baudry, "Ideologische Effekte erzeugt vom Basisapparat," in *Der kinematographische Apparat: Geschichte und Gegenwart einer interdisziplinären Debatte*, ed. Robert Riesinger, Münster 2003, 27–39; Christian Metz, *The Imaginary Signifier: Psychoanalysis and the Cinema*, Bloomington 2000; Laura Mulvey, "Visual Pleasure and Narrative Cinema," *Screen* Vol. 16 (1975), 6–18; Eder, *Die Figur im Film*; Wulff, "Empathie als Dimension des Filmverstehens." On the second variant, see for instance: Plantinga, *Moving Viewers*; Grodal, *Moving Pictures*; Plantinga and Smith (eds.), *Passionate Views*; Smith, *Film Structure and the Emotion System*; Smith, *Engaging Characters*; Tan: *Emotion and the Structure of Narrative Film*.

[88] In light of this problem, Guattari has described film theory as an attempt to subordinate the cinema as a form of poetic making to a logic that seeks to restrict its possibilities. Cf. Felix Guattari, "The Poor Man's Couch," in *Chaosophy: Texts and Interviews*, ed. Sylvère Lotringer, Los Angeles 2009, 257–267.

[89] Cavell, *The World Viewed*, 188f.

Film confronts us with a sensation of perception in which, on the one hand, an experience is conveyed to us that it is our senses that produce a world, which has no basis whatsoever in reality – a world that absolutely belongs to our consciousness alone. On the other hand, this world appears in the mode of our everyday perception; it appears like our everyday world, only that we have no access to it whatsoever. We can be present in it as spectators, but without being able to inhabit it. In the cinema we are confronted with a world that appears like our everyday world of perceptions, but from which we are radically excluded.

Which for one thing confirms our assumption that our everyday reality might very well also be an illusionary perception; and for another, it conveys the idea to us that we as individuals, precisely when this applies, might possess the world as a whole, as an idea of our consciousness. The place from which the world is disclosed as a unified whole is identified by an ego that is not to be found in this world. Film conveys to us – according to Cavell – the uncanny feeling that we, as reflective subjects, are haunting our everyday mode of existence like immortal spirits that return to the locations of their real lives without being able to inhabit them: "A world complete without me which is present to me is the world of my immortality. This is an importance of film – and a danger. It takes my life as my haunting of the world [...]."[90]

The skepticism that our world has no basis in reality becomes a media form in films – a form of visibility that on the one hand conceals its origin, that is, our own sense activities, while on the other hand radically exposing it. The danger of which Cavell speaks consists in the attempt to separate the two sides of this experience (a world through us and world without us) from one another and view the solipsistic ego and the reality devoid of the ego as completely coherent worlds, which could very easily get along without one another: "to be human is to wish, and in particular to wish for a completer identity than one has so far attained; and that such a wish may project a complete world *opposed* to the world one so far shares with others."[91]

We can get quite comfortable in the position of the spectator as a transcendental ego, playing out the entirety of the world projection against the contingency, heterogeneity, fragility, and precarity of the common world. This seems to me to be the case in a great deal of articles in film theory.[92] Whether the spectators

---

90 Ibid., 160.
91 Stanley Cavell, "What Becomes of Things on Film?," in *Themes out of School: Effects and Causes*, Chicago 1984, 173–183, here 181.
92 As a paradigmatic example, see: Baudry, "Ideologische Effekte erzeugt vom Basisapparat," Metz, *The Imaginary Signifier*, or also David Bordwell, *Narration in the Fiction Film*, Madison 1985, esp. chapter 3: "The Viewer's Activity," 30–47.

are conceived as empathetic, whether as identifying, cognitive, or embodying subjects – in these approaches they resemble the ghostly ego that attends the films in transcendental immortality. They take the film world as an opportunity to position themselves as a consistent subject that exists before and outside all media and communication practices, which locate this ego as a matter of the social world.

In fact, Sartre sketched out this kind of spectator in a film script as a mode of existence: *LES JEUX SONT FAITS (THE CHIPS ARE DOWN*, 1943; filmed in 1947 by Jean Delannoy). He describes dead persons who attend and observe a world as living consciousness. Their possibilities for acting in this world are just as radically revoked as their forms of consciousness remain untouched (they are complete, there is nothing to add) by the circumstance that they are long dead to this world.

Watching films, in contrast, also provides the experience of finding ourselves positioned in a radically contingent world of things and bodies that exist independently of us: "I think everyone knows odd moments in which it seems uncanny that one should find oneself just here now, that one's history should have unwound to this room, this road, this promontory. The uncanny is normal experience of film. Escape, rescue, the metamorphosis of a life by a chance encounter or juxtaposition – these conditions of contingency and placement underpin all the genres of film."[93] For Cavell the opposing possibilities in viewing films are completely linked with a moral choice, a political attitude: "This takes moral evil as the will to exempt oneself, to isolate oneself, from the human community. It is a choice of inhumanity, of monstrousness."[94]

But how can spectators be imagined that actually compromise themselves in their subjectivity? How could we theoretically model the activity of watching if it is structured by the experience of a world so dependent on the dangling string of the mutual recognition of relevant subject positions? How could we conceive of spectators to whom this experience is conveyed as a media sensation that concerns them existentially; that neither keeps them at bay as an entertaining game nor as academic abstraction? – Spectators, that is, that know exactly how deceptive the feeling of being sure of themselves as an invariable ego is.

In order to define more precisely such spectating as a mode of experience, we first have to sharpen our understanding of the media technology film as a succession of automatic world projections in the framework of the film phenomenological concept.

---

93 Cavell, *The World Viewed*, 156.
94 Cavell, *Pursuits of Happiness*, 80.

Already at the beginning of this chapter I claimed that films should be reconstructed analytically as visual spaces in which the generation of meaning can be represented as an interaction between projections of moving images and the sense reactions of spectators. Such a reconstruction must make it possible to imagine watching films as a process of embodiment in which the moving image and the activity of watching constantly interlock. Now we can define this interlocking more precisely. In the perspective I have sketched out, we sense the film as a world that arises through our perception alone, in the medium of our sensations alone, our movements of affect and thinking. Only in the medium of the spectators' bodies does the visual space that we call film emerge from the projection of moving images. In the succession of its projections it causes a world to emerge that is due to the sensoriality of our bodies alone, and that has no reality outside this sensorial resonance of constantly being affected by what one has heard and seen.

That is, the world that we perceive as the world of the film is formed in every detail by the same modes of perception, sensation, and thinking that also define our everyday perception. This is why the visual space that emerges through us and for us in the process of watching films has the same evidentiary character as our everyday world. And this is why we sense this space in the same moment as a world that exists completely independently from us; a world that we, the spectators, (re)construct as a visual space; a world that is hermetically shut off from our everyday perception and thus excludes us – as if the perceiving resonating bodies in the form of the spectators were rejected from the visual space.

Such a perspective is diametrically opposed to the idea that films could be read as audiovisual representations; as if the visible things, actions, and people belonged to another world that existed independently of film and the activity of watching films.[95] Rather, the film diegesis only exists as a world that emerges in the experience of watching and hearing films. At the same time, however, it exists as the perception of a way of sensing a world, as the articulation of a specific perceptual perspective, which is utterly external to the spectator.

If audiovisual representations could be detached as meanings from the act of watching films, then there would be no difference between our everyday

---

[95] On this topic Sobchack says: "Positing cinematic vision as merely a mode of objective symbolic representation, and reductively abstracting – 'disincarnating' – the spectator's subjective and full-bodied vision to posit it only as a 'distance sense,' contemporary film theory has had major difficulties in comprehending how it is possible for human bodies to be, in fact, really 'touched' and 'moved' by the movies." Vivian Sobchack, "What My Fingers Knew: The Cinesthetic Subject, or Vision in the Flesh," in *Carnal Thoughts: Embodiment and Moving Image Culture*, Berkeley 2004, 53–84, here 59.

perception and perceiving film. But what separated "spectating" in experiencing film from everyday "seeing" is the experience of a specific kind of seeing and hearing that is constituted and produced through the cinematic image itself. Films are media that manufacture a particular way of being-in-the-world as the temporal process of a perceiving, feeling, and thinking embodied in real spectators. In this sense, films do not reproduce everyday perceptions; rather, they give rise to ever new modes of perceiving the world.

This is how to understand Vivian Sobchack when she outlines the developments of film technology as an arrangement of cinematic forms of expression and perception, which she calls the "history of cinematic embodiment."[96] She envisions the idea through the example of the camera:

> From the initially stationary camera with a fixed gaze at a world that moved, to the capacity of the camera to 'liberate' itself from the paternal studio by virtue of its new found portability, to the development from the awkward jerkiness of hand-held camera to the current invisible immediacy and appropriated fluidity of Steadicam, the technology of the cinema has seemed to respond to the intentional imperatives of the film's body as a series of perceptive and expressive tasks in need of performance.[97]

The term "the film's body" refers to the fact that the spectator, the perceiving act of watching and hearing views, experiences the film in turn as an act of seeing and hearing, as if the film itself were a corporal and perceiving being, an entity capable of sensing, which could be articulated through expressive and perceptual acts:

> More than any other medium of human communication, the moving picture makes itself sensuously and sensibly manifest as the expression of experience by experience. A film is an act of seeing that makes itself seen, an act of hearing that makes itself heard, an act of physical and reflective movement that makes itself reflexively felt and understood.[98]

With the formulations "the expression of experience by experience" Sobchack aims to describe the two interweaving experiential acts in the cinema: Film is a medium of a way of experiencing the world that is not the spectator's; at the same time, however, this world is only brought forward in the first place by the physical, sensed experiences of the spectator.

---

96 Sobchack, *The Address of the Eye*, 256.
97 Ibid., 253–254.
98 Ibid., 3–4.

The process of *meaning making* in film is always anchored in the movement of the sensitive matter: in the perceptual sensations of the affected body of the spectator. To put it the other way around: Film produces a perception that is carried out as a permanent division of its spectator. On the one hand, spectators, as affected bodies with their own movements of sensing, thinking, and feeling, are the media material in which film expressivity is inscribed as a process of the emergence of the visibilities and audibilities of the cinematic visual space.[99] And at the same time, as spectators they are located outside this visual space: in the position of a transcendental ego, from which the world seen and heard can be grasped as a sensed entity, a whole toward which the world projections are organized.

A specific temporality of film images

This division of the spectator in the act of watching defines the specific possibility of the media technology film. It is grounded in the circumstance that the succession of world projections is bifurcated in two series, which are interrelated at every moment. The physiological process of the unfolding sensations of perception and the mechanical process of projection are inseparably bound together as the two sides of the emergence of the film world – a constant interweaving of affecting and being affected. They are inseparably bound as two sides of a repetition.

This is why, in Cavell, genres are to be understood as media, because they realize the media-technological conditions for film to create meaning as a possibility to think our common world in the mode of this split perception. They realize the media-technological possibilities as a specific mode of poetic making and thinking, which conveys to us the experience of seeing how, with every effort of our seeing and hearing, feeling and thinking, we always already do *not* belong to ourselves. This is the uncanny quality of this mode of experience:

> There is a repetition necessary to what we call life, or the animate, necessary for example to the human; and a repetition necessary to what we call death, or the inanimate, necessary for example to the mechanical; and there are no marks or features or criteria or rhetoric by means of which to tell the difference between them.[100]

---

99 The term 'matter' refers to Deleuze's engagement with Bergson's "Matter and Memory" in his cinema books. On the basic conception of the model of film expressivity described here, see: Kappelhoff, *Matrix der Gefühle*.
100 Stanley Cavell, "The Uncanniness of the Ordinary," in *In Quest of the Ordinary: Lines of Scepticism and Romanticism*, Chicago 1988, 153–178, here 158.

In the uncanny quality of the split perceiving consciousness of the film image, as I have attempted to describe it, following Cavell, as a specific possibility grounded in media technology, lies the potential of a genuine film-historical consciousness. In the following I would like to describe another combat report in more detail to show how the split in the perceiving consciousness in the act of watching films founds a specific temporal structure of film images, which is due to the possibility of a memory bank of film images, to which even the horror of the film document refers.

WITH THE MARINES AT TARAWA: a memory image on film

The horror of the film document is at the heart of WITH THE MARINES AT TARAWA from 1944. Like DECEMBER 7TH, the film won the Oscar for best short documentary.[101] It is based on color material, which – like the footage from THE BATTLE OF MIDWAY or BEACHHEAD TO BERLIN – was shot by a military unit while the battle was developing and was produced by the United States Marine Corps Photographic Unit.[102] This combat footage also circulates today in various documentaries of contemporary history channels and internet platforms for web videos.[103]

At the beginning of the film, after the opening credits, which by now have become more complex – they read: *Edited by* WARNER BROS. PICTURES, INC. FOR THE U.S. GOVERNMENT OFFICE OF WAR INFORMATION, *Distributed by* UNIVERSAL PICTURES COMPANY, INC. AND EXHIBITED BY THE WAR ACTIVITIES COMMITTEE– MOTION PICTURE INDUSTRY[104] – we see a naval port.[105] Soldiers are being embarked. The soldiers are briefly and succinctly introduced: "These are the men of the Second Marine Division." While we see the Marines climbing up the guardrails in columns, the off-screen voice switches into speaking in the register of an eyewitness on the scene: "We're now embarking on a full scale amphibious operation after many months of intensive training." While in all the propaganda films that we have considered so far the speakers' voices dramatically shape the off-commentary through intonation and changing speaking perspectives, the voice-over in WITH THE MARINES AT TARAWA largely operates without modeling its expression. The

---

101 Academy Award Ceremony on March 15, 1945 in Los Angeles.
102 A unit of the United States Navy was responsible for THE BATTLE OF MIDWAY, BEACHHEAD TO BERLIN was produced by the US Coastal Guard together with Warner Bros. Studios.
103 https://archive.org/details/WiththeMarinesatTarawa (last viewed January 19, 2016).
104 The film's directors, Richard Brooks and Louis Hayward, were not listed by name.
105 Scene "Aufbruch und Vorbereitung [*departure and preparation*]" (00:00:00:00–00:02:43:23).

steady pitch of the voice suggests extreme objectivity in its cool, laconic diction. Even the fact that it is about film documents that were created during employment does not seem to be worth mentioning.

The even-tempered registering gaze

The camerawork establishes a gaze that imitates the gesture of a chronicling report from a newsreel. We see the destroyers and airplanes in the sky accompanying the transport of the troops. We observe one of the briefings at which the individual platoons are familiarized with the territorial circumstances of the operation area. We get quite close to the soldiers, looking into their faces, lost in thought; they are standing around the model of the island's landscape, or relax squatting on the ground. We see their daily work, cleaning weapons, filling munition belts. The drill appears more as relaxing physical exercise than as strength training; the change in the music takes up the rhythmic movements and gives the scene something almost comical. The camera shots go along in the same laconic brevity as the curt sentences of the off-screen voice, who attributes a precisely defined function to all the activities ("Check and test fire all weapons," "Exercise helps to relieve the tension"), thus integrating them into the wheelwork of the interweaving operations of an all-encompassing machinery: the destroyers guarding the aircraft carriers, the Airforce bombarding in preparation for landing, the briefing of the Marines, the cleaning of small arms ...

The correspondence between the steady intonation, the laconic way of speaking, and the gesture of an objectively recording camera gaze gives the impression that an eyewitness report is being shown, purporting to concentrate exclusively on what is most necessary for the soldiers' work – without any embellishment, padding, or sentimental addition. And still, the words and images, in their strictly corresponding expressive gesture, express nothing more than a subjective sensation of perception. Indeed, very soon the voice switches into the speaking mode of first person plural. It articulates a subjectivity that imagines itself as the "we" of the soldiers. The laconic way of speaking and the gesture of the camerawork articulate an uninvolved, observing perceptive consciousness, registering every detail, in which the second Marine division itself gets a personal contour – it appears as an unflappable, impartial ego that is not mislead by any event, not shocked by any horror, not brought out of the concept by any hardship. In it returns the voice of the dead soldier that we encountered in DECEMBER 7TH. Soldiers in war–whether now dead or still living – speak with one and the same impartial voice; their fate is no longer decided according to individual happiness, but to the life of the community, the We of the platoon, the corps, the nation.

The spectator might initially recognize the staging of military professionalism here, which corresponds to the modern hero image of the soldier responsibly carrying out his work, come what may. Over the course of the film, however – and this gives it its dramatic tension – this attribution will be radically called into question.

For the moment, we once again see the soldiers relaxing on the upper deck of the ship; they are receiving their last instructions before the planned landing. The scene conveys a proximity to the men represented, which is slightly disturbing at first. This footage, the color of which has now largely faded, moves the viewer today in a similar way to photographs of complete strangers whose death we know about. We see faces and bodies of people completely unknown to us, as if we were leafing through an old family picture album, to whom it belongs we cannot say. We study the traits, the clothing, the postures, and the gestures of the soldiers, we look for their gazes, the moment when their emotional life will be disclosed. We do this in complete conviction that they were on the deck of a warship at the time the footage was shot, on the way to the battle of Tarawa. No doubt that the sunlight falling on the camera lens, delineating the faces in the film material, was the same light that burned down on these men's foreheads. Already with the first scenes we sense this effect, which we in fact associate more with photography, as Roland Barthes has described it, and not with film.[106] The laconic impartiality with which the camera delivers the countless details to the spectator's gaze, which shows itself in the faces and the bodies of the soldiers, without insinuating them into a dramaturgical order, seems in fact to take its model in realistic photo reportage.

---

106 In his famous book on photography, Roland Barthes described this affect, opposing it to the effect of film. Cf. Gertrud Koch, "Das Bild als Schrift der Vergangenheit," in *Kunstforum* 128, October 1994, 192–196. In Barthes we read: "In the cinema, no doubt, there is always a photographic referent, but this referent shifts, it does not make a claim in favor of its reality, it does not protest its former existence; it does not cling to me: it is not a *specter*. Like the real world, the filmic world is sustained by the presumption that, as Husserl says, "the experience will constantly continue to flow by in the same constitutive style"; but the Photograph breaks the "constitutive style" (this is its astonishment); it is *without future* (this is its pathos, its melancholy); in it, no protensity, whereas the cinema is protensive, hence in no way melancholic (what is it, then? – It is, then, simply, "normal," like life). Motionless, the Photograph flows back from presentation to retention." *Camera Lucida*, 89–90. I have already discussed this effect in conjunction with the film material of the landing at Omaha Beach.

Elegy of remembering

Also in WITH THE MARINES AT TARAWA – like in the John Ford films – there is a religious service held in open air. But even if the music conveys measured solemnity in a similar way, the scene affects us completely differently; indeed, as spectators we are positioned completely differently than in THE BATTLE OF MIDWAY or DECEMBER 7TH.

Instead of a strict ritual, the staging presents an image of soldiers in their everyday lives. We see faces, unshaven, sweating; men in work clothes, with open shirts and sleeves rolled up; body to body, face to face, row after row piled up in the depth of the picture, arranged as a group image. We try to read into the individual faces; some of them are accentuated by the sunlight, others are obscured by shadows, as if the screen itself as a whole had become a face, connected in its traits out of the many faces, each of which is special and none of which is familiar to us.

Pressed close together, the soldiers stand around the priest. The off-screen voice tells us that they like listening to him because he knows – from his experience of many operations – what words might help them before the battle. We are met by the gaze of a single soldier, he looks up briefly and surreptitiously, turning his eyes upward and looking into the camera positioned above. Almost in the same moment he lowers his eyes again: a child that knows he got caught secretly trying to squint through his fingers despite being told to keep his eyes closed. The soldier's gaze, which breaches the understood rule not to look into a running camera, directly addresses the spectators as the soldiers' counterparts. They see themselves as found out,[107] as recognized, exposed as the hidden eye in the undefined 'up there' of the camera's off-space; as an eye that observes the filmed faces, pondering godlike on the death of these living beings (see Figure 23).

Although some of these young men might indeed have returned to an ordinary life, we seem to be moved in each individual face by the thought that they, precisely in the moment, in the very same second that one of them disregarded the order not to look into the camera under any circumstances, were on board this ship in order to be brought to a military operation in which they will meet their deaths. In the same laconic gesture with which the work had been commented on earlier, only barely broken up by the celebratory music, this thought is also

---

[107] In Barthes we read: "For the Photograph has this power – which it is increasingly losing, the frontal pose being most often considered archaic nowadays – of looking me *straight in the eye* (here, moreover, is another difference: in film, no one ever looks at me: it is forbidden – by the Fiction)." ibid., 111.

Figure 23: WITH THE MARINES AT TARAWA.

spoken out loud. We hear the steadily intoned voice: "Many of these men were killed the following morning." The faces that are shown to us in their unmistakable ordinariness seem to be intractably bound to this one moment, which was already irrevocably past in the fleeting gaze of the camera, in order to be relocated in any spectator's present as the point in time of their own history.

In THE BATTLE OF MIDWAY the soldiers are presented as personal individuals by the maternal voice and by being called out by name; here it happens in the fleeting form of filmed faces, each of which is singular and unique in its ordinariness, although no name is ever ascribed to them, none of them finds any duration beyond the film image in personal consistency. In THE BATTLE OF MIDWAY the soldiers can be grasped in the melodramatic staging as a subjective consciousness that is related to the spectator's empathy. In WITH THE MARINES AT TARAWA their physical appearance is related to the temporal structure of the camera's gaze itself.

The elegy of the scene comes from the temporal split that is inscribed into the film image itself. On the one hand, it is the exposed camera shots that are located precisely in time and space; on the other hand, it is an audiovisual image that only emerges in the spectators' perception. In the documentary mode of the steadily recording gaze of the camera the media form itself becomes the basis of a temporally split perceiving consciousness, which remembers the deaths of the soldiers whose living faces it is only now seeing for the first time. Such consciousness is necessarily linked to the physical presentness of the spectators, who see themselves recognized and called upon as spectators by the fleeting gaze.

Physical presence rather than action

At the same time, the elegy of the scene prepares us for the fall, the dramatic switch to representing battle.

A change in the music accentuates the abrupt cut. We see the palm-covered island in the dawn light; the voice changes its intonation, for a brief moment the manner of speaking becomes dramatic: "D-Day, this is the day we attack!"[108] Then the music goes quiet for the duration of the combat. A montage sequence begins, completely similar to the representation of maneuvers in the Riefenstahl film. The shots alternate in rapid succession; the camera seems to be present everywhere at once, up close with the thundering cannons of the heavy artillery on the warships and at the soldiers' back in the boats; at the guardrail of a large warship, the gaze focused on the small landing boats full of men, swaying on the troubled waters, and at the bow doors of one of the boats, with the island's beach in sight. We see fountains of earth fly up, palms shot up, fireballs blazing up, clouds of smoke. The voice coolly reports on the amount of explosives that had been dropped down on the island in the last three days. We see large warships in the distance on the horizon, and smaller cruisers that run close along the landing boat that is carrying the camera.

The montage suggests a strictly planned succession of the actions: first the artillery, then the airplanes, which first bombard the bunker locations, then go on to shoot free the beach with volleys of machine gun fire, then return again to clear the field of fire for the artillery: "We were a team, working together." The military plan of operations provides the dramaturgical schema in which the landing action appears as a functional intermingling of human material, transport, and weapons technology. For a brief moment one might think that we are moving in the action mode here, which comes to the fore in so many war films whenever staging the fighting power of weapons technology.

But the more insistently the repeating shots of fire-spitting cannons power the montage sequence, the more decidedly the camera moves closer and closer to the

---

[108] Scene "Landung auf Tarawa [*landing on Tarawa*]" (00:02:43:23–00:05:57:03).

soldiers, inserting contemplative gazes into the rapid succession of intermeshing actions. Accompanied by the thunder of cannonry, the camera's gaze once again moves in quite close to the soldiers; so close that we imagine we can almost touch the uniforms, the helmets, sense their texture. We think we can touch the skin on the soldier's neck when he bends over the guardrail of the landing boat, such physical presence do the bodies on the screen have – just for a moment, then the montage is already cutting to a subjective perspective, therefore delegating the prying look of the Marines to the spectator in order to go back to the battle action. In an old wrecked ship an enemy post had been made, from which the landing boats could come under fire. We see an airplane nosediving; then, in a close-up, the radio operator, who had announced the position of the enemy post – and once again the camera turns for a moment to one of the soldiers, we see his hair, his mouth speaking …

At no time does WITH THE MARINES AT TARAWA allow free reign to the pleasure of the action movie. How the battle action is represented, the fighting power of the weapons, measured in tons, is once and for all crosscut with shots in which the bodies and faces of the soldiers are given space in their creaturely vulnerability.

The staging of a non-participatory gaze, but one that registers every detail, gives the footage of the conquering of Tarawa a poignancy that can be compared with the description of battle that Spielberg creates at the beginning of SAVING PRIVATE RYAN. Even if WITH THE MARINES AT TARAWA is miles away from the technical possibilities of the blockbuster movies at the turn of the millennium, possessing neither the temporal depth offset (which combines each moment of the event from a series of multiple camera views), nor the brilliance of resolution (which can cause every random detail to emerge in the highest precision), which defines Spielberg's visual rhetoric: the attention to detail that the film develops in the gesture of non-participatory observation in the middle of battle produces a quite similar effect.

The short film about conquering a small Japanese base hardly omits any horror in the few minutes dedicated to the battle action that might have been associated with such a landing operation. A horror emerges precisely in the gesture of the even-tempered, observing gaze, that horror that Spielberg imitates in the fireworks of special effects. We see the soldiers pressed up against one another on the beach, fixed in place by constant fire, unable to go forward or back.[109] We see their bodies bent over, their uncertain movements, when they try going in one direction or another. One of them remains under cover, almost paralyzed, crouched down deep, obviously shocked by the constant blaze of guns; another stands in the middle of the jagged battlefield, practically impassive, as

---

109 Scene "Battle on the Beach" (00:05:57:03–00:10:57:07).

if he didn't know which way to turn; yet others run from one knoll to the next, without our even being able to guess what the cause or the goal of their overhasty movements might be.

We see the immediate effects of the attacks. The soldiers under fire lose their orientation, their movements appear headless, distraught, paralyzed; as if they were searching for a way out, driven on by the deafening screams of battle, a way out that does not exist. We see how the military structure of precisely aligned, interweaving actions begins to unravel in the situation, according to which all the simulation games, all the training, all the drill had been calculated. The unleashed destructive violence of the war machine set into action leaves the proportions of human sense operations and possible courses of action far behind. In the few minutes of battle action, the beach, the island, the sea become a space for the spectator that seems to explode under the pressure of detonations (see Figure 24).

Time and again the wounded are transported away: whether they are badly injured or shot dead is left to the power of the spectator's imagination. Paramedics recover the wounded, lifting them up on stretchers and hauling them out of the line of fire, or tend to them on the spot, in the tumult of shots firing. We see the wounded

Figure 24: Gestures of imperturbable observation.

being pulled out of fire in daring rescue actions, then only a little later laid out next to one another in rows on large decks to be freighted onto the ships. We see the wounded body of a soldier, his legs, his lower body seem to be in tatters; we see his face, even he appears almost sedate, numbed by the pain-relieving opiates.

The horror: forms of paranoid perception

The camera seems to be present everywhere and is nonetheless radically partisan. The enemy's viewpoint is absolutely excluded from the world of this film. And even the enemy himself remains largely invisible. He is hiding away in bunkers and caves, the scrub of shot down palms and the wrecks of bombed-out military vehicles. His face is equated with the enigmatic threat that embraces all the apparitions lying in wait in every treetop, behind every bush or shrub, behind every hill and in every cave.

THE BATTLE OF MIDWAY or DECEMBER 7TH also thematizes this perceptual consciousness; but there it remains external, a racist caricature – the demonic grimace – or a polemical incantation. In WITH THE MARINES AT TARAWA, however, the paranoid mode of perception itself is the point of the scene: the water, the clouds, the beach – everything that is visible on the island turns into the menacing face of the enemy. Seen from the landing boat the island lies in troubled waters, as if it were a prostrating monster that was shot down in the roar. It spits out earth, fire, and smoke. The commentator even describes this perception curtly and clinically as a procedural problem: "It isn't easy knocking those Japs out of their positions. They're hidden in trees behind revetments, buried pillboxes, bombproofs, bunkers."

In genre cinema the paranoid view of things becomes a central element in the affect rhetorics of the war film. From BATAAN to APOCALYPSE NOW, from the films about the Second World War to the Vietnam movies, nature, the island, the jungle, and the bluff are staged in the mode of the horror film as the menacing face of an invisible enemy. It is a different story in WITH THE MARINES AT TARAWA. Here even the horror unfolds its impact from the documentary gesture. A brief moment of relief: "As we approach the island we have the feeling that the show is just about over."[110] The camera glides – a view from above – almost incidentally past men squatting on the planks of the landing boat; our gaze grazes their faces, then we see one of them in close up. The camera gives us a moment to observe the youthful face; we see the traces of soot, the relieved traits, an almost optimistic look. In the documentary gesture of the impassively observing camera unfolds a

---

110 Scene "Landung auf Tarawa [*landing on Tarawa*]" (00:02:43:23–00:05:57:03).

physical presence of the soldiers, which at the same time is the foundation of the horror. It is based, much like the opening scene of SAVING PRIVATE RYAN, on the precision with which – in the individual shots – the physical details step out of the dynamic flow of the montage sequence.[111]

Here, all of the censorship rules that were in place at that time seem to be void. WITH THE MARINES AT TARAWA shows everything that had so far been omitted from the mobilization and propaganda films. It may be that this represents an effect of the hardening that had already set in by the third year of the war. We see bodies shot up, the burned corpses of the enemy, captives crouching naked on the ground like captured animals; and we see fallen Marines, half-naked bodies, washed up on the beach or floating in the water – shirtless men walk over the sand between the corpses to insure that the dead can still be identified after the end of the battle.[112] The horror comes from the lack of feeling that registers every physical detail along with the camera, as if there were no difference to note between the human and the technological bodies, the shot-up palms and the thundering munitions, no difference between the washed-up corpses on the beach and the bare chests of the soldiers trying to identify them: as if the direction had set in motion a metaphor for the infinitely precarious vulnerability of human bodies, which then became famous as the title of a war novel: the naked flesh that the living share with the dead (see Figure 25).

Narrative enclosure

If we compare the film's scenes with the original material produced by the United States Marine Corps Photographic Unit during the conquest of Tarawa, the losses during the landing action seem to have been enormous. The mode of impartial observation allows for the horror of the war film, the fear of the invisible enemy with its ubiquitous deadly forces, to become a terror lacking any subtlety. The commentary, however, the voice of the 'we' of the battling soldiers, attributes a certain position of observation to the spectators – a way to see the battle as the theater of war. The laconic report turns them into witnesses of an event which

---

111 Siegfried Kracauer has placed this effect of the film image in the center of his poetology of film: "Any film narrative should be edited in such a manner that it does not simply confine itself to implementing the intrigue but also turns away from it toward the objects represented so that they may appear in their suggestive indeterminacy." Kracauer, *Theory of Film*, 71.
112 Scene "Verluste [*losses*]" (00:15:05:01–00:17:42:05).

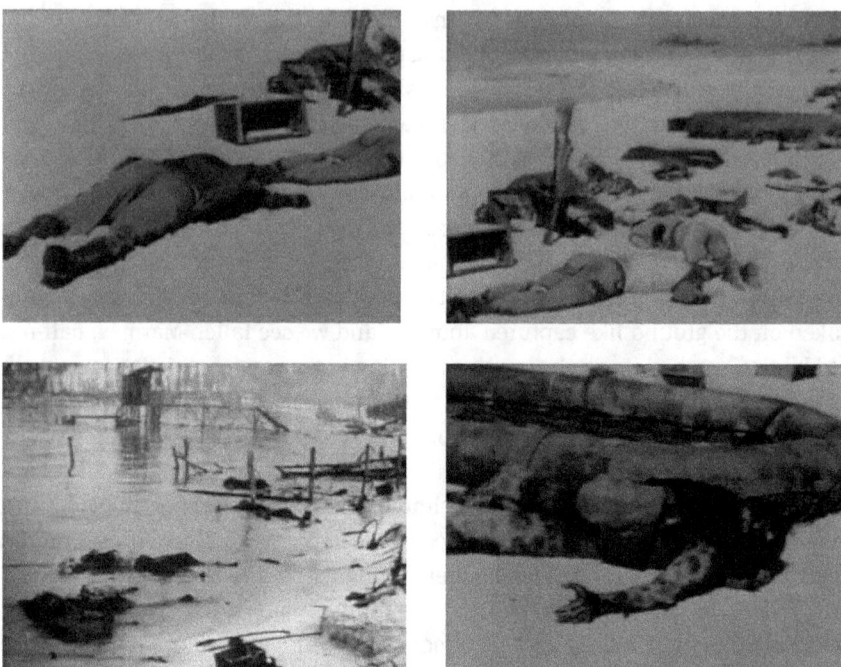

Figure 25: Horror.

they themselves have no part in, but which at the same time would not even exist without their participation.

One could get the impression that WITH THE MARINES AT TARAWA, with its curt, matter-of-fact reporting, mitigates the horror that the film images submit to the spectators in their cinemas back home – not without pointing out a way that the audience can, in fact, help: "Casualties are pretty high. For this, we found out later, blood plasma saves a lot of lives." At any rate, the laconic speech brings a narrative into the visible chaos with which the commandos of the military operation eventually unfold their efficacy, even if this is only for the spectators. It adds a spatio-temporal orientation to the film images and organizes the chaos toward a clear forward motion: "Our men wade ashore from wrecked amphibians. A long pier extending across the fringing reef gives protection to a lot of our boys on the way in. We have a pretty good toehold on the beach, but Jap fire pins us down for hours. [...] When reinforcements arrive we start moving up."[113]

---

[113] Scene "Battle on the Beach" (00:05:57:03–00:10:57:07).

Now it is the American soldiers themselves that deploy the weapons that no living creature can withstand. The technologies by which the enemy posts will be "cleansed" step by step are introduced and named in detail: "We use hand grenades. We use all the firepower we have to blast them up. Our rifle fire is heavy. So are the flamethrowers and the mortars." The battle quickly seems to have been decided. The superior power of the Marines, after persistent battles, has finally held out on Tarawa. Finally, the enemy itself becomes visible; we seem dim shapes running across the image: "The enemy breaks from cover." Like at skeet shooting, they are shot down as they run. Only then does the off-screen voice continue its report: "This bunker is giving us plenty of trouble. It's tough getting in … places like this. You can never be sure where their snipers are placed. We take it slow, easy. We have orders to clean it out." We see the flamethrowers aimed at the ground bunker in which there are presumably survivors. Then we see charred corpses in a foxhole, and we hear the laconic voice: "This is what we found on the other side. They're savage fighters. Their lives mean nothing to them."

A dimension of horror comes into view that is no less terrifying than the battle scenes we have just seen. Only that now the horror is based on our witnessing what happened to the enemy. We see captured Japanese soldiers. They are led off; their faces barely recognizable. Then another group of captives, set up in rank and file; their clothes are cut off from their bodies. The commentator emphasizes that this is for security reasons and that the captives will be cared for medically immediately afterwards. As if to prove this, in the next shot we see bare-chested Japanese soldiers in trousers that are too big for them, their wounds are being tended. One last scene shows us the captives; it is no less terrifying than that with the charred corpses: naked bodies cowering on the ground, weary, faceless flesh (see Figure 26).

If we compare the mobilization films with WITH THE MARINES AT TARAWA, it becomes palpable that the genre films seek to hedge in the horror that confronts us in the combat footage.[114] It is not primarily a matter of seeing human corpses that the sea has washed up onto shore, burned bodies and naked captives. In none of the genre movies do we see soldiers helplessly and confusedly moving about when they are under fire. In none of the films is the disproportion between the demolition power of the weapons and the fragility of the human body so baldly exposed. This is even the case for those films that, like BATAAN, for example, focus on the suffering of the soldiers and which stage the melodrama of a consciousness that finds itself helplessly abandoned to a lost post, forsaken and left for dead. And this is obviously even more the case for the mobilization

---

114 Along with the mobilization films that we have already analyzed here, we could also mention the examples of GUADALCANAL DIARY (Lewis Seiler, 1943) and SAHARA (Zoltan Korda, 1943).

Figure 26: Physical vulnerability.

films that use the mode of action cinema to oppose fear, horror, and melodramatic sentiment with the delight in the elevated powers of an armed corps.

Film memory

While in the propaganda films already discussed – as in all mobilization films – comparable scenes of open combat are always staged in the mode of action cinema, the documentary gesture of the impartially registering gaze of the camera remains formative in WITH THE MARINES AT TARAWA, even in the battle scenes. The physical presence in which the film lets the fighting soldiers become visible for the spectators can be fundamentally distinguished from the films already treated. The effect is precisely not based on the illusion of being-there; much more, as I already mentioned above, it is based on a temporal fold that has its roots in the media structure of the film image itself. The poetic calculation of the film's staging is entirely aimed at keeping the presence of the recording camera present in each moment and in relating it to the presence of the spectator. The film relates the camera's gaze, this is the operative point, to a present that is irretrievably past. *Exactly these soldiers, who I now see before me, anxious, wounded, or dead, were on the ship's deck; they were there at exactly that split second when one of them looked into the camera. Exactly at the moment of this glance they were at this site from which their gaze meets us in our present.*

The moment, in which the light breaks onto the soldiers' bodies, inscribing the movements of their bodies into the film material, works in conjunction with the arbitrary points in time in which the spectators of this material first create the possibility for a film image to emerge from the exposed film material in the act of watching films, in the physical activity of their senses. The physical presence with which the soldiers in WITH THE MARINES AT TARAWA encounter the spectators is a media effect that is due to a poetic calculation – but it is no illusion. What it shows much more is the split structure of perception that Cavell attributes to the media technology film. In view of the film analyses we can now describe this perception structure as a temporal relation in which radically separated presents can be interrelated. In just the same way, it opens a choice for the spectator between two opposing ways of relating to the past, as we find worked out in Cavell as the two main possibilities for how to watch films.

By making a past event from our common world present, the film world of WITH THE MARINES AT TARAWA is an illusion in which the spectators grasp their own world in the audiovisual image as the entirety of the world. But in being aware of this indissoluble singularity, the effect of physical presence rescues the possibility of a way of thinking history that is constituted precisely in the experience of temporal contingency. We imagine the endless production of images of the Second World War as a virtual space in which innumerable shots of the type of the Marine glancing into the camera can exist side by side without any succession, sequence, or hierarchizing, waiting to appear in a cycle of alternating affections between the spectator's body and the film body. The film image provides the spectator with a way to see back into an absolutely past present, back to a world from which they are radically excluded; but the spectators provide the image with the presence of a perceiving and feeling body.

In the poetic calculation of WITH THE MARINES AT TARAWA the possibilities of media technology are worked out into a specific mode of the documentary film image, which I have tried to describe as perception folded in time. We will call this mode the cinematic 'memory image.'[115] This is not meant to create any analogy between individual memory and the production of media images. Instead, memory image means a temporal correlation in which present and past are brought into a mutual relation of definition, without having been linked with one another in a linear temporal arrangement beforehand by such a relation – for instance causal or hierarchical relationships. Deleuze understood such film images as time crystals.[116] But a time crystal can also be reconstructed using Terrence Malick's THE THIN RED LINE.[117] Indeed, in a similar way, one might relate this film to combat footage, which forms the basis of the production of WITH THE MARINES AT TARAWA, just as one can make a connection between the opening sequence of SAVING PRIVATE RYAN with the film production at the landing at Omaha Beach. Except that THE THIN RED LINE composes its staging of images from the standpoint of the film viewer. The troops that meet on the beach, battle

---

115 Cf. Deleuze, *The Time-Image*, 47 ff.
116 Cf.: "Deleuze defines two decisive forms of crystal images. He situates one directly in the past, the other in the present.... The images of the past, the first form, designate the displacement into pure memory, which Deleuze had defined, following Bergson, as an autonomous area, that is, independent of present functions. Projecting into the memory, however, no longer provides any primarily chronological order, but simultaneous sequences of images, for only from the point of view of a present consciousness oriented to an action can time be grasped as successive. Current perception, says Bergson, is thus also oriented in spatial relationships. If, however, we look for memory in its own area, then the images are no longer arranged spatially, but in purely temporal viewpoints. This liberation of time from space is decisive for understanding Deleuze's philosophical approach. Pure memory or retention are exactly such pure time-images, in which the various images coexist instead of following one another. In pure memory, there is no automatism of movement, but regions, sediments, and layers... The second form, the time-images of the present, are the direct expression of the division in time described above. In order to understand an event, we normally assume that it has a present that can be distinguished from its past and future. But this, Deleuze maintains, is a view of the event that basically also ties understanding time to spatial concepts. Namely, we can also understand time as the simultaneity of the present of the past the present of the present and even of the present of the future, for [...] time (occurs) exactly at the intersection of keeping and passing. It is therefore not about what is kept or what passes, but about both at the same time. The actual event contains several temporal moments *simultaneously*, which are commonly thought of as elapsing after one another, it therefore consolidates all these different moments into one event." Oliver Fahle, "Zeitspaltungen: Gedächtnis und Erinnerung bei Gilles Deleuze," in *montage a/v* 11 (1), 2002, 97–112, here 103ff. On this point, see also: Mirjam Schaub, *Gilles Deleuze im Kino: Das Sichtbare und das Sagbare*, Munich 2003, 117ff.
117 On the question of memory in film, cf.: Lehmann, *Affektpoetiken des New Hollywood*.

3.5 On the Historicity of Film Images

weary and exhausted, in order to then ride away from the island on the ship that will take them home, the anonymous faces in the morning sun on the deck of the warship, the monologue of the young soldier, about whom we learn nothing more than what is said at the beginning and the end of the film, when he is briefly singled out from the many unfamiliar faces – each of these audiovisual images is itself part of a multitudinous reminiscence with which the cinema at the turn of the millennium responded to the found footage of the war years. In the contemporary spectator's watching of films emerges a network of relations between the old film images and current cinema, which as a whole behaves as a time crystal.

Perhaps, in the image of the soldier glancing at the camera for a moment, WITH THE MARINES AT TARAWA has completed the decisive turn by which the pathos of the Hollywood war film came to a fixed formula: a face, as singular as it is multifold, as special as it is ordinary, which opens up the space of another time for the spectator for the duration of a glance; just as lightning connects heaven and earth for a second, although it only illuminates the unattainable distance. In the aesthetic experience of the contingency of irretrievable pasts, to which no path leads out of the physical presence of the film-watching spectator, the melodramatic mode gets its particular molding in the war film. In the soldier's face, the pathos of the subjective suffering of a completely exposed, abandoned ego is closely linked with what I have sought to describe as the cinematic memory image: that is, the temporal splitting of the perceiving consciousness, which we defined, following Cavell, as a basic structure of the form of experience that is specific to the medium of film images; the split into an ego that produces the succession of automatic world projections onto its own body as its very own world of perceptions, and one present in this world as a transcendental consciousness. In this link lies the core of a genuine affect poetics of the Hollywood war film, with which the basic modes of aesthetic experience of genre cinema – of action movies, of the melodrama, of the horror film – combine into a new genre.

Seen from here, the film analyses that we have so far presented can be distinguished and summarized in view of three fundamental perceptual politics that contemporary American cinema pursued during the Second World War. On the one hand, this is the function of mobilizing the readiness for war; this corresponds to the development of a specific *affect dramaturgy*, which I have tried to make transparent in its most basic traits in the examples of DECEMBER 7TH and GUNG HO! On the other, it is the reforming of a democratic polity into a military community, which – as I have emphasized for THE BATTLE OF MIDWAY – above all speaks to the *melodramatic modeling of the film document*. Third, it is the *metamorphosis of melodramatic pathos to the memory image*, which I have tried to work out in relation to WITH THE MARINES AT TARAWA; here, the focus – as I brought up in relation to BATAAN – is on commemorating the sacrifice of the soldier. In the interplay of these three reception politics, a level of observation can be constructed by which the genre of the Hollywood war film can be described in its historicity as a history of poetically reconfiguring the sense of commonality. Building from these reflections, I will discuss the following theses in the last part of the book:

1. With the pathos of the cinematic memory image, attention is focused on the question of commemorating the sacrifice, the image of the suffering soldier, and his function for the sense of commonality.
2. With the image of the sacrifice to military communitization, the fundamental contradiction between the liberal ideal of a democratic society and military communitization finally comes to the fore, marking the field of political relations as its constitutive conflict, to which the genre, in its various cycles, is ultimately due.

4 Genre and History

4.1 John Ford's THEY WERE EXPENDABLE: The Matrix of a New Genre

The amount of visual material shot under John Ford's direction at the landing at Normandy must have been enormous. There is apparently only one single interview in which John Ford speaks of his experience directing at Omaha Beach.[1] He talks about incoherent memory images – it was footage without any organization through editing – and about the time that was needed to become aware that one was present at a great massacre. Ford himself obviously never attempted to work with the material. Instead, he began work on THEY WERE EXPENDABLE immediately after the mission at Normandy.

Back to genre films

During the battle at Omaha Beach, Ford meets an officer, John D. Bulkeley, quite by chance, who tells him how, when he was the director of a torpedo boat squadron, he led General MacArthur away to safety from Bataan – after the Philippine post there had in fact already been lost for the American troops.[2] Ford interrupts his work on the footage at the landing in Normandy and begins the preparatory work for THEY WERE EXPENDABLE, in which exactly this story is told. The film shows a small group of soldiers who hold their post in the Pacific despite absolute numerical inferiority, seeking to play for time: the time that was needed for the US Marines to reorganize after the attack at Pearl Harbor. The film deals with the low point of the war, with a state of hopeless abandonment, with the time of waiting in vain for a rescuing armada, which no longer existed. Above all, however, it deals with what it means for soldiers, of which there were thousands, to give up – and with how it feels to be given up.

---

[1] Cf. Peter Martin, "We shot D-Day on Omaha Beach: An Interview with John Ford," in *The American Legion Magazine* 76 (6), June 1964, 14–19 and 44–46.
[2] MGM's intention to make a film of the book on this story (William L. White, *They Were Expendable: An American Torpedo Boat Squadron in the U.S. Retreat from the Philippines*, New York 1942) is even older. Cf. Joseph McBride, *Searching for John Ford: A Life*, New York 2001. I am less interested here in the creation of legends or the production history in all its details than in the constellation that the 'documentary filmmaker' John Ford had reached a point where he was returning to the opening events of the war and to a particular way of making cinema at the same moment.

https://doi.org/10.1515/9783110468083-005

> Today the guns are silent. A great tragedy has ended. A great victory has been won [...] I speak for the thousands of silent lips, forever stilled among the jungles and the beaches and in the deep waters of the Pacific which marked the way.³

John Ford placed these words of General Douglas MacArthur at the beginning of his film THEY WERE EXPENDABLE (USA 1945), and ended the film with his words: "We shall return!" At the beginning of the film is the pathos of remembering the fallen of a war won, at the end the defiant declaration of the beaten American army, after Pearl Harbor and the defeat in the Philippines. Both are affect-charged formulas that are paradoxically linked to the temporality of the Hollywood war film. The pathos of commemorating the dead defines the poetics of the films that were made after the war ended; just as the propagandistic mobilizing after the attack on Pearl Harbor and the defeat in the Pacific, the "We shall return!" designates the historical starting point of the war film and influences its specific poetics, with which it is formed as a new genre within Hollywood cinema.

When I said above that the Hollywood war film emerged out of the propagandistic offensive at the beginning and during the Second World War, this is only the case retrospectively. In fact, cycles of films only emerge after the Second World War in which the opening question of the media mobilization campaign – "Why are we Americans on the march?" – becomes visible as a constitutive conflict that concerns the historical foundation of the political community and the sense of commonality within it. The conflict between military and political community forms the basis for the generic cohesion, the family resemblance⁴ of the films. In a certain sense, an analogous function in the social affective economy had previously been marked by the films of the western genre. It will therefore hardly be possible to understand the genre if we do not take into view the poetics of the western, the specific expressive modalities and affect-dramaturgical moldings with which it relates its spectators to the mythological talk of the birth of the nation.⁵

In this sense – in no way as an explanatory justification for the proximity of the western and the war film – the paradoxical reversal of the temporal formulas of remembrance and declaration of war at the beginning and end of THEY WERE

---

3 Citation from the victory speech by General Douglas MacArthur on September 2, 1945. Cf. Douglas MacArthur, "Signing of the Surrender Instrument by Japan, 2 September 1945," in *Douglas MacArthur: Warrior as Wordsmith*, eds. Bernhard K. Duffy and Ronald H. Carpenter, Westport/London 1997, 173–174, here 173.
4 Cf. Cavell, *Pursuits of Happiness*, 29.
5 Cf. Burgoyne, *Film Nation*, 47ff.

EXPENDABLE also points to the individual history of John Ford's engagement in the Second World War. Ford, who had so far shot documentaries throughout the war for the army,[6] has the experience, during the landing at Normandy, that the events that he is attending at close range overburden any possibility of film documentation – precisely in the fact that the camera's being in the midst of it all is continually pushed, ever further beyond the limits of the bearable. Ford finds an answer to this dilemma by turning back to the first locations of his work as a documentarist. He turns back to the war in the Pacific and – "We shall return!" – to the Hollywood genre cinema that he had so substantially influenced.

An affect-dramaturgical analysis

In the following I would like to attempt to work out the analytical model of the pathos scenes, which I outlined in the chapter on the methodology of analyzing genre, through the example of THEY WERE EXPENDABLE as an affect-poetic concept that is aimed at the participation in a shared feeling of collective remembrance. In doing so, I am very much concerned in allowing the methodological instruments discussed there to be concretely understandable, that is, to establish the terms of the affect-poetic concept of film and to describe it analytically.

Much like BATAAN and many other war films, THEY WERE EXPENDABLE can be understood as an attempt to transform the images of the first defeats in the war into a figuration of sacrifice, which is opposed to the experience of the contingency of historical events. John Ford's THEY WERE EXPENDABLE was meant to show how the feeling for a commonly shared history, for the becoming of a political community, is shaped by the unfolding of a melodramatic image of suffering as a figuration of sacrifice. At the same time, in terms of the war in the Pacific, the film completely takes on a special role in comparison to the older films. Indeed, it stages the film image of past war events as a ritual mode of remembrance. This concerns both the shaping of the expressive modalities of individual episodes and the affect dramaturgy in its relation to the entirety of THEY WERE EXPENDABLE. Precisely here lies the paradigmatic meaning of the film for understanding the expressive modalities and pathos scenes of the genre.

In THEY WERE EXPENDABLE, which was shot before the end of hostilities in 1945, but which only came into American cinemas around Christmastime of the same year, can be seen as a reconfiguration of the affect-dramaturgical model in its focused reduction. Instead of following the model of mobilization films,

---

6 Cf. Gaertner, *Tickets to War*.

in which the first six types of pathos scenes name both the affect-dramaturgical stages and how they develop from one to the next, Ford concentrates on reworking the first field of conflict: the tension between civilian and military forms of communitization, the dissolution of civilian society and the initiation into military order.

The film deals with a small troop of soldiers, a torpedo boat squadron under the command of Lt. 'Brick' Brickley (Robert Montgomery) and Lt. 'Rusty' Ryan (John Wayne), who are trying to hold only their posts in the Pacific despite absolute numerical and technological inferiority and, from retreat order to retreat order, have no other goal than to gain time. The way this troop comes together, gets new recruits and adds them into the paternal order of the military, corresponds for the time being to the basic affective pattern of the second pathos scene, to the tension between the pain of separation in face of unraveling civil relationships and the new communal feeling of a military community. What distinguishes THEY WERE EXPENDABLE from its predecessors is the circumstance that the new military community is not constituted once and for all, but appears as an arrangement, the logic of which constantly requires individual self-abandonment over and over again. The law of the military community is actualized in every of its successful or failed actions, which include the dispensability of individuals, their loss, their staying behind, their death.

To put it another way, the process of initiation into the military community in THEY WERE EXPENDABLE is never concluded, but reactivated time and again by the fact that the changes of the military situation demand a dissolution and reestablishment of the groups at every order to retreat. Like the strokes of a clock, the repetitive loss of men and the partings of parts of the troop structure the time of the film, its affect-dramaturgical shape. It is palpable in the successive loss of the racing speedboats, as it is in the soldiers' increasing dilapidation. The conflict between the representatives of the army in gala uniform on the one hand – later embodied in the figure of General MacArthur – and the ragged figures left behind on the other, is constantly intensified. The latter are only of use to the army in that they hold onto the hopeless posts in order to win time. The soldiers in rags are not simply there, but are peeled out of the bright white dress uniforms in a process of de-uniforming and re-uniforming that is articulated throughout the entire film. Unlike in BATAAN, for example, THEY WERE EXPENDABLE does not develop the subjective experiential perspective of the ones who stay behind, but always only shows how they are left behind. For the spectator of the film, the characters already appear to be positioned outside the time of their suffering, which at the same time is present in the scenes as physically present perception.

Ford treats the pathos complex of initiation in yet another form. He adds a long passage into the middle of the film that practically follows its own dramaturgy: the love story between an officer and a nurse. It puts the representation of initiation, of military order, in a relation of extreme tension to the representation of the phantasm of the feminine, the longing for a woman, and of the pain of separation. This can be seen in the transformations of the feminine that, turned into music, accompany the eruption of war (when the soldiers set out, a patriotic anthem is sung by a Filipino woman) and the commemoration of the sacrifices (a recurring waltz links feelings of romantic love with reports of defeat). From the very beginning, this tension is present in the ways that femininity appears. It becomes transformed from the woman as woman at the evening ball to the woman as nurse in the sick bay, then to the woman at the other end of a telephone line, and finally to the addressee of a letter of which we do not know if it will arrive, nor even if it can be sent at all. Enclosed in the genre scenes of the western and the melodrama, the phantasms of the feminine appear as mirrorings or prisms, in which the historical events that are shaped in the reconstitutions of an increasingly bedraggling military community get reflected as affective figurations that point to individual sensibility and sense of the self.

Starting from the dramaturgical strands mentioned here – the constant reactualization of the *initiation into* the military community and its dissolution in being left behind, of the *exclusion from* this community on the one hand, and the yearning phantasms of the feminine, in which the historical events are reflected as atmospheric echoes and nostalgic feeling on the other – the film's dramaturgy of affect can be described in four rough stages.[7] By arranging the film's dramaturgy into these four stages, a dramaturgical representation of the course of the film as succession, parallelization, and concentration of pathos scenes becomes evident. In such a representation it becomes possible to read and compare the strategies of affect in individual films by means of the following questions: What affective complexes are staged in which succession, amalgamations, and configurations of scenes, and in what duration? Which specific sequences are repeated? Which pathos themes mutually exclude one another and which

---

[7] As noted already, the division into categories of pathos is not about defining narrative stereotypes. Rather, the pathos categories allow us to grasp the visual units of war films as discrete modulation steps in the process of the audiovisual design of a continually unfolding sensation of perception, and to qualify it in terms of the rhetorics of affect. They function as vertices that are in effect in the process of perceiving film as vectorial powers of affectation. The division of this and many other films into pathos scenes and the visualization in diagrams was carried out by means of systematic analyses in the project "Affect Mobilization and the Staging of War in Media" (see footnote 185). Materials on this and the clips related to it are available online in the project's data matrix: July 7, 2017).

concord harmonically with one another?⁸ It is often precisely the relationships that are produced between the various domains of affect within a closed figuration of a scene that make it possible to say something specific about the pathos of a scene and its function within the affect dramaturgy. If we take the diagrammatic visualization of the affective course of THEY WERE EXPENDABLE (see Figure 27) as a transference of the systematic division of the film into pathos scenes that either alternate or run in parallel, as the starting point of the singular analytical perspective, then the four acts can be described as follows:

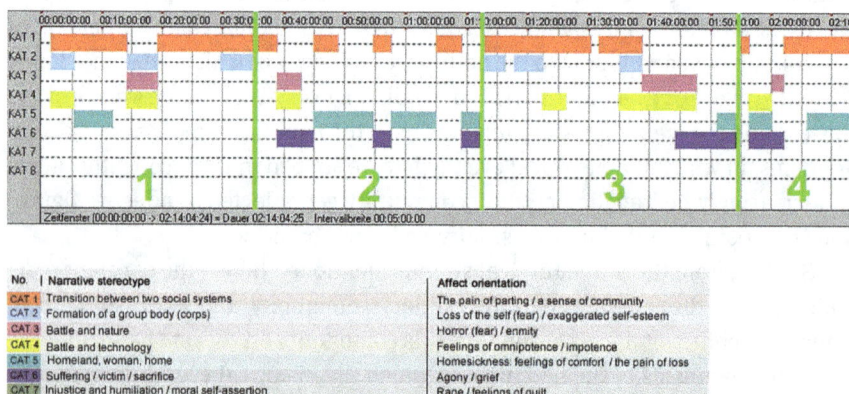

Figure 27: Diagram showing the temporal arrangement of pathos scenes in THEY WERE EXPENDABLE (John Ford, USA 1945) as well as its segmentation into 4 acts.

In the first act⁹ the initiation into the military community is integrated at the moment when war breaks out with audiovisual forms of expression that already inscribe – by means of music, the voice of a Filipino singer, emphatic close-ups

---

8 Using systematic analyses, the films examined were segmented into scenes, which are each definable as staging complexes. As a rule, these scenes can be attributed to one or more categories of pathos scenes. A distinction should also be made between the pathos scene as an abstract category and the action scene as a unit of time, which can also cover several categories of pathos scenes.

9 Scenes 1–8 (00:00:00:00–00:35:39:26); "Drill und Appell [*drill and muster*]," "Einbruch des Krieges [*the irruption of war*]," "Warten auf Befehle [*waiting for orders*]," "Erster Alarm und Kampf [*first alert and combat*]," "Trümmer und Trennung [*wreckage and separation*]," "Neuer Befehl und Aufbruch [*new orders and departure*]," "Versorgungsbelange [*supply matters*]," "Anweisung für die erste Operation [*instructions for the first operation*]." Timecodes and scene titles refer to the systematic compilation of pathos scenes in film, such as the project undertaken and mentioned above.

4.1 John Ford's THEY WERE EXPENDABLE: The Matrix of a New Genre — 239

or long shots of individual characters – the pathos of mourning commemoration into the scenes of the war's beginning. This act ends with the first command to retreat, and thus with the first experience of *being expendable*; the experience of being so as a troop from the viewpoint of military command. The second[10] and third acts[11] stand in a reciprocal relation that can be described as the day and night sides of the staging of battle, defeat, and death. On the night side, in the second act, the representation of sexuality, corporeality, and mortality expands into the phantasmatic, while the day side shows the historical events as a constant repetition and concentration of the scene of reorganization, initiation, and of being left behind. The ideal affect dramaturgical course – from the (re)formation of the military body to the accumulation of tension to release in the ecstasy of the battle and the fall into mourning and disenchantment – becomes a revolving circle in which the event unfolds.

The film's first and fourth acts[12] can both be understood as representing historical defeats, which are almost reduced to the manageable size of a miniature model. In turn, they are arranged into certain aspects as a mirror-symmetrical reversal. On the one hand, at the end we once again see the faces of the boys absorbed into the troop at the beginning – the opposition between the ragged shapes on the beach and the youthful faces could not be greater (see Figure 28).

On the other hand, the images of defeat in the first act are framed by the blind automatism of the military apparatus, while at the end of the film they are marked by the self-assertion of the individual in the act of self-abandonment. This self-assertion is conjured up as the basis of the later victory, which is to be remembered.

In the following, I would like to work out the film's affect-rhetorical calculations by describing selected scenes. In doing so, I will systematically be referring

---

10 Scenes 9–17 (00:35:39:26–01:12:47:15); "Krankenhaus I [*hospital I*]," "Boot unter Beschuss [*boat under fire*]," "Bootsrückkehr [*the boat's return*]," "Krankenhaus II, [*hospital II*]" "Feier und Gespräch [*celebration and conversation*]," "Rückkehr vom Kampf [*returning from battle*]," "Dinner," "Neuer Befehl [*new orders*]," "Krankenhaus III [*hospital III*]."

11 Scenes 18–29 (01:12:47:15–01:54:34:20); "Ansprache [*address*]," "Durch das Telefon getrennt [*separated by telephone*]," "Erneutes Auslaufen der Boote [*the boats head off again*]," "Geleitschutz [*escort*]," "Neue Umstände [*new circumstances*]," "Die Fahrt [*the cruise*]," "Torpedogeschäft [*torpedo business*]," "Jeepfahrt und neuer Einsatz [*jeep drive and new mission*]," "Gefecht zu Wasser [*battle at sea*]," "Ein Luftangriff fordert Opfer [*an airstrike claims victims*]," "Begräbniszeremonie [*funeral ceremony*]," "In der Kneipe [*in the bar*]."

12 Scenes 30–34 (01:54:34:20–02:14:04:24); "Reorganisation," "Wiedersehen und Abschied vom Boot [*reunion and farewell to the boat*]," "Erschöpfung [*exhaustion*]," "Fußmarsch [*march*]," "We shall return."

Figure 28: The child's faces at the beginning and at the end of the film.

back to the division into pathos scenes that I described above. The scenes themselves will be cited on the basis of the analytical and representative methodology of eMAEX, and can be called up as audiovisual citations on an internet platform. As a result, I hope to be able to describe the way THEY WERE EXPENDABLE is staged in such a way that the temporal structure of the staging itself becomes evident as a matrix of spectator feeling.[13]

Act I: dissolution and initiation

The small military unit with its speedboats presents itself to the generals. The soldiers in their grey uniforms present their sleek torpedo boats to the men on the guard tower in their parade uniforms. The music, the camera angles, dominated

---

[13] For reasons of legibility, the references to the timecodes and the scene titles will be given in the footnotes. They are meant to serve to refer back to the definitions formulated above as well as to incite further analysis of the project's data matrix.

by the breadth of the horizon, as well as the harmonic rhythm of the movement of the camera and the boats already form the very first minutes of the film in expressive modalities quite similar to those found in John Ford's westerns.[14] They describe a quite particular relationship between the individual and the landscape, which designates the transition, the threshold between no-longer-wilderness and not-yet-civilization – one might call it a friendly relationship. At any rate, the first scenes are dedicated to the delight in the breadth of the water, flooded over with sun, and in the beauty of the speedboats, but also to the skill of their crews. In the sensual luxuriousness of the images on screen, they are reminiscent of John Ford's westerns; the spectators do not need much imagination to add horses and trumpet calls, and to transform the water into clouds of dust. Either way – what we see is the extraterritorial outposts of American civilization, projected into the infinite breadth of an undefined world.

In stark contrast to the imagined dynamic and the breadth of a world of unlimited opportunity is – still following the mytho-poetic architecture of so many westerns – the stolidity of the generals and the static geometry of the soldiers called to roll call. The delight in movement and speed seems to have exhausted itself in the long run of the boats into the port. Calm, stiff, and straight, the crew awaits the generals inspecting the grey rows in their white parade uniforms. The commanders make no bones of having been able to enjoy the beauty of the maneuver, but in the emergency situation of war there is no use for the torpedo boat squadron; the grey soldiers are really not needed. The opposition between the dynamic of the maneuver and the staticness of the roll call become a metaphor for the looming conflict between the bureaucratic military apparatus in support of the state and the obstinate individualism of the two protagonists Brick and Rusty. The scene ends with Brick giving a loving gaze to one of the boats.

The following scene is also based on a topos that was marked in the western, namely the attempt to develop small forms of sociality in saloons and ballrooms, an ordinary society in a male dominated world.[15] We might compare this scene with the ball scene in Ford's FORT APACHE (1948) three years later, in which the cavalrymen and their wives allow for something like an ordinary communality to emerge for a limited time out in the boondocks and surrounded by enemy Indian tribes; an undertaking that can fail and be interrupted at any moment in light of the military state of exception. The oscillation between civilian normality and state of exception is stressed in THEY WERE EXPENDABLE by the soldiers' Sunday best in their white dress uniforms (see Figure 29). At the same

---

14 Scene "Drill und Appell [*drill and muster*]" (00:01:33:07–00:05:20:29).
15 Scene "Einbruch des Krieges [*the irruption of war*]" (00:05:20:29–00:11:49:16).

Figure 29: Ordinary sociality.

time the homogenous festive uniforms already draw attention to the dividing line at which those in attendance will split up when the announcement comes in about the attack on Pearl Harbor. We see how the crowd of women and men diverge and recognize that the soldiers in their homogenous white uniforms had always already been singled out. From this perspective, the guests at the festivities appear as a parallel montage of the genders in the interior of the frame; or to put it another way, while the women in civilian clothes and men in uniforms do dance with one another, they do not mix; the soldiers are even interchangeable as dance partners in their white uniforms, which increasingly take the upper hand. By the time the comrades are celebrating the parting of the old warhorse 'Doc,' the image space is finally populated exclusively by men. The dialogue and the sequence of the choreographies of the characters, in the interaction of young and old men, varies the topic of initiating the purely male military community – even before the declaration of war definitively drives apart the festive society for good.

The soldiers merrily clink glasses, the orchestra strikes up, we hear the song of a festively dressed Filipino singer – but then there is a disturbance in the scenario of the ball, soldiers in grey uniforms go from table to table, whispering into the ears of the officers dressed in white, after which they abruptly get up: the announcement of the declaration of war. As the party breaks up, it becomes an image that seeks to grasp the dissociation of civilian society under pressure from its militarization, the experience of the pain of separation and threat, condensed into a metaphor. Quite literally, the old strutting dissolves, the community of ordinary cohabitation breaks apart, a mobilization of the senses *en miniature*, in which the men are singled out and separated from the women.

The anthem sung "America (My Country, 'Tis of Thee)," one of the many unofficial national anthems of the USA, in the emphasized presentation of the singer, who overcomes her horror, seems not only to address the characters, but at least as much the spectators; the song, the voice, the singer's face already inscribes the pathos of mourning into the event of the war news without any excitement or surprise, the retrospective consciousness of an inevitable destiny that the soldiers in their dress uniforms will be confronted by. Some of them are singled out as individuals, their faces directly tied to the singing. We see a young recruit, he gets up, hesitating for a moment before incorporating himself into the stream of the other soldiers. The traits on his face seem all the more childlike the more the camera tarries on them. Seen in relation to the spectators, the entire sequence – the boys at the bar between the men, the woman singing, the pensive faces – can be described as a process of suddenly becoming aware: These are children! All these recruits were practically still boys when they entered the male community of the military to go to war.

The war has begun, but there is no use for the torpedo boat unit. The staging is focused on the time spent uselessly waiting for deployment.[16] Only when an enemy plane attacks does the longed-for chance for battle deployment open

---

16 Scene "Warten auf Befehle [*waiting for orders*]" (00:11:49:16–00:14:11:18).

up. The following sequence is staged entirely in the mode of the action film.[17] If the synchronicity of movement and the geometrical spatial arrangement of the boats was the expression of the maneuver's beauty, now the power of the troop as a battle unit is emphatically demonstrated. The movements of the soldiers, the commandos of their boat leaders Brick and Rusty, the interweaving of characters with the technical procedures of their boats and not least the interplay of the boats with one another – all of this, like gears in a machine, is shown and choreographed as dynamic cohesion.

During all of this, the contrast between the small men running around like weasels on their sleek boats and the giant airplane formations in the sky is strikingly presented. The images of the attacking planes are clearly positioned as reminiscent of the documentary footage of aerial warfare. We also understand very quickly why this is the case. Once again the dynamic action ends with the boats heading slowly into the port; the euphoria of the action scenes ends in a scene of dismal mourning. When they return, the soldiers find their port reduced to rubble. The great event of Pearl Harbor is reflected in the attack on this small port somewhere in the Philippines.

Indeed, the image of destruction is an image for Pearl Harbor and at the same time the antithesis to Pearl Harbor: it is precisely not about tons and caliber, but about individual heroism and the sense of commonality.[18] Remembering the images of defeat at the beginning of the war in the Pacific is underscored with a sense of meaning that eludes the enormous amounts of film documents circulating about that event. It is not in the tons of airplane carriers registered in gross, nor in the violence of the heavy artillery, but in the dynamic improvisation of individual fighters, in their sense of commonality that the power to turn the defeat into a victory has its roots. The torpedo boat troop put up resistance, while the military command sought to get the war under control administratively. When they return, the military base is destroyed. Now their boats become transporters to haul the wounded soldiers out of the smoldering ruins; the retreat, the exit of the boats overloaded with wounded men, is underscored with an elegiac accordion.

Here as well, the image of a Filipino woman marks the end of the scene; her gaze bids farewell to the American troops, who are evacuating their base, leaving behind this face, this gaze, just as they had left the singer and her solemn singing in the earlier ball scene. In fact, a significant meaning comes to the circumstance that it is an Asian woman standing in her white dress at the landing for the boats,

---

[17] Scene "Erster Alarm und Kampf [*first alert and combat*]" (00:14:11:18–00:19:15:20).
[18] Scene "Trümmer und Trennung [*wreckage and separation*]" (00:19:15:20–00:21:22:16).

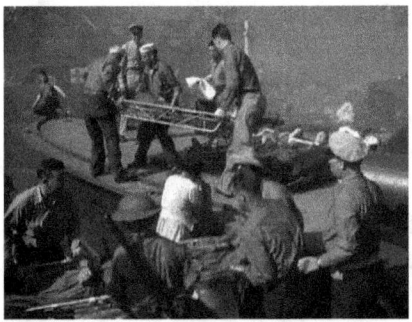 

Figure 30: Iconic formula of elegiac lamentation.

drawing the spectators attention to herself in the middle of and as the calming antithesis to the hectic movements of the soldiers clad in grey. The face of a woman, the dark swathes of smoke, the elegiac music form an expressive figuration that is added to the scene that is reminiscent of the audiovisual documents of the destruction of Pearl Harbor and the first weeks and months of the war in the Pacific, added like a pietà – leaning on a post at the waterfront the woman looks after the soldiers driving away on their boats. The film image of the woman becomes an elegiac lamentation for the spectator (see Figure 30), a pathos formula in which the memory of the anxiety, fear, and mourning of the first weeks of war is called up: the mourning over the loss of a society (the society at the ball earlier), in which men and woman of all races and religions are meant to be joined together in one community.

This is followed by a short intermezzo, which is nonetheless of immense significance for the relations of memory within the film – the moments in which the film, already at its end, remembers its beginning.[19] The emotional ties within this male society are described here at a father-son level. In their destroyed barracks – a tangle of beams and shadows reminiscent of expressionistic forms of expression – the soldiers squat close together on the ground around Brick and Rusty. Among them sit two boys, who can easily be called child soldiers. Trembling, they announce that they are not cold, but that they are afraid. Their facial expression relaxes when Lt. Brick tells them that they have no monopoly on fear, that they shared it with everybody else here. Conveyed by the spatial constriction and the exchange of words, a feeling of connection arises among the individual members of the group.

---

19 Scene "Neuer Befehl und Aufbruch [*new orders and departure*]" (00:21:22:16–00:27:04:15).

We will run into one of the two boys that we see here once again, quite at the end of THEY WERE EXPENDABLE; he will be one of those left behind on the beach – and who watch the planes who are bringing rescue to many others, but not for them. In the reminiscences within the film such as this, a network of relations arises for the spectator in which the feeling unfolds of being expendable for the big picture of the army, for the military machine.

The key words that call up the most difficult defeats of the war in the Pacific – "Pearl Harbor" and the battleship *USS Arizona* that was sunk there; "Bataan" and "Corregidor" – target the contemporary audience's ubiquitous memory of newsreels and combat reports, the newspapers and radio programs of the days of war. By directly or indirectly repeating the motifs and patterns of the images of war, films like THEY WERE EXPENDABLE figure themselves in the image as a medial process of remembering. In the second act of John Ford's film, the principle of repetition and remembering is directly shaped as a process of sensation.

Act II: phantasmagorias of love and death

The following 45 minutes, taken as a whole, can be conceived as a parallel montage in which the randomly told moments of everyday military organization[20] – strategic meetings, scenes of material acquisition, the torpedo boats are used for regular courier service – are linked with a dark side of everyday life: the battle, the scenes in the hospital, the party, and the dinner. The contrast between the dark scenes and the scenes of everyday life, as well as the entirety of the scenes from the first act, is conspicuous, especially at the level of spatial formation and lighting. Previously, the scene was almost continuously defined by a uniform application of light. This allowed for the bodies, things, and spaces to emerge in clearly outlined forms, meaning that even images of destruction were represented in a softly graduated, extensive palette of grey tones. In the second act, however, visual spaces dominate in which the characters seem like islands of light moving over dark, crooked surfaces from which they increasingly become detached.

In the three scenes in the hospital – Rusty had been wounded in the only combat so far – this change becomes especially obvious; these scenes establish the atmospheric tone that then defines the spatiality.[21] The text "Hospital – Corregidor"

---

[20] Scene "Bootsrückkehr [*the boat's return*]" (00:42:51:18–00:44:57:02); Scene "Neuer Befehl [*new orders*]" (01:05:02:16–01:09:08:16).
[21] Scene "Krankenhaus I [*hospital I*]" (00:35:39:26–00:38:55:12); Scene "Krankenhaus II [*hospital II*]" (00:44:57:02–00:48:54:28); Scene "Krankenhaus III [*hospital III*]" (01:09:08:16–01:12:47:15).

appears, and the spectators are placed directly in a channel dominated by a central perspective. In the foreground are two rectangular, occupied beds, behind them in irregular formations are a few room dividers, and from behind, as well as from a sideways, equally channel-like passage, light is cast into the room that is otherwise kept dark. Rusty stands lost in this labyrinth, and his voice echoes from the walls, unpleasantly loud, until he is quietened down, first by a nurse, Sandy (Donna Reed), and then by a thermometer that she sticks in his mouth. The allusion to acting techniques from the screwball comedy can only suppress the disturbing quality of the peculiar spatial arrangement for a moment. What kind of place is this, this cave-like bunker, the roof of which seems on the one hand to stretch endlessly into the depths and on the other to be broken down by a system of rectangular screens, allowing for innumerable parcels to emerge that are shielded from any and all gazes? We might take the space to be grotesque, an allegorical formation in which the body itself, the relation between masculinity and femininity, between power and vulnerability, sexuality and mortality, are made explicit and at the same time are somehow shielded off (see Figure 31). The subjective consciousness of these relations is not represented as an experience of the senses, but in highly symbolic figurations that are practically projected on the separating screens.

This spatiality finds its counterpart in the way that the characters themselves try to shield themselves from the experience of corporeality. The ruthlessness with which Rusty turns against his own body, the insensitivity for his own sensations of pain, the defeat that he experiences in the face of injury and exhaustion – they emerge, again, in the interplay of screen and projection, through the presence of the woman, the nurse Sandy, almost like a behavioral relief that disavows his own corporeality. Rusty himself has shielded himself from the sensorium of pain, exhaustion, and death; and, connected with this, against his longing, his sexuality. Sandy decisively pushes this shielding aside when she literally forces Rusty to drop his trousers. The motif of shielding off continues in the metamorphoses of the woman herself, who conceals her femininity in the overalls, called "potato sacks," and entrenches herself behind her brusque wit in order to find her place in the war. Until even this shield is broken through: an aerial attack – ambulances bring ever more wounded soldiers into the provisional hospital, which itself has come under fire. In the dark cellar spaces the doctor and the nurses attempt to carry out the most urgent operations in the light cone of a single lamp. In the shaky light we see single faces lit up in the dark time and again. They are related to the repetitive close-ups that carve Sandy's sweaty facial features out of the blackness.

For the spectators watching this montage configuration, the motif of disavowed bodily vulnerability, of shielding off from sexuality and mortality, is tied

Figure 31: The allegorical space of the military hospital bunker.

to observing the woman's face. The repeated shift between close-ups of Sandy and flickering, fragmented parts of the faces of wounded soldiers flashing in the dark, which cannot be grasped as either group or as individual, add up into an impression of bodily horror. This conveys a feeling to the spectators of what it might mean to be open to one's own physical sensitivity. The spatial construction is now completely marked by the expressive modalities of the horror genre. At the same time, however, the spectators, in their attentive observation of Sandy's face, are inextricably entangled in the increasing fascination with which Rusty observes the woman, as if she – particularly in this place – were an utterly unreal apparition. So, on the one hand, the scene ends with Sandy asking Rusty to take her to a party in the evening.

On the other hand, the leaving of the exhausted nurses stages an image of death. The three women who have just been fighting for the bodies of the wounded soldiers disappear into the depths of the image. We see them go through a tunnel – a diffuse, weak backlight causes them to appear as silhouettes, while at the same time giving the darkness at the end of the tunnel an impression of infinite depth. The backlight throws the women's shadows right and light onto the walls of the arches of the tunnel. The moving shadows – wildly and grotesquely distorted by the different sources of light – follow them as if they were being accompanied by everyone that they could not save today. All of the shielding now takes on meaning within the staging. It functions as a screen that in the very same moment both reveals and conceals the harsh pain of realizing that one is a vulnerable and mortal body. The variable screens between the sickbeds function equally as thing and as allegory.

Meanwhile, the metamorphosis of everyday locations into nocturnal-unreal allegorical figurations is also inscribed into other scenes. The battle scene, for instance, which is about the sinking of a Japanese ship, is transformed into a form of perception in which the action represented is shaped as an abstract composition that concerns the relationship between seeing, not-seeing, masking, and being-hidden. The enemy is shown as a cone of light, muzzle flash, and blazing explosion. In no shot are the torpedo boats and the Japanese ship related in such a way that we might be able to bring them into a spatial relationship. Instead, in the uncanny quiet of the approach in darkness, in the immobility of the one boat and the movement of the other, and finally in the fireworks in which the enemy ship explodes, a description of a battle emerges that, in its abstraction, is much closer to the grotesque expressive forms of horror than to any realistic representation of combat operations.

Even more telling is the phantasmatic reformation of everyday actions in the scenes that continue the love theme: the dance party[22] and the dinner.[23] In both cases the (male) imagination of civilian sociality, which is presented at the beginning of THEY WERE EXPENDABLE in the ball scene, is taken up once again, and in both cases this imagination is the visual answer in the dramaturgy to a return to combat operations. The first begins with a melancholy waltz and the silhouettes of anonymous, dancing bodies, which can be seen against the wood

---

22 Scene "Feier und Gespräch [*celebration and conversation*]" (00:48:54:28–00:54:46:02).
23 Scene "Dinner" (00:57:35:10–01:05:02:16).

floors illuminated from the right. The shadows of the moonlight fallen through the blinds then fall onto the smiling face of Sandy when Rusty appears at the door; his appearance is already phantasmatically charged by the abstract hazy figurations that can be seen in the background.

This scene is then in no way about the attempt to represent how a nocturnal change from the daily routine of war might have looked – how scenes of civilian sociality might emerge in the midst of war. Rather, the spectator here finds him or herself displaced into an image of longing from the very beginning, in a nocturnal dream of home and romantic relationships. The image of the smiling woman with flowers in her hand, the backdrop of haze, moonlight, and shadows of palm trees, is like a layer of longing laid over the troop's daily reality. The on-screen image functions like a visual equivalent to the photos of loved ones carried around by the soldiers in their shirt pockets, or also the pin-ups on locker doors or hung above the bed. The phantasmagoria of a nocturnal dance party in the midst of war is meant to stage longing, the pain of loss, and the desire that is linked with such photos and posters for anyone who possesses them. The phantasmatic charge – here more in the expressive modalities of the melodrama – by the mise-en-scène, the music, and the verbal invocations, allows for an image space to emerge as the space of an inner reality.

Next to one another, arm in arm, a man and a woman are sitting on a hammock, a dreamy image of remembrance of bodily closeness and intimacy, "rather like back home, isn't it?" But an explosion in the distance and Brick's entrance interrupt the dream – Rusty and Sandy suddenly jump up as if they had just woken up. The follow shot/reverse shot sequence initially frames Sandy alone and Rusty with Brick, and when the two men step into the dark background, Sandy remains alone in the foreground. The separation in the visual composition transforms Rusty back into the soldier and Sandy, who finds herself alone on the hammock, definitively becomes an image of the woman waiting back home.

In both scenes, the music is central to the staging of the feminine, which infiltrates and transforms the purely male society; femininity returns – the voice of the singer, the woman's face at the harbor – after they had already torn themselves away from it. The waltz that is danced to at the party turns up again and again in what follows, very quickly already as a motif of mourning remembrance; and the a cappella singing that is intoned during the dinner scenes by the comrades who are not at the table, but are crouching under the terrace on which the table stands, is none other than singing to the absent beloved, for which the woman present, Sandy, is only an image – an image that the feeling can hold on to, where it can become manifest. The film takes a great deal of time at this point to show us how the image of the beloved is produced. It takes a solid minute until the shadowy figure getting into the jeep turns out to be a nurse in the "potato sack"

Figure 32: The image of the (absent) lover.

uniform that we have already mentioned; and until the nurse finally transforms in front of the mirror, with brushed-out hair and beaming face, into a desirable image, framed in light (see Figure 32).

The awkward silence and the rigid conversation, inept grins on the faces at the beginning and cumbersome farewells at the end frame the minute and a half of the interlude with the singing. Sandy here, by means of the staging of the gazes from the men singing practically beneath her, by her placement into the constellation of characters gathered at the table, and the duration of her close-ups, becomes the pivotal point of the scene and the singing.

The candlelight on her face is similar to the reflection of the flashlights in the close-ups of her face during the emergency operations in the sick bay. Ultimately, it is this connection that is staged in Sandy's metamorphoses. She herself appears as the image in which the consciousness of one's own vulnerability and one's own longing for love, of fear of death and sexual desire, is projected onto the protective screens. These phantasms are staged in the allegorical spatial constructions of the sick bay, of the dance hall, and of the candlelight dinner as the dark side of the military community. They concern physical states that the soldiers are shielded against much like the sick people on their beds are spared having to look at the death pangs of men to their right and left by the screens set up. For the spectators, however, the one gets added to the other in the image space of the film, becoming a whole that increasingly allows, as the perception of a perceiving consciousness, the bright side and the dark side to penetrate the dividing screens that shield off from the experience of being no other reality than that of a wounded, mortal body.

Act III: the cycle of separation and reformation

The passages that come next in the film bring us once again onto the bright side in an increasingly compacted succession of sober scenes of bidding farewell. Farewell to the graves of fallen comrades, farewells between those who are moving on and those who are staying behind, farewell from the woman who is now no longer present as a yearning image, but only through a crackling telephone connection.[24]

Now once again the tension between the calculations of military logic and the needs of individual existence takes the foreground. On the one hand, there is the stern and elevated, stylized corporeality of the commanding officers in their crisp, clean uniforms with the accompanying musical pathos; on the other hand is the heap of ragged soldiers left behind on Bataan. Although there can be no getting away, no reunions, no rescue for them, they smile as they march proudly into the dim half tones of the island, accompanied by the same musical motif as the commanding officers, albeit in a clearly diminished, melancholy form.

---

24 Scene "Ansprache [*address*]" (01:12:47:15–01:16:15:09); Scene "Durch das Telefon getrennt [*separated by telephone*]" (01:16:15:09–01:17:43:03).

Literally between the two move the torpedo boats and their crews. While, at the beginning, their athletic beauty was admired, even if their combat strength was deemed too small to make them suitable for war, they now become the lifesavers of the commander of the American armed forces in the Pacific, General MacArthur. The rescue, in turn, is only conveyed in abstract symbolism in its historical significance – a map shows the passage – since it completely follows the logic of military community formation, which finds its final sense by securing the paternal commander. Perhaps in no other scene in the long history of the Hollywood war film is the archaic principle of military collectivization so clear as in the peculiarly abstract way that this rescue mission is staged, the rescue of the father, to which all individual aspirations, the life of the sons, is radically subordinated.[25] Which lives are expendable, which are to be maintained at any price?

Immediately after the arrival, the pathos-laden music is interrupted when the general continues on by jeep. A somber backdrop of talking and other sounds lets us sense the ordinary life behind the surfaces made up of uniforms, maps, commendations, etc.: the idleness and boredom, the arduous struggle for resources to maintain in some way the strength to fight.[26]

From these scenes of a troop left on its own to waste away, THEY WERE EXPENDABLE once again rises to the occasion and stages the technological prowess, the successful melding of man and machine as a triumphal height of the unchained will to fight.[27] Once again, in the expressive modalities of action movies, the elegance and energy with which the boats navigate the fountains of explosions is presented, once again we see the decisiveness in the faces of the crew, once again comes the highlight of the explosion of the Japanese destroyer, which the little boats had tricked and detonated. The fighting power presented in these scenes is not based on military order, but on individual obstinacy, the capacity for intelligent improvisation, coupled with rowdy readiness and unconditional fidelity to the community. Its foundation is the idea of the American per se, which the film's protagonists embody in the laconic-loyal type of the western; the foundation that rescues the generals and makes it possible to win the war.

---

25 Scene "Erneutes Auslaufen der Boote [*the boats head off again*]" (01:17:43:03–01:22:32:24).
26 Scene "Geleitschutz [*escort*]" (01:22:32:24–01:26:21:14); Scene "Neue Umstände [*new circumstances*]" (01:26:21:14–01:30:15:12); Scene "Torpedogeschäft [*torpedo business*]" (01:31:38:15–01:35:01:22); Scene "Jeepfahrt und neuer Einsatz [*jeep drive and new mission*]" (01:35:01:22–01:38:41:01).
27 Scene "Gefecht zu Wasser [*battle at sea*]" (01:38:41:01–01:44:13:20).

Figure 33: Lust for battle and mournin.

The height of the euphoria of battle is followed immediately by the fall (see Figure 33).[28] The two remaining boats get separated, and we follow Rusty and his people in their vain attempt to get away from the superior air force. First, in a long shot, we see how the boat has to be abandoned, how it is destroyed by

---

[28] Scene "Ein Luftangriff fordert Opfer [*an airstrike claims victims*]" (01:44:13:20–01:47:39:15).

the planes, then the character that forms the maternal center of the troop dies. We do not hear any music while this is happening, only the explosions and the noises created by the huge amounts of water that fly up then crash back down on the characters; on the boy that is rescuing the flag from the boat; on John Wayne, who lets himself sink exhaustedly into the sand, his outstretched body as if paralyzed, solidifying into a visual expression of defeat and mourning.

The two following scenes transform the somber image of mourning into a pathos-laden expressive figuration. At first, the stylized simplicity of the eulogy and John Wayne's broken voice expand, leading to the taps motif from a harmonica.[29] Subsequently, by means of the musical reminiscences interior to the film – it sounds like the waltz from the dance scene – the generic image of men at the saloon and the radio announcement become the experience of an irretrievably lost, happy present, which the characters share with the audience.[30]

After taking stock – two comrades are dead, the troops on Bataan have surrendered – a musical memory of the dance with the woman becomes an audiovisual figuration that appears as a whole as an image of mourning. The men stand in a row at the bar, a standard scene in the western; they no longer add up to the unity of a uniformed troop, to the military order that exceeds the individual. Instead, they are standing next to one another: isolated, roaming westerners, who randomly find themselves together, collectively trying to overcome a hard, dangerous path. The music articulates mourning as the memory of one's own ego, which one once was, before having to leave it behind to become a soldier. It combines the mourning with the figures at the bar. Their exhausted faces already belong to those sacrifices that are being spoken of on the radio: "Flesh must yield at last." The historical memory of the spectators of thousands upon thousands of abandoned and martyred soldiers, perishing in miserable circumstances – of the 70,000 captured Americans that had to surrender to the Japanese forces after General MacArthur's retreat, 16,000 did not survive the "death march of Bataan" – is staged as a present relationship of the spectators to the men at the bar. The spectators become part of the community of mourning that they see represented on screen.

At this point THEY WERE EXPENDABLE combines melodramatic expressive modalities with the character typologies of the western in order to incorporate the self-perception of contemporary spectators into an act of remembrance that concerns the history of the nation itself, of its birth, its endangerment, its renewal.

---

29 Scene "Begräbniszeremonie [*funeral ceremony*]" (01:47:39:15–01:51:04:27).
30 Scene "In der Kneipe [*in the bar*]" (01:51:04:27–01:54:34:20).

256 —— 4 Genre and History

Act IV: the memory image

The bond to the character typology of the western determines how the plot continues. It is the persistent gesture of defiant insistence on the part of an ego claiming to be invulnerable in its moral will. This is expressed succinctly in the scene in which the dissolution of the group around Rusty is described (see Figure 34). Peppered with words of resistance – "Make 'em pay!" – the separation of the

Figure 34: Dissolution of the squad.

group is carried out as a division in which the unity of highly divergent, but complementary forces are represented metaphorically on which the fighting power of the military is based. At first, the majority of the boat crew disappears as a completely improvised troop, the inner cohesion of which is now only supported by gestures and words that conjure up the unifying sense of community.[31] Following this, the bureaucratic commanding level of the army is addressed in the two boys on bicycles, who are supposed to report back to the higher ups. Finally, Rusty's unflinching individualism shows, as he does what he thinks has to be done, thus taking off on his own to look for Brick.

There is, however, a fourth force in the center of this metaphoric configuration: the figure of the old pioneer, who holds the bay in his possession like a settler who has been left at the border of civilization. Fallen completely from the time of the genre, his presence transforms the bay somewhere in the Pacific into a piece of western territory to be conquered. Now the old man refuses to cede to the enemy forces. The power of his insistence becomes the starting point to divide the group, who are diverging in various directions. The camera persists for a long time on the determined face, which, over the course of the shot, calls up images of brave settlers persevering and unflinching trappers, the founding figures of America. His gaze is focused into the distance – no reverse shot is necessary to show us that no American airline carriers or airplanes are to be expected there. Rather, it points to what is outside the world of the film, to the American of the pioneers, to their historical impact.

The following scenes[32] are defined by a specific construction of the image space with which the visual actions are subordinated to a fundamental dynamic. The scenes are linked by a continuous movement that takes place in the depth of the image (see Figure 35). Whether it is the departure of the last remaining boat, whether it is the parading of an army of grotesque and ragged figures, the detonation of a bridge in the background, or Rusty and Brick leaving the crew – what is common to all these scenes is the tension between an entirely unheroic consent to the movement that includes all the actions of the individuals in itself, and the fact that the movement consists in irrevocably separating those who had been left behind, who had been given up from those from whom another task was expected.

The affective force of this sequence of scenes is based in part on the stark contrasts to the film's first scenes. The boat, which glides over the waves so lightly

---

31 Scene "Reorganisation" (01:54:34:20–01:56:23:05).
32 Scene "Wiedersehen und Abschied vom Boot [*reunion and farewell to the boat*]" (01:56:23:05–02:00:12:19); Scene "Erschöpfung [exhaustion]" (02:00:12:19–02:02:08:19); Scene "Fußmarsch [*march*]" (02:02:08:19–02:05:56:06).

Figure 35: Movement into the depth of the image.

and elegantly, is now dragged through the jungle like a dead horse that had to be put down, and the decrepit, broken, hobbling figures can hardly still be associated with the elegantly dressed sailors in their white dress uniforms, who held parades, sang cheerful songs, and entertained the ladies at the ball.

Throughout the duration of THEY WERE EXPENDABLE, a gradual, almost unnoticeable change takes place in the way the military unit appears, a metamorphosis of the film world that causes a feeling to arise on the level of the expressive forms of the film image that is attached to the memory of the news reports and images from the events in Pearl Harbor or Bataan. The film allows what the names and images of this event call up in reflexes of past affects, in which the dramaturgical formation of the metamorphosis of the film world, its spaces, its characters, its rhythm, to become a feeling for the spectator. It thus creates an individual, understandable form for this historical low point in the war. The dramaturgical low point – the boat is lost, the crew dead or scattered to the four winds, the protagonists leave the miserable rest of the troop who were in fact entrusted to them as military officers – is not only represented as a parabolic reduction of the great historical event that is accessible to individual sensation. Rather, a film image is formed in it that becomes the medium of memory for the contemporary spectator of his or her own feelings in light of the news reports and images of the defeat.

The last scene of THEY WERE EXPENDABLE[33] once again brings the two affective poles that structure the film as a whole together into an arc of suspense; the painful separation of the civilian community and the integration into the military body. In doing so, it presents a paradoxical resolution to the opposition by which the opposition itself appears as something that can be affirmed by the individual from out of a feeling for political commonality. In the radical act of separation, in which those who remain behind must abandon all hope of returning home, a kind of comforting feeling emerges. The airplane that the two protagonists – like General MacArthur before – were supposed to fly out on, is about to take off, the last seats have already been assigned, Rusty and Brick turn up too late. With horrible decisiveness and the serenity of inevitability, two soldiers give up the seats they thought were certain, because Rusty and Brick occupy a higher rank in the list of expendables, that is, they are less expendable from the viewpoint of military bureaucracy. The scene's affect is based on the calmness with which the available seats in the last flight back home are assigned, those left behind consent to their fate and getting in one last letter to Sandy, the nurse, as if there was another plane right afterward. The scene shows the quiet triumph of utterly civilian manners over the ruthless, technocratic finality of the list that decides that numbers 31 and 32 have to leave the plane, that decides that Rusty is not allowed to give up his seat voluntarily. Those left behind leave the clearing and are swallowed up by the jungle.

The pathos of separation finds its apotheosis in the upward looking faces of the soldiers, who shortly before had bid farewell to their superiors; broken shapes on the beach watching the airplane as it ascends, flying past a lighthouse without light; the rows of faces begin and end with the face of the boy that had talked about his fear at the end of the first act. The music continually alternates from

---

33 Scene "We shall return!" (02:05:56:06–02:14:04:24).

motifs of deep mourning to announcing the triumphal return in the *Battle Hymn of the Republic*: "Mine eyes have seen the glory of the coming of the Lord [...] Glory, Glory, Hallelujah!"

The contradiction between military and political community is in no way resolved with the end of the war. It continues in a conflict that dominates Hollywood war films after the Second World War: the insistent question of the debt that the community of the living has toward the dead soldiers.

For the only answer to this question of what could justify the orders that cost countless of lives consists in there being a higher value than that of physical life. But it is just this answer that the films cannot give. That is, they can give it if and to the degree to which they refer to the military community. To the political community, however, whose highest value is the happiness of the individual, the sacrifice of the individual must remain an irresolvable conflict. Precisely the morally clear and victoriously settled "good war" causes the irreconcilable contradiction to appear in all its acrimony. By seeking to shape the participation of the experience of the suffering of those who were expendable in the dramaturgy of affect, war films insist on the physical present of remembering this suffering – a pain that binds the spectator to the victims of war.

In the singing that resounds at the beginning and the last shots of THEY WERE EXPENDABLE, in the faces of the women and the young soldiers, who are not much older than children, in the melancholy waltz and the ragged troops that look up at the airplanes, a pathos is staged in which the abstract principle of the triumphant nation collides brusquely with the feeling of individual suffering. In the faces of those that were expendable, who could be sacrificed, in order to achieve victory, THEY WERE EXPENDABLE allows the political community of the pursuit of happiness itself to appear as the sacrifice demanded by the war.

4.2 Cultural Memory and Confabulations of Memory

In THEY WERE EXPENDABLE the individual experience of the soldiers left behind is always already framed by the perspective of the remembering survivors. The film image itself becomes an affective bond that the film tries to draw between the public at home and the sacrifice in war, the fallen American soldier. The poetic concept of the film can be seen as an answer to a historical and social problem: How can war be understood and processed when there is plenty of film material of battle action, but this does not make it possible to experience per se what the event means for the many nameless victims? With THEY WERE EXPENDABLE John Ford forms the war film as a genre that becomes a medium of participating in an experience of suffering, which itself has no language.

The quote from General Douglas MacArthur that Ford places at the beginning of his film succinctly formulates the pathos that will define the Hollywood war film after 1945. These films position their spectators as individuals that participate in a community that is trying to form itself anew in the victim's experience of suffering. The ways they are staged are aimed at placing the spectators' aesthetic sensations and sense of self in a particular relationship to the innumerable visual and audio documents that allowed the cinema to become the space for experiencing the war in the years of the Second World War. They thus started a media practice of communal remembering that aims at renewing the feeling for the communal. In the affect-dramaturgical structure, the films aim at such a media practice, allowing for them to be historically positioned as an intervention into the psycho-social affect economy of forming a political community. They unlock the film material of war propaganda, war reporting, and mobilization films as a media form with which the experience of sensing past days is actualized and ramified in the affection of the contemporary spectator. They thus form the film images of combat reports and newsreels into affect-laden pathos scenes, which very quickly became perceived as stereotypical constellations of plot and characters in a new genre.

If we start from the affect-economic function outlined here, we must necessarily alter our understanding of the historicity of film images. For the films cannot simply be added into the stock of historical source material; rather, they call the concept of the document itself into question; indeed, they are no longer just texts – a file, a letter, a note – to study for what they reveal, but different types of affect generating and modeling media, which are subject to various affect-economic regimes. Their historicizing potential is conveyed through other experiential modalities, through other modes of poetic making than those of reading and writing, for example.[34] Emerging from propaganda and *gung-ho* movies, the war film only gets established by turning to the pathos-laden form of commemoration as a new genre of Hollywood cinema.

---

[34] I have already pointed out that I see a constriction here in Rorty's concept of description that it would do well to get beyond in visual and film theory. On the demarcation of a sign-system understanding of images in the context of visual theory, cf. Gottfried Boehm, "Die Wiederkehr der Bilder," and "Die Bilderfrage," in *Was ist ein Bild?*, Munich 1994, 11–38; Gottfried Boehm, "Iconic Turn: Ein Brief," in *Bilderfragen: die Bildwissenschaften im Aufbruch*, ed. Hans Belting, Munich 2007, 27–36; Gottfried Boehm, "Das Zeigen der Bilder," in *Zeigen: Die Rhetorik des Sichtbaren*, eds. Gottfried Boehm, et al., Munich 2010, 19–53.

Reconstruction of a much-discussed term

A paradigm of historical experience thus takes the foreground, which in turn takes on a prominent position in the discussion about the audiovisual images of war, namely the question of the cultural practices of commemoration and cultural memory.

"The camera, the cinema, and the television worked as apparatuses of perception as well as repositories of cultural memory at the same time."[35] The credo of media theory of numerous historical and cultural-historical studies of the media representation of war is formulated in such sentences. Indeed, the popularity of such a thesis once again stands in stark incongruity to its inconsequentiality. Media technology is in fact claimed as the basis for historical forms of perception of remembrance. But no methodological consequences are drawn from the media-theoretical hypothesis. When analytical work is carried out concretely, many cultural-historical studies move the tracks of well-worn historiographic methods, that is, they describe, analyze, and qualify primarily the contents represented.[36]

The reduction to the represented contents always already disguises the essential characteristic of the film document – the particular aesthetic structure in every media presentation that allows the viewer to establish a specific relation to what is represented in the first place.

What are the represented contents and motifs of audiovisual images at all if we understand the images themselves as historically variable media forms of perception? The blind spot seems to me to be located completely in the terms themselves. Talk about the scope of media technology often seems indifferent to the concrete cultural practice in which media are comprehensible in the first place as concrete forms of perception, that is, as concrete ways of using media technologies. In the common understanding of "cultural memory," a storage metaphor is used to translate an individual psychological concept of remembering into a cultural-theoretical term that often means nothing more than the diverse media practices of transmitting (storing) and reproducing bodies of knowledge. From my point of view, however, storing knowledge is not an appropriate metaphor for sufficiently describing either the media practices of cultural processes of transmission nor the psychic processes of remembering.

---

[35] Paul, *Bilder des Krieges – Krieg der Bilder*, 12.

[36] Rasmus Greiner, for instance, compares the films about the "new wars" to the historical event assumed to have preceded the film in order then to work out representative and reflexive references. Cf. Greiner, *Die neuen Kriege im Film*.

At any rate, the poetic logic of the war film cannot be analytically grasped by theoretically pointing to a wider media-technological *dispositif*; nor is it very useful to describe and historically position the media practice of remembering in genre cinema as storing and reproducing bodies of knowledge. Rather, it should be understood as a concrete poetic making that emphasizes the media forms of perceiving, feeling, and thinking that allow for a space of aesthetic experience to arise that, first and foremost, makes it possible to experience history. This means an experience that cannot be traced back either to the psychic capacity of human individuals for remembering nor to a 'knowledge' that is separable from the media conditions of its own manufacture, transmission, and reproduction.[37]

The relation of memory and political identity (Assmann)

I would therefore like first to reconstruct the term cultural memory in its fundamental provisions, which Jan Assmann developed in a study from 1992 on the cultural practices of memory in early Mediterranean civilizations. The study is characterized – unlike the later concept in cultural theory – by linking the basic reading of Halbwachs's theory of collective memory with a definition of the term that is precisely historically situated.

Since Assmann gets his understanding from comparing various religious and mythological justifications for the politics of memory, its relation to a theory of power comes clearly to the fore. Cultural memory speaks to social practices that belong much more to the area of how totalitarian forms of domination carry out their power and their institutional validation than to individual or collective memory. At any rate, in this study Assmann makes it clear that the term is aimed at media practices of forming community, which implement a strict hierarchical power arrangement in the relation between memory and political identity.[38] The starting forms of such culture of memory are cults of the dead.[39] The social

---

37 Cf Jacques Rancière, "L'historicité du cinéma," in *De l'histoire au cinéma*, eds. Antoine de Baecque and Christian Delage, Paris 1998, 45–60. Siegfried Kracauer, *History: The Last Things before the Last*, Princeton, 2013; Heide Schlüpmann, *Ein Detektiv des Kinos: Studien zu Siegfried Kracauers Filmtheorie*, Basel 1998; Hermann Kappelhoff, *The Politics and Poetics of Cinematic Realism*, New York 2015, 20ff. and 62ff.
38 Cf. Jan Assmann, *Cultural Memory and Early Civilization: Writing, Remembrance, and Political Imagination*, Cambridge 2011.
39 Cf. ibid., 44f.

group is constituted as a 'memory community,'[40] by creating a meaningful world of memory that reaches beyond the present. *"Memory culture is linked to the 'memory that forms a community.'"*[41] Cultural memory therefore concerns forms of community that seek to establish duration by locating themselves in the eternity of the dead. This distinguishes – according to Assmann – cultural memory from tradition. While tradition in itself represents a successful temporal continuum of passing things down,[42] cultural memory refers to a non-dissolvable break, to the unquestionable experience of contingency. While tradition seeks to create a time that is shared by the living and the dead, cults of memory, in their sites and rites, aim for a configuration of time and space that is defined by separating it from the ordinary time of the community.

Assmann adds a further point to this distinction: that between the sacred and the profane, the holy and the ordinary. By bringing things into the present through remembrance, cultural memory is carried out in the mode of official ceremony. The objects of cultural memory can be distinguished from those of ordinary memory by the media practices of ceremonially bringing things into the present, which 'take collective identity out of the daily routine'; they belong to practices of memory in which there is a "possibility of living in two times"[43] – that is, in the time of the dead, which is contrasted in ceremonial remembrance, repetition, and making present as the time of ceremony to an ordinary present of the living.

In light of the various religious and mythological motivations for holiday seasons, ceremonialities, and the agents that carry them out, the theoretical dimension of power as a technology of domination becomes clear. The 'ceremoniality of communication' of cultural acts of remembrance, we could also say: its self-reflexivity, is always already a 'forming (of remembering), that gives way to formings of memory.'[44] This is precisely where its political dimension as a power structure is defined. The ceremonial formations represent topographies that determine the agents, establish positions, and time-places from which significances are announced that can be spoken of in the community. While tradition is accessible to all those who can read, write, and speak, cultural memory – in the understanding sketched out here – always refers to masters and exclusive media, priests and cults, artists and cult objects; to specialists who administer the sites,

---

40 Cf. ibid., 26.
41 Cf. ibid., 16.
42 Cf. ibid., 21.
43 Ibid., 68.
44 Cf. ibid., 38.

objects, and practices with which the radically divided space-times of the dead and the living can be related to one another.

The ceremonial order of practices of remembering, recalling into the present, and repeating establishes the topography of communal life – the positions from them, the relations in them, and the relationships about them that can be spoken of – by projecting them into the parallel world of the realm of the dead. It creates community by establishing a strict hierarchical alignment of the exclusive places, agents, and practices from which the life of the community can be synchronized with the realm of the dead. The great continuities that are produced through cultural memory – mythology, archaic religions – describe forms of community in which ordinary life in the present is defined, regulated, and determined by priestly administrators of the pasts.

All in all, cultural memory concerns forms of domination that seek to perpetuate themselves by organizing their power to link the contingent time of the political community with the eternity of a community of the dead. Assmann speaks in this context of the 'dual time of human life.'[45] Exactly here a problem arises. Namely, if we define life in two times as "one of the universal functions of cultural memory or, to be more precise, of culture as memory,"[46] this applies an authoritarian principle of communitization that was reconstructed from determining the functions of early historical religions[47] for human culture in general. This cultural historical, or perhaps anthropological, generalization blurs the theoretical accuracy of the term.

The problems that arise from this emerge clearly in the categorial distinction between cultural and communicative memory. Assmann speaks of the 'diffuse participation by the group in communicative memory,' which he opposes to the 'always differentiated participation in cultural memory.'[48] Communicative memory means the remembrance of living agents, ultimately grounded in biographical memory, which is embedded in families and group membership. It "comprises memories related to the recent past. These are what the individual shares with his contemporaries. A typical instance would be generational memory that accrues within the group, originating and disappearing with time

---

45 Cf. ibid., 42.
46 Ibid., 68.
47 Cf. ibid, 67f. In this regard, Assmann cites Hubert Cancik and Hubert Mohr, "Erinnerung/Gedächtnis," in *Handbuch religionswissenschaftlicher Grundbegriffe 2*, eds. Hubert Cancik, et al., Stuttgart 1990, 299–323, here 311: "The general function of religion is to convey the non-simultaneous through memory, bringing to mind in the present, and repetition."
48 Cf. Assmann, *Cultural Memory*, 38.

or, to be more precise, with its carriers. Once those who have embodied it have died, it gives way to a new memory."[49]

Cultural memory, on the other hand, means the inventories of available senses, which are added quite generally to the cultural 'techniques of memorization,' that is, media. It restricts the contingence of the dead in a kind of organic accretion of time in which the media are defined by the function of representing the position of the previously alive. "That which continues to be living memory today, may be only transmitted via media tomorrow."[50]

In place of a definition of cultural memory grounded in a theory of power, a cultural-theoretical universalism appears, which gets its definition from the opposition between the living memory of social interaction and the reconstruction of the past that is tied to media technologies and practices – 'foundational memory':[51]

> The foundational mode always functions – even in illiterate societies – through fixed objectifications both linguistic and nonlinguistic, such as rituals, dances, myths, patterns, dress, jewelry, tattoos, paintings, landscapes, and so on, all of which are kinds of sign systems [sic!] and, because of their mnemotechnical function – supporting memory and identity – capable of being subsumed under the general heading of *memoria*. The biographical mode, on the other hand, always depends on social interaction, even in literate societies.[52]

The dichotomy between living memory and the dead media practice of forming cultural memory obscures the question of the political of all memorial culture, which was indeed clearly addressed with the thesis of the "relation between memory and political identity." This means, on the one hand, the "technology of power"[53] that determines the living remembrance of the communicative memory no less than it does the media techniques that define memory. On the other hand, it means the possibility that political communities themselves can be proposed as contingent beginnings; Rorty calls this 'liberal utopia,' Arendt uses the term 'revolution.'

Communities of remembrance, as Assmann has reconstructed, negate the ordinary experience of living individuals in the communities' pursuit of continuity and duration. In the everyday cohabitation of these individuals, time is manifest as an irrefutable experience of the contingency of their physical existence.

---

49 Ibid., 36.
50 Ibid.
51 The "main difference to communicative memory is in its shapedeness and in the ceremonial quality of its sources." Cf. Jan Assmann, *Das kulturelle Gedächtnis. Schrift, Erinnerung und politische Identität in frühen Hochkulturen*, Munich 1992, 58 (this sentence is not included in the English translation).
52 Ibid., 37.
53 Michel Foucault, *Society Must Be Defended*, 242.

From the perspective of the liberal utopia, the history of political communities cannot be located outside this experience. In its pursuit of the transcendental foundations of its continuity and duration, the community of remembrance is diametrically opposed to the political community in Rorty's sense.[54]

In discussion within cultural theory, the term "cultural memory" quickly fulfilled the goal of dislodging "the relation between memory and political identity" from the field of historical-political debates and positioning it in the eternal peace of epistemological topographies. But the media practices of cultural memory can neither be brought together into a universal idea of memory – after all, it is always about historically and culturally distinct politics of memory – nor can a claim be made to a form of memory that is achieved as the pure social interaction of biographical remembrances.

In each act of remembrance the spatial and temporal order of a community gets thematized, the rhythm of communal life (the calendar of festivals that may be 'secular or ecclesiastical, agricultural or military'[55]) and the space of its sensibility.[56] All memory refers to spaces in which communities take on a spatial form: "Group and place take on a symbolic sense of community that the group also adheres to, when it is separated from its own space ..."[57] Ultimately, this means nothing more than that every community is defined by the spatio-temporal order of its sensibility, by a specific "sensory fabric."[58]

The politics of cultural practices of remembrance is thus always already carried out within a communally shared world, which is fixed in its spatio-temporal order of sensibility by exactly such media practices that Assmann has reconstructed as the cultural memory of early civilizations. But the distinction to be made is not between living interaction and media techniques of memoria, but between the various political strategies of constructing the past. These are all to be construed as media practices of poetic making, which refer to the spatio-temporal order of a communally shared world. These practices move within a range between technologies of domination that define, establish, stabilize, and reproduce the life of a community, and those outside interventions that aim to establish political beginnings (Arendt) in new descriptions. Using a terminological dichotomy of Rancière, the polarity can on the one side be called the 'aesthetics of politics,' and on the other the 'politics of aesthetics.'

---

54 Cf. Assmann, *Cultural Memory*, 25ff.
55 Cf. ibid., 24.
56 "Memory needs spaces and tends toward spatialization." Ibid., 25.
57 Ibid.
58 Cf. Rancière, *The Emancipated Spectator*, 56.

Collective memory and individual recollection

The idea of collective memory as developed by Halbwachs also ultimately means nothing more than the circumstance that people are always already connected to communicating communities when they refer themselves to various pasts and remember them. We communicate and act, learn and are taught – and this forms "social frameworks" according to a fundamental hypothesis of Halbwachs, the enclosure and the structure of each individual memory: "A person who has grown up in complete isolation [...] would have no memory."[59] The communication of a community (group, collective) creates the framework in which individual memory, that is, memory fixed to a physical body, is completed. Only here we may not understand "communication" as an exchange between self-conscious subjects, transparent in their intentions. It is precisely the non-transparency of the collective memory for individuals and their remembrances that had concerned Halbwachs.

In summary, he describes the interrelation between the order of a communal world and remembrance as follows:

In short: social beliefs, whatever their origin, have a double character. They are collective traditions or recollections, but they are also ideas or conventions that result from a knowledge of the present. Were it purely conventional (in this sense), social thought would be purely logical. It would allow only that which is serviceable under its present conditions. It would succeed in extinguishing, in all members of the group, all the recollections that hold them back, be it even slightly, and which would permit them to be both part of the society of yesterday and part of the society of today. Were society purely traditional, it would not allow itself to be permeated by any idea – or even by any fact – that was in disagreement, however slight, with its oldest beliefs .... But social thought is not abstract. Even when they correspond to and express the present, the ideas of society are always embodied in persons or groups. Behind a title, a virtue, or a quality, society immediately perceives those who possess them. Those groups and persons exist in the passage of time and leave their traces in the memory of people .... But, on the other hand, society would labor in vain if it attempted to recapture in a purely concrete form a particular figure or event that has left a strong imprint in its memory. As soon as each person and each historical fact has permeated this memory, it is transposed into a teaching, a notion, or a symbol and takes on meaning. It becomes an element of the society's system of ideas."[60]

---

59 Cf. Assmann, *Cultural Memory*, 22.
60 Maurice Halbwachs, *On Collective Memory*, Chicago 1992, 188.

The relation between forms of cultural memory and living remembrance should thus be conceived the other way around from what the theory of cultural memory suggests. Living remembrance – the temporalities of biography, family tradition, friendships – can itself only ever be generated and actualized as relations of a history of the community. These relations are what open up a view of cultural technologies and media practices in the first place, with which individual sensations of time are generated as communally shared worlds of memory. The "ways in which the past is given communicative and cultural presence"[61] are inextricably interrelated. Ultimately, there can be neither individual remembrance nor a communicative memory[62] that is not already embedded in the history of multiple media practices of the poetic making of spatio-temporal arrangements, which allow us to experience the commonly shared world in its historicity in the first place.[63]

Confabulations of memory

This is why I would like to understand the Hollywood war film, following Cavell, as a medium of the poetic making of memory, as "confabulations of memory."[64] But borrowing this term from Sigmund Freud is not in any way meant to put an alternative metaphor in circulation with which individual psychological concepts are transferred to cultural-historical facts. Rather, we can expect that Freud also assumed that individual memories always already include operations of fantasy that in no way have the function of storing and reproducing knowledge about the past. In "Family Romances" the activity of remembering itself can be grasped as a poetic making that can teach us about the subjectivizing function of poetically coming to terms with the past. As an act of subjectivizing, every individual act of remembering is always already entangled in narratives and metaphors, photos, videos, and films, which reach well beyond the stocks of family traditions and predate the remembering ego as an "a priori object."[65] By using the term 'confabulations of memory' I would like to name a generic principle that serves as

---

61 Assmann, *Cultural Memory*, 33.
62 Cf. ibid.
63 I am thinking here of Bakhtin's chronotope, on Jameson's relief of a history of the polity. Cf. Mikhail M. Bakhtin, "Forms of Time and the Chronotope of the Novel," in his: *The Dialogic Imagination: Four Essays*, Austin 1981; Jameson, *Magical Narratives*.
64 Sigmund Freud, "My Views on the Role of Sexuality in the Etiology of the Neuroses," in his: *Selected Papers on Hysteria and Other Psychoneuroses*, New York 1912, 186–193, here 189.
65 Walter Benjamin, *The Origin of German Tragic Drama*, London 1977, 139.

the basis for the widest possible variety of genres of poetic making that aim for the relationship between community and history. This poetic making does not serve to bring historical events into the present through representation, but to create a realm of experience in which a polity refers to itself as an experimental historical configuration.[66] The history of such self-conceptions can neither be reconstructed as the history of agents (the history of politicians, the military, and businessmen), nor as one of the institutions and social systems that operates independently of the history of the forms of sensibility, nor can it be taken to be a cultural memory that might be understood as a media archive of established tradition.

From this perspective, individual memory is always already part of poetic making, which concerns the commonly shared history as a whole. It is less and at the same time more than poetic making; individual memory is always inserted into the history of poetic making, but this history itself only exists in the present actuality of concrete acts of subjectivization – for instance, in the act of watching films. The films of a generic cycle resemble the individuals that narrate their life stories. Their image spaces are always inserted into the historical structure of other poetic conceptions, but this structure is only realized in the actualization of individual films; it should be understood as an affective structure. The films establish an affective relationship to the history of the community in their confabulation of memory. They produce particular perspectives on history in which they take on no less a task than to set up their particular standpoints as positions from which the past presents of a social polity can be related to a possible future of the political community. They produce historical time in the structure of their multiple relations to other poetic concepts.

Celebration and ritual

Seen from this standpoint, the polarity of the ceremonial and the everyday that Assmann offers for cultural memory is also highly suggestive for our topic – as long as we do not understand the ceremonial bringing into the present as the opposite to 'living memory.' In ceremonial time, what is always already in effect behind the social interactions of remembering individuals as a media formation of a commonly shared sense world explicitly enters consciousness. Ceremonial time, as one could interpret Assmann, distinguishes the space/

---

66 Cf. Rorty, *Achieving Our Country*, 22.

time order of the communal sense world as an 'object world'[67] from out of people. It allows the order on which the ordinary sensation of space and time is always already supported to come out into the open as a historical relation. Seen in this way, celebrations and rituals are media practices in which the remembrance of individuals is synchronized with the temporality of the community, the contingencies of social and familial relationships, the time of love, of desire, or aging are interconnected with the rhythms of the history of the community.

In this sense, genre cinema in general, and the war film in particular, can in fact be seen as a ritual practice[68] aimed at asserting the rhythm of the time of the community into the biographical rhythms of the individual – and vice versa. The dramaturgical construction of the films, the arrangement of the pathos scenes of the pain of separation and initiation, fear and fantasies of omnipotence, longing and mourning, can be described as the spectator's passage through a process of affectation that has a completely ceremonial character. In their affect-rhetorical calculation, the films resemble choreographies of ritual procedures; their materials are those sensations that bind their spectators with the images, iconographies, motifs, and events that were formed into affect-laden memory in the cinema of the war years. This is the case for the many small films that are dedicated to the fate of a platoon and for which the war only existed to the degree that it showed itself to the limited perceptual horizon of the fighting community; but it is also the case for the large-scale productions that work on wide-ranging historical panoramas of memory such as THE LONGEST DAY (1962, Ken Annakin, Andrew Marton, Bernhard Wicki, Darryl F. Zanuck). In the affect-dramaturgical arrangement of the pathos scenes, the spectator's sensations are involved in the conflict between the opposing claims of the military and the political community.

This can be succinctly traced in a film made four years after THEY WERE EXPENDABLE and in which a new type of soldier emerges: SANDS OF IWO JIMA (Allan Dwan) from 1949. The circumstance that the new character is developed as the antagonist to exactly that type of officer that, like in THEY WERE EXPENDABLE, is also embodied here by John Wayne, is surely more – if we take Cavell's reflections on the type in cinema as a fundamental generative form into account – than just an anecdotal detail.

---

67 Cf. Assmann, *Das kulturelle Gedächtnis*, 59 (not included in the English translation).
68 Cf. Thomas Schatz, *Old Hollywood, New Hollywood: Ritual, Art and Industry*, Ann Arbor 1983; Will Wright, *Sixguns and Society: A Structural Study of the Western*, Berkeley 1975; Altman, *Film/Genre*, 26ff.

4.3 Interlocking Affects: SANDS OF IWO JIMA

After the end of the war, the contemporary cinema audience – I have already mentioned this several times[69] – was confronted again in fiction films by numerous film images that they were already familiar with from war documentaries and combat reports. One of these films is Allan Dwan's SANDS OF IWO JIMA.[70] Among other things, Dwan uses material that we have already come across in WITH THE MARINES AT TARAWA. But while the combat footage here allows us to sense the discrepancy between the powers of human bodies and the destructive force of weapons, the corresponding footage in SANDS OF IWO JIMA is framed by static scenes of dialogue and group portraits of stoic faces. The film documents are incorporated into a chamber play made up of studio scenes, which consists, in its core, of military briefings and dramatic dialogues between soldiers and their commanding officers during a heightened conflict.

In terms of affect dramaturgy, the basic model of the war film genre is called up, a model that had long been established by 1949; quite as if the drama between emphatic lust for battle and paralyzing fear, between the triumphant 'we' feeling of the troop and the frailty of the individual soldier, who gives up his will and then finally his life, had already been presented so often that it was enough simply to run through the conflict using visual stereotypes. At first glance, the function of the production seems to be to present the film documents of a horror that overcomes all the sense in narrative indifference. Even the acting has a schematic effect, as if it were in fact merely about replaying widely known scenes to call them back to memory.

But things are different when envisioning the historical site which SANDS OF IWO JIMA marks in the history of Hollywood cinema. On closer inspection, it becomes obvious that this film is much more about memories associated with the combat footage than with reproducing a well-worn affect dramaturgical schema of the lust for battle, physical suffering, and the figure of the sacrifice. Even the first film about the conquest of Iwo Jima seems to take the historical event as an occasion to refer – much like Clint Eastwood would do decades later in FLAGS OF OUR FATHERS – to the afterlife of film and photographic documents of the war; although the essential reference point here is the spectators' concrete remembrance of the fear and adversity of those days of war, when they were getting scenes like those from Tarawa at the cinema every day.

---

[69] Cf. the third part of this study.
[70] For instance in the scene "Opfer nach der Schlacht [*victims after the battle*]" (00:56:49:07–00:59:49:24).

Contrary to the film title, which calls up the famous photograph and the American triumph in the Pacific, SANDS OF IWO JIMA, with its reference to wartime cinema, introduces a fundamental change in the structure of the genre. A somber revision of the ideal of the military community can be seen in it. In the apotheosis at the end of the film, it is staged as the disillusionment of the pathos of the sacrifice. The scene, which became an icon of the triumph of the American fighting forces in the Pacific as a press photo, the moment at which the soldiers hoisted the American flag on Japanese soil, is confronted with the death of one of the protagonists and the bitter resignation of the others. He gives up his resistance to the law of military order and throws himself into the fate of the soldiers for whom the war has no end.

The disillusionment of the feeling for military community

At the beginning of SANDS OF IWO JIMA, like in numerous other war films, there is the drill and the training camp, the initiation into the military community. Here the film falls back on documentary footage that we have already seen in GUNG HO! Only the tone has changed significantly. Instead of an officer, who, like a good father, promises the young men identity, direction, and meaningful action, a hard drill instructor appears, who trains the recruits for the emergencies of war; in place of emphasizing a harmoniously intermixed group body, we see the grumbling submission to the will of the commanding machinery (see Figure 36).

The patriarchal form of the military corps now appears as a state of exception and a glaring breach of the soldiers' rights to their individual pursuit of happiness. It is represented as a purely male-paternal form of communitization, based on humiliating submission and sexual resignation. Instead of the good officer, who knows how to gently and lovingly lead his troop – even if to death – father figures appear whose humiliating and abasing actions can only be forgiven at the end, if at all. They are fathers that remain powerful even beyond death; indeed, they justify the power of the military community as fallen heroes, as if the military corps were in fact the body of a transcendental ego that has its soul in the dead fathers. It is part of the laconic way that SANDS OF IWO JIMA is staged that the central conflict is succinctly dealt with in a dialogue between the youthful protagonist, Private Conway (John Agar), and his antagonist, the drill instructor Sergeant Stryker (John Wayne):[71]

---

[71] Scene "Jeep-Szene [*jeep scene*]" (00:24:59:07–00:26:40:23).

Figure 36: SANDS OF IWO JIMA.

Stryker: I hear you've got a girl in town.

Conway: What if I have?

Stryker: They say she is a very nice girl.

Conway: They talk too much.

Stryker: You serious about her? ... You know, with things the way they are, this is no time to start getting serious with a girl. Don't know how long you're gonna be here. Don't know when you'll be back again. Don't even know how long you're gonna be alive.

Conway: Listen Stryker: if it's in the line of duty, you can tell me to do something and I'll do it. But as far as my personal life goes, keep your hands off.

Stryker: It's the same thing your father would have told ya.

Conway: And I wouldn't listen to him, either.

Stryker: That's right, you never did.

Conway: How do you know?

Stryker: He told me.

Conway: What did he say? ... Never mind, I'll tell you what he said: he said, I was a disappointment, right? He said, I didn't have what it takes, right? He said, I wouldn't be able to stand up for myself, right?

Stryker: You're doing the talking.

Conway: No Stryker, my father is doing the talking. Every time you're opening your mouth, my father is doing the talking. Every thought you think is my father's thought. It's as though he were standing at my shoulder all the time. But he didn't always say the right thing. And he didn't always think the right thing. You're gonna find that out. When the time comes, you're gonna find that out. But until then leave me alone!

What gets explicitly articulated in this conversation describes exactly the conflict that would mark the war film over the next 20 years. On the one hand, the military is represented as an authoritarian principle of communitization, in which the commanding characters can replace one another at every level because they are placed in the position of an absent, dead ancestor (the drill instructor holds this position), while, on the other hand, the recruits' wishes for their lives can no longer be transformed into euphoric participation in the military community (the rebellious hero sees himself as forced by his superiors to succeed his father). The occasion for the conversation between the protagonist and his superior was created by a problem that thwarts the patriarchal genealogy. The film has developed it clearly in the previous sequences. The youthful hero has fallen in love. The violence that the recruits encounter at first, the compulsion to submission under the law of forming military community, is opposed to the state of being in love in all its appearances, is even its extreme opposite.

The images of life's sentimental wishes are contrasted to the order of the army, the ideal of a paternal community, as a competing principle of collectivization. The competition is clearly shown in the recurring replacement of fallen soldiers by newly arrived recruits. The topos is as notorious in the Hollywood war film as is the unspectacular, because regulated, transfer of command to the next highest-ranking officer when a troop leader has died. In SANDS OF IWO JIMA, a socializing principle can be seen in these scenes that is based on a kind of asexual, parasitic reproduction – at the expense of the lives of ordinary individuals.

What is described as a conflict in the few sentences of the conversation between the superior and the subordinate would now be found in ever new variations in numerous films of this genre. The forced separation of the genders and sexual abstinence are now no longer dealt with as an effect of war, but as a foundation of the military body. Starting with FROM HERE TO ETERNITY and going on to THE THIN RED LINE and FULL METAL JACKET, this involves the violence that marks military communitization from now on.

At the end of SANDS OF IWO JIMA, Sergeant Stryker, so feared for his severity, gets killed. After the war has been won, he has become as useless as a civilian as he had managed to be a functional warrior. Now he passes the baton to his antagonist: the young man, Private Conway, sensitive, civil, and full of a sense of responsibility for wife and child. We might recognize in him the figure of a new father: different from his father, different from his superiors. Indeed, the apotheosis provides the drama with a disillusioning end. The death of his antagonist, who he so detested, clearly shows Private Conway the fatality of military life: one last look at the victorious flag, the soldiers disappear into the fog-like phantoms – "until the next war." The young hero, the good officer, will hardly be able to found a new civilian order. He is – just like the old warhorse – no longer socially presentable because of having become the perfect soldier.

Obviously, at the end Private Conway has become what at the beginning he absolutely did not want to be: a warrior who, like his father, has been barred from returning to civilian life (see Figure 37). His bitter words, with which he disappears into the fog, already announce the dramas of homecoming; the stories about irate ex-soldiers going berserk after not being able to find peace in the civilian world.

This final scene designates a decisive break in the history of the Hollywood war film. The hated superior is indeed rehabilitated – he was a good soldier, his severity was necessary and just for survival under the special circumstances of war – but the insight into the necessity of his fate also contains the disillusionment.

"They did the impossible," we hear at the end of MERRILL'S MARAUDERS (1961), Sam Fuller's film about the war in the Pacific. This is more than a figure of speech. The victory is a miracle, due to the deaths of countless soldiers. But the miracle of war is rooted in a permanent betrayal. The various superiors continually push the men entrusted to them further and further by misleading them time and again about how hopeless the situation is. The order to the suicide mission is clothed in a lie that comes from paternal love. The logic of a loving betrayal dominates – this is the theme of the film – every step in the hierarchy of command.

The intermediary officer, who loves his boys, tries in vain to protect them, and finally sends them to their deaths, becomes a central figure of many war films. This ambiguity henceforth defines the Hollywood war film. The films after 1949 thematize the debt to the soldiers, whether they have fallen or have become physically of psychologically destroyed – or all at once, like the figure of Joe Costa (Jack Palance) in Robert Aldrich's ATTACK! (1956). They all deal with the guilt of those who survive the orders, who themselves gave the orders, who were able to take that last plane, and who literally ground their survival in the exhaustion,

Figure 37: Death of the father and birth of the warrior.

pain, and death of others. The film material added to SANDS OF IWO JIMA can ultimately be related to just this ambiguity.

The ramifying of affects

For the spectator at the time, seeing the documentary material again would have reactivated just that feeling that was associated with experiencing the film images in the experiential space of the cinema during the war years. Even if the feelings cannot be qualified any more exactly, we can assume that the contemporary audience watching SANDS OF IWO JIMA once again had some relation to the weight of the affect with which the documentary footage of Tarawa had taken hold of their bodies – at a time when the war was not yet decided and the news about fallen fathers, brothers, friends, and relatives was an everyday occurrence. In the memory, the affective violence may have condensed into a spectator feeling that encompassed the reminiscence of all the horrors of war time: fearful expectation, anxiety, animosity, patriotism – but also the helplessness in relation to a state that has ceased to protect freedom and the life of the individual, instead asserting its claims over both. As if the film were creating in the spectatorial feeling – in its power to affect the spectator's body – an affective bond between two separate perceptual spaces: the physical present of currently watching films and the time in which the same spectators encountered the same images in another world; as if it were addressing a perceiving, feeling body that belonged to two different space/times, two different spaces of experience: that is, the cinema of the war years and that of the post-war period. To put it another way, the film allows an image space to emerge for its spectator that in itself (think of the analysis of WITH THE MARINES AT TARAWA) is structured by a temporally split perception in which affect becomes ramified (see Figure 38).

In the affect dramaturgy of SANDS OF IWO JIMA, the spectator's feeling, that is, the spatio-temporal ramifying of affect between film images and spectator bodies from different times, is directly interwoven into the process of disillusionment, which the film stages as its drama and which allows for an ambivalence in the pathos of the sacrifice. The remembered perceptual sensations of film images, which was where the war was at home in the everyday lives of moviegoers, is related to the gesture of resignation in which SANDS OF IWO JIMA finds its apotheosis. It actualizes the fundamental contradiction that we are already familiar with from Capra's propaganda film: the conflict between a civilian society, which imagines itself as a liberal, democratic political society and the military logic of self-protective collectivization. In doing so, it will fundamentally alter the pathos of the war film. This transformation, however, can in no way be inscribed as a stage in the developmental process of the genre; rather, it concerns the historicity of poetic making itself, the form in which the films create the conditions that allow the spectator to make themselves an image of their history.

In the repeated loops of recurring combat footage, as well as in the reenactments of familiar visual or iconographic topoi, the films from the first years after the Second World War relate their spectators to the experiential space of the wartime cinema; to a memory, therefore, which was completely defined by highly ambivalent affections. They involve the spectators in the affect-dramaturgical

Figure 38: Documentary material in SANDS OF IWO JIMA.

structures by means of their own remembered feelings; they turn the spectator's memory of wartime cinema – and the affections of this cinema – itself into the material of the staging. This is precisely why the war films in Hollywood cinema emphasize the historical reference, even when there can be no doubt that the actions represented are pure fiction. The audiovisual reminiscences appeal, in the same way as do the corresponding names that were often used as the titles of films – Iwo Jima, Bataan, Guadalcanal – to a perceiving body in which the memory of the images, events, and places of war is inscribed as affect. They have become the spectators' physical reality, a bodily memory that cannot store historical knowledge without altering its consistency under the weight of affect – mnemonics that Nietzsche had in mind when he saw the very possibility of remembering as linked to pain: "Only what does not cease *to give pain* remains in one's memory."[72]

---

[72] Friedrich Nietzsche, *On the Genealogy of Morality: A Polemic*, trans. Maudmarie Clark and Alan J. Swensen, Indianapolis 1998, 37.

In this respect, the poetic concept of SANDS OF IWO JIMA is completely representative for the strategies that Hollywood developed in the first years after the end of the war. The memory of the war years is restaged as an updating of an affect that is steadfastly ramified between the bodies of film images and the bodies of spectators – an affect that does not cease to give pain.

Making history

The Hollywood war films from the first years after the Second World War provide an impressive example of how such ramifications of affect between individual feeling, aesthetic affections, and official perceptual politics allow for the individual life histories and the history of the polity to become intertwined and to emanate from one another.

It is perfectly possible to speak unmetaphorically of an afterlife of film images that continually branch out ever further in film images of images of the representation of war in media.[73] But we still must bear in mind that the images and audiovisual documents of historical events do not in any way follow us and haunt us on their own impulses, like the ghostly presence of a past trauma. As I have tried to work through in the film analyses here, the powers of affection in film images can neither be traced back to the event represented nor to a power of the images themselves. The affective intertwining of the spectator in the world represented cannot be detached from the unfolding of the structures of representation staged in the media. Referring to the real persons, places, events, and documents of war does not verify or "authenticate" the representation of genre films. It is quite the opposite: the genre itself becomes the medium of an affect event that branches out dynamically in the film images, with which the film material becomes the a priori object of a feeling for the history of the community. Only in the restaging of the genre does it become a historical document in this sense. Historicity is itself

---

[73] In view of this afterlife, much has also been said about "haunting" and trauma, and with good reason. Cf. Burgoyne and the concept of trauma in Elsaesser: Robert Burgoyne, "Haunting in the War Film: Flags of Our Fathers," in *Eastwood's Iwo Jima: Critical Engagement With Flags of Our Fathers and Letters From Iwo Jima*, eds. Anne Gjelsvik and Rikke Schubart, New York 2013, 157–172; Elsaesser, *Terror und Trauma*; Lorenz Engell, "Teil und Spur der Bewegung: Neue Überlegungen zu Iconizität, Indexikalität und Temporalität des Films," in *Der schöne Schein des Wirklichen: Zur Authentizität im Film*, ed. Daniel Sponsel, Konstanz 2007, 15–40.

still an effect, produced by the media structures and staging strategies in which films relate to 'a past event as history.'[74]

In historical film material, the events of the past are not present for us by themselves; but a possibility is retained for us to allow the sense world of a different audience to become present in our own aesthetic sensations in the act of viewing films. Viewed for themselves, the films are nothing more than audiovisual material, as long as they, as media, are not placed into the function that binds us with the audience of a past time, which we take to be part of the history of our own sensibility.

Seen in this way, it is not the film that should be situated historically first and foremost when trying to understand their historical significance and function. Rather, in the films the contemporary audience is historically situated in their sensibility for us. The films allow us to produce history in the perceptual world of another audience as the historicity of our sense world and on our own physicality. In this sense, the films open up for us the opportunity to experience ourselves in our feeling and perceiving – in the specific relation to a past audience in each case – as a historical entity. In the present of their restaging, they allow the sense world of a past audience to become physically present for us today, as a world that appears to be our own, but from which we are radically excluded. The temporal split in film perception here has become the immediate experience of a difference by which historicity itself enters consciousness.[75]

It is not the film images that haunt us as ghostly delegates of guilt and horror, but *we*, the spectators today, that haunt the present of another, past audience, as if we were spectral creatures from an unfamiliar time.

We are like the dead that are no longer concerned about the living, because they are unaware of our presence. The possibility of history consists in understanding the sensations of that audience as the earlier life of our communal world.

---

[74] With regard to historical films, Michael Lück has described historicity itself as an aesthetic effect. Film stagings can on the one hand be described as "modelling the embroilment [of the individual] in history." Here they are related to the modern sense of self, that one's own – biographical – time is interwoven with the time of the community, for example, to which one belongs. On the other hand, they can be described as "modeling the behavior of history." Here they are related to the moral weight of history, to the idea of history as an extrapersonal counterpart that is encapsulated in the topos of the "responsibility to history" – a specific reinterpretation of the classical topos of historia magistra vitae. (Unpublished manuscript.)

[75] In *History: The Last Things Before the Last*, Kracauer almost retrospectively defines this historicity of a self-devouring making of the perceptual forms of perception as the agent of his work on film in media theory. Cf. Kappelhoff, *The Politics and Poetics of Cinematic Realism*, 62ff.

Films are media that allow the spectators present to let the world of a past audience emerge from film images in film images as the physical presence of their senses. To the degree, however, that we recognize and experience ourselves in the one as well as the other as a spectator feeling temporally split in two, we produce something like history.

In the repeating film images (whether direct or indirect), films stage an act of temporally split perception in which history begins to form in the physical states of individual spectators as experiencing different sense worlds. The ramifying of affect between image bodies and spectator bodies in the aesthetic spaces of different presents ultimately defines the dynamic, the driving force for permanent change as the generic principle that is at the basis of the war film genre in the first place.

Between Capra's mobilization films and SANDS OF IWO JIMA the transformation of the pathos of the military community is achieved in the dynamically proceeding ramifying of an affect that I have tried to work through as the constitutive conflict of war films, which leads from the necessary death of the sacrifice to one that is meaningful and finally to the senseless death of the individual – from generating meaning to guilt.[76]

In the first part of this book I qualified the films hypothetically as responses to the disturbance of the feeling for the communal, the sense of commonality. We shall stick to this thesis. Then genre cinema per se is to be conceived as such a ramifying of affects, the generic principle of which should be localized in the political field of conflict itself. But "conflict" here does not mean clashes of interest existing within a given social, political, and cultural order and issues to be resolved. Rather, it concerns the founding shape of a political community in the sense of an order of sensoriality, a principle antagonism aimed at the feeling for the communal world itself.[77]

These are the fundamental aspects of a poetology of genre cinema: Certain genres (if not all) should in fact principally be understood as such dynamic ramifications of affects, in which a generic conflict gets constantly updated that concerns the fundamental structure of the political polity, the feeling for the communal. Affect itself is then addressed as the transcending power that works

---

[76] On feelings of guilt, cf. Matthias Grotkopp, *Filmische Poetiken der Schuld: Die audiovisuelle Anklage der Sinne als Modalität des Gemeinschaftsempfindens*, Berlin/Boston 2017.
[77] Cf. Jacques Rancière, *Disagreement: Politics and Philosophy*, Minneapolis 1999; Jacques Rancière, "The Distribution of the Sensible" in his: *The Politics of Aesthetics*, London 2004, 7–46; Cf. also Kappelhoff, *Cinematic Realism*, 20ff.

toward changing the community within its given orders of sensoriality.⁷⁸ As the capacity of bodies to affect other bodies and to be affected by them, the dynamic of this change works within the symbolic systems, discursive orders, and institutional formations of a community. That is, affect thwarts the stability of the system with every repeating ramification into symbolic forms, images, and signs, and introduces the possibility of differences and deviations into the ordering structure of a community. The affective ramifications are always more than the feelings of individualized bodies and yet they cannot be conceived without them. They are the forces in which the relation between the 'I,' the 'we,' and 'the others' are configured, the subjectivity effect that the shared forms of thinking and feeling in a community themselves are due to. (This is why Massumi calls affect a remnant, what still remains despite all ramifications.)⁷⁹ From this perspective, genre cinema itself can be presented as a network of affect transmissions and allocations organized by media, in which the spectators' bodies themselves are engaged as transmission media. Films are media that relate the technological and organic bodies of different planes of time and separate spaces to one another, figuring them as affective collectivity.

The ramifying of affects thus also does not represent any accidental aspect that could be added into the theory of existing genre poetics; rather, it designates the fundamental generic principle of poetic making, the permanent modulation of the feeling for the communal. Genres are then in no way to be understood as fixed systems of representation, but are a dynamic structure that in principle is expanded, transformed, dissolved, and newly configured with every update, every affective ramification. From this perspective, pathos designates nothing other than the way in which film stagings organize and attempt to further ramify the affective braces between spectators' bodies and the screen image, while pathos formulas mean audiovisual complexes of images in which the tension of the conflict is iconically condensed and fixed. In relation to the history of the Hollywood war film, a poetic making can be worked out that even produces history itself as the basis of a commonly shared world. This does not at all mean the taxonomic classification of films according to characteristic features, stereotypes, and recurring narratives; rather, films are always already to be analyzed as a ramification of affect. Films are affections in which a generic field of conflict is ramified as spectator feeling by being put into relation to other filmic and non-filmic forms of poetic making that belong to the same generic conflict field. The genre relations

---

78 This is the sense in which Deleuze speaks of affect as the new.
79 Cf. Brian Massumi, "Navigating Movements," in *Hope: New Philosophies for Change*, ed. Mary Zournazi, New York 2003, 215.

designate the graduated degrees of relationship in the field of an ultimately indivisible coherence of the history of a community's poetic making.

Genre theory as a poetology of producing history

In fact, in the western tradition, the formulation of genre poetics has always been bound to attempts to open up a way to access history in poetic making itself. Indeed, in the Aristotelian derivation of tragedy, we can understand from the history of poetic making the matrix of a way of thinking history as the history of poetic making. If we, like Rorty, understand poetic making as a permanent reinscription of the limits of community, "which connect the present with the past, on the one hand, and with utopian futures, on the other,"[80] then this implies such an understanding of the production of history itself.

From this perspective, Rorty's idea of description is to be located on the same plane as the term 'mimesis' in Aristotelian poetics. In Aristotle, mimesis is set aside from the philosophical thinking of ideas as an autonomous mode of thinking. It designates a thinking that follows the immanence of human making in its logic and does not try to get outside this immanence.[81] In Rorty, the immanence of making is understood to be a general poeticization of culture, which is opposed to any claim to truth based on transcendence. The immanent logic of poetic making is positioned against a higher truth. It decidedly repudiates the claim that thinking could abandon the immanence of poetic description and redescription of the common world. Of course, these descriptions, as representations, cannot be divorced from media and artistic technologies, from the *téchne* of poetic making. This sets up the task of taking up Rorty's term of description in relation to what had been put forth in the poetics of Aristotle as a historical dynamic of divisions and ramifications of the modes of mimesis in the plurality of the arts, media, and modes of experience as a history of poetic thinking.

Within western tradition, the historical dynamic of poetic making has been interpreted in highly divergent ways. As a rule, this has led to ever new orders of genre poetics, with which the plurality of the arts, genres, and modes of aesthetic experience have been immobilized and subjected to a historically specific regime of power. These interpretations have often followed the familiar schema. They

---

80 Rorty, *Contingency, Irony, and Solidarity*, xvi.
81 Cf. Bernd Seidensticker, "Aristoteles und die griechische Tragödie," in *Die Mimesis und die Künste*, eds. Gertrud Koch, et al., Munich 2010, 15–42.

sought to postulate the relation between the means, the expressive modalities, the objects, and the effects as a legitimate rule.

Given the long history of interpretations, let us now add another one, following Cavell and Rorty, and define "mimesis" as the poetic making of media, the goal of which is to produce a shared perception of the world.[82] For media themselves should not be defined so much by previously established technologies of production; rather, they have to be identified in each case as technologies with which modes of experience, speaking perspectives, and expressive modalities are brought forth that make new re-descriptions of a shared world of perception possible.

Poetic making itself is not any more definable than as an activity of proposing a commonly shared perception of the world. But we do indeed have criteria at our disposal with which this activity can be reconstructed as a history of poetic making. These are the criteria of the differentiations in poetry that Aristotle enumerates in the first chapter of his *Poetics*, namely, 1) the medium, 2) the object, and 3) the mode – one might also say the speaking perspectives and expressive modalities – which they imitate and to which he adds pleasure as a fourth criterion, in the sixth chapter and through the example of catharsis, on the question of affective effect.[83] If the logic of this distinction is intuitively clear at first glance, but seems highly complicated on more careful inspection, there are two reasons for this. On the one hand, western tradition of poetic thinking still moves in translations and interpretations of criteria by means of which Aristotle seeks to grasp the modes of mimesis historically; on the other hand, however, the criteria, following tradition, are often read taxonomically, although they are conceived historically. It is thus anything but chance that the levels of distinguishing genre theories in media studies (mode of production, mode of representation, mode of experience) thoroughly correspond with the criteria that Aristotle had already developed in order to give shape to tragedy as a specific form of mimesis in a historical genesis. By relating the one to the other (the register of genre poetics in film studies to the differentiating criteria in Aristotelian), I would like once again to outline the criteria that should make it possible to get a view of history

---

82 Cf. the chapters on Stanley Cavell in this book (II1. and III.5).
83 Cf. Girshausen, *Ursprungszeiten des Theaters*, 131ff. Aristotle begins his poetics with three of these criteria on the distinctions in poetry in the first chapter – the means, the objects, and the way that they imitate – and adds the fourth – the question of the kind of pleasure – in the sixth chapter using the example of catharsis on the question of affective effect. Aristotle, *The Poetics*, London 1902, chapter 1, 1447a 7ff., and chapter 6, 1449b 23ff.

as the history of poetic making in media, the goal of which is to produce a shared perception of the world.

First, there is the medium. We can define this as the basis in media technology. This includes all the conditions that can be assigned to production. This is the level, for instance, at which we can understand Hollywood films equally as a media technology – as a "succession of automatic world projections" – and as an industrial means of production.

Second are the speaking perspectives and the expressive modalities. Speaking perspectives mean the various generic forms of relation to the common world. Aristotle, for instance, speaks of the difference between the historical report, the epic, and dramatic speech. Literary theory has perpetuated this division as lyric, epic, and dramatic speech.

In relation to film, this means the various media formats: the documentary, the essay film, the genre film, etc.; they can be described as various modes in which a film can relate to a common world. Is there a presumption of a common world – like in the report, the news story, the reportage – in order to relate to a concretely positioned incident? Or are lyric or essayistic worldviews presented, which seek to be seen as subjective reflection of concrete incidents in our shared world? Is a fictional world – the fiction film – presented, which asserts a claim to be able to refer, in its entirety as a constructed world, to the commonly shared world? Or is forensic proof introduced – documentation – that thus places a concrete issue in our common world without any doubt?

It is not difficult to recognize that these referential relations are closely linked to the expressive modalities that we are familiar with as affective perspectives (the sentimental, the horror, the thrill, etc.) on the relation to the world. The speaking perspectives and expressive modalities form the elements of a generative combinatorics that can be extended endlessly. If we understand them as media of producing a shared perception of the world, then they designate the history of the various arts in the broadest sense, the history of the *téchne* of poetic making.

Third would be to examine the constitutive conflicts that arise from the relations of violence and power that form the basis of every political community. In this point the perspective I am developing deviates significantly from the reigning concepts of genre. For from my viewpoint, this does not mean the social or cultural conflicts represented; even if they can certainly be considered expressive forms of constitutive conflicts. Instead, the level to be taken into account here will become clear if we look at the object of Greek tragedy. In no way does it consist in the actions represented themselves, but in the horror that these actions give expression to for the audience. They are the horrors of a past on which the becoming of the polis itself is founded, the horrors of the myth. In tragedy, they are brought into the present in a way which gives rise to possibilities of acting – the possibility of politics.[84] Poetic making is bound to ritual in this, and at the same time can be distinguished from it.[85] The object of poetic making always concerns a field of conflict that is identified in constituting a common world itself. To put it another way: There are always conflicts about the breadth and boundaries of the sense of commonality.

The object of poetic making is therefore closely linked with the fourth distinguishing criterion, the manner of pleasure. In the model of catharsis, we can get a concrete idea of the political function. Poetic making becomes related to the political community in the economy of affect, and distinguished from other kinds of pleasure. But the popularity of this model should not lead us to overly hasty generalizations.[86] The modes of aesthetic enjoyment are not meant to be any stable psycho-physiological mechanisms. They are also not to be conceived as fixed processes that could be schematically repeated. Rather, they are founded on dramaturgical arrangements of heterogeneous expressive modalities and speaking perspectives that allow for highly divergent modulations of affect. This is why it is correct to speak of them as modes of aesthetic experience. In the laughter of the screwball comedy, in the sentimental weepiness of the melodrama, in the patriotic exuberance of the war film, we encounter the affect-dramaturgical model of genre cinema as such modes of experience. These should also not be conceived in any way as a fixed ensemble, but as a dynamic process of ramifications and divisions.

---

84 Ibid., 316ff. Theresia Birkenhauer, "Tragödie: Arbeit an der Demokratie. Auslotung eines Abstandes," in *Theater der Zeit*, November 2004, 27–28.
85 Genre theory in film studies has discussed this aspect in the term 'ritual'; it resorts to an anthropological understanding of myth, which designates the expression of archetypes that are significant for a certain cultural community because they help it to express and to understand the common world experience and/or "collective psychology" of its members. Cf. Schatz, *Old Hollywood, New Hollywood*.

Cf. Wright, *Sixguns and Society*: "More often, as applied to popular media forms, myth in its most neutral formulation designates forms of (culturally specific) social self-representation, the distillation and enactment of core beliefs and values in reduced, usually personalised and narrative, forms. Myth is also characterised by specific kinds of formal stylisation, for example extreme narrative and characterological conventionalisation .... Thus in film genre theory, 'myth' broadly designates the ways in which genres rehearse and work through these shared cultural values and concerns by rendering them in symbolic narratives. 'Ritual' meanwhile redefines the regular consumption of genre films by a mass public as the contractual basis on which such meanings are produced." (18f.) In contrast, myths in the perspective developed here test out the possibilities of actualizing a community's becoming.
86 On the history of catharsis, cf.: Vöhler and Linck, "Zur Einführung."

The modes of aesthetic experience are not separable from the configurations of poetics and politics that must be situated in specific cultural histories in each case. Genre cinema should be viewed as a poetic practice that must be understood as one such configuration in the ramifications of affective modalities and speaking perspectives. In this sense, films are media that generate affective interlockings from which new forms of collective communion arise, new connections between bodies, things, words, and images, in short: new forms of subjectivization. They are as unrelated to the impulse-reaction schemata of the creation and navigation of emotion familiar from reception aesthetics as is Aristotle's catharsis. Rather, they are – like Aristotelian tragedy – to be conceived as cultural practices of intervening into the affect economy of political communities.

4.4 Commemorating the Dead and Community

Memory of the dead, writes Assmann, is "a paradigmatic way of 'establishing the community' (K. Schmidt [sic] 1985)".[87] In fact, the cinema of the immediate postwar period can be understood as an experiential space in which commemoration of the sacrifices of war becomes a mode of communalization. This is the case both for the way that the polity inscribes itself in mourning the dead as a community, and for the media forms in which it seeks to honor the memory of the dead as figures of heroic sacrifice.

A WALK IN THE SUN: a requiem

A WALK IN THE SUN is one of the films that serve to commemorate the dead in the way outlined here. It is not only – like so many other genre productions from those years – based on a short story that was written during the war. Harry Brown's *A Walk in the Sun* (1944) had been published and read serially, almost as a way of accompanying the battle action. The film then, in relaying the experience of the contemporary readers, who had been following the events in the present tense of a narrative, develops a quite specific temporal form.

It starts off with a long opening sequence that establishes a steady atmospheric basic tone over several minutes, which can perhaps be best qualified as

---

[87] Assmann, *Cultural Memory*, 47; Assmann is citing Karl Schmid (ed.), *Gedächtnis, das Gemeinschaft stiftet*, Munich 1985.

that of a nocturne. The screen is very dark; faces swell vaguely from the shadows as illuminated surfaces. Are there seven, nine, twelve, or fifteen faces? The individual soldiers can barely be distinguished from one another. They are pressed together in close quarters on a landing boat – a moving collage of shadowy surfaces of faces. We see neither the sky, nor the sea, nor the coast: a troop of soldiers, enclosed in a night with no horizon. For more than ten minutes the film dwells on this scene. It stages the interweaving of brighter and darker parts of faces as an ornamental shadow play, infused with the voices of the soldiers – and a ballad sung off screen. It tells of the heroic deeds of those who are at that moment gradually becoming visible in the interweaving of illuminating shadows. The singer's voice embraces the entirety of the scene – the shadow play, the soldiers' utterances, the words of the ballad – adding everything up into that aphorisms of an audiovisual anthem.

Even after landing on the Sicilian beach, a twilight reigns that only transitions to the light of day over the duration of the slowly rising morning sun. The characters are introduced as the shadowy figures that they actually are. The long exposition opens the film as an elegiac requiem for the dead soldiers. Even the dramaturgical structure does not follow any principle of tension, but allows the platoon, in a continuing variation of the opening sequence, to become visible as a steadfastly transforming structure of interweaving bodies – grey uniforms, brightly illuminated parts of faces and dark steel helmets – as the ghostly appearance of a body with countless faces.

When the night gives way to day after landing on the coast of Salerno, it seems as if the platoon might once again take shape as a military fighting unit. But even here the sentences spoken, the gestures, the faces all add up into an expression of a body that encompasses the actions of individuals. They form themselves into figurations of interweaving actions and dialogues. One hand motions for a cigarette, another passes it over, yet another hand lights the match at the helm of an uninvolved third party. In such figurations of the body of the group, the platoon gradually comes to life for the contemporary spectators as awakening memory (see Figure 39).

We can understand the world in which these spectators' perception emerges as an embodied hearing and seeing, sensing, feeling, and thinking, as a spirit world in which the dead rise again in order to haunt the living in the film images.[88]

---

[88] As Shaviro writes: Film images are "haunting images," cf. Burgoyne, "Haunting in the War Film," 159 and 167. Burgoyne is referring to: Steven Shaviro, "Response to 'Untimely Bodies: Toward a Comparative Film Theory of Human Figures, Temporalities, and Visibilities,'" Conference Paper, Society for Cinema and Media Studies, Philadelphia, PA, delivered on March 9, 2008.

Figure 39: Figurations of the group body.

In the end, however, it is always the fantasies and memories of the present-day spectators; in the end it is their mourning that approaches the images of war like the slowly brightening morning light does the soldiers on the beach at Salerno; it is their wishes, their longing for meaning and eternity through which the dead are compelled to take shape once again in film images. In a certain sense, they confront us, much like the dead soldiers from DECEMBER 7TH do, speaking directly to the audience through the camera – as images of the dead who are (re-)animated by words and sentences in which good reasons are given for what happened: "Why have we fought?" The film images become a medium that allows the spectators to haunt the past present of the dead with their mourning, but also with their desire for justification. In the perception of living, physically present spectators in the contemporary cinema, A WALK IN THE SUN shows the cinema to be an experiential space in which the present of the dead and that of the survivors can enter into a relationship with one another.

Many of the war films that were made in the first years after May, or rather September 1945, can be understood in this sense as a media practice of commemorating the dead. They position their spectators at a place that was reserved for the gods alone in ancient tragedy; the place from which the fate of the heroes can be overviewed in its irrefutable inevitability, from which the telos that preordains everything that happens can be recognized in the dying and death of the characters. Such pathos can be designated as tragic in a completely strict sense. The world that is visible in the films is defined by the fate of the inalterable death of the heroes. What emerges is a temporal form of film images that can be fundamentally distinguished from the dual temporality of cultural memory in the sense outlined above.

In western twentieth-century culture commemoration of the war refers to the counted and countable bodies of individuals that were violently killed. Every name must be registered, every corpse must have its own final resting place. After the American Civil War this convention was raised to the level of law. Since the First World War it has also been obligatory for European western and middle powers – that is, exactly since the point in time at which "individuals were swallowed up by mass death."[89] And while soldiers could still be buried together regardless of their nationalities until 1917,[90] since World War Two there has been a policy in the United States to transfer fallen American soldiers back home if at all possible, or to bury them at one of the 139 United States National Cemeteries that had been created exclusively on the territory of friendly war allies.[91]

---

89 Reinhart Koselleck, *The Practice of Conceptual History: Timing History, Spacing Concepts*, Stanford 2002, 319.
90 On the 'battlefields of 1870/71, numerous common graves of French and German soldiers' can be found (cf. ibid., 268), and Wilhelm II had a memorial constructed in 1916 that represented both enemy camps; in 1918, at one of the common cemeteries, the French soldiers were exhumed and replaced with German corpses.
91 Until very recently search detachments attempted to retrieve fallen soldiers in the battlefields and to bring them home, so that no American soldier is buried in Germany if it was not his express wish. (cf. ibid., 268).

The formal vocabulary of political sensibility (Koselleck)

In a well-known essay the historian Reinhart Koselleck examines the changes, which can be reconstructed on the practice of war memorials, monuments, and tombs, in what he calls "political sensibility."[92] Like Assmann, Koselleck also questions the forms of commemorating the dead in view of their function in forming political identity.

As late as the eighteenth century, "soldiers appear everywhere on victory monuments but not on war memorials."[93] And even there they have a primarily decorative function. Koselleck cites a dictum of Goethe's that is meant to make it clear that, under the sign of an estates-based society, war was an effective means to deal with political conflicts of interest without calling into question the unity of an overriding society with its culture and customs: "When represented without any clothing – it is the sculptors' right to represent their fighters in this way – both sides become 'completely the same: there are handsome people murdering each other ...'"[94] As long as war was merely an extension of politics by other means, the soldier was not attributed with any representative function with regard to nationality, ethnicity, or ideology. As individuals, they were completely unworthy of any particular commemoration; their fate as killing and killed had no place in the communal world of seeing, counting, and representing – as long as they were not of rank and nobility. The order of the estates-based society and the religious transcendence of death were complementarily interrelated in the practices of memorializing war in a way that can in fact be described as a dual temporality of formations of cultural memory. They belonged to the arsenal of technologies of power with which the nobles secured the privilege of transferring the eternity of death to their office and their lives within the cult of memory. Memorializing the dead was related to an "otherworldly beyond," which sanctioned the existence of the organization of the estates-based society: "As a ruler, he represents his office which is not subject to mortality, but the ruler is also representative as a human being – for human mortality, for everyone."[95]

War memorials that refer to the common soldier only start appearing with the French Revolution. From then on, the equality of individuals is celebrated in

---

92 Ibid., 321.
93 Ibid., 290.
94 Ibid., 313; Koselleck is citing Johann Wolfgang von Goethe, "A Challenge for a Modern Sculptor," in his: *Collected Works, Vol. 3, Essays on Art and Literature*, Princeton 1994, 93–95.
95 Koselleck, *Practice of Conceptual History*, 289f.

practices of cultural memory that point to the victims of war killed in action.[96] The death of the individual is interpreted as a meaningful event and related to the "community of agents,"[97] the community of revolutionaries. Those who had met a violent death in the action of a community of agents were poeticized in war memorials; their lives and efforts became a narrative about the origin, the telos, and the goal of the political community. "War memorials refer to a temporal vanishing line in the future in which the identity of the particular community of agents who had the power to commemorate the dead with monuments was supposed to be safeguarded."[98] The words, images, and architecture of memorials therefore do not primarily apply to the death of soldiers or revolutionaries; instead, the dead, or rather, memorializing the dead, becomes the object of a confabulation of memory in which a political community ensures its own foundation, its origin in the revolutionary or military act, in order to project itself into the future. This means nothing more than that the forms of commemorating the dead become media of a different experience of time than that of the eternity of the dead – namely that of the historicity of a political community.[99] The temporal line between the present of remembering the war dead and the future of monumental remembrance, which is ultimately what the monuments refer to, supercedes the "dual temporality" of the cultural memory of estates-based societies. This is why Capra can call on images of the American Revolution as an appeal to enter the war; indeed, by commemorating the victims of violence, they refer back to the history of a political community that positioned itself, through this violence, as the contingent beginning of just this history.[100]

With the battlefields of the First World War, which left behind thousands upon thousands of unidentified dead and untraceable corpses, the scenes of battles themselves became memorial sites. "The death of hundreds of thousands on a few square miles of contested earth left an obligation to search for justifications that were hard to create with traditional metaphors and concepts."[101] The pathos of commemorating the war was monumentally inflated and at the same time altered its semantics. It transformed into a commemoration of death per se, which set a limit to all continuity of the community and identity of individuals. "The category of the monumental victory memorial from the nineteenth

---

[96] Ibid., 291.
[97] Ibid., 288.
[98] Ibid., 294.
[99] Hannah Arendt analyzed this historicity in view of the American Revolution in *On Revolution*.
[100] Cf. Arendt, *On Revolution*.
[101] Koselleck, *Practice of Conceptual History*, 320.

century turned into an unequivocal memorial to the dead."[102] The personalized memorial, the lists, tables, walls on which each individual name was recorded, replaced the monuments with which the citizens of nineteenth century states had ensured their national identity. In place of creating political meaning, which could still be determined for the late nineteenth century, for example with the motto on a Prussian monument – "In memory of those killed in action, in recognition of the living, for the emulation of future generations"[103] – mourning over the dead itself becomes the focus and the affective material of confabulating memory. The soldier's death finds its meaning in the representation of the survivors' mourning.[104] Mourning over the dead is celebrated as a communally shared feeling, which becomes the powerful source of the feeling for the community. For example, Koselleck cites the dictum on an English war monument: "Pass not this stone in sorrow but in pride/And live your lives as nobly as they died."[105]

From this perspective, the history of war memorials in western societies appears as a process of political functionalization of the memory of the fallen soldiers, which is closely linked with the emergence of modern democracies.[106] In democratic societies the memorial becomes a generic form of poetic making, which, in the ritualized recourse to past wars, reforms the simple passage of time itself, the ordinary time of ordinary life, into the history of the 'community of agents,' that is, the history of a political community. In a wide variety of media practices (monuments and memorials, paintings and photographs, novels, films, music) the time of military foundation or of revolutionary liberation is given perspective and unfolded toward the future of a political community.

The talk of war and the myth of community

Foucault has this political function of memorializing war for the political community in mind when he thematizes "speaking about war" as a discourse in which he assumes the historical-political discourse of western modernity itself is grounded. His reflections allow us to understand that the media stagings of war are related to discourses and institutions that found the civil order of the political community – and are in no way related to the historical fact of war. They report

---

102 Ibid.
103 Cf. ibid., 295.
104 Cf. ibid., 293.
105 Ibid., 320.
106 Cf. ibid., 259f.

4.4 Commemorating the Dead and Community — 295

on war as a bloody violence that is effective as an image of war "beneath and in power relations"; they present war as a mythical event that "presided over the birth of States" and gave birth to their "right, peace, and laws".

The organization and juridical structure of power, of States, monarchies, and societies, does not emerge when the clash of arms ceases. War has not been averted. War obviously presided over the birth of States: right, peace, and laws were born in the blood and mud of battles.[107]

Viewed from this perspective, representations of the suffering, the horror, and the reprehensibility of war could always already be functionally related to the identity of a political community that derives its social territoriality, the integrity as a "political body" of a nation, a people, from producing a form of history. They concern the memory of a contingent violence of the beginning of a history of the people, the nation, and not, as is constantly claimed precisely in view of stagings of war in film and television, the more or less reprehensible derailments of state violence and their horrible consequences, which are always only trivialized or distorted. They concern history as a space in which political entities seek to be constituted as communities, and seek, by speaking about war – the commemoration of war – to project themselves into a 'future of monumental memory.' This is why, according to Foucault, the modern discourse of war is a racist discourse that asserts law as a law apart. "It might be the right of his family or race, the right of superiority or seniority, the right of triumphal invasions, or the right of recent or ancient occupations. In all cases, it is a right that is both grounded in history and decentered from a juridical universality."[108] And further: "The war that is going on beneath order and peace, the war that undermines our society and divides it in a binary mode is, basically, a race war."[109] The discourse of history as western modernity has developed it –and this is the consequence of Foucault's reflections – emerges directly from speaking about war and from memorializing war. In relation to modern democracies, politics would be "the continuation of war by other means."[110]

In part this also concerns the restaging of history in the image spaces of film, as I tried to reconstruct it in the previous studies. It is about films here that project the cinema as an experiential space in which the nation, "the Country," is described as a web of countless biographies and family stories of famous and ordinary individuals, epoch-making and anonymous ones: as "intertwining bodies, passions, and accidents: according to this discourse, that is what constitutes the

---

[107] Foucault, *Society Must Be Defended*, 50.
[108] Ibid., 52.
[109] Ibid., 60.
[110] Ibid., 48.

permanent web of history and societies."[111] We might think here of the thesis of the metafilm, which Hollywood is always restaging:[112]

> Finally, the American cinema constantly shoots and reshoots a single fundamental film, which is the birth of a nation-civilization .... It [organic representation with the Americans] is the whole of history, the germinating stock from which each nation-civilization detaches itself as an organism, each prefiguring America .... A strong ethical judgment must condemn the injustice of 'things,' bring compassion, herald the new civilization on the march, in short, constantly rediscover America.[113]

But neither Deleuze's thesis nor Foucault's reflections can be seamlessly transferred to the Hollywood war film after 1945.

THE STEEL HELMET: the perspective of the dead

In THE STEEL HELMET (1951) Samuel Fuller created a cinematic image space that attempts to describe a relationship between the presence of the dead and that of the survivors, stepping outside of the trajectory of memorializing war that we have described. Only a few of the film's scenes are set in the jungle. Quite obviously, no great efforts were made to get the forest to look like anything other than a set in a film studio. Even the circumstance that the film, only a few years after the end of the Second World War, deals with a different military conflict, namely the Korean War, seems to be completely incidental. The battles continue on seamlessly, and the soldiers who disappeared into the fog in SANDS OF IWO JIMA simply continue fighting as a matter of course in THE STEEL HELMET. They reform themselves, a troop of dispersed survivors, who, after a lost battle, team up for better or worse to move on together somehow.

The troop reaches the grounds of a temple. The gardens, levels, amphorae, galleries, and side rooms are centered around an interior space that is dominated by the gaze of a statue. We see its eyes, a strange idol. Precisely because of its posture, one might grant the statue a certain similarity to cliché representations of the Buddha, the facial features are pure fantasy. This is by no means an inconsequential detail. THE STEEL HELMET presents itself in whole as a confabulation of memory in which the places and times of the action are pure phantasms. In

---

111 Ibid., 54.
112 Robert Burgoyne connected these thoughts of Deleuze to the Hollywood historical film. Cf. Robert Burgoyne, *The Hollywood Historical Film*, Malden/Oxford/Carlton 2008, 74ff.
113 Deleuze, *The Movement-Image*, 148–151. Seen in this way, Griffith would have developed the fundamental pathos that allowed the cinema to become the privileged experiential space of the historical with THE BIRTH OF A NATION.

Figure 40: THE STEEL HELMET: confabulations of memory and chamber play.

what follows, the film compresses the drama of the war film, by now played through hundreds of times, into a chamber play that, much like A WALK IN THE SUN, appears as a "little night music" (see Figure 40).

The face of the statue finds its counterpart in a quite different representation of a face. We have encountered it in the film's exposition; we see a close-up of a helmet lying in the grass, a steel hemisphere with a bullet hole in it; in the foreground the credits roll, underscored by a music with clear echoes of leitmotifs that we associate in westerns with the threat of Indian tribes prepared for battle. The helmet remains visible in the background throughout the entire duration of the credits; gradually, it itself appears to take on the traits of a face; not a shell-shocked face, but – we clearly see the bullet hole left by a targeted shot to the head – an image of the dead soldier per se, steel tomb and face in one.[114] Suddenly the helmet moves, we can make out two eyes, an American infantryman raises his

---

[114] Cf. Torsten Gareis, "Put your helmet on! Der Helm im amerikanischen Kriegsfilm," in *Mobilisierung der Sinne: Der Hollywood-Kriegsfilm zwischen Genrekino und Historie*, ed. Hermann Kappelhoff, et al., Berlin 2013, 345–382, here 358ff.

head; he is, as we will soon find out, the only survivor of his platoon. He meets a Korean boy. Once again an echo of the western: the naked legs that approach the bound and wounded soldier are staged like those of an Indian warrior, trying to complete his work after the carnage.

Only a few minutes later, this boy will be standing devoutly under the gaze of the idol, while the small troop of American soldiers who come together in the jungle follow him into the interior of the temple, gradually gathering behind him. His smile extends the motif that combines the helmet and the repudiating-sullen countenance of the infantryman, brought back to life, with the stiff countenance of the statue, and the cheerful face of the boy into an expressive figuration that, in a certain way, orchestrates the story of the film (see Figure 41). At the end, the boy – the only cheery face in the film – will be dead, and the infantryman will be hit once again by a deadly bullet, which he will once again survive – as a shell-shocked face.

In the interplay of faces, the idol appears as the gaze of an always present, invisible third party. From the first moment on, it is this gaze that is addressed, in the devotion of the Korean boy, in the hesitation of the soldiers gathering together

Figure 41: Steel tomb and face.

under the giant idol, transforming the sacred space into a temporary barracks; they address it in their uncertainty, when they explore the labyrinthine building, always fearing an ambush from the enemy, and then, when one of them, standing at the feet of the stature, gets the creepy feeling that its eyes have moved. He turns around again, trying to fix the eyes of the still image. In fact, the dramatic tension develops in the small chamber play, which gradually causes the obstinacy, preferences, and aversions of the soldiers to become visible as a social structure, from the uncanny feeling of always being watched, without it being possible to grasp the observer himself – until they finally detect an enemy soldier lurking in the shadows to murder from behind.

But even after the soldier has been discovered and overpowered, the oppressive feeling will not give way. Time and again, the montage returns to the shot that simulates the gaze of the looming statue looking down at the soldiers below, so that this gaze remains a burdensome presence. The shot/reverse shot sequences in which the small and large conflicts between the soldiers are developed, are grouped around this shot, as if everything that happened had its uncanny center in the eyes of the statue. The montage therefore establishes an all-seeing eye, whose gaze encompasses the image space as a whole, the room, the temple grounds, almost as if the gaze itself constituted its interiority and hermetically sealed itself off against an indeterminate outside. The paranoid perception that discovers the invisible enemy because of his invisibility in all appearances, has become, in the fixed eyes of the statue, an allegory of a gaze that has a spell on the soldiers.

The battle that can be seen, after all, toward the end of THE STEEL HELMET, the defensive combat in hopeless inferiority, is almost exclusively represented by cutting in found footage; the staging of the film almost seems to be deliberately trying not to mix up the heterogeneity of the various types of audiovisual materials. Even the obviously staged scenes of storming troops, where uniformed extras simulate the attack in which they throw themselves into the line of fire like lemmings – once again a coarse stereotype from the movies about the Indian wars – are spliced in so that they are completely separated from the world of the temple's interior. The images of the war remain as external to the image space of the chamber play as they do for the audience in cinemas back home that watches the images of a newsreel from a far-off war between the main features. The set of the studio jungle, the inserted external shots of arbitrary artillery combat, and the stereotypical battle scenes cause a diffuse phantasmatic exterior to arise that, in turn, allows the hermetic image space of the interior to emerge only more clearly as the spell of the all-seeing eye. In the sound the exterior penetrates into this interior – the whistling bullets that hit and kill the soldiers in the interior of the temple, the corpse of the boy that is carried in after hearing the shot that brought him down ... "It's his own fault. Told him I don't want any kid tagging along. Take him outside and bury him. Go on! Take him out!!" is the only thing the infantryman says when he sees the dead boy. Then he turns away from the others and toward the camera. We see the pain in his sullen face, which explodes in a rage of action in the next moment, drawing in all the others into the uproar of this pain. The infantryman guns down the unarmed prisoner of war, only because he uttered the wrong thing about the boy. The operation table is set up at the foot of the statue, on which the captive is vetted and dies – as if the soldiers were parodying a rite of sacrifice in front of the altar of an idol from the prop room of a cheap theater.

The miracle of survival

Sam Fuller, like many other directors of war films, was an eyewitness to the war. He had fought at various fronts of the Second World War and afterward influenced the poetics of the genre like no other Hollywood director. His first war film – THE STEEL HELMET, in fact – is certainly conceived, not unlike the films of Ford or Capra, as a patriotic tribute to American soldiers. But he creates an image of the sacrifice of soldiers that shies away from providing heroic meaning. The drama that Fuller stages is that of a soldier who knows himself to be constantly watched, detected, and identified by death – and who does not understand, cannot believe, that he, precisely he, is still alive. It is not death, but survival that is actually mysterious in the midst of the all the dying of war. The circumstance that Fuller, a veteran of the Second World War, is directing may in part be expressed in the unbelieving amazement that an infantryman can survive the war at all.

At the beginning, the American soldier tells the Korean boy about the bullet that hit his helmet, but – curiously, miraculously – did not penetrate through to his skull. In the end, the infantryman is once again fatally shot and survives again – against all odds. What we barely understand in the beginning becomes clear in the end. The character himself owes his presence to the miracle of an impossible survival, which repeats itself over and over again. For who survives a firing squad after having previously been struck by a bullet in order then to find himself the prisoner of the ones who have been shot by court martial?

A steel helmet, then a face opening its eyes under the helmet, a soldier that starts to move between the corpses in the bright sunlight – the beginning of THE STEEL HELMET is as ambiguous as the end of SANDS OF IWO JIMA. On the one hand, the reanimation of the dead soldier concerns the reality status of the characters of the film itself. It has the fallen soldiers come alive again as shadowy shapes on the screen, in order to give them all the honor of memorializing the dead; on the other hand, however, it concerns the historical reality of a war that in fact does not want to stop. For the soldiers, the end of one war is only the beginning of another. In this respect, the film's reference to the Korean War is in fact anything but arbitrary. From the viewpoint of THE STEEL HELMET, war is the exceptional state of dying, which has become normality – regardless of which political narrative newly defines the enemy in each case. The question that Capra propounds so emphatically – "Why are we on the march?" – has been resolved. THE STEEL HELMET gives the laconic answer at the end: "There is no end to this story." We might think of a sentence that General MacArthur is supposed to have attributed to Plato in a talk he gave in 1962, and which came to a certain popularity before it was used at the beginning of Ridley Scott's BLACK HAWK DOWN in 2001: "Only the dead have seen the end of war."[115]

For the soldiers – the example here is the hobbling infantryman who miraculously just avoided another attack on his life – it is only a matter of pressing on to the next battle. They leave behind them the gaze that had put a spell on them from the moment that they entered the temple, the place that was designated for their deaths. In fact, the editing separates the gaze from the statue of the idol in order to delegate it to the spectators. In the end, the spectators remain behind in the temple grounds, united with the gaze that always already sees the soldiers as dead men. They watch the soldiers going through the gate and slowly departing.

In THE STEEL HELMET Fuller constructed an image space in which the seeing of the survivors, the seeing of the spectators, is related to the dead of war without allowing the dead to become the heroic sacrifices of the community. At any rate, it is not by chance that the motif of miraculous survival is stretched even further, with the arc reaching back to D-Day.[116] The protagonist is hit; paralyzed, shell-shocked, he calls out to a soldier walking by: "Did you hear the Colonel? Hear what he said? Get off the beach!" The nonsensical sentences refer to the famous words attributed to Colonel Charles Taylor, who is said to have spoken them on

---

[115] "The long gray line has never failed us. Were you to do so, a million ghosts in olive drab, in brown khaki, in blue and gray, would rise from their white crosses, thundering those magic words: Duty, honor, country. This does not mean that you are warmongers. On the contrary, the soldier above all other people prays for peace, for he must suffer and bear the deepest wounds and scars of war. But always in our ears ring the ominous words of Plato, that wisest of all philosophers: 'Only the dead have seen the end of war.'" (MacArthur, *U.S. Military Academy*, 200) I will come back to this truly abysmal speech toward the end of the book.

[116] Cf. the scenes "Abschied und Lob auf die Infanterie [*farewell and praising the infantry*]" (01:02:48:15–01:06:33:15) and "Finale Schlacht [*final battle*]" (01:14:06:11–01:21:33:00).

Omaha Beach. Shortly before, the legend is brought up in an argument with the commander to move him to act:

> Look, I'll tell you about an officer. And he wasn't a 90-day act of Congress like you. He was a colonel, and he didn't have to be there. It was D-day in Normandy, when you were wearing bars in the States and we were pinned down for three hours by kraut fire. This colonel, Colonel Taylor, he got up on Easy Red Beach and he yelled: 'There are two kinds of men on this beach – those who are dead, and those who are about to die. So let's get off the beach and die inland.' That officer I'd give my steel hat to any day.

THE BIG RED ONE: an image of annihilation

It could be that the only reason the sentences became famous was that they were cited in war films over and over again. But they formulate fairly precisely the circumstance that the survival of soldiers is not intended. Fuller wrote the sentence one more time in one of his screenplays, namely in THE BIG RED ONE (1980), his last war film.

In this film, as well, the unbelieving amazement in face of one's own survival is the focus of the staging. Now, however – the complete opposite of the studio chamber play of THE STEEL HELMET – it concerns the staging of a truly monumental film. In THE BIG RED ONE there are four comrades and their leader, all of whom experience all the great battles, from the landing in Africa, Sicily, and Normandy, and then finally the conquest of Germany – without the slightest injury. For the other soldiers, the group becomes the incarnation of a magic invulnerability, which one treats, when it turns up, with the greatest awe and veneration – for all those pulled into battle with these invulnerable lose their lives. With each soldier that joins them, only to be felled in the next armed conflict, these five leave the defeat further and further behind them. Their victory march is literally borne by the death of others, their survival is the miraculous result of a futile effort, an absurd triumph of individual lust for life, which leaves all the physical, technological, and strategic efforts to win the war outshined and eclipsed.

Through all the sites of the invasion of northern Africa and western Europe THE BIG RED ONE traces a military campaign, the stages of which Fuller himself had gone through as an infantryman, up to the liberation of the Flossenbürg concentration camp in Czechoslovakian Falkenau, today Sokolov, in May of 1945. This is where Fuller's actual first film was made. Only many years later did it become known to the public under the title V-E + 1. According to his own statement, Fuller prepared it as an amateur filmmaker who was instructed by his superior to film the citizens of the area as they, on orders from American officers, salvaged the decaying corpses of the murdered concentration camp inmates from the mass graves in order to give them a proper burial.[117] Looking at these three films by Fuller, THE STEEL HELMET, THE BIG RED ONE, and V-E + 1, we can recognize the Korean boy as the Jewish boy who is rescued in THE BIG RED ONE in order to die in dignity. The amateur film of the infantryman Fuller is surely one of the most radical and darkest film documents of the Second World War.[118] Only in his last war film does Fuller refer to this document, but intermixing two historical references with one another, which have remained oddly unconnected in the history of the film images of the Second World War: the images of the liberation of the concentration camps and those of the American troops' battles in Europe and the Pacific.

With THE BIG RED ONE the Holocaust becomes the vanishing point of the representation of the Second World War in American genre cinema.[119] The debate that ignited years later with Spielberg's SCHINDLER'S LIST (1993),[120] of whether it is permissible to use melodramatic pathos to represent the concentration camps, could have been held a good while earlier in relation to these films. The scene in which Fuller shows the discovery of the concentration camps, the incinerators, the corpses, and the completely emaciated survivors, are of the same aesthetic

---

117 Fuller's Film forms the basis for Emil Weiss's 1988 documentary KZ FALKENAU, VISION DE L'IMPOSSIBLE (FALKENAU – THE IMPOSSIBLE), in which the director also appears as an eyewitness. I am referring here to this documentary, which was broadcast in a slightly edited version on the television station arte in 2004 under the title FALKENAU – EINE LEKTION IN MENSCHENWÜRDE. Fuller's film itself did not have its own title, however it has been held in the National Film Registry of the Library of Congress since 2014 under the name V-E + 1.
118 Cf. Georges Didi-Huberman, "Opening the Camps, Closing the Eyes," in *Concentrationary Cinema: Aesthetics as Political Resistance in Alain Resnais's* Night and Fog (1955), eds. Griselda Pollock and Max Silverman, New York 2011, 84–125; Drehli Robnik, "Bilder, die die Welt bewegten: 'The Big Red One' 1980, Regie: Samuel Fuller," in *Spex* 362, July/August 2015, 80–81.
119 On this idea in relation to BAND OF BROTHERS, cf. Robnik, *Kino, Krieg, Gedächtnis*, 133f. In this context, Robnik refers to Anson Rabinbach, "From Explosion to Erosion: Holocaust Memorialization in America since Bitburg," in *History and Memory* 1 (2), 1997, 226–255.
120 At approximately the same time that THE BIG RED ONE was released in cinemas, the American television series HOLOCAUST (1978) made the term Holocaust as popular in Germany as the term "Gung ho" had been during the Second World War in the United States due to the film GUNG HO! The term was included in a list of new popular terms by James F. Bender on December 2, 1945, cf. James F. Bender, "Thirty Thousand New Words," in *New York Times Magazine*, December 2, 1945, 22/2. On the term, which originates in Chinese and was in common usage as US military jargon from the beginning of 1942, the linguist Albert F. Moe surmises: "It is probable that a movie entitled *Gung Ho!* contributed greatly toward making the term popular in general American speech during 1944 and made it possible for the term to be included on Bender's list." Cf. Albert F. Moe, "Gung Ho," in *American Speech* 42 (1), Februar 1967, 19–30, here 22.

brilliance as all the other parts of THE BIG RED ONE. And the scene showing a famished boy taking one more bite from an apple in the arms of a soldier, only to die immediately afterwards, could barely be surpassed in sentimental pathos. But the razor-sharp color images are precisely not trying to be a restaging of historical film documents – although such a document did exist in the director's private collection. The melodramatic scene of the dying child is a confabulation of memory with which audiovisual images of the Holocaust that had been omitted for years are entered in the Hollywood war film genre.

Bearing witness to the death of the dead instead of fictionalizing them as historical victims, granted to them by human beings – this is how we might define the ethos of the poetic concept that defines Fuller's work. Biographical and historical material, individual experience and historical event are transferred into a confabulation of memory and inextricably merged with one another.

The community of survivors

According to Koselleck, what we can assume about the memorializing of the dead in general is particularly so for memorializing them after the Second World War: representational forms and media practices are completely consumed in their political semantics: "No matter how much dying for a cause is thematized in order to derive a particular group identity, dying itself is also always a major additional theme."[121] The attempt to bind the political community with the dead of war in the representation of subjective mourning has brought forth figurations of affect in media that cannot be completely functionally embedded. In their aesthetic imprint, war monuments always also allow something to be sensed from the experience that is linked with the mourning of survivors, "in relation to death itself, not in relation to dying for something."[122]

After the Second World War, the "appeal to political or social identification with the sense of past death"[123] got completely lost. The death violence of war can no longer be represented as creating meaning, but merely exposes the absence, the lack of a community for which these dead might still have sense. "What remains is the identity of the dead with themselves; the capability of memorializing the dead eludes the formal language of political sensibility."[124] Memorializing

---

121 Koselleck, *Practice of Conceptual History*, 309f.
122 Ibid., 312.
123 Ibid., 321.
124 Ibid., 323f.

the dead refers to the experience of radical contingency, which could no longer rest on the "formal language of political sensibility" that the dead linked to the living of the community.[125] This is precisely why – as Koselleck argues – modern commemoration of warriors is tied to the life of the survivors, to their real mourning. Commemorating the warrior becomes an opportunity for the survivors, a ritual practice in which a community is reorganized as a community of survivors.

"The political cult at the old war memorials dries up as soon as the last survivors pass away."[126] What remains behind are the artifacts of media practices of remembering (monuments, memorial sites, cemeteries and gravesites, films, novels, stories, photos, paintings, sculptures, and buildings), which become the testimonial to a community of war survivors. The gap between the survivors' cult of memory and the "political sensibility" of those born afterward "is filled, so to speak, by aesthetics; it interrogates the forms in terms of their own 'statement.' In other words, the 'aesthetic' possibilities for a statement, connected to the sensory receptivity of observers, outlast the political demands for identification that they were supposed to establish."[127]

This idea is significant for the Hollywood war film. The films are initially and above all addressed – we can trace this in the film analyses – to the contemporary audience, the survivors. They draw their affect-rhetorical power from mourning, from the remembered feelings of their spectators. But the affective power does not merge into the contemporary assignation of the feeling of mourning any more than it does in political semantics. The crucial point in this argument seems to me to be affect itself. The affect-poetic constructions of film images of "subjective mourning" become the medium for an affect aimed at the future of a community for which the image of mourning can become the object of a feeling for one's own history.

We can even enter the family of Private Ryan into the line of such a history, looking for an American military cemetery in Normandy at the end of the century in order to perform the sentimental scene par excellence between crosses and stars of David made of white marble.[128] We understand that the family members accompanying the veteran, the woman, the children, the grandchildren, who have no or barely any associations with the names of the dead, are only connected to the experience of survival through the affect of the scene itself – in the old man's tears, surrounded by his family and weeping in front of the grave of the man who

---

125 Ibid., 324.
126 Ibid.
127 Ibid., 325.
128 Cf. 16ff. [in the manuscript] in the present study.

rescued him. In the scene, the appeal lingers on as sentimental emotion, with which the young soldier was obligated to the pursuit of happiness in order to be deserving of what the fallen soldier had given him: survival. For the spectator, however, the sentiment does not merge into the imagination of the feelings of the family or of the soldier. Rather, the sentimental scene becomes the starting point for an altered way of seeing that increases in order to include the military cemetery that stretches out in all directions as a film image. The endless rows of marble memorials, which seem to go beyond the horizon itself in their intersections and lines, become the concrete mathematical formula – every memorial a family scene – with which sentiment, infinitely multiplied, exceeds all power of the imagination. In the film montage the architectural construction of a field of graves that boundlessly stretches out becomes that affect that is aimed at the aesthetic experience of spectators born later.

The confabulation of memory of the Hollywood war film after the Second World War refers to a community of survivors who are not only radically distinct from the community of memory in Assmann's sense. It has also become impossible for this community to continue speaking of war seamlessly as a discourse of the history of the political community.

The community of survivors is based on the experience of radical contingency, on a practice of cultural memory that cannot bridge the temporal split between the dead and the survivors. It has to get by without any narrative, without an idea of community, in which the contingency of historical experience is reinterpreted into a mythology that grounds identity. The liberal utopia of a 'post-metaphysical culture,'[129] as Rorty defines it, corresponds to a community that has survived war, survived the great ideas of community, and the systematic murder of an entire people – the Holocaust. It knows about the impossibility of proposing history as a narrative with which the present of a political community can be described as a seamless connection of its past to a future social utopia.[130]

The "racism" that Foucault ascribed to modern historical-political discourse, like the "ethnocentrism"[131] that Rorty ascribed to it, can only be encountered in the radical affirmation of the experience of contingency. Both can only be corrected again, over and over, by means of 'poetic making,' 'changed descriptions' of the world. The fact that "speaking about war," which Foucault understands as the "birth of history," which declares the rights of the people, the nation, of

---

[129] Rorty, *Contingency, Irony and Solidarity*, xv. Cf. 33ff. [in the manuscript] in the present study.
[130] Ibid., 290.
[131] Rorty, "Solidarity or Objectivity?, " 30.

the country, precisely not as "the universal truth of the philosopher,"¹³² but as the memory of its battles, its defeats, and its victories, might turn out to be a legacy that is as valuable as it is ambivalent. Seen in this way, the confabulation of memory can become an appeal to oppose all attempts to ascribe to the political community the memory of a people, a nation, an ethnicity, or a culture that would ground it as a community, with the "history of making," the "poeticity of culture."

As an aesthetic experience, the mourning of the survivors remains accessible to a later present of spectators to the degree that each of the film images of mourning itself can be sensed as affected; just as it can become aaaan "a priori object" of their feeling for the communal, their sense of commonality. From this perspective, memorializing the warriors of the past is not directly available as a political semantics, as speaking of war, and as a discourse of community; rather, it remains relegated to the detour by means of aesthetic experiences, to the physical presence of the affected spectator. Only by this detour through aesthetic experience can the history of a political sensibility be reconstructed as a history of the 'forms of feeling for a common world,'¹³³ as a history of the sense of commonality. This detour even has to be taken by historical research itself when it seeks to grasp the history of the "formal languages of political sensibility" in films.

4.5 The Irresolvable Conflict

There is a consciousness of a totality of murdering and dying tied to the Hollywood war film that cannot be restricted to any political or cultural conflict, nor even conceived as a conflict at all. In a certain sense, war has become general. If, however, the horror and the murdering, the suffering and dying have become general, any pathos that emphasizes the individuality of the soldiers loses its binding power. This has caused the constitutive conflict of the war film genre, the basic contradiction between military and political community, to become exceedingly intensified.

We should, however, maintain that this intensification of the conflict was foreshadowed early on. This can be seen, for instance, in the success of the novel *From Here to Eternity* (1951) by James Jones and the very successful film version

---

132 Foucault, *Society Must Be Defended*, 52.
133 "L'art est ce qui donne à la communauté politique ces formes de communauté sensible qui unissent les hommes dans des liens vivants, opposés à l'abstraction de la loi. [...] Le mode esthétique de la communauté, c'est le mode d'une communauté pensant ce qu'elle sent et sentant ce qu'elle pense." Rancière, "L'historicité du cinéma," 56.

by the same name, directed by Fred Zinnemann in 1953. It does not seem to me to be by chance that Zinnemann's war film, which actually isn't a war film, shifts the drama of military communitization into the immediate pre-war period. What it thematizes much more than the war are the consequences of militarization for the civilian population. The state of exception of physical subjugation to a foreign, sovereign military authority claims as its first victim the subjectivity and the desires, the aspirations for individual happiness.

Successful boxer Private Prewitt (Montgomery Clift) refuses to fight in the regiment's boxing squadron. He bears all the humiliating punishments and physical exercises without ever doubting his decision, but also without doubting the army. Like the recruits in GUNG HO! he is one of those young delinquents who have found a new identity in the military community. Only when his comrade falls prey to another oppressor does he stab the superior responsible. The humiliation of the drill is reversed as rage against one's own military leadership.

FROM HERE TO ETERNITY describes the training process in the military as an alchemy that forms the warring society from the civilian society. As a result, it produces Burt Lancaster's character, First Sergeant Milton Warden, as that of the officer prepared for war, who is as capable of leaving behind the dying private as he is the women who fall in love with him. The vengeful act of violence is represented as an act of regenerating the military community, which is suffering from the moral insufficiency of particular officers. This narrative is put through a number of variations in numerous subsequent films. Guilt can no longer be staged as a relationship between the survivors and the dead soldiers; rather, it concerns – as we can trace from FROM HERE TO ETERNITY and ATTACK! through THE BRIDGE AT REMAGEN and on to CASUALTIES OF WAR[134] and IN THE VALLEY OF ELAH – the relationship of the military and the State to the political community. The militarized community itself is emphasized as an archaic violence which takes the political community as its victim.[135] The is the basic theme of Vietnam War films.

The irate taxi driver

He is the most well-known film character of the New Hollywood. The taxi driver from the film of the same name by Martin Scorsese (USA 1976) has become the

---

[134] Cf. Grotkopp, *Filmische Poetiken der Schuld*, 222–254.
[135] Sascha Keilholz has shown that the police film of the early seventies indicates a transformation of genre cinema that thematizes the external war, Vietnam, as an internal war in society. Cf. Sascha Keilholz, *Verlustkino: Trauer im amerikanischen Polizeifilm seit 1968*, Marburg 2015.

emblem of this cinema. We remember the melancholy images of nocturnal New York, the extremely stylized shots of the yellow cab, the daydreams of Travis Bickle (Robert De Niro), who cannot sleep and therefore drives a taxi at night, while he spends his days in porno cinemas. We remember the colorful lights of the red-light district, an urban demimonde, the blinking lights advertising striptease bars and nightclubs, the groups of prostitutes, drug dealers, and pimps gathered on the sidewalks. Outside the taxi's window panes, this world floats by; while we, the spectators inside the taxi, follow Travis's monologue, who dreams of a great clean-up: a powerful rain that would simply wash away all this scum.

Travis is a homecomer, a Vietnam veteran, and his insomnia, his job, his sanctuary, the porno cinemas, make himself part of the street life that he so disdains. When all his attempts to make contact with the clean world of good society fail, he thinks back to his purpose as a soldier. Initially, he prepares – a kneejerk reaction to an unrequited love – an attack on a presidential candidate; then he attempts to rescue the prostitute Iris, a very young girl, a child, from the clutches of the drug dealers and pimps. The liberation leads to a desolate killing spree. Everybody and anybody is shot, sinking into a sea of blood. With the newspaper reports of this homecomer's heroic deeds, rescuing the girl from the clutches of prostitution and the drug world, the film ends.

Travis stages a massacre for which he will be celebrated as a liberator the next day. In the accomplished blood bath, he does in fact fulfill his purpose as a soldier. He is now celebrated as a hero for a massacre for which he would have been disdained and criticized during the Vietnam War. The film itself does not give any clue as to the reasons for the trauma that made Travis what he is. The early life of the homecomer remains completely out of the picture. All that gets staged is the rage – without cause, without semantic framing. The rage itself becomes the signature with which the character of the completely shattered anti-social homecomer can be recognized as the return of the archaic war. Indeed, the epic of Achilles's rage is considered the prototype of memorializing the warrior in western culture.

In a certain way, the taxi driver's killing spree is a late manifestation of the war hero that was developed in the Hollywood war film up until the sixties. After 1968, Hollywood's homecoming films are the only variety in which Hollywood explicitly deals with the Vietnam War. (Apart from a very few exceptions,[136] the

---

[136] For instance THE BRIDGE AT REMAGEN (1969, director: John Guillermin); PATTON (1969/70, director: Franklin J. Schaffner) and TORA! TORA! TORA! (1970, directors: Richard Fleischer, Kinji Fukasaku, Toshio Masuda).

Hollywood war film – like Hollywood genre cinema as a whole – seems to have come to an end.) By the time the war film turns up again toward the end of the seventies with Francis Ford Coppola's APOCALYPSE NOW (1979) and Michael Cimino's THE DEER HUNTER (1978), the poetics of Hollywood cinema had changed so radically that academic research differentiates to this day between classical genre cinema and post-classical blockbuster cinema. Of course, what I am trying to work through here for classical Hollywood cinema becomes only too clear in the New Hollywood.[137] The poetics of affect do not follow any rules and taxonomic orders, but should be understood – at least in the more ambitious films – as attempts on the part of a polity to describe itself as a community. Nonetheless, the concrete historical-political constellation has fundamentally changed.

Over the course of the Vietnam War, images of war went out of control as television images and photo reportages. They became witnesses to a fundamental disintegration of the political community; with the news of the Tet Offensive in January 1968 and the massacre at My Lai two months later, the moral legitimacy of the military actions by the warring State were conclusively destroyed. The films that then refer explicitly to Vietnam are staged as flashbacks, attempting, years after the war, to shed light on the annihilation that the war had left behind in the interior of society – as if one could only get an idea of the reality of the horror of the events of war carried out by one's own country in bombastic or intricate dream scenes, which were only gradually starting to clear. The massacre, the napalm war, the battle against the civilian population became visual codes of a slowly dissolving self-deception about the degree of the crisis in one's own political community.

For APOCALYPSE NOW Coppola used all the available technological means of the cinema to allow a monumental image space to emerge with which the metaphor of Joseph Conrad's story, the *Heart of Darkness*, is transposed as an arabesque in a jungle temple, which is decorated not with flowers, but with thousands of human corpses.

On the one hand, the film allows communitization in the anarchic tyranny of ritualized human massacre to appear as the agent of the horror of war; on the other, it unfolds the journey in its stations as a parable about a society whose powers to bind and regulate (myths, laws, ideals) are crumbling, and which can no longer position itself as a political community. The American way of life seems to be a temporary performance on enemy territory, the stage setting of which is always already demolished before the show has even really begun (see Figure 42).

---

[137] Cf. Lehmann, *Affektpoetiken des New Hollywood*.

4.5 The Irresolvable Conflict — **311**

Figure 42: APOCALYPSE NOW.

Figure 42: (continued)

THE DEER HUNTER also develops a visual parable; for all its protruding epic expanse, however, there are small ordinary scenes of living together here that join into a circle of allegorical representations. They find their center in a complex metaphor. The betting games of Russian roulette that the prisoners of war were compelled to play with three bullets in a revolver describe an experience of war in which the killing of the enemy includes and presumes self-destruction. The endless repetition by psychically shattered soldiers, who put their lives on the line in fallen Saigon like Roman gladiators, because they simply can no longer stop themselves, becomes a parable of a society in which the violent acts of war multiply infinitely in its innermost core. In this way, death becomes a mysterious image – neither *sacrifice* nor *victim* – that provides the background in front of which the last scene of the film, the helpless attempts by the mourning community to secure their living present, appears to us, the spectators, as an endlessly precarious attempt to continue living in the community of survivors.

A few years later, Oliver Stone's PLATOON struggles with the task of taking back the broken forms of staging the sacrifice, which had so far defined the Vietnam film, and of restituting an intact image of the sacrifice; an imposition that Brian De Palma's CASUALTIES OF WAR, in turn, seems to reject a few years later with a decisive "No!" And already even in the title: *Casualties* – which means the dead, the injured, and the wounded that are tallied up at the end of a war. It designates the lamentable number of cases of more or less randomly snuffed out lives, from which there can be gratuitously many in an open series. Much like the term 'victim,' it designates the passive agents damaged by an external event – the violence of war, an accident, or a crime. The title emphasizes the fundamental difference to the memorializing of the dead in earlier films, the difference to the heroic sacrifice of the soldier who gives up his physical life through his own actions. The victim has no framing in the narrative of collective commemoration that could form it into a heroic sacrifice as a community-generating symbol.

De Palma's film brings the historic constellation of Hollywood cinema precisely to a point when it has the soldier Max Eriksson (Michael J. Fox) waking up in a bus back home, years after the war, with the face of a young woman in front of him who, like millions of other Americans, is of Asian descent. For a moment – which the film stages as the unending duration of a nightmare – the horror of war becomes alive in the woman's gaze, the butchery, the torture, the rapes.[138] In place of a heroic sacrifice appears the melodramatic implementation of a passive, wordless suffering, which finds its corresponding narrative in the pathologies of the individual psyche.

If we start from the closing sequence of CASUALTIES OF WAR, it is no longer possible to imagine any Hollywood war film. The character of the American soldier seems literally to be exhausted. In fact, the war film only shows up again at the turn of the millennium, with those films that are the object of the opening chapter of this book and that allow, by turning back to the Second World War, a different historical vanishing line to become possible for a brief moment as the continuation of the old genre on the set of the Iraq War.

Celebrating war: JARHEAD

In Vietnam War films, military communitization itself is thematized as an archaic violence that destroys the civilian polity, its culture, its forms of living together. The staging of Wagner's Ride of the Valkyries as a helicopter attack on a Vietnamese village appears like an emblem of this destruction from within the internal forces of culture. The scene from APOCALYPSE NOW became so famous that we can use Wagner's music today as a metonymic reference to the film. Sam Mendes, for instance, uses that scene when he shows the recruits in JARHEAD who have just found out that they are being sent to the deserts of Iraq as they hoot it up in a movie theater, cheering on the helicopters in the background on the movie screen (see Figure 43). We see schoolchildren dressed in white with their teacher, we see the defenseless man in a jeep on the bridge, we see the monumental splendor of the helicopters rushing in thorugh the light-flooded sky, supported by the blustering music; we see the amazed faces of the US soldiers flying along,

---

[138] Cf. Grotkopp, *Filmische Poetiken der Schuld*, 251ff.

Figure 43: JARHEAD: the celebration of the lust for battle and the joy of film viewing.

who don't quite know what hit them – and once again the children, women, men, who are trying to flee the blustering roar of the machine gunning set to music. The recruits in the foreground acknowledge every hit, every woman, every child, every man that is gunned down with wild shouts of encouragement. They celebrate the attack by the helicopters as if they were the ecstatically excited audience at a rock concert. In fact, music in all its forms and media formats, from Wagner to rap, has taken on the job in the Vietnam films and then in the Iraq films that the athletic drill had occupied in the mobilization films of the Second World War.

The topic of JARHEAD is the first American war against Iraq, the deployment of an army numbering in the hundreds of thousands. Anthony Swofford's autobiographical report from 2003, on which Mendes's film is based, also uses the scene above to describe the war deployment as an orgiastic party:

> Then we send a few guys downtown to rent all of the war movies they can get their hands on. They also buy a hell of a lot of beer. For three days we sit in our rec room and drink all of

> the beer and watch all of those damn movies, and we yell *Semper fi* and we head-butt and beat the crap out of each other and we get off on the various visions of carnage and violence and deceit, the raping and killing and pillaging .... Yes, somehow the films convince us that these boys are sweet, even though we know we are much like these boys and that we are no longer sweet.[139]

The video party described here almost marks the opposing pole to the rage of the homecomer: an orgiastic celebration of the thirst for battle, in which young men transform into warriors who are no longer socially acceptable beings.

> There is talk that many Vietnam films are anti-war, that the message is war is inhumane and look what happens when you train young American men to fight and kill, they turn their fighting and killing everywhere, they ignore their targets and desecrate the entire country, shooting fully automatic, forgetting they were trained to aim. But actually, Vietnam War films are all pro-war, no matter what the supposed message, what Kubrick or Coppola or Stone intended .... [We were] excited by them, because the magic brutality of the films celebrates the terrible and despicable beauty of [our] fighting skills. Fight, rape, war, pillage, burn. Filmic images of death and carnage are pornography for the military man; with film you are stroking his cock, tickling his balls with the pink feather of history, getting him ready for his real First Fuck.[140]

In the film we see the hooting soldiers in their uninhibited excitement celebrating the Ride of the Valkyries from APOCALYPSE NOW as a lust that ultimately means the spectator's enjoyment of war movies. Even if spectators try to take a critical position to war, they are still participating in the enjoyment that we are shown in JARHEAD as the pleasure of watching film itself to the degree that they are giving the films a body, a physical reality in their sensibility.

The fact that the metaphors used to describe this pleasure refer to sex acts is no more arbitrary than the fact that Scorsese's taxi driver has failed as a political assassin and a lover – only achieves peak form when he puts himself into the state of a sentimental hero rescuing the defiled virtue of a woman child. What both examples have in common is that the violence of military communitization is linked to the functionalization of male sexuality. The sexualization of the lust for battle and the fury of the man on a rampage describe two sides of one and the same phantasm of war, which has defined the Hollywood war film since the seventies.

---

139 Anthony Swofford, *Jarhead: A Marine's Chronicle of the Gulf War and Other Battle*s, New York 2003, 5f.
140 Ibid., 6–7.

Roger Caillois describes this phantasm as the festivity of military communitization[141] in the celebration of war: "Without doubt, war is horror and catastrophe, the inundation of death, and the festival is consecrated to outbursts of joy and super-abundance of life." War and festival are thus to be conceived as complete opposites in every way. Nonetheless, they assume an analogous position in "their function in collective life," in "the image they imprint on the individual's mind."[142] Like the festivity, war designates the time of excess and of transgressing the rules of living together: "Each has its own discipline, but both see, nevertheless like monstrous and shapeless explosions against the monotonous routine of ordinary life"[143]; both festivity and war "inaugurate a period of vigorous socialization and share instruments, resources, and powers in common"[144], designating a period of dissolving individual activity. The rule of extravagance reigns; here, "reserves accumulated for months, and sometimes for years, are squandered,"[145] there, we allow for all the forms of the social wealth of annihilation.[146]

Such a festivity of lust for the anarchic desecration of all values deemed sacred, for the anarchic debauchery of violence, is staged in JARHEAD; it starts – we recognize the dramaturgical schema – with soldiers' training, cutting their hair, getting into uniform, in order to reach the first high point at the party in the cinema; in the desert metropolis, built out of US Army tents, it starts up again, without the soldiers ever having to move beyond the ritualized preparations for war. The celebration of war circles around in the ritual repetitions of prepared exercises, which do not become an emergency state any more than the constant use of lewd words, images, and gestures ever get beyond one or the other naked parties among drunk young men.

---

141 As a festivity of communitization, it is completely related to those festivities that Jan Assmann has described as practices of ritual memory by authoritarian forms of communitization.
142 Caillois, *Man and the Sacred*, 165.
143 Ibid., 167. Cf. also: "The only hindrance lies in how it is commonly conceived, for despite the rigors of military arts and ceremonial, war and the festival remain images of disorder and confusion. [...] Acts hitherto prohibited and deemed abominable now carry glory and prestige." Ibid., 167.
144 Ibid., 166.
145 Ibid., 169. Like in the festivity, war is associated in its destruction with forces of renewal. Its devastations are celebrated, similar to ritual orgies, as the source of the rejuvenation of civilization. "Everything is created by war, and peace causes everything to perish through engulfment and erosion" (ibid., 171).
146 Ibid., 177. Cf. also: "War, no less than the festival, seems like the time of the sacred, the period of the divine epiphany. It introduces man to an intoxicating world in which the presence of death makes him shiver and confers a superior value upon his various actions." (ibid., 173).

Mendes stages the idleness of waiting, which ends in the early celebration by borrowing the staging principle for the entire film from the recruits' celebration of APOCALYPSE NOW in the movie theater. It is as if the soldiers were playing through the whole repertoire of past war films scene for scene, without ever entering into the action that they are emulating. They are shipped into the giant camp in the Saudi desert, but they remain spectators to the actions that they themselves only imitate; just as the hordes in the movie seats seek to incite the battle action on screen through their hooting gestures. The soldiers' march into the desert is like a great open air festival in which the bands never appear, while the waiting audience plays air guitar.

The soldiers' actions remain restricted to the circle of simulating, preparatory, training exercises, which repeat the initiation into the military community over and over again. The actions are restagings of film scenes that always already repeat even earlier film scenes in which the initiation into the military community is celebrated. Testing out the combat power of the military community, relentlessly celebrating itself, is absent.[147] Like a check list in which the uneventful days are marked off, the off-screen voice of the first-person narrator breaks down the monotonous elapsing of time in the repeated comment, "masturbation ... masturbation ... further masturbation."

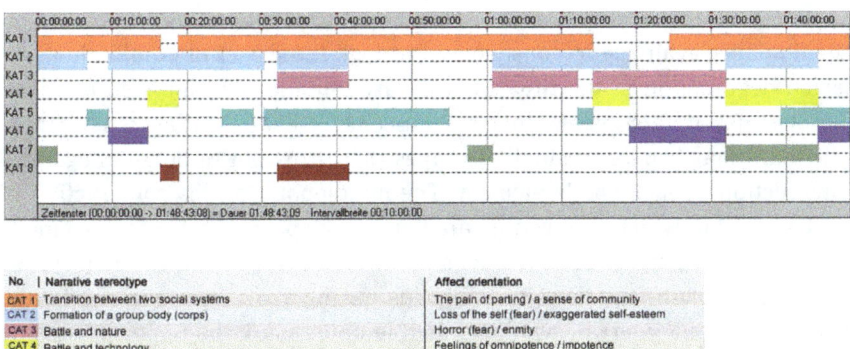

Figure 44: Diagram showing the temporal arrangement of pathos scenes in JARHEAD (Sam Mendes, USA 2005).

---

147 In his analysis of WINDTALKERS, Michael Wedel has attempted to understand this communal experience using terms from Nancy. He shows the degree to which the war film focuses on the experience of community. Cf. Wedel, "Körper, Tod und Technik," 92ff.

Military communitization: FULL METAL JACKET

The film to which JARHEAD relates like to a palimpsest is FULL METAL JACKET from 1987. Stanley Kubrick's film returns the poetics of war films back to the staging of military communitization in order to expose its archaic core. FULL METAL JACKET is conceived as a diptych. The first part depicts the steps of training in a Marine Corps camp, from the first encounter with the trainer to his violent death at the hands of a soldier running amok. The second part uses highly artificial sets to build up an allegorical landscape of war, where the American soldiers lose themselves, like in a labyrinth, in order finally to be killed, one after the other, by a concealed sharpshooter.

The difference between the drill instructors welcoming speech and the encouraging words with which the soldiers in GUNG HO! are received could not be greater:

> **Drill Instructor Hartman:** If you ladies leave my island, if you survive recruit training ... you will be a weapon, you will be a minister of death, praying for war. But until that day you are pukes! You're the lowest form of life on Earth. You are not even human fucking beings! You are nothing but unorganized grabasstic pieces of amphibian shit! ... My orders are to weed out all non-hackers who do not pack the gear to serve in my beloved Corps! Do you maggots understand that![148]

The film once again meticulously plays through the scenes of humiliation and sexual degradation in the rituals of military initiation. In doing so it makes thorough use of stereotypes – that is, film scenes re-enacting film scenes – from which an image space gradually emerges that turns out to be an allegorical construction in each single element. The middlepoint of this construction is the barracks in which the recruits are housed: a space of extremely symmetrical reflections, synchronous actions, and serial arrangements. The recruits' dormitory contains two rows of bunkbeds, facing apart from one another at exactly the same interval, two large double doors mark the opposite ends of the room; one leads to the toilets, in which two rows of lavatory sinks stand opposite one another. And when the recruits perform their cleaning duties in snow-white underwear, this also happens in precise duality and symmetrical doubling. The cleaning couple in the dormitory finds its synchronous counterpart in the washroom. Here as there, the floors get washed, on which dirt is never seen.

---

[148] Stanley Kubrick, et al., *Full Metal Jacket. The screenplay*, New York 1987. Scene "Antrittsappell [*forming up*]" (00:01:29:01–00:07:12:01).

4.5 The Irresolvable Conflict — 319

In place of the "duality of man"[149] – which Joker (Matthew Modine) talks about when he is asked about the contradiction between the peace sign and the martial slogans that adorn his helmet – in place of the ambivalence and dualism of people, comes the symmetrical multiplication of the masculine: Hartmann, "the hard man," the name of the trainer; on the other side the long row of exercising boys.

The world of complete symmetry, geometrical order, and immaculate cleanliness stands in contrast to "the world of shit" in the second part of the film. In the training camp there are lawns, asphalt, tiled bathrooms, artfully constructed barriers, and exclusively men; in Vietnam there is the character of unorderly forms: advertising panels, big city bustle, thieves – and above all women.[150]

The two Marines in a street café in Saigon let themselves be messed around with by the first prostitute that comes along; while they attempt to make a deal with her, their camera equipment gets stolen. Nancy Sinatra's famous song "These boots are made for walkin'" is laid over the scene like a speech bubble on the mouth of the character in an allegorical painting:

> You keep playing where you shouldn't be playing
> And you keep thinking that you'll never get burnt (HAH)
> Well, I've just found me a brand new box of matches (YEAH)
> And what he knows you ain't had time to learn
> These boots are made for walkin', and that's just what they'll do
> One of these days these boots are gonna walk all over you

"Are you ready, boots? Start walkin'!": We subsequently see the war itself as an effort, as persistent as it is futile, to rebuild the landscape according to the order of clear symmetrical block constructions (see Figure 45).

The war is finally reduced to the impact of lethal bullets from an invisible sharpshooter. When the soldiers finally get him in his hiding-place, they find themselves face to face with a woman: alone, by herself, she shot down man after man on her own account. Now she lies wounded and unarmed on the ground in front of the soldiers, placidly awaiting her death (see Figure 46).

Positioned in the allegorical image space, all action, all movement becomes part of the transformation that is manifest in the metamorphosis of young men

---

[149] "I think I was trying to suggest something about the duality of man, sir." Scene "The duality of man" (01:00:29:18–01:02:59:01).
[150] The first image of the war shows a street; a prostitute comes into the foreground of the image, crosses the street and approaches two GIs. Scene "These Boots" (00:43:34:20–00:45:48:00).

Figure 45: Symmetry and chaos (FULL METAL JACKET).

Figure 46: The female sniper.

as a driving force of the whole. It is completed in the first part of the film as a sequence of ritualized actions, orchestrated by gestures and songs, in which the bellowing drill instructor behaves like a conductor trying to assemble a multi-voiced symphony orchestra into a single body of sound. Just so, as we can see in the running exercises, when the tempo and the rhythm of completely synchronized courses of movement are given by the call-and-response singing that devours all the obstinate impulses of individual bodies.

The immortal body: the corps

Within the allegorical construction of FULL METAL JACKET even the singing, as much as we are familiar with it as a movie stereotype, becomes legible as a practice in the structure of desires of a new body, that of the "Marine Corps":

> Left right left right left right left
> I love working for Uncle Sam (2x)
> Lets me know just who I am (2x)
> Lets me know just who I am (2x)
> 1 2 3 4 United States Marine Corps (2x)
> 1 2 3 4 I love the Marine Corps (2x)
> My Corps your Corps Our Corps Marine Corps
> Mmm good
>
> [...]
>
> I don't want no teenage queen (2x)
> I just want my M14 (2x)
> If I die in the combat zone (2x)
> Box me up and ship me home (2x)
> Pin my medals on my chest (2x)
> Tell my Mom I done my best (2x)
>
> [...]151

Kubrick's film describes how the soldier is born from the ritualized violence of the drill; a process that causes the body born of women to disappear in order for the geometry of the military body to appear.

The filth that threatens the symmetrical order of the corps is the very physical reality of the recruits. It is personified in the character of Private Pyle (Vincent D'Onofrio). He is "the maggot," fat, soft, always hungry, moronic; he cannot climb; he cannot jump; he does not even know right from left. He embodies the baby, the imbecilic desire of a hungry maggot which everybody else perceives as the repulsive ugliness of their own desires that they violently try to shake off. In the punishment ritual – at night in the dormitory all the recruits line up to beat Private Pyle with a piece of soap wrapped up in a towel – every stroke concerns their own neediness, which is literally expelled in their comrade's disgusting voracity.

At the end of training, even the ever-hungry child, which had such trouble leaving the world of the mother, is "definitely born again": as an exemplary

---

151 Scene "Pvt. Pyles Verstoß [*Pvt. Pyle's offense*]" (00:21:54:07–00:26:58:01) and "Pvt. Pyles Entwicklung [*Pvt. Pyle's development*]" (00:29:00:06–00:36:10:00).

Marine.¹⁵² Still, Private Pyle exhibits a malfunction. He goes berserk and kills first the officer, then himself: a bloodbath in cold white-blue, "unorganized grabasstic pieces of amphibian shit" on the sparkling clean toilet, an early birth, a premature explosion of the pent-up violence.

"The military is a specific type of illusion machine that essentially produces the construct of masculinity,"¹⁵³ writes Mario Erdheim. The means – we can add in view of the Hollywood war film – the illusion of melding with an invulnerable, immortal body, the military corps. The corps proposes a topographical order of bodies, actions, and relations in which contingent social relationships of the sexualized, vulnerable, and mortal body are harnessed in a network of strictly hierarchized symbolic significance.¹⁵⁴ Its idealized "we" is therefore grounded in the discrimination of all the attributes that are attributed to the organic body, the child, the woman, the foreign ethnicity.¹⁵⁵

FULL METAL JACKET describes ritualized communitization as an alchemistic process in which the panic of loss of the self combines with the desire for melding, and humiliating self-denial combines with the we-feeling into an affect that finds its resolution in the killing spree. In the ritual transition from ordinary individual existence to its effacement in the unity of the military corps, from a civilian being-in-society to a society in a state of exception, from a body of sexual desires to a functional part within the armed corps, FULL METAL JACKET stages the calculation of transforming sexual desire into the lust for violence.

The explosive state of going berserk, ready to burn out in rage at any moment, turns the soldiers, "our boys," into warriors, ready to kill. They become bombs in

---

152 Hartman (R. Lee Ermey), amazed at the recruits' transformation, says: "Private Pyle, you are definitely born again hard!" "Pvt. Pyles Entwicklung [*Pvt. Pyle's development*]" (00:29:00:06–00:36:10:00).
153 Mario Erdheim, "Heiße Gesellschaften, kaltes Militär," in his: *Psychoanalyse und Unbewußtheit in der Kultur*, Frankfurt am Main 1988, 311–344, here 336. In the drill and in the barracks, 'ritual traits of initiating and male bonding could almost be placed on ice, held in the center of modern society;' cf. ibid., 337ff.
154 "In the traditional cultures, enclosed in a fixed cosmos of values, initiation leads to a reorganization of omnipotence. On the psychic level, this is above all because the omnipotence (of the childhood self-image) of the individual is transferred to the group, the clan, or the tribe. The sphere that absorbs and preserves this omnipotence is, as a rule, the sacred." Mario Erdheim, "Ritual und Reflexion," in *Rituale heute: Theorien – Kontroversen – Entwürfe*, eds. Corina Caduff and Joanna Pfaff-Czarnecka, Berlin 1999, 165–178, here 172.
155 When the practice of initiation is culturally as widespread as it is uniform, then this is also because the state that it seeks to secure is highly precarious and endangered. Indeed, participating in a transcendental body signifies a highly illusionary form of identity formation. Cf. Ulrike Brunotte, "Krieg und Kino: No Mail Days Are Sad Days," in *Frauen und Film* 61, 2000, 5–21.

the flesh, tuned to the brief moment of an eruptive outbreak of violence, in which what had been humiliated and obliterated in the procedure of militarizing the body is once again created in the intoxicating feeling of power: a subjective sense of self-worth. THE THIN RED LINE shows the moment of ecstasy associated with the first successful, deadly shot; JARHEAD shows the frustration when this shot is not taken. The rage of the warrior is the product of a calculated disregard for his dignity as an individual; of course, this dignity can be understood as "male honor" exactly to the degree that the individual's personality, his subjectivity, can be measured on his masculinity.

In the endlessly repeated exercises of subjugating the individual body under the higher will of the corps, bodies emerge that obliterate themselves in the act of violence that they carry out. "Marines die – that's what we're here for!" – the trainer's speech, with which he sends his charges into war, formulates the logic of this making in straight-forward clarity.

> Today you people are no longer maggots. Today you are Marines. You're part of a brotherhood. From now on, until the day you die, wherever you are, every Marine is your brother.
>
> Most of you will go to Vietnam. Some of you will not come back. But always remember this: Marines die – that's what we're here for. But the Marine Corps lives forever – and that means you live forever.[156]

The main character, Joker, lives up to his name by being able to insert himself into any environment without losing his peculiar underdetermination as a man of all possible qualities. He carries the peace sign with the same equanimity as the martial "Born to Kill" on his helmet; he traverses the horror of war while still clinging to everything that is devalued and detested in the military ritual of communitization: the invalidity of individual existence and the all too banal sexual desires and fantasies; belonging to the press corps, he always remains associated with the state of the civilian; he always remains close to the hungry, soft, fat maggot that even he, especially he, recognizes in its weakness: infinitely vulnerable because it is infinitely in need of love. The last words in FULL METAL JACKET, with which the obscene sayings of the drill instructor are reversed into their opposite, belong to him, this most unheroic of all heroes:

> My thoughts drift back to erect nipple wet dreams
> about Mary Jane Rottencrotch
> and the Great Homecoming Fuck Fantasy.

---

156 Scene "Graduation" (00:36:10:00–00:38:20:18).

> *I am so happy that I am alive, in one piece and short.*
> *I'm in a world of shit ... yes. But I am alive.*
> *And I am not afraid.*[157]

The sentences identify Joker as the antagonist of all those soldiers who, like the protagonist in PLATOON, pass through the atrocity of war in order to come back home as ethically mature men. No contradiction could be greater than that between Joker's last words and the ethos of the first-person narrator who announces at the end of PLATOON:

> As I am sure Elias will be fighting with Barnes for what Rhah called possession of my soul ... There are times since I have felt like the child born of those two fathers ... but be that as it may, those of us who did make it have an obligation to build again, to teach to others what we know and to try with what's left of our lives to find a goodness and meaning to this life.[158]

The one reclaims the meaning of life, which was gambled away in the death of the others (those that did not manage); the other is happy to have survived. He takes his experience home with him, which cannot be taught, because it does not reach beyond the "But I am alive." We might speak of an experience that follows from the disenchantment of those who have even survived the community itself. The philosopher Nancy has described this experience with the following words:

> Generations of citizens and militants, of workers and servants of the States have imagined their death reabsorbed or sublated in a community, yet to come, that would attain immanence. But by now we have nothing more than the bitter consciousness of the increasing remoteness of such a community, be it the people, the nation, or the society of producers. However, this consciousness, like that of the "loss" of community, is superficial. In truth, death is not sublated. The communion to come does not grow distant, it is not deferred: it was never to come; it would be incapable of coming about or forming a future. What forms a future, and consequently what truly comes about, is always the singular death.[159]

Viewed in this way, Joker's last words, as well – like De Palma's CASUALTIES OF WAR – could have meant the end of the Hollywood war film.

---

[157] Scene "Von Menschen und Mäusen [*of mice and men*]" (01:41:52:01–01:48:15:21).
[158] Scene "Abflug [*takeoff*]" (01:45:19:18–01:50:32:00).
[159] Jean-Luc Nancy, *The Inoperative Community*, Minneapolis 1991, 13; Cited in: Anja Streiter: "Das 'Kino der Körper' und die Frage der Gemeinschaft. Autorenkino und Filmschauspiel," in *Nach dem Film* 5 [Ausgabe "Werkstatt Filmwissenschaft"], 2004, http://www.nachdemfilm.de/content/das-kino-der-k%C3%B6rper-und-die-frage-der-gemeinschaft, (November 30, 2016).

The heroic epic: PATTON

At the culminating point of the crisis in the wake of the Vietnam War, western moviegoers, who had gone to the movies in the early seventies with great esteem for the art of film rarely seen before, were confronted with a general from the Second World War who seemed to have fallen completely out of time. PATTON by Franklin J. Schaffner from 1970 begins with a speech by its protagonist that precedes the film like a prologue. After only a few sentences it is clear that the spectator should not expect any biopic in the typical sense, no hero's tale about the general who was as famous as he was politically dubious. His bawdy sentences and obscene metaphors unmask similar speeches given by commanding officers to their men, repeated hundreds of times in the history of the Hollywood war film, the core statements of military life, stripped of all their trivializing rhetoric. The speech, which is meant to rile up the will to fight and to commit the soldiers to the unity of the troop, becomes a blatant appeal to the lust to kill, which is triumphantly hurled at a listening audience who believes they can withdraw into a world of the good, the beautiful, and the true. The cynical manner of the speech speaks openly of the conviction of stating a truth that goes much deeper than the listeners' political opinions and positions. Walking back and forth in front of a giant American flag like a famous actor savoring his effect on the audience, Patton (George C. Scott) speaks directly into the movie theater, his gaze fixed squarely at the camera, aimed at the spectator. The flag in the background becomes a velvet curtain in front of which a master of ceremonies appears who has an important announcement to make before the film begins. Looking down from above, from the height of the screen in old movie theaters from the early seventies, the coarse words come down to the spectators, vilifying everything that they have brought with them about the ideals of a democratic society – above all the idea that the pursuit of happiness by the individual, even the individual life at all, could have any particular value.

Patton does not confront his spectators as a heroic warrior from the Second World War, but as a ghost that covers the audience's belief in liberal democracy with the scorn of one calling on his millennia-long experience, which always keeps the last word for him, the warrior. He is the personified shape of the "haunting of history,"[160] only that his "unfinished business" reaches much further back than the history of the United States. He is the eternally returning war hero to whom

---

[160] Cf. the literature listed in footnote 73 (part IV).

the historical course of time of the west, of the occident (or however else we might address a cultural history in sweeping terms) gets retracted to a sequence of great wars and battles (see Figure 47).

Figure 47: PATTON.

The film begins with a battlefield. We see a vulture, a long panning shot; the camera's gaze stretches over a bare, deserted landscape: abandoned buildings, decaying ruins between which goats are moving, and masked figures. Then we see slaughtered soldiers between shot-up military equipment, burnt-out tanks, shot down airplanes, scattered in the barren landscape. Through this wasteland, like shortly before among the ruins, we see children moving, masked men and women. They are plundering the corpses, quickly stealing their helmets, trousers, jewelry, leaving them naked among the wreckage, abandoning them to the vultures to feed on. The music turns the panning shot into the beginnings of an overture in which the musical leitmotifs are played out, while for the spectator the desert landscape with herds of goats and shepherds becomes an iconographic formula for the cultures of the Berber populations in the Maghreb.

Over the duration of the panning shot, the landscape becomes the chronotope of an archaic culture that allows us to perceive the battlefield, the soldiers' corpses between the bombed-out military equipment, as if all this were being projected into the space of another time. At any rate, we get this impression in retrospect when we see Patton a few minutes later being driven in a jeep to the battlefield on the next day, accompanied by another officer, to inspect the "heavy losses" of people and weapons. Suddenly he insists on changing course:

> Patton: Hold it. Turn right, here.
> Driver: Sir, the battlefield is straight ahead.
> Patton: Please don't argue with me, sergeant, I can smell a battlefield.
> Bradley: He was out here just yesterday, George.
> Patton: It's over there. Turn right, damn it.

Patton is perceiving a battlefield from a completely different war than the one in which he and his companions find themselves when he, caught up in excitement, follows his own nose and not his companions' knowledge of the place. Only slight aside from the site of the current carnage are the ruins of ancient Carthage. He devoutly reflects on the great battle in which Carthage fell; a plane stretches out before him into infinity.

> It was here. The battlefield was here.

> The Carthaginians defending the city were attacked by three Roman legions. The Carthaginians were proud and brave, but they couldn't hold. They were massacred. Arab women stripped them of their tunics and their swords and lances. The soldiers lay naked in the sun. 2000 years ago ...

> I was here.

With these last words, we once again hear the trumpet echo that had started the panning shot, making the following sentences sound like an echo of an old heroic song:

> You don't believe me, do you, Brad? You know what the poet said:

> Through the travail of ages
> Midst the pomp and toils of war
> Have I fought and strove and perished
> Countless times upon the star
> As if through a glass and darkly
> The age-old strife I see
> Where I fought in many guises
> Many names
> But always me.

> You know who the poet was?

When Bradley shakes his head, Patton answers: "Me."[161]

The general indulges here in a melancholy for which Alexander the Great is exemplary in western history, who is said to have wept at the grave of Achilles because there was no more Homer to sing of his crusades.[162]

While Patton seeks to bring the hall of fame of heroic ages into the present in the ruins of Carthage, the spectators tarry in their feelings and thoughts with the images of the battlefield that showed the corpses in ghastly actuality, robbed of their clothing – exactly as Patton describes the historical scene: 'They were massacred. Arab women stripped them of their tunics and their swords and lances.' The war that Patton is speaking about has lasted for millennia; it is an eternal war that is not any means to a political end, but an art that turns generals into heroes who poets sing about. If we follow Patton's words, the goal of history is fulfilled in war. It is the time in which the heroes return.

As ancient as the character of Patton and his behavior might seem, the type that enters into Hollywood cinema with him is completely contemporary as a type in genre cinema in the sense of Cavell. It finds its sharply outlined counterpart in Marlon Brando's Colonel Kurtz from APOCALYPSE NOW.[163] The highly decorated officer in the American army, who has become a deserter due to philosophical considerations, orders ritual butchery that serves no other purpose that to turn his field camp in the depths of the jungle into a stage for the return of the mythical war hero by decorating it with corpses.

Without this mythical superelevation, Patton as a type is a singular polemical provocation. He lays bare the establishment of State and military by cynically referring to the values of the civil rights and anti-Vietnam movements that do indeed critically confront this State. He counters the technocratic reflex with which the officers who are first to reach the scene painstakingly take the corpses left to the vultures as *casualties*, contrary to the art of the commander, which grants the dead the honor of being addressed as soldiers that he was prepared to sacrifice in order to set the return of the war hero in place. The corpses there are nothing more than nameless losses in the balance of bureaucratic warfare; here they are the rank and file in the hero's triumphant procession, which he leads as if he were on a transmigration through the times of war, from century to century. With all the means of art – those of the poet, those of the orator, and not least

---

161 On these sentences, cf. the scene "Schlachtenruhm [*battle glory*]" (00:26:19:07–00:29:09:15).
162 Cf. Aleida Assmann, *Erinnerungsräume: Formen und Wandlungen des kulturellen Gedächtnisses*, Munich 2010, 40f.
163 Nick Nolte and John Travolta in THE THIN RED LINE by Terrence Malick are further variations of this type.

those of the director of monumental battle paintings – Patton struggles against the post-heroic age; as if he wanted to call to his audience that it had to brace itself for "heavy casualties" because it despised the heroic sacrifice.

In his ruthless attacks and nitpicking obstructions against all attempts to restrict and end war, we finally distinguish a military event that the Hollywood war film generally does not thematize, or only in metaphorical cover – for instance in the napalm war in APOCALYPSE NOW. In the vanishing line of the crusade dreamt up by Patton, on towards the east, against the Russians, ever onward by land to the other side of the Pacific, what happened on August 6 and 10, 1945, comes clearly into view: the casting of atomic bombs on Hiroshima and Nagasaki.

The present of military communities

"Who put us in the uniform? Why are we Americans on the march?" – you can hardly find a Hollywood war film that negates the argument with which Capra justifies the Americans' war from the enmity of liberal democracy to the military communitization of fascist states as radically as PATTON does. From the viewpoint of the Hollywood war film, there is no way back to the clear antagonism in which the world of freedom confronts the world of slaves; there is no way back to a political community to which the militarization of society appears as an alien, but necessary evil, which freely allows itself to be restricted to the temporary emergency state of defending freedom.

That the film character of the versifying commander very much concerns the political reality of the military, which draws its legitimacy from the sentinel of liberal democracy, can also be seen in another American general in the speech, who also knew a lot about the art of poetry. We can read his speech on the internet, and even order the poster that goes along with it. It illustrates the farewell speech that General Douglas MacArthur gave to the officer cadets at the Military Academy in Westpoint in 1962 on the occasion of being awarded the Sylvanus Thayer Medal, the highest award granted by the United States Military Academy. The disaster of the Korean War was not even a decade behind, that of the Vietnam War was just getting started.

If we read the speech, it becomes clear that the image of the devoutly listening cadets that are haunted by the dead soldiers of all wars illustrates a process of remembering that MacArthur presents metaphorically:

> And what sort of soldiers are those you are to lead? Are they reliable? Are they brave? Are they capable of victory?

Figure 48: "... The Long Gray Line has never failed us. Were you to do so, a million ghosts in olive drab, in brown khaki, in blue and gray, would rise from their white crosses thundering those magic words, 'Duty, Honor, Country!'... "Paul Steucke, "Duty-Honor-Country".

> Their story is known to all of you. It is the story of the American man-at-arms. My estimate of him was formed on the battlefield many, many years ago, and has never changed. I regarded him then, as I regard him now, as one of the world's noblest figures; not only as one of the finest military characters, but also as one of the most stainless.
>
> His name and fame are the birthright of every American citizen. In his youth and strength, his love and loyalty, he gave all that mortality can give. He needs no eulogy from me, or from any other man. He has written his own history and written it in red on his enemy's breast.
>
> But when I think of his patience in adversity, of his courage under fire, and of his modesty in victory, I am filled with an emotion of admiration I cannot put into words. He belongs to history as furnishing one of the greatest examples of successful patriotism. He belongs to posterity as the instructor of future generations in the principles of liberty and freedom. He belongs to the present, to us, by his virtues and by his achievements.
>
> [...] In memory's eye I could see those staggering columns of the First World War, bending under soggy packs on many a weary march, from dripping dusk to drizzling dawn, slogging ankle deep through the mire of shell-pocked roads: to form grimly for the attack, blue-lipped, covered with sludge and mud, chilled by the wind and rain, driving home to their objective, and, for many, to the judgment seat of God. I do not know the dignity of their birth, but I do know the glory of their death. They died, unquestioning, uncomplaining, with faith in their hearts, and on their lips the hope that we would go on to victory. Always for them: Duty, honor, country. Always their blood, and sweat, and tears, as we sought the way and the light and the truth.[164]

---

[164] MacArthur, *U.S. Military Academy*, 198.

The speech plainly shows an ethos of the military community that took shape as a type in genre cinema in the figure of Patton. But it has an utterly comedic effect when the speaker's metaphors successively allow for a scene to emerge that corresponds fairly precisely to a ritual of memory, in which – if we follow Assmann – the ancient Egyptians had already sought to bridge the gap that, as the experience of death, destroys the continuity of power and domination. In the farewell party for the general, in the gala uniforms, the conferring of medals, the devout listening, and the aged commander himself, who, quite a poet, sings of past battles, the elements of a festive ceremonial become palpable: a ceremonial that seeks to seal off the eternity of the community of soldiers against the experience of contingency that defines the ordinary lives of ordinary people. By singing the anthem to fallen soldiers, it allows the past wars to be brought to mind in the present as the one, eternal war. Step by step, it allows the dual temporality of a memory of the military community to emerge, which is opposed to the contingent history of political communities:

> ... The long gray line has never failed us. Were you to do so, a million ghosts in olive drab, in brown khaki, in blue and gray, would rise from their white crosses thundering those magic words, Duty, honor, country.[165]

In the ritual stagings of dual temporality – this goes for the celebration that Leni Riefenstahl stages in TAG DER FREIHEIT, as much as it does for Patton's art of poetry and MacArthur's speech – the death of the individual becomes the elixir of life for the military community. But the soldier's duty is thus claimed as an ontological mode of its own, which is solely due to the military victory that is always to be gained anew, and not to the mandate of democratic society. Ritualized memory itself is the decisive motif for a communitization that is completed within a liberal democratic polity without itself being defined by this democracy. Think back once again to the dead soldier in DECEMBER 7TH, who speaks at the Arlington Cemetery in a similar way – his gaze focused directly into the camera – to how Patton addresses the film spectators. We can no longer shake the ghosts of the military communitization once they have been called up in the first place.

The irreconcilable opposition between the authoritarian forms of wartime communitization and the ideal of a political community has found a highly precarious solution in the territorialization inside democratic society. The consequences of this 'solution' are the topic of the Hollywood war films that deal with the Iraq War after 2006.

---

165 Ibid.

Genre and Sense of Commonality: An Epilogue

The Pixelated Revolution

Documenta 13 (2012) included a cycle of works by Rabih Mroué. The object: videos downloaded from the internet, all recorded with simple mobile phone cameras. The images seem to be familiar from television: houses, streets, courtyards somewhere in Syria, or Libya, or Iran. They reproduce the movement of the person who shot the videos – until a gunman comes into the field of view. As soon as the gunman notices that he is being filmed, he shoots at the person holding the telephone; he shoots, as it were, into the camera's gaze. The image shakes, there are rattling noises, darkness.

In a black box at the end of the exhibition space we see Rabih Mroué himself: the video recording of a lecture performance. He is analyzing these videos, using all the rules of film theory; he plays them in slow motion, breaks them down frame by frame, inspects the dramaturgy of the sequence. At the same time, he develops basic theoretical questions: How dangerous these video images must be, if people are shot on sight when they are discovered filming them! What is the status of these images, whose producers were shot during production? Were they in fact killed? When, at what moment in the video, do we see their death? And this witnessing eye, disseminated worldwide in the internet as seeing and hearing, has it not survived this death, released from the body that had been shot?

One leaves the screening room, moving back, passing once again through the installation. Only now does it become clear what all of this has to do with the things presented there.

This is meant to be taken literally. On the longer wall, there are large posters; they show the pixilated faces of the gunmen, as if they were responding to what you felt when the lecture was taking apart the internet videos. You wanted to know more about these monstrous events, you wanted to see the perpetrator's face, the victim behind the camera, you wanted to get closer, you wanted bigger images. Well, here they are, hanging there, absurd abstract enlargements, in which all contour is lost.

And on the opposite wall is the reverse shot: the video image, washed in red; in razor-sharp silhouette you see an actor positioned as in a duel, only that instead of a Colt he is holding a mobile phone camera. He is slumped into himself, as if hit by the bullet, then stands upright again, only to slump again, and again, and again ... Finally, at the front entrance is the counter with the handy little booklets: series of images printed out on paper that work like a flip-book. The soundtrack can be turned on by pressing a button. You can reconstruct the clip – almost like crafting it yourself. And you listen to the sounds like a sound engineer, trying to get the recording to match the sound in a meaningful way, to make it fit to the moving image. Then there is a super8 film that you can start up by hand: razor-sharp images, which can be moved backwards and forwards on the editing table: zooming in on the face of the perpetrator, quite close ... (see Figure 49)

Visitors find themselves in a film analysis workshop, groping their way through the perceptual possibilities given in the space. They create a film image for themselves based on the audiovisual data. This image alters the legibility of the data base. It calls the representational structure of the video images themselves into question. Indeed, it is not at all about imagining a victim, fatally shot in the off space of the video camera. Instead, a gaze becomes established in the audience itself that witnesses and that pronounces judgment (see Figure 49).

Figure 49: Rabih Mroué's *The Pixelated Revolution*.

The film image developed as we make our way through the installation at *documenta* stands in stark opposition to the images of victims that have been circulating – since the occupation of Iraq by western armed forces – among users of such internet platforms as YouTube. The clips there have provided television news reports and talk shows with images of the victims of unrest in Iran following the last presidential election, as well as of the violent acts in the last Iraq War or in the contemporary civil wars in the Arab world. They have long been the object of broad debates about the function of these media in the new civil wars and revolutions. But these flickering, blurry video images have also already become the aesthetic signature of most recent Hollywood war films. These films reproduce the conventional patterns of the genre only to a very limited degree. Rather, they focus much more on the ordinary, everyday usage of media images of war – the private as well as the public, the political-strategic as well as the personal-sentimental. The films thematize the various uses of audiovisual media, and they show how new media-technological configurations alter the way war appears, how they change the interaction of things and people. As a result, they produce a new visuality of a reality of experience that is changing in terms of media: This is the experience of the historical.

But what does it mean to transform the audiovisual material of contemporary war events into the images of genre cinema that we watch at home as a DVD or an internet video or as a film projected in the cinema?

THE WAR TAPES

The film THE WAR TAPES (USA 2006) is based on video images that are quite similar to those analyzed by Mroué.[1] All of the film material comes from American soldiers who recorded it during their military deployment in the region around Baghdad and Fallujah. The soldiers could volunteer for a project in which they were required to keep audiovisual logbooks during the deployment. A total of 21 soldiers took part. They were provided with hand-held mini-DV cameras. During combat operations they sometimes wore them mounted on their helmets or their gun barrels. Five of the soldiers filmed over the entire year of their deployment,

---

[1] I am referring in the following to an analysis carried out by Cilli Pogodda. Cf.: Cilli Pogodda and Danny Gronmaier, "The War Tapes and the Poetics of Affect of the Hollywood War Film Genre," in *Frames Cinema Journal* (7), June 2015. Online at: http://framescinemajournal.com/article/the-war-tapes-and-the-poetics-of-affect-of-the-hollywood-war-film-genre/ (last viewed on December 8, 2016).

and of these, three were chosen whose video diaries became the basic material of the documentary film. This footage was combined with scenes from the home front, in which the everyday life of the soldiers' families was documented and presented by professional film teams. Both of these were mixed with video chats between the soldiers and their wives and children. The arrangement of videotapes and home stories follows a strictly symmetrical ordering of military routine, combat operations, and home front. Only at a single moment is this symmetry broken: A girl is run over by a patrol convoy (see Figure 50).

Figure 50: THE WAR TAPES: soldiers' camcorder recordings.

But the presence of horror in this film – like in every genre film – is a completely fictional presence. Only that the fiction of THE WAR TAPES draws its aesthetic appeal from an operation of emphatic authentication. But what would it be if we were not reassured: This moment, here and now, is the moment of horror, which was utterly real there at that place at that point in time? How would it be if we did not know that these images were candid, prepared by the soldiers in a combat mission? If we were not told from the beginning that we are seeing a girl that fell victim to the mission of just these soldiers? What if we were not aware at every moment: This is the moment in which the morally reprehensible effect of war, the collateral damage, is disclosed? Undoubtedly, there is a temporality suggested by the aspect ratio, which seeks to link back to the witnessing quality of the photographic document: the presence of the man who, in service of his army, took part in the death of this girl lying on this very street – and who used his camcorder as agreed.

Viewing THE WAR TAPES as a whole, the dramaturgical arrangements of alternating video recordings from various perspectives seem like indirect subjective monologues. They successively allow for the three filming soldiers to appear as protagonists of a film employing characters that completely correspond to the typical personnel of the war film genre (see Figure 51). Framed by this dramaturgical arrangement, the effect of this moment of witnessing horror is not simply dislodged in a peculiar way. We can indeed share the experience of this horror, we can literally feel it along with the soldiers, as if it were part of our world – and yet the horror occurs in a segment of space/time that is utterly separate from our own, and to which we have no access.

But how would it be if we were not told: These video images originate from the area of Baghdad and the region around Fallujah; they were recorded by three soldiers in the Army National Guard (Stephen Pink, Mike Moriarty and Zack Bazzi,

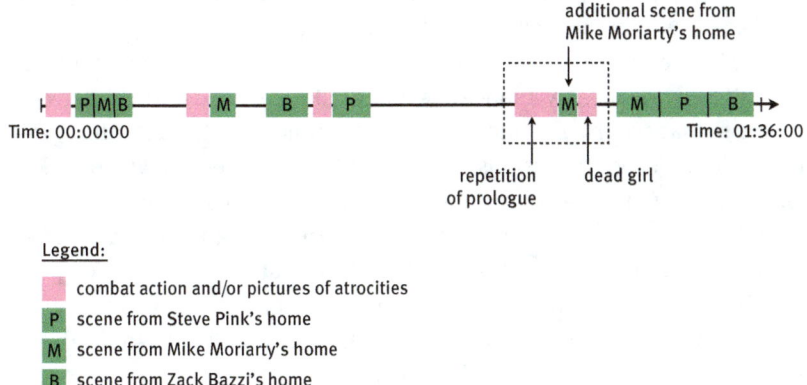

Figure 51: Diagram showing the dramaturgical structure of THE WAR TAPES (Deborah Scranton, USA 2006), created by Cilli Pogodda.

Charlie Company, 3rd of the 172nd Infantry) while stationed in Camp Anaconda, which lies about 110 kilometers north of Baghdad in the Sunni Triangle? The answer to this question is almost banal. We would no longer see anything but the flow of audiovisual signals. We would not really be able to distinguish the footage in THE WAR TAPES from those fictional films, for example from all the nocturnal video footage in REDACTED.

REDACTED

Accordingly, Brian De Palma's 2007 film expressly begins with the notice that all the characters and their actions are purely invented, although they are based on events that occurred in Samarra (a city in Iraq, north of Baghdad). This somewhat old-fashioned notice is necessary due to the aesthetic process chosen by the film. *Redacted* – edited or reworked; on the one hand, the title is a euphemistic synonym for television censorship and the politics of embedded journalism. On the other, it indicates the aesthetic process of the film itself. For the film fictionalizes a director's strategy that, like in television, reworks and edits existing film and video footage without establishing the neutral viewpoint of an objectively narrating camera. Instead, the fictional video diary of a soldier becomes the overriding point of reference; of a soldier who joined the army after being rejected from film school, hoping to become famous in this way – the dream of a YouTube user – with spectacular war videos.

The focus is thus on the indirect subjective perspective of the soldier, who actually wants to make films, and who is now trying to make a bid for Hollywood with a video diary from the theater of war. Around these videos, the film groups clearly defined audiovisual material through marked perspectives and moral stances (see Figure 52): the videos of other soldiers, news images from Arabic television, static shots from surveillance cameras in the camp and during interrogations by the military court, and internet videos over and over; the despairing wife of a dead soldier or the confessions of an anonymous soldier in a video chat or the then latest weapons of warfare; video clips of Arab insurgents, which show a successful bomb attack or the sentencing and beheading of an American soldier.

The construction of the montage in REDACTED creates a fictional viewpoint from which all the audiovisual images that had been omitted and edited out in western television become visible. It creates a gaze that is only brought forth as a space of perception in the act of viewing films.

Even the brilliant cinematic images that follow the hero's first video recording, in order to cast a critical eye on the procedures at an American checkpoint, are produced in the best tradition of the European auteur film. They are – a

Figure 52: Mediated points of observation and moral views (REDACTED).

film title and the off-screen commentary leave no doubt to this – the pastiche of a French film that stages the equally banal and existentially physical suffering of the soldiers, who persevere doing nothing in the sun, heavily armed and covered up to the chin in their protective uniforms. Close ups of the soldiers' faces alternate with shots showing them watching children playing and pedestrians occasionally passing by; an endlessly repeating course of the same. We see in the soldiers' faces the physical suffering of the guard duty that never seems to end. The music from Handel's *Sarabande*, which constantly underscores the scene, gives concrete shape to the temporality of this agonized perseverance: the monotony of an endless striding, which appears as unlimited as it does aimless in its circular arrangement, until one of the cars driving into the barrier – which happens rarely enough – abruptly alters the whole situation, placing everyone involved on high alert. While the music keeps up its steady tempo, the images are accelerated, repeating the same situation over and over in fast-forward.

Suddenly the Baroque arrangement is loudly and dramatically shattered by the television images of an Iraqi station reporting on an incident at this border post. A woman in labor pains has been shot to death because her brother misunderstood the orders of the soldiers at the checkpoint while driving her to the hospital. We see the victim, the blood-soaked pregnant woman, who is hastily rushed into the operating room by doctors. Our hero's video diary then shows the perpetrator, his comrade, back in the barracks. Like in a real interview, he is coolly asked about his feelings. What is it like for a soldier, when he has shot his first civilian, when he has killed a woman and her unborn baby? But this interview is also just a game to kill time, the enervating boredom of the men sitting between the pallets and the chairs. And in fact, for a moment, there is trouble: a fight breaks out, a kind of blackboard in the background, covered with strokes that count off the days remaining until going home. For the biggest problem is the fact that time will simply not go by; they just need a deployment order, and the longed-for end of waiting will become the beginning of a new round. The only thing left to do is to keep playing cards decorated with naked women, to flip through porno magazines, to read novels, or even to surf the internet. No daylight seems to fall in this cavern beyond everyday social life; there is nothing but boredom and monotony.

Suddenly, the atmosphere of debilitated, tense stagnation turns into depravation: there is an assault on an Arab family, the daughter is raped, killed, burned, the mother and the grandfather shot. In the style of an anonymous internet video we see our hero condemned by an Arab court of Arab resistance fighters. He was there with his camera when the lecherous fantasies became real, he filmed the murder and the rape. For this he is decapitated – in front of another running video camera. We see, in the internet video, how the knife cuts through his throat, the way one would kill a lamb. The head is held up for the camera.

His accomplices are condemned by a military court. We see video footage of their interrogation; the Baroque tables and armchairs, adorned with gold leaf, mark the spot; we are familiar with this furniture from images in the newspaper announcing the victory over Iraq; they showed American soldiers spreading their legs out in the expensive furnishings of the conquered rulers, before the administration of the US military requisitioned the palaces for their quarters.

Moral judgments and transformations in genre poetics

One might find these and similar Hollywood films dubious with regard to their artistic dignity or their political-moral value – or award them with an Oscar. What I wanted to demonstrate by means of this analytical sketch concerns the ways these films, in their aesthetic construction, lay the groundwork for making a moral judgment in the first place. REDACTED – not unlike other Hollywood films about the Iraq War – refers in a variety of ways to the history of genre cinema in general, and to the war film genre in particular.

For the Iraq films, the depiction of an aimlessly extended waiting, whether that is manning a checkpoint or off-duty time in the barracks and tents, is as typical as the no less aimless patrols. The convoys that wind their way through the desert or the streets of Arab cities remind us of the cavalry marching out in a western, leaving the safe fort, forced to expose themselves to a completely hostile world, somewhere between prairie and jungle, only to come back to the safety of this or another fort shortly afterwards. In fact, the barracks, tents, and dugouts where the soldiers, like exposed foreign matter, wait for nothing more than the time to pass are without foothold or cover in a western-style world cleared empty. They are transitory places, not outposts of civilization; these places are always already slated for destruction, only provisionally concentrated into bases that turn up in the landscape for the short term and then disappear again without a trace, like the military convoys that wind their way through the desert. The sites are literally only temporary – a specific temporality materializes in them: the long waiting for one's own disappearance, a waiting that, measured by the eternity of the desert, is indeed just a fleeting moment in time.

Another example of this are the unrecognizable night shots from mobile phone cameras – a reminiscence of the horror figurations from war films of past decades. What was connected to the motif of an impenetrable, hostile nature in those films, here becomes the static flow of undecipherable video signals. For the spectator, such motivic allusions and references give rise to what Bakhtin called a chronotope: a specific space/time configuration that is completely saturated with meaning; a form of thinking that discloses a world that refers back in multiple ways to the history of making such forms of thinking.

By modifying the aesthetic operations, dramaturgical patterns, and poetic concepts of earlier films, REDACTED allows for the genre itself to emerge as a historical space of experience. The history of the wars of the last century can be grasped in it as a permanent alteration of forms in which we perceive and comprehend wars as part of our reality.

The logic of this poetic making can be succinctly summarized in the transformation of the figure of the victim – indeed, it can be comprehended in the experiential space of genre cinema, in the reconfiguration of old film images by new films, as the hallmark of historical-political shifts. In Hollywood Vietnam films, the American soldier was still described as a disillusioned, lost individual, who despaired at the senselessness of his activity. Only in the reality of the clinic did those returning from Vietnam become traumatized victims. Jonathan Shay has portrayed these post-heroic heroes from the viewpoint of psychiatric practice. With great accuracy, he chose the occidental war epos per se, Homer's *Iliad*, as the dramaturgical blueprint on which to trace the clinical pattern in the *Undoing of Character* through the stages of growing rage, which leads Achilles first into mania and finally to death.[2] We encounter such psychiatrized soldiers in the Iraq films.

A new figure of victim

We can observe this shift in THE WAR TAPES if we understand the presentation of the three soldiers as a specific image of the victim. For the appeal to the feeling for moral reprehensibility in the film does not refer to injured and murdered children, men, or women, and not to the killed enemy soldiers, not to the civilians. Rather, it is the American soldiers themselves that appear as *Casualties of War*. They are wounded by hearing and seeing, by perceiving the collateral damage of their own military operations, by seeing the victims of their military action. As if viewing these atrocities itself hit them like a bullet – at any rate, one gets the impression that the Iraq films link the soldiers' suffering primarily to the moral dubiousness of the military operation itself. In this respect, THE WAR TAPES articulates a reversal that defines the American Iraq war film as a whole. The melodramatic staging of the victim refers to the psychic suffering of American soldiers in the moral culpability of their own acts of war.

The last amateur video in REDACTED shows a celebration at home; people applaud the returning soldier, the only one from the group who got away, who left the scene of the crime to look away, who betrayed his comrades and who survived the grind of the court martial that blatantly turned this betrayal into an accusation. He speaks of his guilt feelings; his stammering and his weeping face mark out a conceivable post-heroic victim (see Figure 53). No narrative can insert his suffering into a meaningful context of community. He is the *Casualty of War* par excellence, traumatized, wounded by what he has seen and heard and done.

In the character of the soldier falling to pieces in his feelings of guilt, the legacy of the Hollywood Vietnam War film is recapitulated and brought to a point. What appears in films about the Second World War as a heroic figure of self-sacrifice for the community and in the Vietnam war movie as meaninglessly wasted human material – the victim and the soldiers' suffering – can now be seen

---

2 Cf. Jonathan Shay: *Achill in Vietnam: Kampftrauma und Persönlichkeitsverlust*, Hamburg 1998.

Figure 53: The physical suffering of the soldier as a melodramatic staging of sacrifice.

as miserable self-referentiality, which counters the lament of the victim of war with the collateral damage of one's own psychic trauma.

Brian De Palma contrasts the last video with photographs of the civil victims of war, a collage of those who go unseen, closing with a photograph of the burned body of a raped and murdered girl – an image in which the horror of the invisible enemy, which runs through the history of the Hollywood war film, becomes visible as the thousand-fold tormented victim of oppressed civil society.[3]

From here, not only do the images of military violence become legible in a different way, but so do the innumerable video images that circulate online, in

---

[3] This photograph by Taryn Simon has itself absorbed several layers of context in its circulation.

which a seemingly anarchic production of the net community transfers the affect poetics of Hollywood's mobilization films, war memorial films, and homecoming movies to the format of the music video clip. In internet production it is made evident that the history of poetic making in relation to recent cinema means the making of the spectators themselves, their tactical appropriation in the act of consuming films.[4] Against this backdrop, the question that Rabih Mroué poses with his cycle of works at *documenta* becomes comprehensible: Who is the subject of the eye that survives the death of its user? Mroué suggests an answer that has become central to the genre-theoretical approach that I would like to develop here. The subject, one might respond, is the inconclusive community of those who share the rage about what they get to see and hear; it is the community of those who take part in this moral indignation with their sensations and feelings; it is all those who can agree with this feeling.

The sensus communis and aesthetic judgment

Such participation, in which a community feels a sense of being connected in its moral values, is what Rorty is referring to when he makes morality, not unlike truth, a matter of belonging to a community, a question of the *sense of commonality*. Rorty's term, as I already mentioned in the first part of the book, touches on the decisive point of Kantian "sensus communis" [*Gemeinsinn*], which maintains its conceptual dignity precisely in being distinct from the common understanding of *sensus communis* or *common sense* as the general knowledge derived from sanity and reason. Now the term *common sense* or *sensus communis*, due to its long tradition in the history of philosophy, is so enigmatic and ambiguous[5] that it may raise serious doubts about whether turning back to Kant can meaningfully add anything to Rorty's clear definitions. But only in the Kantian turn does the term take on a distinctive precision in which the genuine political dimension of poetic making – which Rorty calls solidarity – becomes palpable. Indeed, solidarity – as we have run up against time and again over the course of this book – is to be located at the level of a feeling for a common world, at the level of shared sensibility.[6]

---

4 Cf. Michel de Certeau, *Kunst des Handelns*, Berlin 1988.
5 This problem is carved out in detail in Sophia Rosenfeld's reconstruction. Cf. Sophia Rosenfeld, *Common Sense: A Political History*, Cambridge/London 2011.
6 Cf. Jacques Rancière, *The Politics of Aesthetics: The Distribution of the Sensible*, London 2004; for further reading: Kappelhoff, *Cinematic Realism*, 1ff.

What is decisive here, which I have tried to demonstrate in the film analyses in the previous chapters, is that the feeling for the communal is always only reflected and defined in the form of an aesthetic judgment, from which it can also be interrogated – because it concerns the feeling of living in a commonly shared world, and not any facts or discourses that can be grasped intellectually; because it is exactly not grounded, as Kant maintains, in terminological operations. Rorty himself points in this direction when he links the term 'solidarity' inextricably with the irony of poetic making.[7]

The basic hypothesis of the work here thus brings us to this point: *Only by making a detour via the aesthetic judgment can the poetics of genre cinema be qualified as the media practice of a particular culture – in its relation to the political, historical, and moral problems of a community.*[8] The thesis is that genre cinema in general, and the Hollywood war film in particular, relates to a politically operative common sense in the same way as does the artistic work of Mroué. In order to qualify this relation politically, historically, and morally, we must reflect on the aesthetic judgment. Such a judgment is oriented to the question of whether the events represented, as the reality of a common world, concern me in my sense of self in a way that is valid not only for me, but for all others that I presume to share the common world with me. It concerns a sense that verifies sensibility itself – this is the willful interpretation that Hannah Arendt gives to the sense of taste. In the following I would like to sketch out briefly Arendt's attempt to define aesthetic judgment, that is, the judgment of taste, as an agent of political thinking, before coming back one last time to the Hollywood war film.

In matters of taste, shame is the feeling that shows us whether we are right or wrong in our assessment. Hannah Arendt emphasizes this in her reading of Kant's *Critique of the Power of Judgment* (1790). Shame lets us know whether we appear to be without taste in our outward appearance, our household fixtures. It shows us that when we are concerned with attire and beauty in the most ordinary of things, this always has a tangible socio-political component. We can recognize an empirical interest in the beautiful in such aspirations. For Kant, this interest is called "sociality"; for him, according to Arendt, an aspiration for sociality is expressed in all questions of the beautiful, and this aspiration defines the human being as a species. The interest in the beautiful finds its aim in "affecting common feelings and feeling of commonality through such ideas."[9] For Arendt, Kant sees

---

7 Cf. Rorty, *Contingency, Irony, and Solidarity*.
8 Cf. Jameson, *Magical Narratives*.
9 Georg Kohler, "Gemeinsinn oder: über das Gute am Schönen. Von der Geschmackslehre zur Teleologie (§§ 39–42)," in: Immanuel Kant: *Kritik der Urteilskraft*, ed. Otfried Höffe, Berlin 2008,

this aspiration for sociality as the "full dimensions of ... the determination of proper human ends."[10]

Wanting to belong, wanting to converse, to ensure belonging to one another, these are wishes that – from such a perspective – name a fundamental aspiration of all human beings for sociality, from which arises all interest in the beautiful. Seen in this way, sociality, conversation, and reasoning, that is, those things that we tirelessly devalue as feuilletonistic blustering and a gratuitous addition to what is actually artistic in the art business, would then completely match up with the social interest in being concerned with art and the beautiful. We produce the beautiful as art because the experience of the beautiful opens a space for the social to us.

Dewey also pursues these thoughts when he – counter to Kant – grounds the experience of art in an aesthetic behavior, an anthropological aspiration to decoration and ornament. From here this thought leads up to contemporary attempts to identify an empiricism of aesthetics based on evolutionary theory; in another strain it leads straight to the theory of habitus, which describes a subtle, but highly effective instrument of domination in judgments of taste sanctioned by shame. And once again, it is not least the institutions and discourses of the art and entertainment industries where this form of domination has its tools.

Kant may have had both directions in mind when he decided to keep to the beauty of nature and not of art in order to define the experience of the beautiful.[11] In art, aesthetic judgments are always intermingled with other empirical goals; they are completed in spaces of sociality, which are always also social spaces, in which the force of prestige and social distinction are in effect. This is why art only comes to the center of Kant's reflections when it is a question of making things that we then experience as beautiful.

Arendt stresses that Kant is in no way skeptical of the aspiration of sociality when he maintains a certain distance to the empirical interest in the beautiful. It should be situated at the definition of a pure aesthetic judgment – without empirical additives. Appeal and emotion should be excluded from this judgment as should the feeling of an embarrassed breach of what is appropriate. And this is

---

137–150, here: 149. Cf. also: "Empirisch interessiert das Schöne nur in der Gesellschaft (...)," in Immanuel Kant: *Kritik der Urteilskraft*, Werkausgabe Band X, Frankfurt am Main 1990, 229 (§ 41). This is also the connection to: "Geselligkeit [...] als zur Humanität gehörige Eigenschaft" (ibid.).
10 Hannah Arendt, *Das Urteilen*, Munich 2012, 18. She is citing Kant's "Mutmaßlicher Anfang der Menschheitsgeschichte" (Kant-Werke, Band 9, 86; cf. also Arendt, *Das Urteilen*, 98f.)
11 Cf. Kant: *Critique of Judgment*, § 42, 165ff.

exactly why the conditions of pure aesthetic judgment are developed in relation to the experience of the beauty of nature.

That is also what justifies the special position of the beautiful among all possible judgments of taste. The purely aesthetic judgment lays claim to being a feeling that everyone can share because it concerns the harmonic accord of all aspirations. As the experience of such a feeling, the beauty of nature becomes an indicator of a generally shared feeling. The experience of the beautiful is the feeling for a sensibility equally shared by all people. In reverse, the possibility of a generally shared feeling is the condition for the existence of the beautiful – bereft of all empirical goals – in the first place. And it is this transcendental basis, a feeling for a common feeling, that Kant calls *sensus communis*.

Sensus communis as sense of commonality (Arendt)

In short, one can say that the *Critique of the Power of Judgment* is not at all about the beautiful and even more not about art – but about the term *sensus communis*.[12] At least this is how Hannah Arendt sees it. For her, Kant, with his understanding of the sensus communis as a transcendental feeling for the social, is translating an ancient, often revised anthropological concept into a completely new category of political thought.

When I experience something as beautiful, then I place my feeling in relation to others, who experience the phenomena in the same way. And if I sense an action as hideous, then this judgment is founded on the strong feeling of sharing my sensation with all those who, like me, belong to the human community. I do not relate to an object or an issue, but to a feeling, which I share with everyone for whom this issue becomes an event in this experience of the world.

In this reading, "judging" does not mean forming an opinion by making an argument. It does not tell me what I have to do or to allow. Judging – as Arendt emphasizes – precisely does not follow the moral reasoning of practical rationality. It is carried out, like tasting or smelling, without mediation: I like it, I don't like it.[13] "We could even define taste," as Arendt cites Kant once again at the close

---

12 In fact, "common sense" is introduced as an a priori definition that facilitates judgments of feeling, such as taste in general (cf. ibid. and Marc Düwell, *Ästhetische Erfahrung und Moral: Zur Bedeutung des Ästhetischen für die Handlungsspielräume des Menschen*, Freiburg/Munich 1999).
13 Arendt, *Das Urteilen*, 103.

of her argument, "as the faculty of judging of that which makes generally communicable [...] our feeling."[14]

With this turn of phrase she works out a meaning of the term that is fundamentally distinct from that of common sense. In this meaning, the term famously takes on a key position in theories on communication societies and on communicative action. Kantian *sensus communis*, on the other hand, names a feeling for the social, a sense of commonality, and not the common sense of convictions, opinions, and knowledge grounded in rationality.

In this sense – as a feeling for the social, as a sense of commonality and not as common sense – *sensus communis* in judgments of taste forms the basis for what Arendt calls an "enlarged mentality." For her, the *sensus communis* still functions as an a priori condition; but no longer in order to justify a purely aesthetic judgment of the beautiful, but to account for judgment itself as a specific mode of thinking: as a mode of thinking that does not become detached from the particular case of the feeling for a particular thing.

The Kantian beautiful almost becomes a ladder that is pushed away, since the term *sensus communis* is defined as a feeling for a common feeling in the first place. The only thing remaining for Arendt is the judgment of taste, indeed in all its empirical messiness. What is up for discussion in the *Critique of the Power of Judgment* – according to Hannah Arendt – is not any understanding of the being of human beings, nor the moral being that is the human being as a species, but "men in the plural," the 'actual inhabitants of the earth,' whose '"end" is ... *sociality*.'[15] This judging thinking always remains related to the plurality of subjective feeling in its particularities in the given situation. It would always be a judgment about something particular – "'this is good,' 'this is bad,' 'this is right,' 'this is wrong,' 'this is beautiful,' 'this is ugly,'" as we read in Arendt.[16]

But does such thinking not once again presume the *sensus communis* to be an anthropological fact, even in its reinterpretation as a feeling for a common feeling? How else should this thinking be carried out if not by detaching from the plurality of each particular sensation among many others? In the answer to this question Arendt gives *sensus communis* a decidedly historico-political slant. Namely, she reverses the judgment of taste into an agent of the *sensus communis*. The judgment of taste allows us, every time we reflect on something to judge, to

---

[14] Ibid., 111. Arendt is citing from § 40 of *Critique of Judgment* (Kant, *Critique of Judgment*, 159ff.).
[15] Ibid., 44.
[16] Transcript from Arendt's "Remarks on American Society for Christian Ethics," Richmond, VA, January 21, 1973, Library of Congress, cited in Elisabeth Young-Bruehl, *Hannah Arendt. Leben, Werk und Zeit*, Frankfurt am Main 1986, 615.

verify the *sensus communis* anew for its generalizability. It compels us to question the *sensus communis* itself as something that limits our way of thinking at all times, and is thus infinitely in need of extension. The judgment of taste is the basis for an "enlarged mentality," which necessarily has to be extended with every reflective judgment to include this one particular case of feeling for a thing. This, however, means radically historicizing the *sensus communis* as how taste is organized in a concrete cultural community.

The judgment of taste becomes an "enlarged mentality" by positioning itself in a world that it proposes, fictionalizes, and thinks as a combination of contrary and mutually exclusive positions of sense experience. This judging thinking is carried out in the imaginary arena of a public space where an audience assembles, and the wide variety of their particularities of taste implies every possible standpoint of judging. This aesthetic parliament does not have its medium in the better argument of an ideal community of communication, but in judging as a constant process of extending the positions of taste. This means that the judgment of taste necessarily gives expression to the borders of the *sensus communis*, its need to be extended.

Genre cinema as a space of experiencing competing senses of the communal

It is also entirely possible to imagine this aesthetic parliament, along with Cavell, as the experiential space of genre cinema.[17] His analysis of Stella Dallas, the woman who attempts to usurp the style of more respectable society in order to come up in the world, but fails over and over again; who in every failure senses ever more potently the discrepancy between her eccentric preferences, which appear as vulgar, exaggerated, and repulsive to the others, and what is considered good taste for them. But, we can also think of Stella Dallas, as Cavell does, as the type that effortlessly anticipates every position of taste, able to refer to its own eccentric self-image; the type that commands a way to calculate the right outfit for any social constellation. We can think of the cinema spectator in the position of Stella when we trace how the judgment of a common woman in inappropriate clothing changes according to the perspective that she is viewed from. We can describe the dramaturgy of the film, the heroine of which is Stella, as a spectator feeling that is inextricably caught up in the object of observation while watching

---

17 Cf. Cavell, "Stella's Taste: Reading Stella Dallas."

the character's faux pas, still experiencing itself in its sense of self as part of this change in perspective, with witch the feeling for the character turns over in starkly opposing valuations; a spectator feeling that finally becomes aware of the dynamic process of the stark shifts of each concrete sensual-affective relation in the whole, embracing it in a mental movement that understands "too Stella Dallas"[18] as an innate feeling for the self. This means that only from the spectator's position can the dynamic of the judgment of taste be realized as an extended way of thinking, as a mode of thinking.

But in Arendt judgments do not mean any kind of thinking in the perceptual space of the cinema with its multiple perspectives. She conceives the imaginary arena, in which the infinitely multipliable perceptual positions take place, precisely as a parliament that requires spoken language and terminological thinking. This is why, when she turns Kant's world citizen into a world spectator, she resorts to the philosophically reliable metaphor of theater.[19] The judgment of taste initiates a thought process that is implemented like a spectacle in front of the critically judging audience of world spectators. The metaphor of the theater takes on a variety of meanings in Arendt's political writings. But at this significant spot – the interpretation of the Kantian world citizen as a world spectator – she remains oddly abstract. The extended way of thinking ultimately means a theater of the imagination of the philosopher who thinks politically.

This has its reasons. Namely, Arendt detaches the judgment of taste from the concept of that activity which has the goal of putting this imaginary theater in place as a concrete experience – the concept of art. By dismissing art-making, she shifts the focus away from just that area in which the mode of judging thinking meets the question of the concrete making of experiential spaces, in which thinking, in the spectacle of judgment, cannot be separated from the "*this* is beautiful, *this* is ugly, *this* is right, *this* is wrong" of each given particularity. Using the work of Rorty, we have defined this connection between making and thinking in describing and redescribing the boundaries of our shared world as poetic making.

---

18 Cavell uses this expression to name the disciplinary judgment of taste when he talks about his mother, who, when she was using too much color in her fashion choices, would ask if it was "too Stella Dallas?" "When my mother asked for an opinion from my father and me about a new garment or ornament she had on, a characteristic form she gave her question was 'Too Stella Dallas?'" (ibid., 200).

19 See for instance: "The general viewpoint or standpoint is occupied, rather, by the spectator, who is a 'world citizen' or, rather, a 'world spectator'." (Arendt, *Lectures on Kant's Political Philosophy*, 58.) And: "The spectacle before the spectator – enacted, as it were, for his judgment – is history as a whole, and the true hero of this spectacle is mankind in the 'series of generations proceeding' into some 'infinity'." (Ibid., 58).

In view of the aesthetic judgment as a driving force behind the sense of community, I would like to propose no longer reading description and redescription as writing and reading, but thinking it as seeing and hearing, and to view filming and viewing films as paradigmatic metaphors for poetic making. Then genre cinema, precisely in the plurality of its modes of experience and modalities of expression, can be written as a history of creating 'spaces of separated sensibilities.'[20] In historical (re)constructions – there are countless examples of this, from Siegfried Kracauer to Stanley Cavell – this cinema can be grasped as a space of experience from which the limitations and contingency of existing orders of taste can be viewed. Admittedly, this view does not match up with a utopia of the aesthetic community. Instead, the boundaries of this community are constantly becoming visible in the medium of the judgment of taste.

From this perspective, community is always an ad hoc event, which is formed around the discovery that something or someone is missing. It would always be tied to proposing a fictional world in which this lack can be felt, can be perceived in the first place. It would always be – and here I am referring to one of the most important theorists of genre cinema, Rick Altman – a particular community, based on the dissident judgment of taste. It is not by chance that Altman explains this idea in reference to those films that group their audiences as friends of esoteric tastes, and not generally socially acceptable taste. Through such films we can learn that the sense of community itself has to be seen as a fissured field of ever new particular communities of taste. Indeed, cult and trash films are merely particularly striking manifestations of a kind of thinking guided by the judgment of taste.

If we follow Altman's ideas about the particular communities that are formed as the audience of a dissident taste, then we can describe the political community in the history of genre cinema as a battlefield of heterogeneous, unstable, and competing ad hoc communities. The judgment of taste is the guide in a description in which the visual spaces of genre cinema can relate to society as a field of competing proposals for the sense of community – to society as a political community – without laying claim to any essence of this community (a people, a nation, or communism as the telos of history).

I have attempted to reconstruct such a field as the history of the Hollywood war film: from the original constellation of making films between military reconnaissance, propagandistic public relations, and entertainment for the home front through the affect poetics of mobilization films, of war commemoration and lamentation for the dead, to films that thematize the terror of militarizing a society

---

20 Cf. Jacques Rancière, *Aesthetics and its Discontents*, Cambridge 2009, 24ff.

and focus on the destruction of the sense of commonality, or that seek to organize its reconstruction. Each of these historical constellations can be described as a conflict between highly contradictory politics; those that are focused on establishing, controlling, and stabilizing forms of sense experience (the "formal language of political sensibility") according to dominant power relations; and those that bring exactly these limitations into view and make efforts to dissolve them, those that provide polemic counterproposals or subtle boundary shifts in the sense of community in the spaces of the film image.

Seen from this perspective, the photos at the end of Brian De Palma's REDACTED act no differently than the reverse shot of the mobile phone camera in Mroué's installation. They oppose a violence that is aimed at perceptibility itself in order to fix it within its borders. They make war's military politics of perception visible as an attempt to erase the gaze that recognizes the enemy as a victim who belongs to the socially shared world.

This is the sense in which I have attempted, drawing on Rorty, to unlock the history of the Hollywood war film as a history of contingent descriptions and redescriptions, of continuously refiguring the limits of community. I have attempted to understand genre cinema itself as a poetic making that should always be related to the temporal depths of the history of poetic making. At this level, films can be located in the tension between exclusion and inclusion, belonging, ostracism, and animosity in the field of opposing forms of community and practices of communalizing.

In any given single case we may only be able to get a hazy picture of this, or it may be exhausted in the simple repetitions of long-familiar patterns – but spectators will always place films in a particular relation to this history. This is why films can always be described as a figuration of the relation between poetics and politics. Which means nothing other than viewing history itself as a history of poetic making whenever analyzing films.

Bibliography

Agamben, Giorgio, et al. *Demokratie? Eine Debatte*. Frankfurt am Main: Suhrkamp, 2012.
Altman, Rick. *Film/Genre*. London: British Film Institute, 1999.
Anderegg, Michael, ed. *Inventing Vietnam: The War in Film and Television*. Philadelphia: Temple University Press, 1991.
Antze, Paul, and Michael Lambek, eds. *Tense Past: Cultural Essays in Trauma and Memory*. New York/London: Routledge, 1996.
Arendt, Hannah. *Lectures on Kant's Political Philosophy*. Chicago: University of Chicago Press, 1992.
Arendt, Hannah. *On Revolution*. London: Faber & Faber, 2016.
Aristotle. *Poetics*, ed. Anthony Kenny. Oxford: Oxford University Press, 2013.
Ascherson, Neal. "Missing in Action," *The Observer* (6. September 1998), 7.
Assmann, Aleida. *Erinnerungsräume. Formen und Wandlungen des kulturellen Gedächtnisses*. Munich: C.H. Beck, 2010.
Assmann, Jan. *Cultural Memory and Early Civilization: Writing, Remembrance, and Political Imagination*. Cambridge/New York: Cambridge University Press, 2011.
Auster, Albert. "Saving Private Ryan' and American Triumphalism." In *The War Film*, ed. Robert Eberwein. New Brunswick/London: Rutgers University Press, 2005, 205–213.
Bakhtin, M. M. "Forms of Time and the Chronotope of the Novel." In *The Dialogic Imagination: Four Essays*, Austin: University of Texas, 1981.
Bakels, Jan-Hendrik. *Audiovisuelle Rhythmen: Filmmusik, Bewegungskomposition und die dynamische Affizierung des Zuschauers*. Berlin/Boston: De Gruyter, 2017.
Balázs, Béla. *Early Film Theory: Visible Man and The Spirit of Film*. Oxford: Berghahn, 2010.
Barker, Martin. *"A Toxic Genre:" The Iraq War Films*. London: Pluto Press, 2011.
Barthes, Roland. *Camera Lucida: Reflections on Photography*. New York: The Noonday Press, 1981.
Basinger, Jeanine. *The World War II Combat Film: Anatomy of a Genre*. Middletown, Conn.: Wesleyan University Press, 2003.
Baudry, Jean-Louis. "Ideologische Effekte erzeugt vom Basisapparat." In *Der kinematographische Apparat: Geschichte und Gegenwart einer interdisziplinären Debatte*, ed. Robert Riesinger. Münster: Nodus Publikationen, 2003, 27–39.
Bazin, André. "Evolution du Western," *Cahiers du cinéma* 9, 54 (1955): 22–26.
Bazin, André. "The Evolution of the Western." In *What is Cinema? Vol. 2*. Berkeley/Los Angeles: University of California Press, 2004.
Bazin, André. "The Ontology of the Photographic Image." In *What is Cinema? Vol. 1*. Berkeley/Los Angeles: University of California Press, 2005.
Bellour, Raymond. "Le déplides émotions," *Trafic* 42 (2002), 93–128.
Belton, John. "American Cinema and Film History." In *American Cinema and Hollywood*, eds. John Hill, and Pamela Church Gibson. Oxford: Oxford University Press, 2000, 1–11.
Belton, John. *American Cinema, American Culture*. Boston: McGraw-Hill, 2005.
Bender, James F. "Thirty Thousand New Words," *New York Times Magazine* (December 2, 1945), 22.
Benjamin, Walter. *The Origin of German Tragic Drama*, ed. John Osborne. London: New Left Books, 1977.
Benjamin, Walter. "Theories of German Fascism: On the Collection of Essays in War and Warriors, edited by Ernst Jünger." In *Selected Writings, Volume 2, 1927–1934*. Cambridge/London: The Belknap Press of Harvard University Press, 1999.

Benjamin, Walter. "The Work of Art in the Age of Its Technological Reproducibility." In *Walter Benjamin: Selected Writings, Volume 4, 1938–1940*, eds. Howard Eiland, and Michael William Jennings, Cambridge: Harvard University Press, 2003.

Birkenhauer, Theresia. "Tragödie: Arbeit an der Demokratie. Auslotung eines Abstandes," *Theater der Zeit 11* (November 2004), 27–28.

Blunt, Alison. *Domicile and Diaspora: Anglo-Indian Women and the Spatial Politics of Home*. Oxford: Blackwell, 2005.

Boehm, Gottfried. "Die Bilderfrage." In *Was ist ein Bild?*, ed. Gottfried Boehm. Munich: Fink, 1994, 325–343.

Boehm, Gottfried. "Die Wiederkehr der Bilder." In *Was ist ein Bild?*, ed. Gottfried Boehm. Munich: Fink, 1994, 11–38.

Boehm, Gottfried. "Iconic Turn: Ein Brief." In *Bilderfragen: Die Bildwissenschaften im Aufbruch*, ed. Hans Belting, Munich: Fink, 2007, 27–36.

Boehm, Gottfried. "Das Zeigen der Bilder." In *Zeigen: Die Rhetorik des Sichtbaren*, eds. Gottfried Boehm, Sebastian Egenhofer, and Christian Spies. Munich: Fink, 2010, 19–53.

Bordwell, David. *Narration in the Fiction Film*. Madison: University of Wisconsin Press, 1985.

Bordwell, David, and Kristin Thompson. "Film Genres." In *Film Art: An Introduction*. New York: McGraw-Hill, 2010, 328–348.

Bordwell, David, Kristin Thompson, and Janet Staiger. *The Classical Hollywood Cinema: Film Style and Mode of Production to 1960*. New York: Columbia University Press, 1985.

Boyle, Brenda M. *Masculinity in Vietnam War Narratives: A Critical Study of Fiction, Films, and Nonfiction Writings*. Jefferson, NC: McFarland, 2009.

Boym, Svetlana. *The Future of Nostalgia*. New York: Basic Books, 2001.

Braudy, Leo. "Flags of Our Fathers/Letters from Iwo Jima," *Film Quarterly* 60 (2007), 16–23.

Brinkley, Douglas. "The Color of War: John Ford stormed to the Beach at Normandy on D-Day, armed with Full-Color Film. What happened to the Footage he shot?" *The New Yorker* 74 (20) (1998), 34–36.

Bronfen, Elisabeth. *Specters of War: Hollywood's Engagement with Military Conflict*. New Brunswick, N.J.: Rutgers University Press, 2012.

Brooks, Peter. *The Melodramatic Imagination: Balzac, Henry James, Melodrama, and the Mode of Excess*. New Haven/London: Yale University Press, 1976.

Brunotte, Ulrike. "Krieg und Kino: No Mail Days Are Sad Days," *Frauen und Film* 61 (2000), 5–21.

Bühler, Karl. *Ausdruckstheorie: Das System an der Geschichte aufgezeigt*. Jena: G. Fischer, 1933.

Burgoyne, Robert. *The Hollywood Historical Film*. Malden/Oxford/Carlton: Blackwell Pub., 2008.

Burgoyne, Robert. *Film Nation. Hollywood Looks at U.S. History*. Minneapolis, Minn.: University of Minnesota Press, 2010.

Burgoyne, Robert. "Generational Memory and Affect in 'Letters from Iwo Jima'." In *A Companion to the Historical Film*, eds. Robert A. Rosenstone and Constantin Parvulescu. Malden, MA: Wiley-Blackwell, 2013, 349–364.

Burgoyne, Robert. "Haunting in the War Film: 'Flags of Our Fathers'." In *Eastwood's Iwo Jima: Critical Engagement With 'Flags of Our Fathers' and 'Letters from Iwo Jima,'* eds. Anne Gjelsvik, and Rikke Schubart. New York: Wallflower Press, 2013, 157–172.

Caillois, Roger. *Man and The Sacred*. Westport: Greenwood Press, 1980.

Cancik, Hubert, and Hubert Mohr. "Erinnerung/Gedächtnis." In *Handbuch religionswissen-schaftlicher Grundbegriffe 2*, eds. Hubert Cancik, Burkhard Gladigow, and Karl-Heinz Kohl. Stuttgart: Kohlhammer, 1990, 299–323.

Capra, Frank. *The Name above the Title: An Autobiography*. New York: Bantam Books, 1971.

Carroll, Noël. "Film, Emotion, and Genre." In *Passionate Views: Film, Cognition, and Emotion*, eds. Carl Plantinga, and Greg M. Smith. Baltimore: The Johns Hopkins University Press, 1999, 21–47.

Caruth, Cathy ed. *Trauma: Explorations in Memory*. Baltimore: Johns Hopkins University Press, 1992.

Caruth, Cathy. *Unclaimed Experience: Trauma, Narrative and History*. Baltimore: Johns Hopkins University Press, 1996.

Cavell, Stanley. *The World Viewed: Reflections on the Ontology of Film*, Cambridge: Harvard University Press, 1979.

Cavell, Stanley. "What Becomes of Things on Film?" In *Themes out of School. Effects and Causes*. Chicago: University of Chicago Press, 1984, 173–183.

Cavell, Stanley. *Themes out of School: Effects and Causes*. Chicago: University of Chicago Press, 1988.

Cavell, Stanley. "The Uncanniness of the Ordinary." In *In Quest of the Ordinary: Lines of Scepticism and Romanticism*, Chicago: University of Chicago Press, 1988, 153–178.

Cavell, Stanley. "Stella's Taste: Reading Stella Dallas." In *Contesting Tears: The Hollywood Melodrama of the Unknown Woman*. Chicago: University of Chicago Press 1996, 197–222.

Cavell, Stanley. *Pursuits of Happiness: The Hollywood Comedy of Remarriage*, Cambridge, Mass.: Harvard University Press, 1997.

Cawelti, John G. *The Six-Gun Mystique Sequel*. Bowling Green, Ohio: Bowling Green State University Popular Press, 1999.

Certeau, Michel de. *Kunst des Handelns*. Berlin: Merve, 1988.

Chadwick, Bruce. *Reel Civil War: Mythmaking in American Film*. London: Vintage, 2002.

Chambers II, John Whiteclay. "'All Quiet on the Western Front' (1930): The Anti-War Film and the Image of the First World War," *Historical Journal of Film, Radio and Television* 14 (4) (1994), 377–411.

Chambers II, John Whiteclay. *World War II: Film and History*. New York/Oxford: Oxford University Press, 1996.

Chion, Michel. *The Thin Red Line*. London: BFI, 2004.

Christie, Israel C., and Bruce H. Friedman. "Autonomic Specificity of Discrete Emotion and Dimensions of Affective Space: A Multivariate Approach," *International Journal of Psychophysiology* 51 (2004), 143–153.

Conrad, Dennis, and Burkhard Röwekamp. "Krieg ohne Krieg: Zur Dramatik der Ereignislosigkeit in 'Jarhead'." In *All Quiet on the Genre Front: Zur Praxis und Theorie des Kriegsfilms*, eds. Heinz B. Heller, Burkhard Röwekamp, and Matthias Steinle. Marburg: Schüren, 2007, 194–207.

Cook, Bernie. "Over My Dead Body. The Ideological Use of Dead Bodies in Network News Coverage of Vietnam," *Quarterly Review of Film and Video* 18 (2) (2001), 203–216.

Culbert, David, ed. *Film and Propaganda in America: A Documentary History, Volume II, World War II Part 1*. New York/Westport/London: Greenwood, 1990.

Culbert, David. *Film and Propaganda in America: A Documentary History, Volume III, World War II Part 2*. New York/Westport/London: Greenwood, 1990.

Curtis, Robin. "Embedded Images: Der Kriegsfilm als Viszerale Erfahrung," *Nach dem Film 7* (2005), http://www.nachdemfilm.de/content/embedded-images (July 24, 2015).
Damasio, Antonio. *The Feeling of what Happens: Body and Emotion in the Making of Consciousness*. New York: Harcourt Brace, 1999.
Deleuze, Gilles. *Cinema 1- The Movement-Image*. London: Athlone, 1986.
Deleuze, Gilles. *Cinema 2- The Time-Image*. London: Athlone, 1989.
Deleuze, Gilles, and Félix Guattari. *What is Philosophy?*. New York: Verso, 1994.
Deleuze, Gilles, and Félix Guattari. *A Thousand Plateaus: Capitalism and Schizophrenia*. London/New York: Continuum, 2008.
Derrida, Jacques. "Otobiographies: The Teaching of Nietzsche and the Politics of the Proper Name." In *The Ear of the Other*, Lincoln: University of Nebraska Press, 1985.
Derrida, Jacques. "Declaration of Independence." In *Negotiations: Interventions and Interviews 1971–2001*, ed. Elizabeth Rottenberg. Stanford: Stanford University Press, 2002, 46–54.
Devine, Jeremy M. *Vietnam at 24 Frames a Second: A Critical and Thematic Analysis of over 400 Films about the Vietnam War*. Austin: University of Texas Press, 1999.
Dewey, John. *Art as Experience*. New York: Perigree Books, 1980.
Didi-Huberman, Georges. "Opening the Camps, Closing the Eyes." In *Concentrationary Cinema: Aesthetics as Political Resistance in Alain Resnais's Night and Fog (1955)*, ed. Griselda Pollock, and Max Silverman. New York: Berghahn Books, 2011.
Didi-Huberman, Georges. *Remontagen der erlittenen Zeit: Das Auge der Geschichte II*. Paderborn: Fink, 2014.
Distelmeyer, Jan. "Transparente Zeichen: Hollywood, Vietnam, Krieg," *Nach dem Film 7* (2005), http://www.nachdemfilm.de/content/transparente-zeichen (July 24, 2015).
Dittmar, Linda, and Gene Michaud. *From Hanoi to Hollywood: The Vietnam War in American Film*. New Brunswick: Rutgers University Press, 1997.
Doherty, Thomas. *Projections of War: Hollywood, American Culture, and World War II*. New York: Columbia University Press, 1993.
Doherty, Thomas. "Documenting the 1940s." In *Boom and Bust: The American Cinema in the 1940s*, ed. Thomas Schatz. Berkeley/Los Angeles: University of California Press, 1997, 397–421.
Düwell, Marc. *Ästhetische Erfahrung und Moral: Zur Bedeutung des Ästhetischen für die Handlungsspielräume des Menschen*. Freiburg/Munich: Alber, 1999.
Eder, Jens. *Die Figur im Film: Grundlagen der Figurenanalyse*. Marburg: Schüren, 2008.
Eisenstein, Sergej. "The Filmic Fourth Dimension" In *Film Form: Essays in Film Theory*, ed. Jay Leyda. New York: Harcourt, 1977.
Elsaesser, Thomas. "Postmodernism as Mourning Work," *Screen 42* (2) (2001), 193–201.
Elsaesser, Thomas. *Terror und Trauma: Zur Gewalt des Vergangenen in der BRD*. Berlin: Kulturverlag Kadmos, 2007.
Elsaesser, Thomas. "'Saving Private Ryan.' Retrospektion, Überlebensschuld und affektives Gedächtnis." In *Mobilisierung der Sinne: Der Hollywood-Kriegsfilm zwischen Genrekino und Historie*, eds. Hermann Kappelhoff, David Gaertner and Cilli Pogodda. Berlin: Vorwerk 8, 2013, 61–87.
Elsaesser, Thomas, and Michael Wedel. "The Hollow Heart of Hollywood: 'Apocalypse Now' and the new Sound Space" In *Conrad on Film*, ed. Gene M. Moore. Cambridge: Cambridge University Press, 1997, 151–175.
Elsaesser, Thomas, and Michael Wedel. *Körper, Tod und Technik. Metamorphosen des Kriegsfilms*. Paderborn: Konstanz University Press, 2016.

Engell, Lorenz. "Teil und Spur der Bewegung: Neue Überlegungen zu Iconizität, Indexikalität und Temporalität des Films." In *Der schöne Schein des Wirklichen: Zur Authentizität im Film*, ed. Daniel Sponsel. Konstanz: UVK Verlagsgesellschaft, 2007, 15–40.

Erdheim, Mario. "Heiße Gesellschaften, kaltes Militär." In *Psychoanalyse und Unbewußtheit in der Kultur*. Frankfurt am Main: Suhrkamp, 1988, 311–344.

Erdheim, Mario. "Ritual und Reflexion." In *Rituale heute: Theorien – Kontroversen – Entwürfe*, eds. Corina Caduff and Joanna Pfaff-Czarnecka. Berlin: Reimer, 1999, 165–178.

Fahle, Oliver. "Zeitspaltungen: Gedächtnis und Erinnerung bei Gilles Deleuze," *montage a/v 11 (1)* (2002), 97–112.

Fauth, Søren R. Krejberg, Kasper Green, and Jan Süselbeck eds. *Repräsentationen des Krieges: Emotionalisierungsstrategien in der Literatur und in den audiovisuellen Medien vom 18. bis zum 21. Jahrhundert*. Göttingen: Wallstein, 2012.

Fiedler, Konrad. "Moderner Naturalismus und künstlerische Wahrheit [1881]." In *Schriften zur Kunst I*. Munich: Fink, 1991, 82–110.

Fiedler, Konrad. "Über den Ursprung der künstlerischen Tätigkeit [1887]." In *Schriften zur Kunst I*. Munich: Fink, 1991, 112–220.

Fisch, Valentijn T., and Ed S. Tan. "Categorizing Moving Objects into Film Genres. The Effect of Animacy Attribution, Emotional Response, and the Deviation from Non-Fiction," *Cognition 110* (2009), 265–272.

Fluck, Winfried. *Das kulturelle Imaginäre: Eine Funktionsgeschichte des amerikanischen Romans 1790–1900*. Frankfurt am Main: Suhrkamp, 1997.

Fluck, Winfried. "The 'Imperfect Past.' Vietnam According to the Movies." In *The Merits of Memory: Concepts, Contexts, Debates*, eds. Hans-Jürgen Grabbe and Sabine Schindler. Heidelberg: Winter, 2008, 353–385.

Foster, Hal. "Obscene, Abject, Traumatic," *October 78* (1996), 106–124.

Foucault, Michel. *Society Must Be Defended: Lectures at the Collège de France, 1975–1976*. New York: Picador, 2003.

Freud, Sigmund. "My Views on the Role of Sexuality in the Etiology of the Neuroses." In *Selected Papers on Hysteria and Other Psychoneuroses*, New York: Journal of Nervous and Mental Disease Pub. Co., 1912, 186–193.

Fried, Michael. *Absorption and Theatricality: Painting and Beholder in the Age of Diderot*. Berkeley: University of California Press, 1980.

Frijda, Nico H. *The Emotions*. Cambridge: Cambridge University Press, 1986.

Frijda, Nico H. "Emotions, Cognitive Structure and Action Tendency," *Cognition and Emotion 1*, 1987, 115–144.

Frijda, Nico H. *The Laws of Emotion*. Mahwah, NJ: Erlbaum, 2006.

Frye, Northrop. *Anatomy of Criticism: Four Essays*. Princeton: Princeton University Press, 1957.

Fuchs, Thomas. *Leib, Raum, Person: Entwurf einer phänomenologischen Anthropologie*. Stuttgart: Klett-Cotta, 2000.

Gaertner, David. "Mit allen Mitteln: Hollywoods Propagandafilme am Beispiel von Frank Capras 'Why We Fight'-Reihe." In *Mobilisierung der Sinne: Der Hollywood-Kriegsfilm zwischen Genrekino und Historie*, eds. Hermann Kappelhoff, David Gaertner, and Cilli Pogodda. Berlin: Vorwerk 8, 2013, 307–344.

Gaertner, David. "World War II in American Movie Theatres from 1942–45. On Images of Civilian and Military Casualties and the Negotiation of a Shared Experience," *mediaesthetics* (2016), http://www.mediaesthetics.org/index.php/mae/ article/view/50.

Gaertner, David. "Tickets to War. Propaganda, Kino und Mobilisierung in den USA von 1939–1945," dissertation manuscript: Free University, Berlin, unpublished.
Gallagher, Tad: *John Ford. The Man and His Films*. Berkeley: University of California Press, 1988.
Gansera, Rainer. "'Krieg und Geilheit, die bleiben immer in Mode' (Shakespeare)." In *Kino und Krieg: Von der Faszination eines tödlichen Genres*, eds. Ernst Karpf, and Doron Kiesel. Frankfurt am Main: Gemeinschaftswerk der Evangelischen Publizistik, 1989, 33–46.
Gareis, Torsten. "Put your Helmet on! Der Helm im amerikanischen Kriegsfilm." In *Mobilisierung der Sinne: Der Hollywood-Kriegsfilm zwischen Genrekino und Historie*, eds. Hermann Kappelhoff, David Gaertner, and Cilli Pogodda. Berlin: Vorwerk 8, 2013, 345–382.
Gary, Brett. "Communication Research, the Rockefeller Foundation, and Mobilization for the War on Words, 1938–1944," *Journal of Communication 46 (3)* (1996), 124–148.
Gary, Brett. *The Nervous Liberals. Propaganda Anxieties from World War I to the Cold War*. New York: Columbia University Press, 1999.
Gates, Philippa. "'Fighting the Good Fight.' The Real and the Moral in the Contemporary Hollywood Combat Film," *Quarterly Review of Film and Video 22 (4)*, (2005), 297–310.
Girshausen, Theo. *Ursprungszeiten des Theaters: Das Theater der Antike*. Berlin: Vorwerk 8, 1999.
Gledhill, Christine. "Rethinking Genre." In *Reinventing Film Studies*, eds. Christine Gledhill, and Linda Williams. London/New York: Arnold, 2000, 221–243.
Godfrey, Richard, and Simon Lilley. "Visual Consumption, Collective Memory and the Representation of War," *Consumption Markets & Culture 12 (4)* (2009), 275–300.
Goethe, Johann Wolfgang von. "A Challenge for a Modern Sculptor." In *Collected Works, Vol. 3, Essays on Art and Literature*. Princeton: Princeton University Press, 1994, 93–95.
Goldin, Philippe R., et al. "The Neural Bases of Amusement and Sadness: A Comparison of Block Contrast and Subject-specific Emotion Intensity Regression Approaches," *NeuroImage 27*, 2005, 26–36.
Goldin, Philippe R., Kateri McRae, Wiveka Ramel, and James J. Gross. "The Neural Bases of Emotion Regulation: Reappraisal and Suppression of Negative Emotion," *Biological Psychiatry 63 (6)* (2008), 577–586.
Greifenstein, Sarah, and Hauke Lehmann. "Manipulation der Sinne im Modus des Suspense," *Cinema 58* (2013), 102–112.
Greiner, Rasmus. *Die neuen Kriege im Film: Jugoslawien – Zentralafrika – Irak – Afghanistan*. Marburg: Schüren, 2012.
Grodal, Torben K. *Moving Pictures: A New Theory of Film Genres, Feelings and Cognition*. Oxford: Clarendon Press, 1997.
Grodal, Torben K. *Embodied Visions: Evolution, Emotion, Culture, and Film*. Oxford: Oxford University Press, 2009.
Gross, James J., and Robert W. Levenson. "Emotion Elicitation Using Films," *Cognition and Emotion 9 (1)*, (1995), 87–108.
Grotkopp, Matthias. *Filmische Poetiken der Schuld: Die audiovisuelle Anklage der Sinne als Modalität des Gemeinschaftsempfindens*. Berlin/Boston: De Gruyter, 2017.
Grotkopp, Matthias, and Hermann Kappelhoff. "Film Genre and Modality: The Incestuous Nature of Genre exemplified by the War Film." In *In Praise of Cinematic Bastardy*, eds. Sebastien Léfait, and Philippe Ortoli. Newcastle upon Tyne: Cambridge Scholars Publishing, 2012, 29–39.
Guattari, Félix. "The Poor Man's Couch." In *Chaosophy: Texts and Interviews*, ed. Sylvère Lotringer. Los Angeles: Semiotext, 2009, 257–267.

Haggith, Toby. "D-Day Filming for Real: A Comparison of 'Truth' and 'Reality' in 'Saving Private Ryan' and 'Combat Film' by the British Army's Film and Photographic Unit," *Film History 14* (2002), 332–353.
Halbwachs, Maurice. *On Collective Memory*, Chicago: University of Chicago Press, 1992.
Hallin, Daniel. *The Uncensored War: The Media and Vietnam*. New York: Oxford University Press, 1986.
Hammond, Paul. "Some Smothering Dreams: The Combat Film in Contemporary Hollywood." In *Genre and Contemporary Hollywood*, ed. Steve Neale. London: British Film Institute, 2002, 62–79.
Hansen, William P., Fred L. Israel, Fred L., and June Rephan, eds. *The Gallup Poll. Public Opinion 1935–1971 Volume 1, 1935–1948*. New York: Random House, 1972.
Harris, Mark. *Five Came Back: A Story of Hollywood and the Second World War*. New York: The Penguin Press, 2014.
Hebekus, Uwe, and Jan Völker. *Neue Philosophien des Politischen zur Einführung*. Hamburg: Junius, 2012.
Heberle, Mark ed. *Thirty Years After: New Essays on Vietnam War Literature, Film, and Art*. Newcastle upon Tyne: Cambridge Scholars Publishing, 2009.
Hegel, Georg Friedrich Wilhelm. *Lectures on Fine Art*, Vol. 2. Oxford: Clarendon Press, 1975.
Hellmann, John. "Vietnam and the Hollywood Genre Film: Inversions of American Mythology in 'The Deer Hunter' and 'Apocalypse Now'," *American Quarterly 34 (4)* (1982), 418–439.
Hess Wright, Judith. "Genre Films and the Status Quo [1974]." In *Film Genre Reader II*, ed. Barry Keith Grant. Austin: University of Texas Press, 1995.
Hölzl, Gebhard, and Matthias Peipp. *Fahr zur Hölle, Charlie! Der Vietnamkrieg im amerikanischen Film*. Munich: W. Heyne, 1991.
Hooks, Bell. *Belonging: A Culture of Place*. New York: Routledge, 2009.
Jameson, Fredric. "Magical Narratives: On the Dialectical Use of Genre Criticism." In *The Political Unconscious: Narrative as a Socially Symbolic Act*. London: Cornell University Press, 1981, 103–150.
Kaltenbeck, Franz, and Peter Weibel, eds. *Trauma und Erinnerung/Trauma and Memory: Cross-Cultural Perspectives*. Vienna: Passagen, 2000.
Kant, Immanuel. *Critique of Judgment*, trans. and with an introduction by Werner S. Pluhar. Indianapolis/Cambridge: Hackett Publishing, 1987.
Kaplan, E. Ann. "Melodrama, Cinema and Trauma," *Screen 42 (2)* (2001), 201–205.
Kappelhoff, Hermann. *Matrix der Gefühle: Das Kino, das Melodrama und das Theater der Empfindsamkeit*, Berlin: Vorwerk 8, 2004.
Kappelhoff, Hermann. "Unerreichbar, unberührbar, zu spät: Das Gesicht als kinematografische Form der Erfahrung," *montage a/v 13 (2)* (2004), 29–53.
Kappelhoff, Hermann. "Der Bildraum des Kinos: Modulationen einer ästhetischen Erfahrungsform." In *Umwidmungen – architektonische und kinematographische Räume*, ed. Gertrud Koch. Berlin: Vorwerk 8, 2005, 138–149.
Kappelhoff, Hermann. "Apriorische Gegenstände des Gefühls: Recherchen zur Bildtheorie des Films." In *Bildtheorie und Film*, eds. Thomas Koebner, Fabienne Liptay, and Thomas Meder. Munich: Edition Text + Kritik 2006, 404–421.
Kappelhoff, Hermann. "Das Wunderbare der Filmkunst: Die Illusion des lebendigen Ausdrucks." In *...kraft der Illusion. Illusion und Filmästhetik*, eds. Gertrud Koch, and Christiane Voss. Munich: Fink, 2006, 175–189.

Kappelhoff, Hermann. "Shell Shocked Face: Einige Überlegungen zur rituellen Funktion des US-amerikanischen Kriegsfilms." In *Verklärte Körper*, eds. Nicola Suthor, and Erika Fischer-Lichte. Munich: Fink, 2006, 69–89.

Kappelhoff, Hermann. "Ausdrucksbewegung und Zuschauerempfinden: Eisensteins Konzept des Bewegungsbildes." In *Synchronisierung der Künste*, eds. Robin Curtis, Gertrud Koch, and Marc Siegel. Munich: Fink, 2012, 73–84.

Kappelhoff, Hermann. "Sense of Community: Die filmische Komposition eines moralischen Gefühls." In *Repräsentationen des Krieges: Emotionalisierungsstrategien in der Literatur und in den audiovisuellen Medien vom 18. bis zum 21. Jahrhundert*, eds. Søren R. Fauth, Kasper Green Krejberg, and Jan Süselbeck. Göttingen: Wallstein, 2012, 43–57.

Kappelhoff, Hermann. "Artificial Emotions: Melodramatic Practices of Shared Interiority." In *Rethinking Emotion: Interiority and Exteriority in Pre-Modern, Modern, and Contemporary Thought*, eds. Rüdiger Campe, and Julia Weber. Berlin/Boston: De Gruyter, 2014, 264–288.

Kappelhoff, Hermann. *The Politics and Poetics of Cinematic Realism*. New York: Columbia University Press, 2015.

Kappelhoff, Hermann. "Melodrama and War in Hollywood Genre Cinema." In *After the Tears: New Perspectives on the Politics of Victimhood*, eds. Scott Loren, and Jörg Metelmann. Amsterdam: Amsterdam University Press, 2016.

Kappelhoff, Hermann, and Jan-Hendrik Bakels. "Das Zuschauergefühl – Möglichkeiten qualitativer Medienanalyse," *ZfM – Zeitschrift für Medienwissenschaft 5 (2)*, (2011), 78–96.

Kappelhoff, Hermann, Helga Gläser, and Bernhard Groß, eds. *Blick – Macht – Gesicht*, Berlin: Vorwerk 8, 2001.

Kappelhoff, Hermann, et al. "eMAEX: Ansätze und Potentiale einer systematisierten Methode zur Untersuchung filmischer Ausdrucksqualitäten," http://www.empirische-medienaesthetik.fu-berlin.de/media/emaex_methode_deutsch/eMAEX-_-Ansaetze-und-Potentiale-einer-systematisierten-Methode-zur-Untersuchung-filmischer-Ausdrucks-qualitaeten.pdf?1401464494 (Dezember 5, 2015).

Kappelhoff, Hermann, and Cornelia Müller. "Embodied Meaning Construction. Multimodal Metaphor and Expressive Movement in Speech, Gesture, and Feature Film," *Metaphor and the Social World 1 (2)* (2011), 121–153.

Karpf, Ernst. "Kriegsmythos und Gesellschaftskritik: Zu Coppolas 'Apocalypse Now'." In *Kino und Krieg: Von der Faszination eines tödlichen Genres*, eds. Ernst Karpf, and Doron Kiesel. Frankfurt am Main: Gemeinschaftswerk der Evangelischen Publizistik, 1989, 106–112.

Katzman, Jason. "From Outcast to Cliché: How Film Shaped, Warped and Developed the Image of the Vietnam Veteran, 1967–1990," *Journal of American Culture 16* (1993), 7–24.

Keilholz, Sascha. *Verlustkino: Trauer im amerikanischen Polizeifilm seit 1968*. Marburg: Schüren, 2015.

King, Geoff. "Seriously Spectacular: 'Authenticity' and 'Art' in the War Epic." In *Hollywood and War: The Film Reader*, ed. J. D. Slocum. New York/London: Routledge, 2006, 287–301.

Kittler, Friedrich. *Grammophone Film Typewriter*. Stanford: Writing Science, 1999.

Koch, Gertrud. "Das Bild als Schrift der Vergangenheit," *Kunstforum 128* (October 1994), 192–196.

Koch, Gertrud. "Müssen wir glauben, was wir sehen?" In *... kraft der Illusion: Illusion und Filmästhetik*, eds. Gertrud Koch, and Christiane Voss. Munich: Fink, 2006, 53–70.

Kodat, Catherine Gunther. "Saving Private Property: Steven Spielberg's American DreamWorks," *Representations 71* (2000), 77–105.

Kohler, Georg. "Gemeinsinn oder: Über das Gute am Schönen. Von der Geschmackslehre zur Teleologie (§§ 39–42)." In *Immanuel Kant. Kritik der Urteilskraft*, ed. Otfried Höffe. Berlin: Akademie Verlag Berlin, 2008, 137–150.
Koppes, Clayton R., and Gregory D. Black. *Hollywood Goes to War: Patriotism, Movies and the Second World War from "Ninotchka" to "Mrs. Miniver."* London/New York: Tauris, 1988.
Koschorke, Albrecht. *Körperströme und Schriftverkehr: Mediologie des 18. Jahrhunderts.* Munich: Fink, 1999.
Koselleck, Reinhart. *The Practice of Conceptual History: Timing History, Spacing Concepts.* Stanford: Stanford University Press, 2002.
Kracauer, Siegfried. *Theory of Film: The Redemption of Physical Reality.* New York: Oxford University Press, 1960.
Kracauer, Siegfried. *History: The Last Things before the Last.* Princeton: Wiener, 2013.
Kubrick, Stanley, Michael Herr, and Gustav Hasford. *Full Metal Jacket: The Screenplay.* New York: Knopf, 1987.
Kuhn, Markus, Irina Scheidgen, and Nicola Valeska Weber, eds. *Filmwissenschaftliche Genreanalyse.* Berlin/Boston: De Gruyter, 2013.
Kurtz, Rudolf. *Expressionismus und Film.* Berlin: Verlag der Lichtbildbühne, 1926.
Laclau, Ernesto. "Why do Empty Signifiers Matter to Politics?" In *Emancipation(s)*. London: Verso, 1996, 36–46.
Landweer, Hilge. *Scham und Macht: Phänomenologische Untersuchungen zur Sozialität eines Gefühls.* Tübingen: Siebeck, 1999.
Langford, Barry. *Film Genre: Hollywood and Beyond.* Edinburgh: Edinburgh University Press, 2005.
Leder, Helmut, Benno Belke, Andries Oeberst, and Dorothee Augustin. "A Model of Aesthetic Appreciation and Aesthetic Judgements," *British Journal of Psychology 95*, (2004), 489–508.
Lehmann, Hans-Thies. "Die Raumfabrik – Mythos im Kino und Kinomythos." In *Mythos und Moderne: Begriff und Bild einer Rekonstruktion*, ed. Karl Heinz Bohrer. Frankfurt am Main: Suhrkamp, 1983, 572–609.
Lehmann, Hauke. *Affektpoetiken des New Hollywood – Suspense, Paranoia und Melancholie.* Berlin/Boston: De Gruyter, 2016.
Löffler, Petra. *Affektbilder: Eine Mediengeschichte der Mimik.* Bielefeld: transcript, 2004.
Loiperdinger, Martin. "'Why We Fight' contra 'Triumph des Willens' – Feindbilder in der amerikanischen Gegenpropaganda." In *Widergänger: Faschismus und Antifaschismus im Film*, ed. Joachim Schmidt-Sasse. Münster: MAkS Publikationen, 1993, 76–90.
MacArthur, Douglas. "Signing of the Surrender Instrument by Japan 2 September 1945" In *Douglas MacArthur. Warrior as Wordsmith*, eds. Bernhard K. Duffy, and Ronald H. Carpenter. Westport/London: Greenwood Press, 1997, 173–174.
MacArthur, Douglas. "U.S. Military Academy, West Point, NY, 12 May 1962" In *Douglas MacArthur. Warrior as Wordsmith*, eds. Bernhard K. Duffy, and Ronald H. Carpenter. Westport/London: Greenwood Press, 1997, 197–200.
Madsen, Axel. *William Wyler: The Authorized Biography.* New York: Crowell, 1973.
Maltby, Richard. *Hollywood Cinema.* Oxford: Blackwell, 2003.
Martin, Peter. "We shot D-Day on Omaha Beach: An Interview with John Ford," *The American Legion Magazine 76 (6)* (June 1964).
Massumi, Brian. "Navigating Movements." In *Hope: New Philosophies for Change*, ed. Mary Zournazi. New York: Routledge, 2003, 210–243.

McBride, Jospeh. *Searching for John Ford: A Life*. New York: St. Martin's Press, 2001.
Merleau-Ponty, Maurice. *On Collective Memory*. Chicago: University of Chicago Press, 1992.
Metz, Christian. "On the Impression of Reality in the Cinema." in *Film Language: A Semiotics of the Cinema*. Chicago: University of Chicago Press, 1991, 3–15.
Metz, Christian. "The Impersonal Enunciation, or the Site of Film." In *The Film Spectator: From Sign to Mind*, ed. Warren Buckland. Amsterdam: Amsterdam University Press, 1995.
Metz, Christian. *The Imaginary Signifier: Psychoanalysis and the Cinema*. Bloomington: Indiana University Press, 2000.
Modleski, Tania. "Clint Eastwood and Male Weepies," *American Literary History 22 (1)* (2010), 136–158.
Moe, Albert F. "Gung Ho," *American Speech 42 (1)* (Februar 1967), 19–30.
Montserrat, Guibernau. *Belonging: Solidarity and Division in Modern Societies*. Cambridge: Polity, 2013.
Mulvey, Laura. "*Visual Pleasure and Narrative Cinema*," Screen 16 (1975), 6–18.
Münsterberg, Hugo. *The Photoplay: A Psychological Study*. New York/London: Appleton, 1916.
Nancy, Jean-Luc. *La communauté désoeuvrée*. Paris: Bourgois, 1986.
Neale, Steve. *Genre and Hollywood*. London/New York: Routledge, 2000.
Neale, Steve. "Questions of Genre." In *Film Genre Reader III*, ed. Barry Keith Grant. Austin: University of Texas Press, 2003, 160–184.
Nichols, Bill. *Representing Reality: Issues and Concepts in Documentary*. Bloomington: Indiana University Press, 1991.
Nietzsche, Friedrich. *On the Genealogy of Morality: A Polemic*, trans. Maudmarie Clark, and Alan J. Swensen. Indianapolis: Hackett, 1998.
Niney, François. *Die Wirklichkeit des Dokumentarfilms. 50 Fragen zur Theorie und Praxis des Dokumentarischen*. Marburg: Schüren, 2012.
Niney, Francois. "Filming Pearl Harbor(s)," *Motion Picture Herald 146 (7)*, (February 14, 1942), 9.
Paris, Michael, ed. *The First World War and Popular Cinema: 1914 to the Present*. Edinburgh: Edinburgh University Press, 1999.
Parrish, Robert. *Growing Up in Hollywood*. New York: Harcourt Brace Jovanovich, 1976.
Pasolini, Pier Paolo. "Il 'cinema di poesia'" In *Empirismo eretico*. Milan: Garzanti, 1981, 167–187.
Pasolini, Pier Paolo. "The 'Cinema of Poetry'." In *Heretical Empiricism*, ed. Louise K. Barnett. Bloomington: Indiana University Press, 1988, 167–186. Italian original: "Il 'cinema di poesia'." In *Empirismo eretico*, Milan: Garzanti, 1981, 167–187.
Paul, Gerhard. *Bilder des Krieges – Krieg der Bilder. Die Visualisierung des modernen Krieges*. Paderborn/Munich: Fink, 2004.
Plantinga, Carl. "Die Szene der Empathie und das menschliche Gesicht im Film," *montage a/v 13 (2)*, (2004), 6–27.
Plantinga, Carl. *Moving Viewers. American Film and the Spectator's Experience*. Berkeley: University of California Press, 2009.
Plantinga, Carl, and Greg M. Smith. eds. *Passionate Views: Film, Cognition and Emotion*. Baltimore: The Johns Hopkins University Press, 1999.
Plessner, Helmuth. *Lachen und Weinen: Eine Untersuchung nach den Grenzen des menschlichen Verhaltens*. Munich: Lehnen, 1950.
Plessner, Helmuth. "Die Deutung des mimischen Ausdrucks: Ein Beitrag zur Lehre vom Bewußtsein des anderen Ichs [1925]." In *Gesammelte Schriften VII. Ausdruck und menschliche Natur*. Frankfurt am Main: Suhrkamp, 1982, 67–130.

Plessner, Helmuth. "Zur Hermeneutik nichtsprachlichen Ausdrucks." In *Gesammelte Schriften VII. Ausdruck und menschliche Natur*. Frankfurt am Main: Suhrkamp, 1982, 67–130.
Pogodda, Cilli, and Danny Gronmaier. "The War Tapes and the Poetics of Affect of the Hollywood War Film Genre," *Frames Cinema Journal (7)* (June 2015), (http://framescinemajournal.com/article/the-war-tapes-and-the-poetics-of-affect-of-the-hollywood-war-film-genre/ December 8, 2015).
Polan, Dana. "Auteurism and War-teurism: Terence Malick's War Movie." In *The War Film*, ed. Robert Eberwein. New Brunswick: Rutgers University Press, 2005, 53–62.
Probyn, Elspeth. *Outside Belongings*. New York/London: Routledge, 1996.
Rabinbach, Anson. "From Explosion to Erosion: Holocaust Memorialization in America since Bitburg," *History and Memory 1 (2)* (1997), 226–255.
Radstone, Susannah. "Screening Trauma: 'Forrest Gump,' Film and Memory." In *Memory and Methodology* ed. Susannah Radstone. Oxford: Berg, 2000, 79–110.
Radstone, Susannah. "Trauma and Screen Studies: Opening the Debate," *Screen 42 (2)* (2001), 188–193.
Rancière, Jacques. *The Names of History: On the Poetics of Knowledge*. Minneapolis: University of Minnesota Press, 1994.
Rancière, Jacques. *La fable cinématographique*. Paris: Seuil, 2001.
Rancière, Jacques. *Disagreement: Politics and Philosophy*. Minneapolis: University of Minnesota Press, 1999.
Rancière, Jacques. "L'historicité du cinema." In *De l'histoire au cinema*, ed. Antoine de Baecque, and Christian Delage. Paris: Editions Complexe, 1998, 45–60.
Rancière, Jacques. "The Distribution of the Sensible." In *The Politics of Aesthetics*. London: Continuum, 2004, 7–46.
Rancière, Jacques. *Film Fables*. London: Berg, 2006.
Rancière, Jacques. *Das Unbehagen in der Ästhetik*. Vienna: Passagen-Verlag, 2007.
Rancière, Jacques. *Aesthetics and its Discontents*. Cambridge: Polity Press, 2009.
Rancière, Jacques. *The Emancipated Spectator*. London: Verso, 2009.
Reinecke, Stefan. *Hollywood goes Vietnam. Der Vietnamkrieg im US-amerikanischen Film*. Marburg: Hitzeroth, 1993.
Robnik, Drehli. "Körper-Erfahrung und Film-Phänomenologie" In *Moderne Film Theorie*, ed. Jürgen Felix. Mainz: Bender, 2002, 246–285.
Robnik, Drehli. *Kino, Krieg, Gedächtnis: Affekt-Ästhetik, Nachträglichkeit und Geschichts- politik im deutschen und amerikanischen Gegenwartskino*, unpublished dissertation: Universiteit van Amsterdam, Amsterdam 2007, http://dare.uva.nl/document/50897 (August 17, 2013).
Robnik, Drehli. "Bilder, die die Welt bewegten: 'The Big Red One' 1980, Regie: Samuel Fuller," *Spex 362*, (2015), 80–81.
Rodowick, David N. *Gilles Deleuze's Time Machine*. Durham: Duke University Press, 1997.
Rorty, Richard. "Pragmatism, Relativism, Irrationalism." In *Consequences of Pragmatism. Essays: 1972–1980*. Minneapolis: University of Minnesota Press, 1982, 160–175.
Rorty, Richard. *Contingency, Irony, and Solidarity*. Cambridge: Cambridge University Press, 1989.
Rorty, Richard. *Achieving Our Country: Leftist Thought in Twentieth-Century America*. Cambridge: Harvard University Press, 1998.
Rorty, Richard. *Objectivity, Relativism, and Truth*. Cambridge: Cambridge University Press, 1995.
Rorty, Richard. "A Defense of Minimalist Liberalism." In *Debating Democracy's Discontent: Essays on American Politics, Law, and Public Philosophy* eds. Anita L. Allen, and Milton C. Regan. Oxford/New York: Oxford University Press, 1998, 117–125.

Rosenfeld, Sophia. *Common Sense: A Political History*. Cambridge/London: Harvard University Press, 2011.
Rowe, John Carlos, and Rick Berg eds. *The Vietnam War and American Culture*. New York: Columbia University Press, 1991.
Schatz, Thomas. *Hollywood Genres: Formulas, Filmmaking, and the Studio System*. Philadelphia: Temple University Press, 1981.
Schatz, Thomas. *Old Hollywood, New Hollywood. Ritual, Art and Industry*. Ann Arbor, Mich.: UMI Research Press, 1983.
Schatz, Thomas. "World War II and the Hollywood 'War Film'." In *Refiguring American Film Genres: History and Theory*, ed. Nick Browne. Los Angeles/London: University of California Press, 1998, 89–128.
Schaub, Mirjam. *Gilles Deleuze im Kino: Das Sichtbare und das Sagbare*. Munich: Fink, 2003.
Scherer, Klaus R. "What Are Emotions? And How Can They Be Measured?" *Social Science Information 44 (4)* (2005), 693–727.
Scherer, Thomas, Sarah Greifenstein, and Hermann Kappelhoff. "Expressive Movement in Audio-Visual Media: Modulating Affective Experience." In *Body – Language – Communication: An International Handbook on Multimodality in Human Interaction*, Handbooks of Linguistics and Communication Science 38.2., eds. Cornelia Müller, Alan Cienki, Ellen Fricke, Silva H. Ladewig, David McNeill, and Jana Bressem. Berlin/Boston: De Gruyter, 2014, 2081–2092.
Schlüpmann, Heide. *Ein Detektiv des Kinos: Studien zu Siegfried Kracauers Filmtheorie*. Basel: Stroemfeld, 1998.
Schmid, Karl ed. *Gedächtnis, das Gemeinschaft stiftet*. Munich/Zurich: Schnell & Steiner, 1985.
Schreiner-Seip, Claudia. *Film- und Informationspolitik als Mittel der nationalen Verteidigung in den USA, 1939–1941*. Frankfurt am Main/Bern/New York: Lang, 1985.
Schubart, Rikke, Anne Gjelsvik eds. *Eastwood's Iwo Jima: Critical Engagement with "Flags of Our Fathers" and "Letters From Iwo Jima,"* New York: Wallflower Press, 2013.
Schweinitz, Jörg. "Genre und lebendiges Genrebewußtsein," *montage a/v 3 (2)* (1994), 99–118.
Seeßlen, Georg. "Von Stahlgewittern zur Dschungelkampfmaschine: Veränderungen des Krieges und des Kriegsfilms." In *Kino und Krieg. Von der Faszination eines tödlichen Genres*, eds. Ernst Karpf, and Doron Kiesel. Frankfurt am Main: Gemeinschaftswerk der Evangelischen Publizistik, 1989, 15–32.
Seeßlen, Georg. *Steven Spielberg und seine Filme*. Marburg: Schüren, 2001.
Seidensticker, Bernd. "Aristoteles und die griechische Tragödie." In *Die Mimesis und ihre Künste*, eds. Gertrud Koch, Martin Vöhler, and Christiane Voss. Munich: Fink, 2010, 15–42.
Shaviro, Steven. "Response to 'Untimely Bodies: Toward a Comparative Film Theory of Human Figures, Temporalities, and Visibilities'," Conference Paper, Society for Cinema and Media Studies. Philadelphia, PA, delivered on March 9, 2008.
Shaviro, Steven. *The Cinematic Body*. Minneapolis: University of Minnesota Press, 1993.
Shay, Jonathan. *Achill in Vietnam: Kampftrauma und Persönlichkeitsverlust*. Hamburg: Hamburger Edition, 1998.
Silet, Charles L. P. ed. *Oliver Stone: Interviews*. Jackson: University Press of Mississippi, 2001, 39–49.
Simmel, Georg. "Aesthetik des Porträts [1905]." In *Aufsätze und Abhandlungen 1901–1908 (Bd. I)*. Frankfurt am Main: Suhrkamp, 1995, 321–332.
Simmel, Georg. "Die ästhetische Bedeutung des Gesichts [1901]." In *Aufsätze und Abhandlungen 1901–1908 (Bd. I)*. Frankfurt am Main: Suhrkamp, 1995, 36–42.

Sinclair, Andrew. "John Ford's War," *Sight and Sound 48 (2)* (1979), 99–104.
Singer, Ben. *Melodrama and Modernity*. New York: Columbia University Press, 2001.
Skinner, James M. "'December 7.' Filmic Myth Masquerading as Historical Fact," *The Journal of Military History 55 (4)* (1991), 507–516.
Slaby, Jan, Achim Stephan, and Henrik Walter, eds. *Affektive Intentionalität: Beiträge zur welterschließenden Funktion der menschlichen Gefühle*. Paderborn: Mentis, 2011.
Smith, Greg M. *Film Structure and the Emotion System*. Cambridge: Cambridge University Press, 2003.
Smith, Julian. *Looking Away: Hollywood and Vietnam*. New York: Scribner, 1975.
Smith, Murray. *Engaging Characters: Fiction, Emotion, and the Cinema*. Oxford: Clarendon Press, 1995.
Sobchack, Thomas. "Genre Film: A Classical Experience [1975]." In *Film Genre Reader IV*, ed. Barry Keith Grant. Austin: University of Texas Press, 2012, 121–132.
Sobchack, Vivian. *The Address of the Eye: A Phenomenology of Film Experience*. Princeton, NJ: Princeton University Press, 1992.
Sobchack, Vivian. *Carnal Thoughts: Embodiment and Moving Image Culture*. Berkeley: University of California Press, 2004.
Sobchack, Vivian. "What My Fingers Knew: The Cinesthetic Subject, or Vision in the Flesh." In *Carnal Thoughts. Embodiment and Moving Image Culture*. Berkeley: University of California Press, 2004, 53–84.
Sproule, J. Michael. *Propaganda and Democracy: The American Experience of Media and Mass Persuasion*. Cambridge: Cambridge University Press, 1997.
Stewart, Garrett. "Digital Fatigue: Imaging War in Recent American Film," *Film Quarterly 62 (4)* (2009), 45–55.
Streiter, Anja. "Das 'Kino der Körper' und die Frage der Gemeinschaft. Autorenkino und Filmschauspiel," *Nach dem Film 5*, (2004), http://www.nachdemfilm.de/content/das-kino-der-k%C3%B6rper-und-die-frage-der-gemeinschaft (November 30, 2015).
Streiter, Anja. "Die Frage der Gemeinschaft und die 'Theorie des Politischen'." In *Die Frage der Gemeinschaft: Das westeuropäische Kino nach 1945*, eds. Hermann Kappelhoff, and Anja Streiter. Berlin: Vorwerk 8, 2012, 21–37.
Swofford, Anthony. *Jarhead. A Marine's Chronicle of the Gulf War and Other Battles*. New York/London: Scribner, 2003.
Tan, Ed S. *Emotion and the Structure of Narrative Film: Film as an Emotion Machine*. Mahwah, New Jersey: Erlbaum, 1996.
Tudor, Andrew. "Genre." In *Film Genre Reader IV*, ed. Barry Keith Grant. Austin: University of Texas Press, 2012, 3–11.
Turim, Maureen. "The Trauma of History: Flashbacks Upon Flashbacks," *Screen 42* (2001), 205–210.
Virilio, Paul. *War and Cinema: The Logistics of Perception*. London/New York: Verso, 1989.
Visarius, Karsten. "Wegtauchen oder Eintauchen? Schreckbild, Lockbild, Feindbild: Der inszenierte Krieg." In *Kino und Krieg: Von der Faszination eines tödlichen Genres*, eds. Ernst Karpf, and Doron Kiesel. Frankfurt am Main: Gemeinschaftswerk der Evangelischen Publizistik, 1989, 9–13.
Vogl, Joseph. "Einleitung." In *Gemeinschaften: Positionen zu einer Philosophie des Politischen* ed. Joseph Vogl. Frankfurt am Main: Suhrkamp, 1994, 7–27.
Vöhler, Martin. "katharsis/Katharsis." In *Aristoteles-Lexikon*, ed. Otfried Höffe. Stuttgart: A. Kröner, 2005, 304–306.

Völler, Martin. "Reinigung in der griechischen Kultur." In *Un/Reinheit. Konzepte und Praktiken im Kulturvergleich*, eds. Angelika Malinar, and Martin Völler. Paderborn: Fink, 2008, 169–185.

Völler, Martin, and Dirck Linck. "Zur Einführung" In *Grenzen der Katharsis in den modernen Künsten: Transformationen des aristotelischen Modells seit Bernays, Nietzsche und Freud*, eds. Martin Völler, and Dirck Linck. Berlin/Boston: De Gruyter, 2009, IX–VIV.

Völler, Martin, and Bernd Seidensticker. "Zur Einführung Katharsiskonzeptionen vor Aristoteles." In *Katharsiskonzeptionen vor Aristoteles*, eds. Martin Völler, and Bernd Seidensticker. Berlin/Boston: De Gruyter, 2007, VII–XII.

Walker, Janet. "Trauma Cinema: False Memories and True Experience," *Screen* 42 (2) (2001), 211–216.

Walker, Janet. *Trauma Cinema: Documenting Incest and the Holocaust*. Berkeley: University of California Press, 2005.

Walker, Mark. *Vietnam Veteran Films*. Lanham: Scarecrow Press, 1991.

Warburg, Aby. "Einleitung zum Mnemosyne-Atlas (1929)." In *Der Bilderatlas Mnemosyne: Gesammelte Schriften, Bd. II 1.2*. Berlin: Akademie Verlag, 2008, 3–6.

Warburg, Aby. "Dürer und die italienische Antike." In *Werke in einem Band*, ed. and comm. Martin Treml, Sigrid Weigel, and Perdita Ladwig, Berlin: Suhrkamp, 2010, 176–184.

Wedel, Michael. *Der deutsche Musikfilm: Archäologie eines Genres 1914–1945*. Munich: Text + Kritik, 2007.

Wedel, Michael. "Körper, Tod und Technik: Der postklassische Hollywood-Kriegsfilm als reflexives 'Body Genre'." In *Körperästhetiken. Filmische Inszenierungen von Körperlichkeit*, ed. Dagmar Hoffmann. Bielefeld: Transcript, 2010, 77–99.

Westwell, Guy. "Accidental Napalm Attack and Hegemonic Visions of America's War in Vietnam," *Critical Studies in Media Communication* 28 (5) (2011), 407–423.

White, William L. *They Were Expendable: An American Torpedo Boat Squadron in the U.S. Retreat from the Philippines*. New York: Harcourt, 1942.

Williams, Alan. "Is a Radical Genre Criticism Possible?" *Quarterly Review of Film Studies* 9 (2), (1984), 121–125.

Williams, Linda. "Film Bodies: Gender, Genre, and Excess." In *Film Genre Reader III*, ed. Barry Keith Grant. Austin: University of Texas Press, 2003, 141–159.

Wilsbacher, Greg. "Al Brick: The Forgotten Newsreel Man at Pearl Harbor," *The Moving Image* 10 (2010), 30–59.

Woodman, Brian J. "Represented in the Margins: Images of African American Soldiers in Vietnam War Combat Films." In *The War Film*, ed. Robert Eberwein. Brunswick N.J.: Rutgers University Press, 2005, 90–114.

Worland, Rick. "The Other Living-Room War: Prime Time Combat Series, 1962–1975," *Journal of Film and Video* 50 (3), (1998), 3–23.

Wright, Will. *Sixguns and Society: A Structural Study of the Western*. Berkeley: University of California Press, 1975.

Wulff, Hans J. "Empathie als Dimension des Filmverstehens: Ein Thesenpapier," *montage a/v* 12 (1) (2003), 136–161.

Wundt, Wilhelm. *Grundzüge der physiologischen Psychologie, Bd. 2*. Leipzig: Engelmann, 1880.

Wundt, Wilhelm. *Grundriss der Psychologie*. Leipzig: Engelmann, 1896.

Young-Bruehl, Elisabeth. *Hannah Arendt: Leben, Werk und Zeit*. Frankfurt am Main: S. Fischer, 1986.

Yuval-Davis, Nira. *The Politics of Belonging: Intersectional Contestations*. Los Angeles: Sage, 2011.

Name index

Achilles 72, 309, 329, 342
Altman, Rick 10, 78, 79, 83, 86, 95, 96, 101, 271, 351
Arendt, Hannah vi, 32, 266, 267, 293, 345–348, 350
Aristotle 33, 96, 97, 102, 103, 284, 285, 286, 288
Assmann, Jan 263, 264–271, 288, 292, 306, 316, 332

Bakhtin, Mikhail M. 23, 94, 269, 341
Balázs, Béla 24, 121
Basinger, Jeanine 13, 84, 87, 89, 125, 151
Bazin, André 151, 173, 208
Benjamin, Walter 54–56, 269
Bernays, Edward 147
Bordwell, David 84, 211
Brando, Marlon 38, 329
Brinkley, Douglas 139, 141
Brooks, Peter 83, 84, 91, 92, 125
Brown, Harry 288
Bühler, Karl 119

Caillois, Roger 66, 88, 203, 316
Capra, Frank vi, 49–51, 56, 58, 61–72, 76, 90, 99, 101, 138, 148, 149, 152, 160, 161, 163, 172, 278, 282, 293, 300, 301, 330
Cavell, Stanley vi, vii, 64, 72–90, 98, 100, 136, 137, 205, 207, 208, 210–212, 215, 216, 229, 231, 234, 269, 271, 285, 329, 349, 350, 351
Clift, Montgomery 4, 308
Conrad, Joseph 38, 310
Cooper, James Fenimore 19, 22
Coppola, Francis Ford 4, 37, 40, 42, 310, 315

Damasio, Antonio 109, 110
Deleuze, Gilles 4, 6, 23, 49, 109, 119–123, 189, 215, 230, 283, 296
De Palma, Brian 312, 313, 325, 338, 343, 352
Dewey, John 29, 110–112, 115, 116, 147, 346
Diderot, Denis 14
Dwan, Allan 271, 272

Eastwood, Clint 144, 175, 272
Eisenstein, Sergej M. 114, 120, 121, 148
Emerson, Ralph Waldo 22, 24
Erdheim, Mario 323

Fiedler, Konrad 119
Ford, John vi, 18, 45, 50, 138–140, 142, 148–155, 157, 158, 160, 162, 164, 171, 172, 175–178, 219, 233–238, 241, 246, 260, 261, 300
Foucault, Michel 28, 88, 91, 266, 294, 295, 296, 306, 307
Fried, Michael 15
Frijda, Nico 104, 105
Fuller, Samuel vi, 18, 177, 276, 296, 300, 301, 302, 303, 304

Gledhill, Christine 83–85, 91–97, 99, 123, 124, 138

Halbwachs, Maurice 263, 268
Hanks, Tom 4, 13
Herr, Michael 39–41, 318
Hitler, Adolf 51, 55, 56
Homer 25, 56, 329, 342

James, William 29
Jameson, Fredric 80, 84, 269, 345
Jones, James 22, 23, 307

Kant, Immanuel 32, 111, 344–348, 350
Koselleck, Reinhart 291–294, 304, 305
Kracauer, Siegfried 147, 173, 208, 225, 263, 281, 351
Kurtz, Rudolf 121

Lincoln, Abraham 65
Loiperdinger, Martin 50

MacArthur, Douglas 233, 234, 236, 253, 255, 259, 261, 301, 330, 331, 332
Malick, Terrence 1, 9, 11, 21, 23, 24, 30, 230, 329

Massumi, Brian 109, 119, 283
McCullin, Don 1, 2, 3, 5
Mendes, Sam 313, 314, 317
Metz, Christian 67, 173, 208, 210, 211
Mroué, Rabih 333–335, 344, 345, 352
Münsterberg, Hugo 121

Nancy, Jean-Luc v, 17, 317, 325
Neale, Steve 79, 82, 86, 92, 144
Nietzsche, Friedrich 32, 279
Nolte, Nick 329

Pasolini, Pier Paolo 23
Patton, George S. 326, 328, 329, 330, 332
Peirce, Charles S. 120
Plato 103, 301
Plessner, Helmuth v, 3, 102, 119, 120

Rancière, Jacques v, 64, 77, 145, 152, 205, 263, 267, 282, 307, 344, 351
Riefenstahl, Leni 49, 50, 51, 54, 55, 56, 58, 61, 63, 64, 69, 71, 76, 101, 161, 177, 183, 184, 221, 332
Roosevelt, James 171, 172
Rorty, Richard v–vii, 8, 29–37, 46–48, 50, 74, 76, 145, 261, 266, 267, 270, 284, 285, 306, 344, 345, 350, 352
Rosenthal, Joe 175

Schmid, Karl 288
Shay, Jonathan 341, 342

Sheen, Martin 4, 38, 40
Simmel, Georg 119
Skinner, James M. 153–158
Smith, Greg M. 95, 104, 106, 107, 122, 210
Sobchack, Vivian 112–115, 121, 145, 213, 214
Spielberg, Steven 4, 9–14, 20, 21, 142, 143, 144, 146, 222, 303
Stevens, George 149
Stone, Oliver 5, 37, 43, 177, 312, 315
Swofford, Anthony 314, 315

Tan, Ed S. 105, 106
Thompson, Kristin 84
Thoreau, Henry David 22
Toland, Gregg 153, 154, 158, 160, 161, 164
Travolta, John 329

Vertov, Dziga 53–55, 148, 184
Virilio, Paul 178

Wagner, Richard 313, 314
Warburg, Aby 6, 126
Wayne, John 236, 255, 271, 273
Whitman, Walt 29
Woo, John 9, 11, 16, 20, 21
Wundt, Wilhelm 119
Wyler, William vi, 138, 148, 149, 152, 176

Zanuck, Darryl F. 148

Film index

APOCALYPSE NOW (1979, Francis Ford Coppola) 4, 37–42, 132, 224, 310, 311, 313, 315, 317, 329, 330
ATTACK! (1956, Robert Aldrich) 67, 276, 308
A WALK IN THE SUN (1945, Lewis Milestone) 24, 288, 291, 297

BAND OF BROTHERS (2001) 303
BATAAN (1943, Tay Garnett) 129, 132, 190–198, 202, 203, 204, 206, 224, 227, 231, 235, 236
BEACHHEAD TO BERLIN (1945) 141, 144, 145, 216
BLACK HAWK DOWN (2001, Ridley Scott) 301

CASUALTIES OF WAR (1989, Brian de Palma) 308, 312, 313, 325

D-DAY IN COLOUR (2004) 143
DECEMBER 7TH (1943, John Ford, Gregg Toland) 50, 149, 150, 153–160, 162–164, 170, 174–176, 203, 206, 216, 217, 219, 224, 231, 290, 332
DUEL IN THE SUN (1946, King Vidor) 151

FIRST BLOOD (1982, Ted Kotcheff) 179
FIVE GRAVES TO CAIRO (1943, Billy Wilder) 150
FLAGS OF OUR FATHERS (2006, Clint Eastwood) 88, 144, 175, 272, 280
FORT APACHE (1948, John Ford) 241
FROM HERE TO ETERNITY (1953, Fred Zinnemann) 4, 67, 129, 276, 308
FULL METAL JACKET (1987, Stanley Kubrick) 4, 276, 318, 320–324

GONE WITH THE WIND (1939, George Cukor, Victor Fleming, Sam Wood) 141
GUNG HO!: THE STORY OF CARLSON'S MAKIN ISLAND RAIDERS (1943, Ray Enright) 129, 152, 180–190, 192, 195, 203, 206, 231, 273, 303, 308, 318

HAMBURGER HILL (1987, John Irvin) 5
HOLOCAUST (1978) 303

IMMORTAL SERGEANT (1943, John M. Stahl) 150
IN THE VALLEY OF ELAH (2007, Paul Haggis) 308

JARHEAD (2005, Sam Mendes) 313–318, 324

KZ FALKENAU, VISION DE L'IMPOSSIBLE (1988, Emil Weiss) 303

LES JEUX SONT FAITS (1947, Jean Delannoy) 212
LETTERS FROM IWO JIMA (2006, Clint Eastwood) 88, 144, 175, 280

MERRILL'S MARAUDERS (1961, Samuel Fuller) 276
MR. SMITH GOES TO WASHINGTON (1939, Frank Capra) 64, 65
MY DARLING CLEMENTINE (1946, John Ford) 151

PATTON (1969/70, Franklin J. Schaffner) 309, 326–330, 332
PEARL HARBOR (2001, Michael Bay) 10
PLATOON (1986, Oliver Stone) 5, 37, 43–46, 312, 325
PRELUDE TO WAR (1942, Frank Capra) 56, 57, 59, 62, 65, 66, 67, 69, 71, 75, 90, 99, 101, 149, 163

REDACTED (2007, Brian de Palma) 338, 339, 341, 342, 352
RED RIVER (1948, Howard Hawks, Arthur Rosson) 151

SANDS OF IWO JIMA (1949, Allan Dwan) 152, 181, 271–280, 282, 296, 300
SAVING PRIVATE RYAN (1998, Steven Spielberg) 4, 9–15, 21, 27–29, 35, 46, 142–144, 152, 222, 225, 230
SCHINDLER'S LIST (1993, Steven Spielberg) 9, 303
SEX HYGIENE (1942, Otto Brower, John Ford) 148
STELLA DALLAS (1937, King Vidor) 73, 74, 349, 350

https://doi.org/10.1515/9783110468083-009

TAG DER FREIHEIT – UNSERE WEHRMACHT (1935, Leni Riefenstahl) 50, 51, 52, 55, 56, 62, 69, 101, 332
TAXI DRIVER (1976, Martin Scorsese) 308, 309, 315
TERMINATOR 3 – RISE OF THE MACHINES (2003, Jonathan Mostow) 179
THE ADVENTURES OF ROBIN HOOD (1938, Michael Curtiz, William Keighley) 141
THE BATTLE OF MIDWAY (1942, John Ford) 50, 149, 164–172, 175–178, 203, 206, 216, 219, 220, 224, 231
THE BATTLE OF SAN PIETRO (1945, John Huston) 172
THE BIG RED ONE (1980, Samuel Fuller) 302–304
THE BRIDGE AT REMAGEN (1969, John Guillermin) 67, 308, 309
THE DEER HUNTER (1978, Michael Cimino) 4, 44, 87, 310, 312
THE LONGEST DAY (1962, Ken Annakin, Andrew Marton, Bernhard Wicki, Darryl F. Zanuck) 10, 67, 271
THE MEMPHIS BELLE: A STORY OF A FLYING FORTRESS (1944, William Wyler) 149
THE NEGRO SOLDIER (1944, Stuart Heisler) 149
THE OX-BOW INCIDENT (1943, William A. Wellman) 151
THE PERILOUS FIGHT: AMERICA'S WORLD WAR II IN COLOR (2003) 143
THE SECOND WORLD WAR IN COLOUR (1999) 143
THE STEEL HELMET (1953, Samuel Fuller) 5, 132, 296–303
THE THIN RED LINE (1964, Andrew Marton) 67
THE THIN RED LINE (1998, Terrence Malick) 1, 3, 9, 10, 11, 21–30, 35, 47, 132, 230, 276, 324, 329
THE WAR TAPES (2006, Deborah Scranton) 335–338, 342
THEY WERE EXPENDABLE (1956, John Ford) 45, 233–241, 246, 249, 253, 255, 258, 259, 260, 271
THUNDERBOLT (1947, John Sturges, William Wyler) 149
TORA! TORA! TORA! (1970, Richard Fleischer, Kinji Fukasaku, Toshio Masuda) 309
TRIUMPH DES WILLENS (1935, Leni Riefenstahl) 50, 56
TUNISIAN VICTORY (1943, Frank Capra, Hugh Stewart, John Huston) 149

WE WERE SOLDIERS (2002, Randall Wallace) 10
WHY WE FIGHT (1943–1945, Frank Capra) 49, 50, 56, 65, 149, 172
WINDTALKERS (2002, John Woo) 9, 10, 15–22, 27, 28, 35, 46, 317
WITH THE MARINES AT TARAWA (1944, Louis Hayward) 134, 216, 219–231, 272, 278

Subject index

Action 92, 96, 97, 128, 158, 169, 185, 188, 190
Action cinema 67, 97, 124, 125, 130, 149, 177, 179, 184, 185, 189, 204, 207, 222, 228, 231, 253
Adventure 135, 184
Aesthetic pleasure/aesthetic enjoyment 7, 35, 38, 55, 56, 97, 108, 117, 177, 179, 204, 287
Affect
– Affect dramaturgy 72, 96, 102–103, 126, 127, 135, 162, 231, 235, 238, 260, 272, 278
– Affect economy 97, 102, 103, 151, 234, 261, 287, 288
– Affect poetics 8, 100–104, 118, 123, 125, 126, 128, 135, 152, 164, 231, 310, 344, 351
– Affect rhetoric 103, 127, 162, 164, 165, 168, 170, 174, 176, 177, 224, 237, 239, 271, 305
– Interaffectivity 111, 113, 115, 119, 121, 136
Affection-image 4, 6, 121, 189, 202
Anthropology 6, 119, 126, 265, 287, 346, 347, 348
Aesthetics of politics 152, 205, 267
Aesthetic experience 10, 28, 35, 36, 44, 55, 58, 62, 69, 85, 89–93, 95–101, 106–112, 116, 122–125, 130, 136, 138, 144, 145, 177, 178, 203, 205, 231, 263, 284, 287, 288, 306, 307
Aesthetic judgment 62, 112, 344–347, 348, 351
Authenticity 135, 139, 143, 145, 173, 174, 176, 177, 189, 207
Avant-garde 48, 53, 55, 59, 63, 64, 69, 71, 147, 148, 173

Being-in-the-world 98, 109, 111, 112, 115, 178, 214
Berserk 4, 134, 203, 276, 323

Casualties 226, 312, 329, 330, 342
Catharsis 96, 97, 102, 103, 285, 287, 288

Censorship 85, 148, 150, 153, 160, 162, 225, 338
Chronotope 269, 327, 341
Cognitive film theory 98, 104, 105, 106
Combat film 10, 50, 79, 84, 151,
Combat footage 156, 158, 159, 164, 216, 227, 230, 272
Combat reports 134, 149, 152, 216, 246, 261, 272
Comedy 92, 93, 96, 102, 166, 168, 247, 287
Commemoration of the sacrifices of war 47, 126, 134, 202, 237, 288, *see also* sacrifice
Commemoration of the dead 67, 234, 288, 291, 292, 293, 351
Commemoration of the warrior 67, 305, 307, 309
Common sense 31, 32, 90, 95, 101, 344, 345, 348
Community
– Limits of community v, viii, 34, 78, 152, 284, 352
– Communities of taste 351
– Community of survivors 304, 305, 306, 312
– Memory community 264
– Military community 23, 27, 63, 66, 68, 128, 129, 130, 132, 133, 134, 135, 136, 180, 188, 190, 192, 194, 202, 204, 205, 231, 236, 237, 238, 243, 252, 253, 260, 273, 275, 282, 308, 317, 332
– Political community v, vii, 5, 6, 7, 8, 14, 16, 17, 18, 20, 28, 29, 30, 31, 32, 35, 37, 42, 43, 46, 47, 48, 61, 65, 66, 67, 69, 72, 75, 78, 90, 91, 95, 99, 100, 103, 125, 135, 145, 146, 152, 161, 234, 260, 261, 267, 270, 271, 282, 286, 287, 288, 293, 294, 295, 304, 306, 307, 308, 310, 330, 332, 351
– Communitization vi, vii, 20, 48, 55, 63, 65, 133, 188, 194, 232, 236, 265, 273, 275, 276, 308, 310, 313, 315, 316, 318, 323, 324, 330, 332
Constitutive conflict 65, 69, 75, 99, 232, 234, 282, 286, 307
Corporeality 129, 132, 168, 183, 239, 247, 252

372 — Subject index

Cult film 351
Cycle 74, 75, 79, 100, 136, 234, 270

Democracy v–viii, 7, 32, 33, 64, 160, 176, 326, 330, 332
Document 10, 13, 24, 77, 78, 139, 143–146, 150, 151, 152, 153, 158, 173, 174, 175, 176, 177, 204, 205, 206, 207, 216, 217, 231, 244, 261, 262, 272, 280, 303, 304
Documentary 49, 50, 60, 134, 138, 142, 144, 145, 148, 149, 153, 154, 155, 171, 172, 205, 206, 207, 208, 220, 224, 229, 244, 273, 277, 278, 279, 286, 303, 336

eMAEX 115, 240
Embodiment 70, 114, 118, 121, 210, 213, 214
Emotion 4, 45, 103, 104–111, 118, 136, 164, 346
Entertainment culture 7, 14, 15, 55, 83, 91, 92, 93, 138
Epic 18, 25, 142, 180, 181, 286, 309, 326
Essay film 206, 286
Ethos 36, 44, 51, 64, 65, 68, 137, 172, 175, 177, 304, 325, 332
Experiential space 99, 100, 143, 144, 146, 153, 278, 288, 291, 295, 296, 349, 350
Expressivity 1, 42, 74, 75, 92, 96, 113, 117, 118, 121, 125, 128, 156, 197, 215
Expressive Movement 58, 115, 121, 122, 124, 128, 130, 135, 191, 193
Expressive Movement Units (EMU) 122, 193, 196, 197, 198, 200

Face 1, 3, 4, 5, 6, 7, 11, 12, 13, 14, 15, 17, 20, 21, 22, 23, 24, 25, 26, 27, 39, 40, 41, 42, 45, 51, 57, 63, 66, 75, 132, 140, 161, 162, 166, 169, 186, 188, 195, 198, 200, 217, 218, 219, 220, 221, 222, 224, 227, 231, 239, 243, 244, 247, 248, 250, 251, 252, 253, 255, 257, 259, 260, 272, 289, 297, 298, 300, 313, 333, 334, 339, 342
Family melodrama viii, 62, 101
Fascism 54, 55, 56, 57, 62, 63, 64, 66, 330
Feeling viii, 4, 24, 27, 28, 30, 31, 32, 35, 36, 40, 42, 44, 45, 46, 47, 49, 62, 90, 91, 97, 98, 103, 108, 109, 110, 111, 112, 113, 116, 117, 119, 120, 121, 123, 124, 125, 127, 128, 129, 130, 132, 133, 134, 135, 137, 146, 147, 153, 155, 159, 160, 163, 164, 174, 176, 177, 178, 179, 181, 182, 185, 186, 188, 192, 198, 235, 236, 237, 246, 248, 258, 259, 260, 261, 272, 277, 278, 279, 280, 282, 283, 294, 305, 307, 323, 324, 329, 342, 345, 347, 348, 349, 350
Film viewing 40, 69, 108, 113, 114, 116, 117, 155, 210, 281, 314, 338, 351
Formal vocabulary of political sensibility 292
Found footage, 24, 57, 139, 143, 146, 152, 164, 231, 299

Gangster film 61, 63, 71, 97, 101
Genre
– Function of genre 7, 28, 46, 49, 55, 76, 82–84, 86, 89, 90, 93, 95, 96, 98–100, 102, 117, 148, 153, 204, 234
– Generic form 4, 6, 75, 77, 124, 125, 126, 135, 185, 286, 294
– Genre poetics/poetics of genre 7, 36, 72, 77, 79, 80, 83, 84, 86, 92–102, 153, 283–285, 340, 345,
– Genre system 7, 64, 80, 82–86, 91, 92, 96–101, 124, 137, 138, 151, 283
– Genre theory viii, 73, 74, 78–80, 82, 83, 89, 91, 93, 101, 102, 284, 287
Group body (corps) 21, 51, 66, 67, 129, 130, 131, 181, 182, 184–187, 204, 217, 228, 273, 289, 290, 322, 323, 324, see also pathos scene, category 2
Gung-ho film 66, 261, see also mobilization film

History of making 32, 36, 47, 78, 79, 81, 93, 95, 99, 100, 101, 137, 270, 278, 284, 285, 286, 307, 341, 344, 352, see also poetic making
Homecomer 309, 315
Homecoming films 309, 344
Horror 3, 5, 13, 23, 38, 42, 63, 92, 97, 117, 124, 131, 135, 159, 162, 164, 172, 178, 186, 189, 199, 202, 208, 216, 217, 222, 224, 225, 227, 228, 248, 249, 278, 281, 286, 295, 307, 310, 313, 316, 336, 337, 341, 343

Horror film 12, 96, 125, 131, 132, 135, 162, 189, 198, 202, 224, 231, 248
Ideology 48, 49, 61, 70, 85, 185, 292
Individualities 69, 73, 74, 75 see type
Iraq War film 81, 82, 313, 314, 332, 335, 341, 342
Image Space 40, 42, 47, 68, 82, 130, 201, 243, 250, 252, 257, 270, 278, 295, 296, 299, 301, 310, 318, 319, see also visual space

Judgment of taste 112, 345–351

Meaning making 117, 118, 215
Memory
– Collective memory 6, 9, 263, 268
– Communicative memory 265, 266, 269
– Cultural memory 260, 262, 263, 264, 265, 266, 267, 269, 270, 291, 292, 293, 306
– Memory image 216, 230, 231, 232, 233, 256
– Confabulations of memory 260, 261, 269, 297
– Living memory/living remembrance 266, 269, 270
Melodrama viii, 18, 20, 60, 62, 63, 71, 73, 74, 91, 92, 93, 94, 96, 97, 101, 125, 128, 133, 135, 151, 168, 169, 179, 185, 189, 202, 227, 231, 237, 250, 287
Mimesis 97, 103, 106, 284, 285
Mobilization film 130, 137, 149, 150, 151, 152, 180, 181, 183, 184, 185, 188, 189, 192, 195, 204, 227, 228, 235, 261, 282, 314, 344, 351
Modality 7, 36, 38, 48, 49, 55, 60, 64, 91, 92, 93, 95, 96, 97, 98, 99, 101, 105, 111, 117, 122, 123, 124, 125, 130, 131, 137, 138, 150, 151, 153, 162, 173, 177, 203, 204, 261, 288, 351
– Expressive Modality 97, 99, 117, 124, 125, 126, 128, 131, 132, 133, 135, 136, 137, 152, 162, 163, 166, 177, 185, 189, 190, 198, 202, 203, 234, 235, 241, 248, 250, 253, 255, 285, 286, 287
Mode 13, 23, 35, 36, 37, 58, 61, 63, 64, 67, 71, 72, 77, 78, 83, 85, 89, 91, 92, 94, 96, 97, 98, 101, 111, 117, 123, 124, 125, 135, 136, 137, 138, 140, 144, 146, 150, 156, 159, 177, 178, 180, 184, 188, 203, 205, 206, 207, 208, 211, 212, 213, 214, 215, 220, 224, 225, 230, 264, 266, 285, 286, 287, 288, 332, 348, 350
– Action mode. *See* action
– Comic mode. *See* comedy
– Horror mode. *See* horror
Mode of experience 35, 36, 37, 42, 45, 53, 69, 85, 89, 90, 91, 92, 93, 97, 98, 99, 100, 101, 106, 107, 108, 112, 117, 121, 124, 125, 128, 130, 132, 136, 137, 138, 152, 177, 203, 205, 207, 210, 215, 231, 284, 285, 287, 288, 351
Mode of production 85, 98, 285
Mode of representation 61, 63, 64, 85, 86, 88, 98, 285
Melodramatic mode 67, 92, 93, 94, 96, 124, 125, 132, 136, 178
Myth 5, 18, 20, 38, 82, 88, 90, 91, 99, 266, 286, 287, 294, 310

Newsreels 49, 50, 56, 57, 134, 141, 145, 148, 150, 156, 159, 181, 204, 205, 246, 261

Orientation films 149, 152

Pathos 5, 6, 7, 8, 14, 19, 20, 28, 35, 36, 38, 42, 44, 45, 46, 48, 49, 51, 52, 56, 62, 63, 65, 66, 67, 69, 70, 72, 73, 74, 75, 92, 93, 96, 103, 104, 133, 137, 138, 152, 158, 160, 165, 168, 169, 170, 176, 177, 180, 192, 195, 202, 204, 218, 231, 232, 234, 237, 238, 239, 243, 252, 253, 255, 259, 260, 261, 273, 278, 282, 291, 293, 296, 303, 304, 307
Pathos formula 5, 6, 7, 14, 45, 57, 74, 75, 126, 152, 175, 245, 283
Pathos scene 20, 126, 127, 128, 129, 130, 131, 132, 134, 135, 136, 190, 195, 235, 236, 237, 238, 240, 261, 271, 317
– Category 1 (Transition between two social systems) 67, 128, 136, 156, 165, 180, 183, 184, 190, 192, 195, 236, 237, 242, 244, 252, 253, 259, 273, 316, 318, 323

Pathos scene (*continued*)
- Category 2 (Formation of a group body) 11, 26, 51, 67, 129, 135, 136, 165, 180, 181, 184, 188, 190, 194, 195, 221, 236, 241, 244, 272, 273, 316, 318, 322, 323, 324
- Category 3 (Battle and nature) 11, 41, 57, 124, 131, 135, 179, 189, 190, 191, 192, 196, 199, 222, 224, 249, 341, 343
- Category 4 (Battle and technology) 11, 41, 52, 53, 55, 57, 67, 124, 130, 135, 169, 179, 184, 185, 188, 190, 192, 200, 221, 241, 244, 253, 272
- Category 5 (Homeland, woman, home) 132, 156, 159, 166, 198, 241, 249, 250, 251, 252, 255, 259
- Category 6 (Suffering/victim/sacrifice) 5, 7, 11, 13, 14, 67, 72, 125, 133, 135, 136, 180, 184, 188, 195, 202, 223, 227, 255, 342
- Category 7 (Injustice and humiliation/moral self-assertion) 14, 133, 276
- Category 8 (Sense of community as shared filmic remembrance of shared suffering) 10, 134, 143, 158, 159, 164, 272, 278

Perception
- Everyday perception/ordinary perception 55, 114, 125, 211, 213, 214
- Perceptual politics 151, 152, 153, 162, 163, 203, 204, 231, 280
- Split perceiving consciousness 216, 221, 231, 281
- Shared perception of the world 75, 78, 89, 90, 100, 178, 203, 205, 285, 286, 352

Phenomenology 49, 109
Photography 1, 5, 10, 140, 148, 152, 178, 218, 272, 337
Poetic making 33, 35, 36, 46, 47, 71, 76, 77, 78, 79, 81, 91, 93, 94, 95, 96, 97, 98, 99, 100, 101, 137, 138, 148, 152, 205, 207, 209, 210, 215, 261, 263, 267, 269, 270, 278, 283, 284, 285, 286, 287, 294, 306, 341, 344, 345, 350, 351, 352
Poetics and politics 33, 46, 48, 69, 79, 94, 95, 97, 100, 101, 152, 288, 352

Poetics of affect, *see* affect poetics
Poetology 70, 73, 79, 100, 148, 225, 282, 284
Politics of aesthetics 267
Practice
- Media practice 6, 8, 36, 46, 103, 108, 109, 124, 138, 150, 153, 160, 164, 261, 262, 263, 264, 266, 267, 269, 271, 291, 294, 304, 305, 345
- Poetic practice 28, 33, 47, 48, 95, 288
Propaganda, 16, 48, 49, 50, 57, 62, 66, 77, 90, 138, 147, 150, 152, 153, 158, 162, 163, 175, 204, 261
Propaganda film 7, 48, 49, 50, 58, 63, 67, 68, 69, 70, 71, 173, 175, 176, 204, 206, 216, 225, 228, 278
Psychology 13, 98, 103, 104, 105, 106, 121, 287
Pursuit of happiness vii, ix, 14, 19, 30, 31, 62, 66, 69, 260, 306, 326

Rage 6, 17, 57, 63, 72, 126, 127, 133, 134, 155, 163, 164, 170, 192, 203, 300, 308, 309, 315, 323, 324, 342, 344
Reception aesthetics 98, 103, 107, 288
Representation of war 4, 9, 20, 78, 82, 88, 127, 128, 139, 143, 153, 164, 203, 204, 205, 262
Ritual 6, 8, 21, 38, 39, 45, 48, 52, 57, 62, 63, 66, 88, 96, 108, 129, 134, 160, 170, 171, 184, 202, 204, 219, 235, 266, 270, 271, 287, 305, 316, 322, 323, 324, 329, 332
Rule-governed poetics 77, 82, 83, 93, 94, 95, 97

Sacrifice 5, 6, 7, 13, 14, 15, 21, 45, 47, 51, 54, 67, 87, 93, 125, 126, 127, 133, 134, 136, 137, 183, 184, 188, 192, 195, 198, 202, 231, 232, 235, 237, 255, 260, 272, 278, 282, 288, 300, 301, 312, 313, 329, 330, 342, 343
Screwball comedy 247, 287
Sense of Commonality v–viii, 7, 9, 30, 31, 32, 34, 35, 36, 37, 44, 46, 47, 48, 50, 64, 66, 69, 74, 75, 90, 103, 136, 160, 161, 162, 163, 164, 176, 178, 206, 232, 234, 244, 282, 287, 307, 333, 347, 348, 352
Sensoriality 213, 282, 283

Sensus communis 344, 345, 347, 348, 349
Sentimentality 7, 11, 14, 15, 20, 21, 62, 64, 92, 93, 96, 97, 124, 125, 135, 151, 166, 167, 169, 189, 202, 286, 304, 305, 306, 315, 335
Sexuality 203, 239, 247, 315
shell-shocked face 1, 2, 3, 4, 5, 6, 7, 12, 13, 14, 17, 26, 42, 45, 72, 74, 75, 126, 297
Speaking perspective 24, 97, 98, 99, 152, 163, 206, 208, 216, 285–288
Spectator's body 70, 113, 119, 123, 188, 229, 278, *see also* embodiment
Spectator feeling 113, 116, 117, 118, 126, 127, 138, 240, 278, 282, 283, 349, 350
Subjectification 73, 74, 75, 108, 111, 190
Succession of automatic world projections 208, 209, 212, 286
Suspense 96, 117, 259

Taxonomy 7, 77, 82, 83, 84, 85, 93, 94, 95, 98
téchne 81, 138, 209, 284, 286
Technology
– Media technology 51, 53, 76, 80, 81, 90, 121, 124, 130, 138, 144, 178, 179, 205, 207, 208, 209, 210, 212, 215, 216, 229, 230, 262, 286
– War technology 38, 54, 55, 178, 184, 192
– Weapons technology 54, 57, 124, 130, 135, 178, 184, 185, 190, 221

Terror 38, 61, 62, 125, 131, 135, 163, 198, 200, 225, 351
Thrill 97, 123, 125, 135, 286
Thriller 92, 96, 117
Time crystal 230, 231
Time-image 121, 230
Tragedy 92, 96, 97, 102, 103, 108, 119, 137, 284, 285, 286, 288, 291
Trash film 351
Trauma 14, 18, 43, 280, 309, 343
Type 4, 39, 40, 58, 72, 73, 74, 75, 79, 97, 119, 127, 183, 229, 253, 271, 329, 332, 349

Utopia 34, 35, 54, 266, 267, 284, 306, 351

Victim 5, 19, 34, 133, 153, 191, 192, 202, 260, 261, 293, 304, 308, 312, 313, 333, 335, 340, 341, 342, 343, 352
Vietnam War film 9, 18, 37, 42, 43, 44, 81, 82, 162, 191, 224, 308, 310, 312, 313, 314, 315, 341, 342
Visual space 11, 28, 70, 113, 114, 117, 122, 123, 124, 132, 136, 188, 191, 195, 196, 199, 200, 201, 202, 209, 213, 215, 246, 351, *see also* image space

Western (genre) 18, 21, 86, 97, 101, 125, 128, 135, 136, 151, 158, 169, 234, 241, 253, 255, 256, 297, 298, 341

www.ingramcontent.com/pod-product-compliance
Lightning Source LLC
Chambersburg PA
CBHW051555230426
43668CB00013B/1862